EXPLORING AND PROCLAIMING

The Apostles' Creed

EXPLORING AND PROCLAIMING

The Apostles' Creed

Edited by

Roger E. Van Harn

WILLIAM B. EERDMANS PUBLISHING COMPANY

GRAND RAPIDS, MICHIGAN / CAMBRIDGE, U.K.

Wm. B. Eerdmans Publishing Co.
255 Jefferson Ave. S.E., Grand Rapids, Michigan 49503 /
P.O. Box 163, Cambridge CB3 9PU U.K.

Printed in the United States of America

09 08 07 06 05 04   7 6 5 4 3 2 1

Library of Congress Cataloging-in-Publication Data

Exploring and proclaiming the Apostles' Creed /
edited by Roger E. Van Harn.
p.   cm.
Includes bibliographical references.
ISBN 0-8028-2120-0 (pbk.: alk. paper)
1. Apostles' Creed 2. Doctrinal preaching. 3. Apostles' Creed —
Sermons. 4. Sermons, American — 21st century.
I. Van Harn, Roger E., 1932-
BT993.3.E96   2004

238′.11 — dc22

2004047870

www.eerdmans.com

Contents

Contents

Foreword

When, in a student's essay, I come across the solecism "Apostle's Creed," the misplaced apostrophe always provokes me to inquire in the margin: Which apostle? More importantly, I take the next opportunity to tell the class how the Apostles' Creed came to be. Having received at Pentecost the necessary linguistic gifts, the apostles set out to propagate the gospel in all the world: "As they were on the point of taking leave of each other, they first settled an agreed norm for their future preaching, so that they might not find themselves, widely separated as they would be, giving out different doctrines to the people they invited to believe in Christ. So they met together in one spot and, being filled with the Holy Spirit, compiled this brief token of their future preaching, each making the contribution he thought fit; and they decreed that it should be handed out as standard teaching to believers."

That was the story making the rounds at the turn into the fifth century when Rufinus of Aquileia wrote his commentary on the Creed. J. N. D. Kelly, in *Early Christian Creeds*, recalls that tale and then recounts how the details were filled in, so that from an eighth-century sermon that traveled under the name of Saint Augustine we can attribute each creedal clause to a particular figure, with the association between the man and his phrase not lacking a certain biblical plausibility. Peter, as usual, spoke first: "I believe in God the Father Almighty, Maker of heaven and earth" (cf. Matt. 16:17). Then Andrew: "And in Jesus Christ his Son our only Lord" (cf. John 1:41). And so on, down to Matthias, the replacement for the dead and doomed Judas: "And the life ev-

ix

erlasting" (cf. Acts 1:15-26). In sculpture and stained glass this account of the Creed's apostolic origin persisted into medieval pedagogy and aesthetics.

In the present book the themes of the Creed have been redistributed under fifteen heads, and the number of the contributors has been increased, so that an essayist and a preacher can go out two by two (cf. Luke 10:1), and we are given fifteen chapters in which a sermon is each time paired with a historical and theological exposition of a creedal phrase. The content and the purpose remain as of old: a statement of "the faith once delivered to the saints" (Jude 3) in such wise as to assist its spread and the making of disciples to Christ. A pleasant feature is that some who are perhaps best known for their academic work are here allowed to appear as homileticians. And certainly we are confronted with a remarkably coherent, consistent, and (under God) persuasive version of classic Christian beliefs and the message of the gospel.

The writers take pains to display the broader scriptural witness to the truths that the Creed encapsulates. They show how the Creed attained its basic structure and how particular clauses were inserted or refined. They explain why certain articles of the faith needed, in the face of misunderstandings and controversies, to be formulated more fully and precisely at the councils of Nicea, Constantinople, and Chalcedon, so that the Apostles' Creed, as the baptismal symbol of the West, is properly professed in light of the Nicene-Constantinopolitan Creed which the Western churches followed the East in taking into their eucharistic liturgies (the Orthodox employ that creed at both baptism and Eucharist). In that connection I recall a significant moment from the early stages of the "apostolic faith study" in the Faith and Order Commission of the World Council of Churches in the 1980s. We had long been discussing what to take as the basis of that study, and the mood swung finally and decisively in favor of the Nicene-Constantinopolitan Creed when a Jamaican Baptist member — who by culture and denomination might have been expected to be suspicious of "Greek metaphysics" and the text of "imperial councils" — declared that he recognized his own faith in the advocates of that creed rather than in those up-to-date critics who were dubious about taking any creedal base at all.

In matters presently under theological discussion I am encouraged by the tendencies represented in this book. Thus, apart perhaps from an occasional slippage, Christianity is *not* presented as one species in a putative genus of "great monotheistic religions." Again, while showing respect to Judaism, our authors stake the Christian claim to the Old Testament — in the sense of both writing and event — as the history which Jesus fulfills and interprets. Or again: in expounding the saving death of Christ our writers are not afraid of such words as "sin," "wrath," "judgment," "sacrifice," and "redemption," so that the field is not entirely abandoned to Abelard but room is left also for Anselm (with due warning about not setting the Son against the Father). Several of our authors tend toward a universal final hope, but, like Karl Barth and Hans Urs von Balthasar, they take seriously the biblical warnings about damnation; it was not a fundamentalist preacher but a liberal sociologist who remarked that "deeds that cry out to heaven also cry out for hell" (Peter L. Berger, *A Rumor of Angels*).

All in all, this is a splendid book in both concept and execution. I intend to make it required reading in my introduction to theology course. It will lighten my burden, and might indeed save me from having to teach at all — although I would be loath to forgo that privilege and joy.

GEOFFREY WAINWRIGHT
Durham, North Carolina
All Saints' Day 2003

Preface

When the confirmation class was concluding its preparatory sessions with a weekend retreat, Pastor Mary decided it was time for a no-holds-barred wrestling with church doctrines. The sessions to date were laced with "what do you believe about . . . ?" and "what would you do if . . . ?" questions. Discussions were animated. It seemed time to take on "this is what the church believes about (creation, providence, covenant, atonement, etc.)." When she finished outlining the doctrine of the Trinity, a fourteen-year-old responded with, "I think I'm getting it, but it makes my head hurt."

No preacher would want to send his congregants home from worship with their heads hurting, but there is a growing sense that the church could benefit these days from a revival of doctrinal preaching. The topical "three points and a poem" sermons from the North American mid–twentieth century need not be the model for the revival. But sermons designed to teach what the church has received in and with the gospel of Jesus Christ may be the witness that satisfies a growing hunger. Ironically, the mood of postmodernism which relativizes faith convictions into mere personal opinions may well increase the appetite and make more room for church doctrine on the table.

This book was conceived in the hope that it will stimulate renewed interest in doctrinal preaching. The Apostles' Creed was chosen as the basis because of its narrative structure, confessional character, liturgical familiarity, and ecumenical appeal. Anchoring doctrinal reflection in this historic creed can focus our faith and restrain our eccentric tendencies.

Each chapter includes an essay and a sermon to assist exploration and proclamation of the Creed. Essay contributors identify biblical sources, trace how this doctrine functioned and fared in the history of the church, and reflect theologically on the confession for our time. Sermon contributors provide models to show how these articles can be preached as good news today.

Two satisfying discoveries occurred in the creation of this book. First, the variety of traditions represented by the contributors has not muted the proclamation of the good news. Second, while the sermons were offered to encourage doctrinal preaching, they also bear marks of pastoral, evangelistic, ethical, expository, and prophetic preaching. The words of two contributors written in another context may be more true than they knew: "Before they counsel, instruct, warn, or comfort, preachers proclaim."[1] Had they been describing the sermons in this book, they may have said that when preachers proclaim what the Creed confesses, they also "counsel, instruct, warn, or comfort."

Whatever else they do, these essays will assist students, teachers, and preachers to explore the Apostles' Creed and the sermons will model preaching possibilities.

The publishers and contributors lament the long shadow of death cast by the sudden and — for us — untimely passing of Colin Gunton, of King's College, London, on May 6, 2003. His death warrants added attention to his sermon, "The Almighty God," with its closing line: ". . . in the long term we shall all die, but we shall die in the hope of the resurrection."

Roger E. Van Harn
Pentecost 2003

---

1. Thomas G. Long and Cornelius Plantinga, Jr., *A Chorus of Witnesses* (Grand Rapids: Eerdmans, 1994), p. 73.

Contributors

Walter R. Bouman
Edward C. Fendt Professor Emeritus of Systematic Theology
Trinity Lutheran Seminary
Columbus, Ohio

Richard A. Burridge
The Dean, King's College
London, UK

Philip W. Butin
President and Professor of Theology
San Francisco Theological Seminary
San Anselmo, California

Gabriel Fackre
Abbot Professor of Christian Theology Emeritus
Andover Newton Theological School
Newton Centre, Massachusetts

David F. Ford
Regius Professor of Divinity
University of Cambridge
Cambridge, UK

Colin Gunton († May 6, 2003)
Professor of Christian Doctrine
King's College
London, UK

Richard B. Hays
George Washington Ivey Professor of New Testament
Duke University Divinity School
Durham, North Carolina

Craig C. Hill
Professor of New Testament
Wesley Theological Seminary
Washington, D.C.

Scott E. Hoezee
Minister of Preaching and Administration
Calvin Christian Reformed Church
Grand Rapids, Michigan

Leslie J. Hoppe, O.F.M.
Professor of Old Testament Studies, Catholic Theological Union
Chicago, Illinois

George Hunsinger
Hazel Thompson McCord Professor of Systematic Theology
Princeton Theological Seminary
Princeton, New Jersey

Scott Black Johnston
Pastor, Trinity Presbyterian Church
Atlanta, Georgia

James F. Kay
Joe R. Engle Professor of Homiletics and Liturgics
Princeton Theological Seminary
Princeton, New Jersey

Richard A. Lischer
James T. and Alice Mead Cleland Professor of Preaching
Duke University Divinity School
Durham, North Carolina

Thomas G. Long
Bandy Professor of Preaching
Candler School of Theology
Atlanta, Georgia

Lois Malcolm
Associate Professor of Systematic Theology
Luther Seminary
Saint Paul, Minnesota

Daniel L. Migliore
Charles Hodge Professor of Systematic Theology
Princeton Theological Seminary
Princeton, New Jersey

Richard A. Norris, Jr.
Emeritus Professor of Church History
Union Theological Seminary in the
City of New York

Steven D. Paulson
Associate Professor of Systematic Theology
Luther Seminary
St. Paul, Minnesota

Cornelius Plantinga
President and Professor of Systematic Theology
Calvin Theological Seminary
Grand Rapids, Michigan

Cynthia L. Rigby
W. C. Brown Associate Professor of Theology
Austin Presbyterian Theological Seminary
Austin, Texas

Fleming Rutledge
Priest of the Episcopal Church
Diocese of New York

William M. Shand III
Rector, Saint Francis Episcopal Church
Potomac, Maryland

Marguerite Shuster
Professor of Preaching
Fuller Theological Seminary
Pasadena, California

Wm. C. Turner
Associate Professor of the Practice of Homiletics
Duke University Divinity School
Pastor, Mt. Level Missionary Baptist Church
Durham, North California

Geoffrey Wainwright
Robert Earl Cushman Professor of Christian Theology
Duke University Divinity School
Durham, North Carolina

Robert Louis Wilken
William R. Kenan, Jr., Professor of the History of Christianity
University of Virginia
Charlottesville, Virginia

Ralph C. Wood
University Professor of Theology and Literature
Baylor University
Waco, Texas

Susan K. Wood
Professor of Theology and Associate Dean
St. John's University
Collegeville, Minnesota

Frances M. Young
Cadbury Professor of Theology
University of Birmingham
Birmingham, UK

Robin Darling Young
Associate Professor of Theology
University of Notre Dame
South Bend, Indiana

The Apostles' Creed

I believe in God, the Father almighty,
creator of heaven and earth.

And in Jesus Christ, his only Son, our Lord;
who was conceived by the Holy Spirit
and born of the virgin Mary.
He suffered under Pontius Pilate,
was crucified, died, and was buried;
he descended into hell.
The third day he rose again from the dead.
He ascended into heaven
and is seated at the right hand of God the Father almighty.
From there he will come to judge the living and the dead.

I believe in the Holy Spirit,
the holy catholic church,
the communion of saints,
the forgiveness of sins,
the resurrection of the body,
and the life everlasting. AMEN.

Credo in deum patrem omnipotentem,
creatorem coeli et terrae;

Et in Iesum Christum,
filium eius unicum, dominum nostrum,
qui conceptus est de Spiritu sancto,
natus ex Maria virgine,
passus sub Pontio Pilato,
crucifixus, mortuus et sepultus,
descendit ad inferna,
tertia die resurrexit a mortuis,
ascendit ad coelos,
sedet ad dexteram dei patris omnipotentis,
inde venturus est iudicare vivus et mortuos;

Credo in Spiritum sanctum,
sanctam ecclesiam catholicam,
sanctorum communionem,
remissionem peccatorum,
carnis resurrectionem,
et vitam aeternam. Amen.

CHAPTER 1

The Triune God

Credo in deum patrem, in Iesum Christum, et in Spiritum sanctum

MARGUERITE SHUSTER

When one first glances at the Apostles' Creed, one may be struck by the fact that the Creed, like the Bible itself, does not mention by name a doctrine so absolutely central and crucial to the Christian faith as the Trinity. Yet a second glance in each case reveals something quite different from this seeming oversight, for the structure of the Creed, like the structure of biblical revelation itself, is trinitarian in form.[1] The Creed moves from Father to Son to Spirit; God's self-revelation moves from the God who made himself known by name to Moses, to Christmas, to Pentecost. And because Christians believe that revelation would not be revelation if who God *is* did not correspond to who he[2] shows himself to be, they believe that from all eternity a fundamental threeness as well as an essential oneness characterize the one they worship as the sole Lord of heaven and earth.[3]

---

1. According to J. N. D. Kelly, the Creed was understood this way — understood as affirming the coequal, coeternal deity of the Holy Spirit as well as of the Son — by the time it reached its final shape (*Early Christian Creeds,* 3rd ed. [London: Longman, 1972], pp. 383-84).

2. I reluctantly use male pronouns for God, not because I attribute gender to God or consider God to be more like the male than like the female of the human species, but because I worry about the subtle depersonalization that takes place by repeated use of "God" and "Godself."

3. Several church fathers doubted that number can properly be attributed to God, who transcends number; even so, human language virtually requires that we say "three" in order rightly to maintain the distinctions within the Godhead, even as we must say "one" of the divine essence.

Thus, while no Christian wishes to be understood as other than monotheistic in her faith, there is something at least partially misleading in lumping Christianity together with Judaism and Islam under some such rubric as "the great monotheistic faiths," without further ado. Indeed, it is precisely what makes Christianity Christian — affirmation of the full deity of Jesus Christ (and of the Holy Spirit as a distinct member of the Trinity) — that these other great religions reject. Likewise, groups like the Jehovah's Witnesses and Mormons, who do not affirm these things, are not generally recognized as Christian. Even when Mormons, say, use a trinitarian baptismal formula, their baptism is not recognized by most churches as *Christian* baptism because they do not mean by the words what the Christian church has meant. It is not only a form of words but a particular, carefully defined content that is critical to Christian identity. *Christian* faith is *trinitarian* faith.

Biblical Sources

In Scripture we find no "doctrine" of the Trinity, but we do find the materials that necessitated the development of the doctrine. A particularly significant point is that the preferred designation of the early Christians for Jesus was not his own favorite phrase, "Son of Man," but rather "Lord," the Greek translation of the tetragrammaton, Yahweh, the sacred name of the Old Testament — a name identified with God himself. Not only did early Christians use this form of address in ways that involved worship, appropriate to God alone (especially prominently in John 20:28, Thomas's confession, "My Lord and my God"; but also in prayers, hymns, and christological benedictions), but they applied to Jesus Old Testament passages clearly referring to God, for instance, Philippians 2:9-11 (Isa. 45:23), Romans 10:11 (Isa. 28:16), and Romans 10:13 (Joel 2:32).[4] Lordship is likewise affirmed of the Spirit (2 Cor. 3:17).[5] How can such practice of worship and use of language possibly be made to mesh with the Shema (Deut. 6:4), the great affirmation of God's oneness cited by Jesus himself (Mark 12:29)?

It would seem clear that an incipient, unarticulated trinitarianism deeply

4. For these sources and much helpful discussion, see Donald A. Hagner, "Paul's Christology and Jewish Monotheism," in *Perspectives on Christology: Essays in Honor of Paul K. Jewett*, ed. Marguerite Shuster and Richard Muller (Grand Rapids: Zondervan, 1991), pp. 19-38.

5. I do not, obviously, see this text as establishing the identity of Jesus and the Spirit, but rather as declaring the Spirit's deity; though the language is admittedly slippery. See Paul K. Jewett, *God, Creation, and Revelation* (Grand Rapids: Eerdmans, 1991), p. 290 n. 28; I have greatly profited from the whole section on the Trinity, pp. 261-325.

shapes the thought and expression of the writers of the New Testament, including their understanding and appropriation of the Old Testament. That is, they knew, even if they did not say it in so many words, that it was the one God, and no other, who met them in Jesus Christ and whose Spirit, poured out upon them, enabled them to live in newness of life. Thus, right from the beginning of the Gospel narratives, we find all three persons of the Trinity represented, in the annunciation (Luke 1:35), and in the stories of the baptism of Jesus in all four Gospels (Matt. 3:13-17; Mark 1:9-11; Luke 3:21-22; John 1:31-34). During his earthly ministry Jesus referred to the Father as uniquely related to him (e.g., Luke 10:22; John 5:18) and to the Spirit as the one by whom he worked (Matt. 12:28). In John's Gospel come particularly strong affirmations of the unity of Father and Son (John 10:30; 14:9), as well as of Jesus' sending of the Spirit (14:16-17; 16:6-15). And of course, there is the baptismal formula of Matthew 28:19, as clear a trinitarian formulation as can be found in the New Testament.[6] This statement is remarkable not least because the name of the three persons into which the convert is to be baptized is a singular name, yet the designation of each person is preceded by an article: singularity and plurality are held firmly together.

When we turn to the Pauline and deutero-Pauline epistles, we find the same sort of consciousness, and not only in the great trinitarian benediction of 2 Corinthians 13:13, "The grace of the Lord Jesus Christ, the love of God, and the communion of the Holy Spirit be with all of you" (in which "God," strikingly, is listed not first but second). Paul uses language like "God," "God the Father," "Son of God," "our Lord Jesus Christ," "Spirit," "Holy Spirit" constantly and in such a way that the terms are by no means interchangeable (even though Christ and Spirit occasionally seem to merge). He prays to Jesus (2 Cor. 12:8). He says the Spirit of God is related to God as the human spirit is related to a human being (1 Cor. 2:11). In Colossians 1:19 we are told that the fullness of God was pleased to dwell in Christ.[7] But the depth of the trinitarian flavor of the texts cannot be seen in single verses alone. The number of longer passages in which the work of all the persons of the Trinity is represented (particularly as regards salvation) is impressive: see, to take but a sample, Romans 8:3-4, 15-17; 1 Corinthians 1:4-7; 2:4-5; 6:11; 12:4-6; 2 Corinthians 1:21-22; Galatians 4:4-6; Ephesians 1:3-14; 4:4-6; 1 Thessalonians 1:2-6; 2 Thessalonians 2:13. Similar threefold references also appear in non-Pauline epis-

---

6. We of course exclude 1 John 5:7 as not part of the original text of Scripture. By contrast, the text of Matt. 28:19 is secure, according to the best manuscripts we have.

7. I am also inclined to understand Titus 2:13 as referring to Jesus Christ as God, given the single article: τοῦ μεγάλου θεοῦ καὶ σωτῆρος ἡμῶν Ἰησοῦ Χριστοῦ.

tles, as in 1 Peter 1:2 and Jude 20-21. The New Testament writers could not say what they needed to say without frequent reference to Father, Son, and Spirit, in ways that give virtually equal dignity to each.

What, though, about the Old Testament? To say that the Old Testament contains no such evidence of the Trinity as we find in the New Testament would seem simply to state the obvious, especially as we have identified knowledge of the Trinity with the events of salvation history. Nonetheless, Christians continue to believe that in Old Testament and in New, we deal with the same God; and the writers of the New Testament clearly read the Old with the assumption that Christ was to be found in it — even if later exegetes have struggled with meager success to discern where Jesus, on the road to Emmaus, might have looked to expound, "beginning with Moses and all the prophets . . . the things about himself in all the scriptures" (Luke 24:27). Certainly we no longer presume to see the Trinity every time we find three of anything;[8] but conversely, interpreting the plurals of Genesis 1 simply as "plurals of majesty" that presume singularity of subject is a strategy that has fallen on rather hard times, on the grounds that such usage was not in fact characteristic of the Hebrews. At the very least, that the commonly used Hebrew term for God, *Elohim*, is a plural form is surprising for a rigidly monotheistic people. Similarly, even if one does not wish to go as far as Barth in identifying the divine image with humankind being male and female, that there is this plurality and hint of relationship in the image is suggestive.

Other possible adumbrations include the appearances of the Angel of the Lord, a being who seems separate from God and yet evokes a response that goes beyond that produced by an ordinary messenger, bringing a sense of the divine presence itself (see, for instance, Gen. 16:7-14; 18:1-19; 22:11; Exod. 3:1-15; Num. 22:22-35; Judg. 13:20-22, among many others). Some have seen in such appearances, as well as in other Old Testament theophanies, the presence of the preincarnate Christ, or at least a prefiguring of the incarnation.[9] Some have referred to the personification of a preexistent Wisdom, particularly in

8. The threefold ascription of holiness in Isa. 6:3 and the threefold use of the divine name in Num. 6:24-26 nonetheless remain suggestive and find their place comfortably in Christian worship; these are certainly not trinitarian affirmations, but they fit readily into trinitarian settings. Note, too, the "us" of Isa. 6:8, similar to that of Gen. 1:26, though today generally understood in both cases as address to a sort of heavenly court.

9. The idea goes all the way back to Justin Martyr. For illumining discussion, see J. Andrew Dearman, "Theophany, Anthropomorphism, and the *Imago Dei*: Some Observations about the Incarnation in the Light of the Old Testament," in *The Incarnation*, ed. Stephen T. Davis, Daniel Kendall, S.J., and Gerald O'Collins, S.J. (Oxford and New York: Oxford University Press, 2002), pp. 31-46.

Proverbs 8, as consonant with the preexistent Logos of John 1 (though one must be cautious to observe that preexistence as such does not necessarily entail divinity). And of course, there is the messianic strand of the Old Testament as represented in Psalms 45:6-7 and 110:1, both of which make a distinction between God and God or Lord and Lord, interpreted in Hebrews 1:8 and Matthew 22:41-45, respectively, as a distinction between the Father and the Son. None of these is likely to be persuasive to one not reading with Christian spectacles on, yet early Jewish Christians who were wearing such spectacles found in such texts a way to affirm the fundamental continuity of their religious convictions and experience.

Historical Sketch

It took several hundred years — until the final form of what we now refer to as the Nicene Creed (more precisely the Niceno-Constantinopolitan Creed, framed in Constantinople, 381), with further "fine tuning" in the so-called Athanasian Creed (fifth century) — for the incipient trinitarianism of the Scriptures and of early Christian faith and worship to reach the developed form in which it has long been universally accepted by Christians.[10] The formal doctrine, to state briefly its technical terms, is that God is one in his essential being (*ousia* — substance, nature, or essence) but subsists eternally in three persons *(hypostases)*, Father, Son, and Holy Spirit.[11] The Father is of none, neither begotten nor proceeding; the Son is eternally begotten by the Father; and the Spirit proceeds eternally from the Father (and the Son). This logical order of Father, Son, Spirit is the source of the language of first, second, and third persons of the Trinity; but it must be emphasized that this is a *logical* order, not a temporal order or an order of comparative dignity, for all the persons are coequal and coeternal.

The working out of the details took time. However, once the church had to face squarely the seeming contradiction between strict monotheism and the fact that Christians worshiped Jesus — particularly in the challenge of Arius, who taught that the Son was not coeternal and coequal with the Father, but was the first and best of the creatures — extension of the christological

---

10. Accepted with some nuancing, of course, and an asterisk concerning the ongoing debate about the *filioque* clause, the question of whether the Spirit proceeds from the Father and the Son, or from the Father alone (the Eastern Church rejects the *filioque*).

11. While I have used common translations of *ousia* and *hypostasis,* these terms are notoriously slippery. Precisely what the Fathers meant by them continues to be debated (not to mention that, early on, they were used as synonyms).

principles articulated at the Council of Nicea (325) to the Holy Spirit followed
with a sort of necessity of internal logic. Just as orthodox understanding of
the person of Christ involved not only his full divinity but also rejection of
Adoptionistic and Docetic heresies, so understanding of the Trinity involved
not only affirming the full divinity of the Holy Spirit as well, but also steering
somehow between tritheism (three Gods) and modalism (also called Sabel-
lianism: the one God appearing in different modes at different times, often
understood sequentially — first as Father, then as Son, now as Spirit). Significantly to oversimplify a complex picture, attention to "threeness" has traditionally been associated with the Eastern Church, particularly the Cappa-
docian Fathers, while emphasis on "oneness" has been associated with the
Western or Latin tradition, particularly with Augustine, leading respectively
to "social" versus "psychological" or "individual" or "Latin" trinitarian models. These are, however, to be seen as matters of weight and emphasis, not of
fundamental doctrinal disparity: the church as a whole affirms one God in
three persons, and affirms that just how this can be is a mystery in a strict
sense, inscrutable to the human mind.[12] Until recent challenges we shall mention briefly below, this orthodox formulation has stood the test of time, apart
from objections taking shape in the various forms of Unitarianism that have
cropped up since the time of the Reformation.

While the technical language of trinitarian theology is unlikely to prove
edifying in the preaching ministry of the church, certain points nonetheless
bear comment, in order that the language of preaching might remain suffi-
ciently precise so as not inadvertently to betray fundamentals of the doctrine
of the Trinity. One of these is the importance of the terms "beget" about the
Son and "proceed" about the Spirit. As C. S. Lewis observed, one "begets"
something fundamentally like oneself (and similarly for what proceeds from
oneself), while one "creates" or "makes" something unlike oneself. Use of
such language seeks to protect the substantial oneness of God. Reference to
"substantial" oneness provokes the caution that when thinking of "substance"
in trinitarian discussion, it is better not to picture some sort of quasi-material

---

12. That the mystery is such as to be finally impenetrable to finite minds is not to be seen as
a breaking of the canons of logic: the Fathers were careful not to say that God is one and three *in
the same sense*. Hence the differentiation of *ousia* and *hypostasis*, however difficult these may be
to define. It is also important to note that the affirmation that there are three and only three divine persons is a conclusion reached not by logic but by revelation: one does not do well to seek
behind revelation for allegedly more fundamental constraints; nor does one do well to hypothe-
size that if there can be three, why not more. Again, the constraint is not a logical one, but one of
the divine nature as God has made himself known to us (which is the only way we can know
him at all).

"God stuff" that the persons of the Trinity share or is parceled out among them, but rather simply what makes all the persons God, as when one speaks of the *substance* of an argument.[13] Another fruitful way of speaking, developed by the late seventh- to early eighth-century theologian John of Damascus, is that of the *perichoresis* (Greek; Latin, *circumincession;* English, "co-inherence"), or mutual indwelling, of the divine persons. We do well to picture Father, Son, and Spirit not, as it were, in a line (which evokes tritheism), but rather *inside* one another (as suggested by Jesus' words in John 10:38; 14:8-11). Although that figure might sound paradoxical, we get a hint of what is entailed when we think of two people who love each other so deeply that their concerns, perceptions, and interests interpenetrate one another such that they can in no way be separated, much less set at odds; yet these persons would say they are in no way lessened but rather more themselves because of this relationship. This idea was particularly important in the East because it protected the equality as well as the unity of the persons; and equality had been somewhat at risk because of the Eastern Church's emphasis on the monarchy of the Father.[14] Since the Father is one way or another the "fount" of the Trinity, subordination of the other divine persons to the Father has always been a tendency, especially given biblical language that affirms in particular the subordination of the Son to the Father (e.g., John 14:28; Phil. 2; 1 Cor. 15:27-28). Such passages have, however, traditionally been referred to the Son as incarnate, not in his essential deity.

That distinction, between the Godhead in its essential nature, prior to and apart from the creation, as differentiated from the Trinity as revealed in the created order through creation, incarnation, and Pentecost, is the distinction between the so-called essential or ontological or immanent Trinity, on the one hand, and the economic Trinity on the other. It cannot be emphasized too strongly that there are not two trinities but only one: it is the eternal Son of the Father (who may also be identified as the Logos, as in John 1) who becomes incarnate in Jesus of Nazareth; it is the eternal Spirit of God who is poured forth on Pentecost. Nonetheless, it is not meaningless to speak of God apart from what he has made, even if we ourselves, being creatures, can speak of him only from within the creation. There are obvious differences between

13. Dorothy Sayers makes this point with particular clarity in comments in her translation of Dante's *Purgatory* (Baltimore: Penguin Books, 1959), p. 212.

14. Ralph Del Colle notes that the situation was a little different in the West, where the Son was understood as begotten and the Spirit proceeding more from the *being* (*ousia,* which all the persons share) than from the *person* (*hypostasis,* unique to each person) of the Father ("The Triune God," in *The Cambridge Companion to Christian Doctrine,* ed. Colin Gunton [Cambridge: Cambridge University Press, 1997], p. 132).

God related to himself and God relating to us, and members of the Trinity play particular roles with respect to the created order that they do not play apart from it. The Son, not the Father, dies on the cross. The Spirit, not the Son, is sent to remain with us always. The Father is called by the Creed, "Creator of heaven and earth." However, always insistent upon maintaining the principle of fundamental unity despite diversity in the Trinity, the church has long affirmed Augustine's dictum that the works of the Trinity *ad extra* (with respect to the created order) are indivisible. Particular roles are assigned "by appropriation," but that should not be taken to mean that all the members of the Trinity are not involved. Thus, while we call the Father "Creator" by appropriation (the act of creation being particularly appropriate to the Father), Scripture does not hesitate to speak of the creative work of Son (John 1:3) and Spirit (Ps. 104:30), nor does the church hesitate to compose a grand hymn, "Veni Creator Spiritus." Likewise, while the work of redemption is particularly appropriated to the Son, Father and Spirit are also involved in our salvation, and so on. This idea of appropriation helps us understand the flexibility with which Scripture speaks of these matters. In all his works on our behalf we see the triune God truly revealed, but not exhaustively revealed, for the creature is not capable of the infinite.

While in a rough way this understanding of the Trinity has persisted for centuries (always allowing for differences of emphasis between East and West, and according to the predilections of particular traditions and theologians), recent theological developments and a sudden spurt of interest in the Trinity have brought various challenges. Some of these have to do with detailed historical and theological analysis of traditional sources that questions whether traditional readings of these sources are exact;[15] others have to do with larger changes in the theological and social scene. Among the more important of the former challenges are those that point out that the translation "person" for *hypostasis* has always been inexact and becomes increasingly hazardous in a day when personhood carries connotations of individualism, independence, and personality that are very far from anything the Fathers intended. That God is personal is orthodox theology; that God resembles a committee is not.

On the latter sorts of challenges we might note at least in passing those that come from process theology, with its emphasis on becoming rather than being. "Substance" and "being" language seems to have a static quality at odds

---

15. See, for various examples, contributions by historians and systematicians to the volume *The Trinity*, ed. Stephen T. Davis, Daniel Kendall, S.J., and Gerald O'Collins, S.J. (Oxford and New York: Oxford University Press, 1999).

with the activity and energy process theologians associate with God, which suggests to them that a whole wrong metaphysics is involved in the traditional formulation of the doctrine of the Trinity (and in the doctrine of the church as a whole).[16] Some feminist theologians, troubled by the seeming "boys' club" character of the Trinity, have sought to emphasize a feminine principle, whether by seeing the Holy Spirit as feminine or by developing a wisdom Christology (since the word for wisdom in both Greek and Hebrew is feminine — though it can hardly be denied that the second person as incarnate was, as a simple matter of historical fact, male; and grammatical gender can hardly be assumed to imply personal gender).[17] Others have worked with the language of worship, particularly the baptismal formula, and have suggested that we move to more gender-neutral wording, such as baptizing in the name of "the Creator, the Redeemer, and the Sustainer" (of which tactic I shall say more below). Moltmann in particular has reinvigorated the question of whether God, traditionally understood as impassible, experiences suffering: When Jesus died, did he suffer as man only, or as God?[18] If his suffering did indeed entail that of the second person of the Trinity, what does that mean for our understanding of the Godhead as a whole? And as far as the Holy Spirit, given short shrift for centuries, is concerned, the astonishing growth of Pentecostal and charismatic churches worldwide has given the Spirit a whole new prominence. The theological implications of this new prominence have not been fully explored, but since theological reflection has long developed out of the worship life of the people of God, we may surely anticipate that the relative neglect of the Spirit will be remedied in the writings of younger, and especially Two-Thirds World, theologians.

16. To this complaint we might at the very least reply that the verb "to be" is used by Scripture in speaking of God; indeed, even the divine name is related to it (though some have given the name a future sense, viz., "I will be what I will be").

17. I affirm as strongly as anyone that there is no gender in the incorporeal God, and I likewise affirm that the masculinity of the incarnate Christ is a contingent and not an ontologically necessary fact, though it was probably culturally necessary that the incarnation take a male form.

18. Theologians have traditionally said that the second person of the Trinity assumed humanity, not that a human being somehow became God: the *person* is and remains divine while taking full humanity unto himself, which raises the question of whether Jesus could suffer only in his human nature.

Contemporary Reflections

Given how closely theological reflection has followed upon the worship life of God's people, it is perhaps fitting to begin thinking about the contemporary scene with an eye on the worshiping congregation. A moment's thought reveals that the Trinity is everywhere assumed in Christian worship — not only in explicit ways, as in the baptismal formula, but also in the trinitarian form of common benedictions and in service music such as the Doxology and the Gloria Patri, as well as in the trinitarian design of many classic hymns, which take up the work of the different persons in successive stanzas. Though we may most frequently pray to the Father, through the Son, with the implied or implored aid of the Spirit (Rom. 8:26), we may address our prayers to any member of the Trinity: Stephen prayed to Jesus, that he might receive his spirit (Acts 7:59), and we often invoke the Spirit in prayers of invocation or before the Eucharist. It can indeed be a useful exercise some Sunday to observe and think about all the ways the doctrine of the Trinity informs worship.

At the same time, it may be important to think carefully about how presumably innocuous liturgical practices and changes, not to mention sheer sloppiness, compromise the trinitarian theology that shapes congregants' thinking at a level below that of conscious awareness, but that profoundly influences their way of picturing and relating to God. In earlier days the common practice of leaving out the third verse of hymns contributed to the lack of lively awareness of the Holy Spirit. Today many repetitive choruses and worship songs focus on one divine person only. Efforts at inclusive language (which I support in principle, but not always in practice) may generate not a trinitarian consciousness but a wrenching sense of God-who-suffers-from-gender-confusion, insofar as the unity of the Trinity is maintained, or a sort of pagan-style divine family, insofar as there is a slide toward tritheism.[19] The substitution of economic language (Creator, Redeemer, Sustainer) for immanent language (Father, Son, Spirit) in the baptismal formula not only substitutes a "job description" for the triune name, at the same time obscuring the unity of the works *ad extra*. Ironically, it also feeds by a back door into the very gender problem it is trying to avoid, in that there is subordination in the economic Trinity, and the subordination applies precisely to the persons associated with the feminine (generally the Spirit, but also the Son in Sophia Christologies).

Sloppiness is particularly rife in prayer language, where address slips and

---

19. Note, here, that what I take to be the truth that God is without gender is obliterated by focus on gender.

slides, and proper distinctions among the persons frequently are not maintained; but also in sermons preachers commit virtually the whole range of heresies by what often appears to be sheer inattention and inadvertence.[20] Speaking of heresies, one will find especially rich sources in children's sermons. For instance, one could scarcely ask for a finer illustration of modalism than the common children's sermon explaining the unity and diversity of the Trinity by the example of water in the three forms of gas, liquid, and solid. When one remembers that this sort of analogy sticks like glue in the minds of *adults* in the congregation, one may be moved to instruct and supervise the youth ministry team a bit more closely.

Another instructive sort of observation has to do with whether a congregation's worship life, or a preacher's sermons, or one's personal piety, reveals a marked preference for one person of the Trinity over the others.[21] Insofar as it does (and I suspect that it is as psychologically difficult to *relate* to God as Trinity as it is intellectually difficult to conceive God in this way), one does well to reflect on what is being gained and what is being lost. What does a Jesus-centered piety offer that a Father-centered one lacks, and vice versa? What has mainline neglect of the Spirit cost it?

As soon as one begins to put questions of this kind, however, one must quickly return to basics of trinitarian thought and take care that one is not succumbing to the temptation to give "personalities" in the modern sense to the members of the Godhead. It is simply a mistake to say, or even to feel in one's heart, that the Father is the rigid lawgiver who is angry with one while gentle Jesus, meek and mild, understands and forgives. Attributing to one person what one cannot imagine attributing to another, or setting the persons up in opposition to one another, should immediately raise a red flag. It easily follows that recent flaps about "child abuse" theories of the atonement are first of all mistakes in trinitarian theology. Charges that the Father unjustly punishes the Son ignore the unity of the works *ad extra,* as well as the willing self-sacrifice of the one who freely gives himself on our behalf.

A right understanding of the Trinity, then, is absolutely critical to soundness both in worship and in doctrinal exploration, for what one believes about the basic nature of God underlies everything else. But when one is faced with questions about the nature and work of God, one does well not just to say "Trinity" and stop, as if the word itself answered the questions.

---

20. For examples in published sermons, see my article, "Preaching the Trinity: A Preliminary Investigation," in *The Trinity,* pp. 357-81.

21. I owe this point to a chapel address by Richard Mouw, who in turn credited H. R. Niebuhr.

Rather, in my judgment, one ought immediately to ponder implications of *both* the individual *and* the social models of the Trinity (and not, either, come down firmly on one side or the other and *then* stop, as many involved in contemporary debates are prone to do). Precisely because the mystery of the Trinity, being the mystery of God himself, is finally beyond us, we need both analogies. From the individual analogy we learn that it is one God, and one God alone, whom we must worship and obey. We may not conceive plural agendas that we may pit against one another, or plural demands that catch us on the horns of a dilemma (e.g., "the Father wants me to be just; Jesus wants me to be merciful"; or "the Father set down these rules, but the Spirit gives me freedom to do otherwise" — no; the one Lord is holy love, both just and merciful, a God of order and of freedom). God's purposes are not compromised by intratrinitarian competition or conflict; the persons do not thwart one another or appease one another. Talk implying such splits is simply a mistake. The social analogy, however, better captures the personal nature of God and God's character as love. Were God a mere monad, he could perhaps be confused with an "It"; the God who is eternally Father, Son, and Spirit, united in the perfect love that means perfect joy, can rightly be conceived only in personal terms. Furthermore, because the members of the Trinity have within the Trinity perfect objects of love, there can be no thought either of love as narcissism (love without an outgoing quality is scarcely love at all in the proper sense) or of need for a creation in order to have an object of love. The creation is thus an act of God's freedom, an overflow of love from the God who is love from all eternity. It is *this* God whom we are to worship and proclaim, *this* God who invites our love in return, and enables it by his own Spirit.

The Triune God Who Seeks and Finds Us

Ezekiel 34:11-16; Matthew 28:16-20

PHILIP W. BUTIN

I

Some people spend their entire lives searching for a "spirituality" that seems right to them. A "faith" that matches their own perceptions of what God ought to be like. A way of believing that fits who they are, that corresponds to what they're looking for in life.

I'd like to tell you about three people like this whom I've known over the years. One friend of mine was baptized in a Presbyterian church in a middle-sized city in the East. She grew up and was confirmed there. She went to a Presbyterian college. But as a young woman she decided traditional Christian beliefs weren't broad enough for her. That certain things Christians thought conflicted with what she thought. So she went out on a search for a way of connecting with God that better fit her aspirations and intuitions.

Eventually she found a group of people who supported most of her personal beliefs. They took the same stands she did on controversial political and ethical issues. They emphasized Christian teachings she agreed with. They played down Christian teachings she disagreed with.

That's where she settled in. And that's where she worships today. Finally she seems to have found a faith that matches her personal convictions. But in the process she's ended up with a pretty tame God. A God quite under her own control. She seems to have lost the sense that God is actively involved in her life and in the world. She's lost confidence in prayer. She's lost the conviction that God can really offer her the help she needs in life's crises.

13

A successful young man I know has spent his life searching for the confidence that he really belongs to God. In his search he's been through various Christian denominations. In each tradition he's hoped he would finally find a secure sense of salvation. But on each point of his search he's struggled with a sense that his relationship with God really depends on what he does or doesn't do, on what he has or hasn't experienced.

He grew up Nazarene. The leaders in his congregation emphasized personal holiness. He tried his best to be the person God wanted him to be. But he always found himself slipping back into old habits. Then he'd start to wonder again if he really belonged to God.

A Baptist friend suggested that if he were baptized in their tradition, he could find assurance of salvation. For a while he felt better. But eventually he began to doubt his standing with God again.

This time he went to a Pentecostal church. They told him about what they called "the baptism of the Holy Spirit." He prayed for it, and his prayers were followed by a remarkable experience of God's power. But he didn't feel different for long, and eventually he moved on.

After a long period outside the church he finally became Episcopalian. The formality of the liturgy and the dignity of church tradition and the weekly celebration of the Eucharist seemed to offer him a stability and a sense of security he hadn't found elsewhere.

But from my perspective he still struggles with grave doubts about God's relationship to him. When his wife wanted a divorce, he blamed himself. God must be punishing him. He redoubled his participation in worship and agreed to serve on the vestry, but none of this really helped him to know that he belonged to God.

When his children began to experiment with drugs in their teenage years, he decided it was because he hadn't been a sufficient Christian example. He tried to spend more time in prayer. To be more consistent in putting his faith into practice. But it didn't seem to work. In fact, they strayed even further from Christian faith. And he blamed himself.

When my wife Jan and I were in seminary, we were co–youth directors in California. I had the honor of being invited by about fifteen teenagers who had been addicted to drugs or alcohol to lead a weekly Bible discussion and prayer time. They were just starting out on the twelve steps, in a meeting at the church building where we served.

These young people had been taught in their hospital recovery programs that it didn't really matter what god they placed their trust in, as long as it was a "higher power" beyond themselves. One of them told me matter-of-factly that she didn't have any patience with Christianity. As far as she was concerned, her higher power could be a doorknob, as long as she wasn't trusting herself.

I'm highly supportive of twelve-step recovery programs. When they're coupled with the love of a church community, they can be a wonderful beginning on the path of Christian faith. And in this case, that was particularly true. These young people asked to meet on a weekly basis with a Presbyterian youth director because they sensed that it really did matter what god they trusted. They wanted to place their faith in the God who really is. They knew that a so-called god who was no more than a projection of their own needs or beliefs didn't have any real power to help them with their addiction. To answer their prayers. To give them a strength greater than their own.

Each of these three stories is unique. But I'd like to focus on what they have in common. In each story religion was a "search" to find something that seemed to be missing. In each story the person was actively looking for a God or a sense of God that could meet his or her needs. And in each story the human being was the one in the active, defining, seeking role. God was out there somewhere. But the person had to find God by defining God in a way that fit his or her personal sense of how the world ought to be. By discovering an experience or religious style that finally "fit." By identifying or choosing a power greater than himself or herself.

The searches I've described assume that finding God is something that we do, by looking for a group of people who will support and reinforce the convictions that we've come to on our own. By searching until we find a faith tradition that meets our needs or fits our tastes. By defining things in a way that works for us.

II

All these people want to be Christians. But ironically, the approaches to faith in God that I've been describing are exactly the opposite of the approach that prevails in the Scriptures and the early church.

Let's listen to an Old Testament version of this latter approach. It begins with the moving shepherd images of Ezekiel 34:11-16, as the God of Israel is revealed as the one who seeks and find us. "For thus says the Lord God: I myself will search for my sheep, and will seek them out. As shepherds seek out their flocks when they are among their scattered sheep, so I will seek out my sheep. . . . I will seek the lost, and I will bring back the strayed, and I will bind up the injured, and I will strengthen the weak."

In the stories I told you, people were searching for God. In the faith of

Scripture and the early church, it's God who's searching for us. In the stories I told you, people assumed that the outcome of their search depended on what set of religious beliefs we come up with, or how hard we look, or what we do. In the faith of Scripture and the early church, no precise set of doctrines that we subscribe to or struggle with, no religious experience that we search for or discover, nothing that we do or don't do is the ultimate basis of our standing with God.

In the stories I told you, religious commitment can begin when a human being finally discovers the God he or she is looking for. In the faith of the New Testament and the early church, the life of Christian discipleship has its beginning in baptism.

Let's think for a moment about what happens in baptism. Whether the person being baptized is an adult or a tiny, helpless infant, baptism is something that is done to us and for us. It's not something we do.

The person kneels in a posture of spiritual receptivity and prayer. Or a baby is held tenderly in the arms of another who represents God's grace and love expressed in and through the church.

Then three times, in the name of the Father, and of the Son, and of the Holy Spirit, the person is immersed or dipped in water, or water is sprinkled or poured on the person: by someone else.

One of my teachers had a way of putting this very clearly: "Baptism is not related primarily to what we do, to our faith, or to our decision or confession of faith, but to that which is done for us, to that on which our faith is set." "[Baptism] invites both ourselves and others to look first at the one who is the object of our faith and whose gracious work we acknowledge when we confess our faith." "The connection of baptism is not with what we do, with our conversion or confession, but with what God does for and in us in Jesus Christ and by the Holy Spirit, the forgiveness of sins and regeneration."[1]

The faith of the New Testament and the early church is the faith of our common baptism. And in that faith everything depends not on us but on our triune God. As the Holy Spirit, God searches us out and finds us by grace, uniting us to Jesus Christ. Our salvation depends on what God has done for us in Christ by the Holy Spirit, not on what we do or don't do for God. Our beliefs are structured and patterned not around our own ideas of the kind of God or ethical stances or liturgical environment we believe we need, but rather around what God has shown us of the divine nature through Jesus Christ, by means of the Holy Spirit.

The trinitarian faith of the New Testament and the early church — the

---

1. Geoffrey Bromiley, *Children of Promise* (Grand Rapids: Eerdmans, 1979), p. 32.

common faith of our one baptism — is summed up in what we now call the Apostles' Creed.

The Apostles' Creed begins with four little words that seem so obvious at first for any religious person that we're tempted to jump over them and miss their importance. "I believe in God. . . ." In Greek, "faith" or "trust" are the nouns for which "believe" is the usual verb. "I believe" means "I place my faith in . . . ," "I place my trust in . . ."

When we say the Creed, we're not just coolly summarizing doctrines to which we assent. We're confessing our faith in the God of the biblical story. What separates Christian faith from every religious search or quest is not human faith itself. Especially not its quality or intensity or earnestness or sincerity. What separates Christian faith from every religious search or quest is the object of our faith. The God on whom we set our faith. The God in whom we place our trust.

Notice who this God is in whom we believe through our baptism. It's the one God to whom the three paragraphs of the Creed point: our heavenly Parent and sovereign Creator; the Son who entered our human story as God and suffered, died, and was raised in our place; the Spirit who lives in the church and makes God's grace and eternal life ours. It's the same God to whom the risen Jesus referred in our sermon text for today in Matthew 28:19, when he said, "Go therefore and make disciples of all nations, baptizing them in the name of the Father and of the Son and of the Holy Spirit. . . ." The God who, by the Holy Spirit, seeks out and finds lost humanity in Jesus Christ.

The Creed developed gradually but very consistently, throughout the early church, in many, many different locations. It developed as a primary way of identifying the God into whom Christians are baptized. Individual congregations worked out the clauses of the Creed in common with one another. Together, in this way, they identified and confessed what it meant to place their faith in the one God of Israel, the God of the biblical story beginning with Abraham and Sarah and reaching its climax in Jesus, the God whose gracious search for us was acknowledged and culminated in our baptism.

Karl Barth once put it like this: "God is gracious to us — this is what the confession of the Father, Son, and Holy Spirit says."[2]

In its three parts the Creed identifies the gracious triune God of the biblical story, in whom we place our faith, and into whom we are baptized.

---

2. Karl Barth, *Dogmatics in Outline*, trans. G. T. Thomson (London: SCM Press, 1949), p. 16.

III

Why does this matter? What difference does it make what God we believe in? Why believe in this God and not some other? Why embrace a trinitarian apprehension of God over competing conceptions? Why not make up a god who fits our sense of our needs or aspirations or beliefs or "search"?

From the very beginning Christian faith has begun not with a human search, but with a divine search that culminates in our baptism. From the very beginning Christian faith has begun with the triune God who seeks and finds us.

As Christians we've each been baptized in this triune name. As the Great Commission in our Matthew text shows us, trinitarian baptism is rooted in the mandate of Jesus himself. The faith of our baptism is precisely the faith in the triune God summarized for us in the Apostles' Creed.

In baptism we place our faith in God the Father almighty, Creator of heaven and earth. As we do we can be sure that the one in whom we believe is the true God: Yahweh — the one who made the universe and who made each of us. In Jesus Christ, through the Holy Spirit, this mighty, sovereign, ineffable God is our divine Parent, the God of everlasting covenant faithfulness, steadfast love, and mercy.

In baptism we place our faith in Jesus Christ, God the only Son our Lord. As we do we gain dependable knowledge of who God is, and the assurance that God is both with us and for us. Because God was incarnate in Jesus Christ, who lived a fully human life in our own flesh and blood, we know that we have God with us. In Jesus' life and teaching, his passion and resurrection, we know that even in the face of suffering and death our God is for us.

In baptism we place our faith in the Holy Spirit. As we do we have the firm confidence that God is present in us as the fulfillment of God's purpose for us. The Spirit lives in all of us as the church — the body of Christ: the living presence of Christ to gather God's people in worship, to extend and seal God's grace and life, and to send us out in mission. And the Spirit lives in each of us — in our hearts and lives — reassuring us that we're adopted as God's own daughters and sons, and offering us the power to be transformed into all that God intends us to be.

How can we have confidence that we really belong to God? That God's grace counts for us? That our sin is forgiven? That nothing we do or fail to do can ever separate us from the love of God in Christ Jesus our Lord? That searching for God anywhere else is fruitless, because in Christ we have the words of eternal life?

For Reformed Christians that confidence comes from our baptism in the strong name of the triune God who seeks and finds us.

Calvin put it beautifully in a catechism he wrote in Strasbourg to teach young adults the basis of their faith and their salvation:

Are you, my child, a Christian in fact as well as in name?
Yes, my father.

How do you know yourself to be?
Because I am baptized in the name of the Father and of the Son and of the
    Holy Spirit.

What knowledge do you have of the Father and of the Son and of the Holy
    Spirit?
I have that knowledge which the principal articles of our religion teach,
    which we make our profession through individual confession.

What is that confession?
(And here, the new Christian would confess the faith, using the words of
    the Apostles' Creed.)[3]

Is your life this morning a search for something — a spirituality, a faith, a god — that always seems just beyond your grasp?

Look no further. The good news of the Christian message is that the triune God to whom the Creed directs our faith is the God who seek and finds us. The God to whom our baptism binds us in faith. Assurance, confidence, spiritual rest, peace — all are elusive if we seek them by making up a god we like. Or in an endless search through every religious option available. Or by squeezing our concept of God into the self-centered box of our own personal priorities and experiences and beliefs.

But assurance and confidence and spiritual rest and peace do become ours — unshakably and inalterably ours — as we are encountered by the triune God who seeks and finds us: the faithful, covenant God of our baptism.

---

3. Hughes O. Old, *The Shaping of the Reformed Baptismal Rite* (Grand Rapids: Eerdmans, 1992), p. 207.

CHAPTER 2

I Believe in God, the Father Almighty

Credo in deum patrem omnipotentem

RICHARD A. NORRIS, JR.

I believe . . .

The label "creed" is a medieval English corruption of the Latin word that means "I believe" *(credo)*. Thus its proper reference is to a specific class of formulas, that of publicly authorized declaratory professions of faith which open with the words "I believe." Only two formulas of this type are now in widespread use: the so-called creed "of the apostles," a Western and Latin formula, and the Niceno-Constantinopolitan Creed, which was originally composed in Greek and whose text is known through the minutes of the ecumenical Council of Chalcedon (451). The latter formula gradually, after the fifth century, became the established baptismal creed of all Eastern churches and, since it has been widely used in the West as well, is in fact the one genuinely ecumenical confession of faith.

The ancient churches never gave in to the sort of offhand informality represented by a term like "creed." Instead they called their baptismal confessions by hefty names like "the symbol of the faith" or simply "the faith." The texts that originally bore these names had grown up locally and regionally and hence were, to begin with, fairly numerous.[1] They varied in wording from

---

1. Though, of course, such texts are not easily come by, since they were never written down save as they were quoted in formal expositions. Thus Augustine typically instructs his catechumens to remember the *symbolum* and recite it daily, but never to write it down (*De symbolo ad catechumenos* 1).

city to city (i.e., from church to church), though not in basic form or substance, and in any case tended to cohere into "families." The symbol Western tradition has attributed to "the apostles" — no doubt in order to emphasize its authority — is an eighth-century descendant of a whole family of Latin creeds that derived from the Roman baptismal confession of the third century — the latter, in its earliest form, set in Greek. That the creed now called "of the apostles" eventually became the baptismal creed of all churches under the jurisdiction of the Church of Rome was no doubt due in significant part to the esteem in which it was held by Charlemagne, who imposed it on all his dominions and strongly advised Pope Leo III to employ it. He thus unwittingly restored to the Roman Church a developed form of its own original baptismal formula.

Like its Eastern cousins, of which the Niceno-Constantinopolitan Creed is a representative, this formula was derived, in both content and form, from two closely related sources: (1) the interrogatory confession of faith which was the most widespread second-century baptismal "formula," and (2) the so-called "rule of truth" or "rule of faith." The latter, in its earliest forms, was not in the strict sense a "formula" at all. Rather, in widely differing shapes and wordings, it summarized the heads of what was inculcated in standard baptismal catechesis, and so was taken to be a norm of authentic Christian belief. Eventually, of course, it came to be identified with — or perhaps one should say *as* — the formula(s) now named by the word "creed." Creeds, then, were initially shaped in, and had their primary use in, the catechetical and liturgical procedures associated with baptism. Their content became standardized, like the New Testament canon itself, in the course of the second and later centuries. Given their baptismal setting, they functioned at one and the same time (a) as confessions of faith that marked a decisive turn in an individual's life — i.e., entrance, through the gift of the Spirit and forgiveness of sins, upon a new relationship with God in Christ; and (b) as the churches' syllabi for doctrinal instruction. When later introduced into the liturgy of the Eucharist, the Niceno-Constantinopolitan formula came to function, in addition, as a hymn of praise — and thus as a "confession" in that sense.[2] These several functions, moreover, attest the twofold character of creedal formulas, for they represent on the one hand an individual's personal confession —

2. Consider the use of *confiteor* (confess) in the hymn *Te Deum* ("We *acknowledge* thee to be the Lord"), and of *exomologeō* in the Septuagint translation of the Psalter (for example, in Ps. 104:1 [LXX]). See also Maximus the Confessor, *Mystagogy* 13 ("When they [the congregation at the eucharistic liturgy] have been brought together with one another and with [God] by the kiss, they gratefully offer him, in return for his innumerable benefits to them, the confession of thanksgiving for their salvation, which the divine Symbol of the Faith conveys"); cf. 18.

whether of faith or of praise — and at the same time the whole church's public testimony to God, for neither the terms of the confession nor the relationship it enacts is merely or even primarily individual. Both are the shared property of the entire believing community, which embraces the individual as he or she cries, "Abba, Father!"

I believe in . . .

Furthermore, this baptismal setting of creedal formulas surely determines the sense that is to be assigned to their opening words (in English): "I believe in . . ." Traditional debates about whether those words betoken primarily an assent to certain statements or propositions (Heb. 11:3, 6) or an act expressive of a radical, and thankful, confidence and trust (Gen. 15:6; Mark 1:15) are perhaps, given the original baptismal context of the creeds, pointless. In that context "I believe" plainly expresses a glad commitment that is understood to grow out of serious — and altogether risky — conviction, and to represent in principle a life-changing act. The words in question represent a public acknowledgment and attestation of God's salvation in Christ, and thus constitute an act of what F. D. Maurice called "affiance." They are words that buy into a covenant with the God to whom the creed makes reference. Like a marriage vow, "I believe" is therefore an expression of the sort that the philosopher J. L. Austin has taught us to call "performative": it brings about a new state of affairs of some sort. (Thomas Aquinas, indeed, suggested that baptismal faith joins the soul to God in a kind of "matrimony.")[3]

This sort of believing, however, is a complex affair, as Augustine of Hippo insisted in his comments on John 6:29 (". . . that you believe in him whom he has sent"). There he argued that there is a distinction to be noted between believing God and believing in God.[4] It is possible to believe that God exists, and indeed to believe what God "says," without believing in God. On the other hand, it is not possible to believe in God without (a) believing that God exists and (b) believing God. The mature act of faith, Augustine thought, involves a motion of the self in the direction of God. It is among other things a trustful wanting of God, a desiring what God has promised in Christ, and so a setting out upon a pilgrimage into God — a journey empowered by God's gift

---

3. N. Ayo, trans., *The Sermon-Conferences of St. Thomas Aquinas on the Apostles' Creed* (Notre Dame, Ind.: University of Notre Dame Press, 1988), p. 19.

4. The Latin preposition *in,* when followed by a noun in the accusative case, normally implies motion *into* or *toward* whatever the noun in question designates.

of the Spirit.[5] Indeed, it is fair to say that in the first instance this understanding of faith explains, from a certain perspective, what for Augustine — and not for him alone — the word "God" initially denotes: namely, the sole "good" which is truly ultimate, that is, capable of being loved and sought for its own sake. It is entirely correct, then, to point out that such faith cannot be a mere expression of assent to certain statements. It is also true, however, that such faith cannot exist apart from a relatively wide range of convictions — about the reality of God, about the world as God's gift, about a revelatory course of events — that specify the context in which alone such faith can make sense. Such convictions, in a word, indicate what is essentially presupposed by the commitment that faith makes as a response to the gospel of God's grace in Christ, and thus in the end contribute further to the task of framing the sense of "God" in Christian discourse.

Once this is said and affirmed, however, one must add a stiff denial that mere acquiescence in certain "beliefs" can ever qualify as faith. Even the belief of the demons, "mere" though it is, is said to be accompanied by a heartfelt shudder (James 2:19); this suggests not that their condition satisfies the definition of "faith" but that their real faith is ultimately lodged elsewhere: that they do in fact confess God, but only as their enemy. To be sure, there can be — and is — such a thing as an "elementary" faith, or faith in what one might call a preliminary form. This is not, however, simply a matter of cool, correct belief free of all self-involvement, an objective assent from which one might then graduate, as it were, to faith-as-glad-commitment. Elementary faith is perhaps closer to being a wistful contemplation of God and the things of God as possibilities. In such faith glad commitment is already present to the extent that these possibilities are entertained as real possibilities, entrancing and engaging, but at the same time doubtful just because they may seem, as the saying goes, too good to be true. On the other hand, such commitment is absent to the extent that other, inconsistent and competitive, possibilities seem just as real and continue to have their own attraction. Nor is it easy to specify with any precision the steps that lie between such elementary faith and the mature faith that, in response to the church's witness, entrusts itself to the God who had at first seemed no more than a distant possibility, a hope-filled vision or dream. One may, like Augustine of Hippo, be sure that grace in the shape of the Holy Spirit has more than a little to do with it,[6] but that assertion, justi-

---

5. Augustine, *Tractates on the Gospel of John* 29 (Nicene and Post-Nicene Fathers, 1st ser., 7:185); cf. Thomas Aquinas, *Summa Theologiae* 2-2 q.2 a.1.

6. Cf. Rom. 5:5 — in either or both of the interpretations that the controverted genitive can have. See Augustine, *On the Spirit and the Letter* 3.5.

fied though it be, merely removes the process and its explanation from the realm of human calculation (though not of human description), and at the same time, in doing so, accentuates the labors and struggles, the falls and recoveries that mark the road to an honest — though, to be sure, never completely placid — faith.

I believe in God the Father . . .

It may be better to use the words of Saint Paul as quoted in the Niceno-Constantinopolitan Creed: "I believe in 'one God the Father' . . ." (1 Cor. 8:6). The New Testament is full of references to God as "Father." Plainly, however, the word as used there bears more than one connotation, even if, as Paul's language insists, it has a unique denotation. In fact, there are three principal "senses" of "father" in its theological use — all of them, needless to say, metaphorical;[7] they require first to be disentangled and then to be brought into a coherent relation with one another if the creed's basic understanding of God is to be grasped.

The first of these — and the one closest to the surface in Paul's language at 1 Corinthians 8:6 — employs "Father" to characterize God as the ultimate ground of the cosmos, the one "from whom are all things," the one who generates all things. This sense of the term is already an established commonplace in the writings of Philo of Alexandria. Thus in his treatise *On the Making of the World,* God is called "Maker and Father" — which is no doubt a recollection of Plato (*Timaeus* 28C) — and characterized as one who exercises a providential care over all creatures.[8] These characterizations or their equivalents are reiterated regularly by Philo,[9] and of course they recur in Stoic sources. The Stoic sage Epictetus — who was a rough contemporary of the second Christian generation — refers to God as "Maker, Father, and Guardian" of human beings, and asserts that in virtue of this relationship the latter are entitled to think of themselves as citizens of the cosmos;[10] his testimony is

---

7. Note here the admonition of Justin Martyr (*2 Apology* 6.1f.): "To the Father of all things, no name is assigned, because he is unbegotten. . . . 'Father' and 'God' and 'Creator' and 'Lord' and 'Master' are not names but designations drawn from beneficent deeds and functions."

8. Philo, *On the Making of the World* 7.10.

9. See, just for example, *De cherubim* 44 ("the Father of things that exist, the unbegotten God that begets all things"); *De decalogo* 64 ("All created things are brothers, just inasfar as they are created, since the Father of all is the one Maker of the universe"); *De specialibus legibus* 2.198 ("God the Begetter and Father and Savior of the cosmos and of everything in it").

10. Epictetus, *Discourses* 1.9.7.

reiterated by Diogenes Laertius, who tells us that the Stoics conceived the many-named God, the Spirit that pervades the universe, as "the Artisan and, so to speak, the Father of all things" — a title that above all emphasized deity's role as the providential ruler of the cosmos, the "formula" (logos) according to which things come to pass.[11] Early Christian writers too seem often, in the first instance, to explain "Father" in this way; i.e., in the framework of God's relation to the created order as a whole. Thus 1 *Clement* speaks of God as "Father and Creator of the whole world" (19.2), who is an "ever-merciful and beneficent Father" (23.1), or as "the Craftsman and Father of the ages and the all-holy One" (35.3). 2 *Clement* names God "Father of truth" (3.1). In the same spirit Theophilus of Antioch describes the Almighty as "God and Father and Maker" of the universe,[12] while Tatian describes God as "the Father of things perceptible and visible."[13] The most interesting example of this way of taking "Father," however, may be that found in Novatian's third-century treatise *On the Trinity* (which is perhaps best read not as a treatise on the doctrine of the Trinity but as a commentary on the three members of the "rule of truth," i.e., in this case, the baptismal profession of faith). For him the opening words of the confession refer to "God, the Father and almighty Lord, that is, the most perfect Founder [*conditorem*] of all things" — a description he glosses first with a paraphrase of the Genesis story of creation and fall, and then with an account of God as the one who contains all things, who has no "origin," who knows no time *(non habet tempus),* and who utterly escapes human speech and understanding[14] — characterizations that might have been garnered from Irenaeus of Lyon in his earlier polemic against Christian gnosticism.

In the Pauline corpus, however, a different sense of "Father" predominates. According to this second usage, "Father" portrays God as the loving Father of believers — as "our Father" (cf. Matt. 6:9 with Gal. 1:4 and 4:6), not to mention the references to "your Father" or "your heavenly Father" in Matthew 6 and Paul's habitual phrase, "God our Father and the Lord Jesus Christ." Ignatius of Antioch too knows God as the Father of believers;[15] this seems to be the general sense in which "Father" is employed of God — on the relatively few occasions it is so employed — in the Old Testament and the Apocrypha. In 3 Maccabees the persecuted people of God in Egypt call upon "their merciful God and Father" for help, even as Tobit tells "the sons of Israel" to make known the greatness of the God who "is our Father for ever"

11. Diogenes Laertius, *Lives of the Philosophers* 7.147.
12. Theophilus, *Ad Autolycum* 2.34.
13. Tatian, *Oratio ad Graecos* 4.2.
14. Novatian, *On the Trinity* 1-2.
15. Ignatius, *Trallians* 13.3; cf. *Romans* 8.2.

(13:4). In the introductory chapters of 2 Esdras — chapters that contain a first-century Christian composition sometimes referred to separately as 4 Ezra — God complains to his people that they have forsaken him even though he had "entreated [them] as a father entreats his sons or a mother her daughters or a nurse her children" (1:28). Such language, moreover, echoes certain — infrequent but significant — passages in the Pentateuch, the Prophets, and the Psalms. In Psalm 89:26ff., for example, God is Father of the king and of the people in his covenant with them. In the time of trouble it is God, not Abraham or Jacob, that is Israel's Father (Isa. 63:16; cf. 64:8) — even the God who is "Father of the fatherless, and protector of widows" (Ps. 68:5). Hence God complains that the people have not honored him as their Father, but have "forgotten the Lord their God" (Jer. 3:19-22); a similar complaint is found even earlier, in the prophecy of Hosea (11:1ff.).

This usage did not disappear in Christian theological discourse after the close of the period in which the books now contained in the New Testament were written — far from it. It is important, however, to note that in the catechetical tradition the normal occasion for taking up this use of "Father" was provided — logically enough — by the opening phrase of the Lord's Prayer rather than by the language of the first member of the Creed. Thus Origen appeals, as precedent for the words "Our Father" in the Lord's Prayer, to Deuteronomy (23:6; 32:18, 20), but he insists at the same time that there is no prayer in the Old Testament "in which someone calls God 'Father,'" the explanation of this being that only after the advent of Christ do "those who desire it 'receive the adoption of sons' [Gal. 4:5; cf. Rom. 8:15]" and are able to address God as "Abba, Father!" To the same end he recalls Johannine passages that speak of believers' birth from God (John 1:12; 1 John 3:9).[16] In this, moreover, he seems to have the support of Ephesians, whose author speaks of "one God and Father of all" (4:6), signifying by the word "all" those who (also) share in the "one baptism." This understanding is maintained by later expositors of the Lord's Prayer. Cyril of Jerusalem, for example, in his exposition of the Eucharist, directly connects the church's custom of addressing God in the words "our Father" with the bestowal of forgiveness and the participation in grace that accompany baptism.[17] The same view is taken by Ambrose, who explains to his catechumens that God has begotten them as his children by the washing of baptism, just as he has redeemed them in Christ, so that they can lift up their eyes to God and say, "Father."[18] Theodore of Mopsuestia

---

16. Origen, *On the Prayer* 22.1-2; cf. Tertullian, *On the Prayer* 2.1-3.

17. Cyril of Jerusalem, *Mystagogical Catecheses* 5.11.

18. Ambrose, *De sacramentis* 5.19.

dwells at length, in his exposition of "Our Father," on the baptismal bestowal of the Spirit, which brings about the "adoption of sons" and the *parrêsia*, the freedom, that enables believers to address God as "Father."[19] For Christians, as traditionally for Jews, then, divine fatherhood is revealed — and so becomes, as it were, operative — within the covenant relationships symbolized by baptism and circumcision respectively. God is Father not primarily in his relation to humanity understood simply as part of the created order, but rather in his electing and redeeming action within that order. It is interesting to observe that in the Johannine Gospel it is only after the resurrection that Jesus openly refers to God as the "Father" of his disciples (John 20:17, but note 16:27 and 8:41f.).

This theme of filial adoption, however, which is rooted, as Origen and patristic tradition knew well enough, in the argument of Galatians 4:1-7, depends in principle upon a third connotation of "Father" — that according to which the Son to whom the Father is directly related is not, in the first instance, the collective people of Israel or the body of Christian believers, but that "unique Son" who is, as the Creed insists, "Jesus Christ our Lord," and who was manifested as such when, at his baptism by John, the Spirit of God descended upon him as Love's gift to attest this status. It is hardly necessary to enumerate the occurrences in the New Testament of phrases like "God and the Father of our Lord Jesus Christ" (Col. 1:3; cf. Rom. 15:6); it is sufficient merely to note that Mark's Gospel seems to entitle itself "The Gospel of Jesus Christ the Son of God," or to weigh the testimony of the opening verses of Hebrews, where this Son of God is presented as that very divine offspring and Wisdom (Prov. 8:22f.; Wisd. of Sol. 7:21ff.) "through whom [God] made the ages" (Heb. 1:2; cf. 1 Cor. 8:6; Col. 1:15f.; John 1:1ff.), or to enumerate the roughly twenty-five times the Johannine Christ refers to God as "my Father."

It is this usage, moreover, that has dominated expositions of the creedal description of God as "Father" — and understandably, inasmuch as the sense of "God the Father" in the first member of the Creed seems to be determined by the words *filium eius unicum* of the second member,[20] rather than by the word "Creator" that more or less immediately follows it. Typical is the interpretation put on the word by Cyril of Jerusalem, who observes straightforwardly: "in the thought of God, let the thought of Father be included, so that the glory which we ascribe to the Father and the Son with the Holy Spirit may

---

19. Theodore of Mopsuestia, *Catechetical Homilies* 11.7-8 (in R. Tonneau, trans., *Les homélies catéchétiques de Théodore de Mopsueste* [Vatican City, 1949], pp. 297f.).

20. And, of course, in the Niceno-Constantinopolitan formula, *ton huion tou theou ton monogene.*

be perfectly free from difference." "God the Father," then, means the first hypostasis of the Trinity, the begetter of the Word and breather of the Spirit. Augustine for his part dwells at length upon the meaning of "Almighty," but only mentions "Father" when he comes to the opening words of the second member of the Creed: "we believe also in his Son, that is to say, the Son of God the Father Almighty, 'his only Son, our Lord.'"[21] Karl Barth — to take one obvious example from more modern times — read the Creed in the same way: "God is Father in respect to Jesus Christ, and Jesus Christ is his eternal Son."[22]

No doubt this way of interpreting "God the Father" can from a certain perspective seem strange. One might have thought that, where the Creed is concerned, the word "Creator" would be taken to govern the sense of "Father," so that the text could be construed as if it said "God the Almighty Father-Creator." In this way emphasis would be laid upon the role of God as the one who not only summons a world into being but also exercises a providential care over all its parts. Saint Paul, moreover, in his letter to the Romans (1:19-21), seems to suggest that the universal first step in human awareness of God is acknowledgment of the reality of God as evoked by the beauty and harmony of the cosmos; the psalmist, after all, asserts that "the heavens declare the glory of God, and the firmament shows his handiwork" (Ps. 19:1). Presumably Paul in Romans 1 is referring not to any formal "argument from design" but, in the manner of all the ancients, Jew and Greek alike, to an insight that in his view all but infallibly presents itself to anyone who contemplates the splendor and order of the heavens, an insight that discerns in and behind them what Joseph Addison, sharing this wonder, once called "their great Original." Paul also knows, however, what Calvin later learned from him and formulated tersely: such knowledge does not produce "real piety," for all, it seems, "fall away from true knowledge" of God,[23] into idolatry as Paul would have it, or into pride and superstition (which, after all, look like forms of idolatry). Any honest modern, however, is bound to acknowledge that it may also involve a large dose of simple doubtfulness, inspired not only by a scientific discourse that seems to do nicely without the hypothesis of God, but also by goings-on in the world created by human beings for themselves that seem to call in question the vision which the heavens were taken to inspire. It might be better, then, to say that what this "general revelation" or

---

21. Augustine, *De symbolo ad catechumenos* 3.

22. Karl Barth, *The Faith of the Church*, trans. G. Vahanian (New York: Meridian Books, 1960), p. 45.

23. Calvin, *Institutes* 1.4.1; cf. Paul's quotation of Ps. 14 at Rom. 3:11-12.

"natural knowledge" — Calvin's *sensus divinitatis* — amounts to in most cases is not so much a clear awareness of God as a vague awareness that "God" is the label of a question at once inevitable, difficult, and embarrassing. In any case, when Hebrews alleges that it is "by faith" that "we understand that the world was created by the word of God" (11:3), it is impossible not to wonder and to ask where such faith originates. How does one get to see the created order in all its multiplicity and, to human eyes, confusion as well, as a manifestation of the glory of God?

In both the Old and the New Testaments what is, at least in the order of learning, first seen, and hence what primarily evokes serious faith, is the "good news" embodied in happenings that set people free for God — free to accept and seek the promises uncovered and exemplified in those happenings themselves. In both cases, moreover, the events in question are those associated with Passover: the exodus of the people from slavery in Egypt, and the exodus that God's "Son" and "Chosen One" "was to carry through in Jerusalem" (Luke 9:31, 35). No doubt these events occurred against backgrounds in which the title "God" had already been seriously spoken, and moreover, referred to one who was thought to have more than a little to do with the way things go and therefore with the way they got started. Nevertheless, it is these "saving" events alone which make it essential for faith to affirm that God — i.e., the God who redeems and liberates — must be, and is, the one who is ultimately responsible for everything, for the way things are and indeed for there being any "things" at all. Otherwise it would be hard to understand how such a redemption and liberation could come to pass in this world.

The Father of the cosmos, then, is known first of all as the Father of that eternal Word in whose incarnate work the exodus from Egypt is somehow repeated, renewed, and extended, and hence as the source of that Spirit by whose power this one Son becomes the companion and leader *(archegos)* who brings "many sons and daughters into glory" (Heb. 2:10). In the order of logic, creation may come before redemption, but in the order of learning, people's perception of the world as God's creation depends for its plausibility upon God's work of redemption in the incarnate Word. It is the "grace and truth" given in Christ that allow the world itself to be seen clearly as a work of grace, as God's gift that comes out of nowhere and therefore has no presupposition save God's eternally spoken Word and God's life-giving Breath (cf. Ps. 33:6).

But then plainly, and merely on the basis of what we have already said, the eternal Son of God the Father is not the sole object of the Father's love. He stands before God, he says, together with "the children God has given me" (Heb. 2:13). With these children he has shared "in flesh and blood," partaking of their nature (2:10-14). The Word through whom the world was created (cf. 1:2) acknowledges, in the incarnation, that the love with which the Father loves him is the very love with which God loves his entire creation and an errant humanity within it. Hence "John" can say to his community: "Beloved, we are children of God now. It does not yet appear what we shall be, but we know that when he appears, we shall be like him, for we shall see him as he is" (1 John 3:2). The love with which God knows the Son who is his very self eternally reiterated overflows upon those creatures with whom, in the Son, he shares his life (4:9), so that they may truly come to be after his image. Hence, as Paul had said, this God is their Father too — our Father. "For by one Spirit we were all baptized into one body" — the body whose name is Christ (1 Cor. 12:12-13) and child of God. Since, further, this relationship of Father and children presupposes the divine work of creation, the three "paternities" of which Christian language speaks are different indeed, but, it seems, mutually entailing.

. . . the Father almighty

The English word "almighty" translates the Latin *omnipotens* (omnipotent), which translates the Greek *pantokratōr* ("all-ruler," "ruler of all things"). It is therefore *pantokratōr* whose sense must be explored here. There is little to be learned from its use in the Scriptures: the Septuagint employs it to render the Hebrew *sabaoth*, as in the expression "Lord of hosts" — though it is not consistent in this practice.[24] In the New Testament, apart from a Pauline citation of 2 Samuel 7:14,[25] it occurs only in the Revelation to John (where the RSV renders it regularly as "the Almighty"), and there, it seems, principally as a rhetorical device to emphasize the power and grandeur of God. In Job the term tends to occur independently ("the Almighty"), no doubt to accentuate the power and hence the answerability of God.

On the other hand, *pantokratōr* figures prominently in *1 Clement* and certain other works associated with the literature of the apostolic fathers. The *Letter to Diognetus* refers to the "all-ruling and all-creating and invisible God."[26] In *1 Clement* too, *pantokratōr* is associated with God in his role as "Father and Creator" (62.2; cf. 2.3), but the Roman Church's letter also associates the term with God in his redeeming activity: *pantokratōr theos*, we learn, is the one who

24. The translators of Isaiah, for example, simply write *kurios sabaōth,* as at Isa. 6:3, while in Jeremiah the phrase *kurios (theos) pantokratōr* is used habitually. Neither phrase occurs in the Pentateuch.

25. Cf. 2 Cor. 6:18.

26. *Diognetus* 7.2.

has justified men and women by faith "from the beginning of the age" (32.4). It is he, moreover, who through Jesus Christ causes grace and peace to burgeon for the church, as we are told in the letter's greeting. The *Didache* identifies God as the "Lord Almighty" who "created all things for the sake of thy Name."[27] Among the apologists, Justin Martyr too associates the title *pantokratōr* with "the Maker of the Universe," and indeed, in one place, with "Father":[28] in his usage the expression "Almighty God" *(theos pantokratōr)* seems to be roughly synonymous with "the true God," i.e., the God of Jewish and Christian tradition. Hermas, on the other hand, in his *Shepherd,* uses *pantokratōr* to specify an attribute of God's "glorious Name,"[29] which — or rather who — is the founder of the church; this usage, which clearly intends the Christ, is also found in *1 Clement,* who similarly refers to God's "almighty and glorious Name" (60.4; cf. John 17:11).

Augustine, whose creed has the Latin *omnipotens* for *pantokratōr,* hastens to explain what "almighty" does not mean. It does not mean that "God is able to do anything," for there are "many things that he cannot do, and yet is almighty — indeed, is almighty precisely because he cannot do these things. For if he could die, he would not be almighty; if to lie, to be deceived, to do unjustly, were possible for him, he would not be almighty: because if this were in him, he would not be worthy to be called almighty. For our almighty Father, it is quite impossible to sin. He does whatever he wills: that is omnipotence. He does whatever he rightly wills, whatever he justly wills."[30] Having thus dismissed a possible sense of the Latin *omnipotens,* Augustine goes on to suggest that it is the work of world-creation that most obviously characterizes God as the true All-Ruler;[31] in fact, he refers to the term as indicating a ground for belief that the world was created ex nihilo[32] — in this respect, it seems, agreeing substantively with the tradition before him: if God is "in charge" of everything, God must also be the source and ground of everything.

It is this line of thought that is illustrated by Irenaeus's contention that one must choose between two alternatives: confessing the one God who "contains all things without being contained" and is therefore responsible for the creation of all things, or admitting "Makers and Gods" in unlimited numbers, each of whom is, as it were, responsible for some localized partition of reality. The latter hypothesis, however, if adopted — so Irenaeus argues — would

---

27. *Didache* 10.3.
28. Justin, *Dialogue* 16.4; 38.2; 139.4.
29. Hermas, *Vision* 3.3.5.
30. Augustine, *De symbolo ad catechumenos* 2.
31. Augustine, *De symbolo ad catechumenos* 2.
32. Augustine, *De fide et symbolo* 2.2.

mean that the very word *pantokratōr* would disappear from use.[33] *Panto-kratōr*, then, entails an assertion of God's unlimited character (and so of God's incomprehensibility); for the uncontained has no boundaries (2.30.9). It further entails acknowledgment that the Almighty is intimately close to all creatures in that he "works everything in all things" (4.20.6), and further that the *pantokratōr* has always acted to save his creatures from demonic evil, and did so even before the advent of Christ, because he was and is the one to whom all things are ever subject — "God over all" (2.6.2). Hence Irenaeus likes to characterize God by use of the two words *dives* and *multus:* God is "rich" and "many" not only in the sense that he is rightly known "by different designations and many names" (3.10.6), but also in the sense that through his many differing "dispensations" *(oikonomiai)* — i.e., the varying devices by which he equips humanity for growth toward salvation — he realizes the purposes implicit in the act of creation in multifarious ways (4.20.11).

In the creeds, then, "Almighty" has a function partially but significantly distinct from that of "Father." It accentuates the role of God as the active founder and administrator of all that is — one who actively fulfills the work of creation in exercising providence and in the work of redemption. It further stresses the double relation of God to the cosmos as the one "who is everything in all things by transcending all things infinitely."[34] In performing these tasks, however, *pantokratōr* raises in an acute form the question of evil and of God's relation to it, and thus inevitably, like "Father," looks ahead to the second member of the Creed.

33. Irenaeus, *Adversus haereses* 2.1.5. See the note of A. Rousseau in Sources chrétiennes, 293:206. Parenthetical references in the remainder of this paragraph are to Irenaeus.

34. Maximus the Confessor, *Mystagogia* 1.

The Almighty God

Isaiah 45:1-8; 2 Thessalonians 2:1-12; Luke 13:1-9

COLIN GUNTON

Text: Isaiah 45:6, 7: "I am the Lord and there is no other. I form light and create darkness, I bring prosperity and create disaster; I, the Lord, do all these things."

I

Many of our traditional prayers begin with the words "Almighty God." There is much in our theology about God's power. We say God is omnipotent — that he is all-powerful, can do anything he likes, and all the rest. Indeed, that is in our creed: "I believe in God, the Father almighty. . . ." Not surprisingly, many people have problems with this, two of which stand out. First, the words of the Creed may cause God to be depicted as a heavenly tyrant, one who by sheer power forces things into his mold; against this notion there has arisen in recent centuries a movement known as "protest atheism." If God is like that, say a number of moderns, then we will reject him. They have come to regard God as an enemy to be opposed.

The second problem is similar, though it appears on the surface to be the opposite. If God is so powerful, why does he not see to it that his world is run somewhat more benevolently? Why, to use a common way of putting it, does God allow crazed terrorists to fly aircraft into buildings — to kill indiscriminately? If God is all-powerful, could he not intervene to stop such a great evil? There is a famous portrayal of that challenge in a novel by the great Christian novelist Fyodor Dostoyevsky. A character in the novel makes the claim that if God allows the suffering of even one innocent child, that is enough to reject him. If God gives a free ticket to life, isn't the fact that God allows this suffering sufficient reason simply to return the ticket?

The terrible events of September 11, 2001, in New York and Washington, D.C., whose long-term outcome is still difficult to predict, crystallize all the problems we have with the idea that God is omnipotent. Sometimes the world seems too uncertain, too wicked, too overwhelmingly hostile to be the work of a good and all-powerful God. The problem becomes worse when the perpetrators of the evil claim to be obeying God's will in what they call "holy war." What, then, shall we make of it all?

We can appeal to human freedom — as many do. Are we not free to do evil if we choose to? Why blame God? That view, however, simply pushes the problem back a step. Who creates these beings with this overwhelming capacity for evil? The questions keep coming. The Creed calls God "almighty," and in doing so it is being true to Scripture. But what does it mean?

II

The writer we call Second Isaiah ministered to the people of Israel in their exile in Babylon. Carried away from their home and alone in a foreign country, they began to wonder if God still cared about them. Isaiah's message is straightforward: they should not suppose that because they are away from their homeland, they are outside God's care. The God of chapters 40–55 of the book of Isaiah is the universal creator who rules heaven and earth — and everything that happens therein. Nor is God's authority restricted to calling on only those who believe in him. Even kings who refuse to acknowledge him bring about his purposes despite themselves. Thus, in an astonishing passage, the prophet calls King Cyrus of Persia "God's anointed," the servant who will bring about his purposes of destroying the power of Babylon: "Cyrus, whose right hand I take hold of to subdue nations before him . . . though you do not acknowledge me . . . though you have not acknowledged me" (45:1, 4, 5). And God does it for the sake of his people Israel, so that they may return to the land from which they had been taken ("for the sake of Jacob my servant, of Israel my chosen").

But the purposes of God stretch beyond Israel, who is his servant for a purpose, "so that from the rising of the sun to its setting people may know that there is none besides me." And he continues in words that provide the text for today: "I am the Lord and there is no other. I form light and create darkness, I bring prosperity and create disaster; I, the Lord, do all these things." That is the difficult thing for us to encompass. Does God actually bring about disaster and evil? Isaiah is not the only biblical writer to suggest that; Amos 3:6 is similar in its thrust: "When disaster comes to a city, has not the Lord caused it?" We need to accept the full implications of these words. Nothing, not even the worst thing that might happen, is outside God's control, at least in the sense that he permits it to happen. That does not mean, of course, either that the Americans killed by terrorists deserved what happened to them or that those innocent civilians caught in the retaliatory cross fire will deserve what happens to them. Things are much more complicated than that. Remember what Jesus said about a similar, if smaller, disaster: "Or those eighteen who died when the tower in Siloam fell on them — do you think they were more guilty than all the others living in Jerusalem?" (Luke 13:4). What God is doing — and why — is rarely clear to us at the time it happens, except that we know that events and actions are not outside his ordering.

There are three things about the way God works that teach us how to view what "happens." First, God works long term, allowing events to take their course. Rome was not built in a day, a child does not become an adult overnight, and glaciers are not known for their speed. So it is with everything in God's creation. Already in Genesis 1 we learned that creation took place over a period of "days" and that God made a world that only became what it is over a long period of time. And once evil corrupted the good creation, processes in nature and history have taken even longer. God allows things to take their course, not because he cannot do anything else, but because that is the nature of the created order. They neither become what they are instantly, nor are they healed of their sickness overnight. There is no instant salvation, no magical removal of evil at a stroke, not at least until God's time has run its full course.

Second, God never allows evil to run out of control. It is true that evil can become entrenched in whole nations, as we saw happen in Germany last century, so that even innocent people seem to get caught up into complacency or following leaders that are quite against their true selves. And it seems true that a present rogue form of Islam has a similar way of creating fanaticism and moral blindness in which killing becomes an end in itself. But the way of all these systems is doomed. The reading from 2 Thessalonians makes a similar point: Paul speaks of someone "who sets himself up in God's temple, proclaiming himself to be God"; he will do appalling damage, but there is one who holds the evil one back "till he is taken out of the way." Notice, too, the way the story of the coming of evil into God's good world is told in Genesis. At each stage it brings disaster in its train, yet at each stage God in his mercy sees to it that its toll is restricted. My favorite example is Cain, who is punished for his murder and yet given a mark so that no one will punish him further. So we can believe in God's superintendence in the events we fear so much. They may indeed be fearful, but in the mercy of God they will be restricted within limits, so that some good will eventually result.

Third, and most important of all, where does God reveal his power and his defeat of evil? It is in the cross of Jesus. There we see the power, the wisdom, and the mercy of God in action. There evil, indeed the greatest evil that would destroy goodness and love, is faced and overcome, and its doom ensured. This is the basis of our confidence that God allows matters to take their time, and yet it shows that from within our time and space he takes charge of them in an omnipotent way. It is omnipotent because evil has no answer to the one who conquers it by love alone, refusing to use the weapons of the enemy. In that power we can trust.

This does not mean that we may never support the use of force, even war, to overcome the threats to our world. But it certainly means that, as Christians, we rule out revenge as a proper Christian response in daily life toward those who would do us harm. But proper punishment is not revenge, nor is the forcible restraint of the violent. When the war against the evil of Nazism broke out in the last century, my father was a pacifist. By the end of the war he decided that he had been wrong. He came to realize that there is no peace without a justice tempered by the light of the victorious power of the cross.

III

In the light of all this, what are we to make of our creed? Notice the actual language the Creed uses. First of all, it speaks of "God, the Father almighty. . . ." The almighty God, the omnipotent, the one who is Lord of all things ("I am the Lord and there is no other") is not simply an omnipotent tyrant. This God is the Lord and Father of our Lord Jesus Christ.

On my sixtieth birthday some of my students gave me an icon of Jesus, the Pantocrator, a representation of the risen and ascended Lord in glory. It portrays a heavenly monarch and ruler, awesome in his power, but he remains the Crucified One. His power is the greatest possible power we can imagine, because it achieves its end through the merciful means of the cross. He lets evil take its course, but only to a degree; he answers evil with good, hatred with love. In sum, this is the power that takes shape in the love of the one who died even for those who sought to put him to death. This is real, omnipotent power, though it does not achieve its ends overnight. It is firm and relentless, and it will not let go until evil is driven from the earth and tears are wiped from all eyes. In the meantime we, the people of God, can live by the faith that God almighty will accomplish his saving purposes, and we can live in a hope that is grounded in the resurrection.

Second, the Creed associates that power with the act of creation: "the Father almighty, creator of heaven and earth." This takes us right back to our text, to the words of Second Isaiah: "I am the Lord and there is no other. I form light and create darkness, I bring prosperity and create disaster; I, the Lord, do all these things." The crucified Jesus wields the power of the Lord of all creation.

What, then, should our attitude be toward events of terror and those unknown consequences that we fear? Our response is, first, to pray that God will work all things together for good, including the evil in the world, as he turned the evil of the crucifixion to the world's salvation. And our second response must come in the light of how the cross and resurrection infuse our long-term vision with hope. John Maynard Keynes famously observed that in the long term we are all dead. The Christian response is rather different: in the long term we shall all die, but we shall die in the hope of the resurrection.

CHAPTER 3

Creator of Heaven and Earth

Creatorem coeli et terrae

LESLIE J. HOPPE, O.F.M.

Almost every religious tradition makes some attempt to explain the origins of the world. People have gazed at the wonders of the universe with a mixture of awe, curiosity, and fear, and they have looked to their belief systems to make this world and its mysteries understandable. That the Bible begins with a story about the origins of the universe is not at all surprising. Affirming that God had a purpose in creating and that the world is a comprehensible place is important for biblical religion. At the same time, it is clear that ancient Israel did not devote as much attention to the beginnings of the universe as did other peoples of the ancient Near East. In comparison with its neighbors, Israel does not give as much sustained attention to matters of cosmogony. Ancient Israel simply assumed much about creation from the cultural heritage to which it was an heir. But it is a mistake to hold that creation has only a marginal place in biblical theology compared with the doctrine of salvation. That the Scriptures begin with an account of creation shows that the question of origins is very significant for biblical religion.

Creation in the Old Testament

Two characteristics of the Old Testament treatment of creation are important. First, there is no uniformity or consistency in the way the Hebrew Bible understands the process of the way God brought the cosmos into being. The story of creation found in Genesis 1:1–2:4a is usually identified as *the* biblical account of creation. It is not difficult to see why. This story begins the Old Testament. Also, its aesthetic character, comprehensiveness, and elevated tone have contributed to its status as the normative biblical text on creation for both Jews and Christians. But scattered throughout the Bible is evidence of other ways that ancient Israel confessed its faith in God as the creator. One of these is obvious from the many allusions to a cosmic battle waged by God against the forces of chaos. God defeated these forces, and this led to the creation of the universe. Other texts describe personified Wisdom's role in the creation of an orderly, rational universe. The Bible carefully preserves these quite different theological approaches to creation, so identifying Genesis 1 as *the* biblical account of creation is imprecise. Second, nowhere does the Old Testament betray its ancient Near Eastern origins more clearly than in its treatment of creation. The Bible is the product of a people who developed their cultural and religious identity after Egyptian, Mesopotamian, and Syrian cultures were flourishing many centuries before the Israelite tribes emerged in Canaan. Like the creation stories from these older cultures, ancient Israel's creation traditions are fundamentally mythic and reflect patterns found in earlier ancient Near Eastern treatments of the origins of the world.

The most obviously mythic of ancient Israel's creation traditions are found in poetic texts. Many such texts imply that a primordial battle between God and the forces of chaos took place before the creation of the world. The Bible's poetry identifies the sea and the monsters that dwell in it as these forces of chaos. For example, Psalm 74:12-17 is devoted to creation, but it does not derive its imagery from Genesis 1; rather, it celebrates God's victory over the sea and the monsters living in it — a victory that was the prelude to the creation of the world. Psalm 89:9-10 (MT 89:10-11) praises God for the victory over the sea and the defeat of the dragon Rahab. Amos 9:2-3 describes God as commanding the sea serpent that dwells in the underworld. Habakkuk 3:8 lists the "river" and the "sea" among God's enemies. Isaiah 51:9-10 takes the reader back to the beginnings of the cosmos when God killed Rahab and the dragon and dried up the waters of the sea. Psalm 104 is a hymn entirely devoted to the praise of God for creation. It mentions Leviathan (v. 26) and notes that God built God's palace "upon the waters" (v. 3).

These vague allusions to a battle God waged and won with the sea and the monsters that dwelt in it would be unintelligible had we no knowledge of the Akkadian and Ugaritic epics. These tell of a primeval battle between the creator god and the forces of chaos and death named in the Ugaritic epics Prince Sea and Judge River and in the Akkadian epics Tiamat, "the Deep." According to these ancient Near Eastern epics, the world as humans experience it resulted from the victory the divine warrior won over the forces of chaos identified with the sea. Following his victory the divine warrior ascends his throne on a mountain and utters the powerful words that lead to the production of the world that human beings inhabit. In Canaan the imagery of the sea and rivers as chaotic powers probably had its setting in the transition that takes place between the dry and rainy seasons. At this time the Mediterranean Sea is very rough and difficult to navigate. It threatens low-lying areas with flooding. The rivers, swollen by violent rainstorms, become destructive torrents.

Ancient Israel's poetic celebration of Yahweh as creator simply adopts what was traditional imagery to speak about creation. Though the Bible does not contain a complete story of God's battle with the sea and its monsters, it should be obvious that those for whom these texts were first intended were familiar with at least the basic outline of the epics that celebrated the divine warrior's victory in a cosmic battle that ended with the creation of the world human beings inhabit. The allusions to the sea, the dragon, the splitting of a sea monster in two depended on people's familiarity with the myth as a whole; otherwise the metaphors would have been unintelligible for those who first heard or read the Hebrew Bible.

The imagery of a great cosmic battle reemerges in some of the latest texts from the Hebrew Bible. Apocalyptic literature looks to the future and describes the re-creation of the universe using the same conflict imagery that earlier texts used to describe the creation of this world. Apocalyptic eschatology describes the creation of "new heavens and a new earth" (Isa. 65:17) after a great battle that will bring this world to an end. In other words, apocalyptic texts describe the origin of the world to come with the same conflict imagery used to describe the origins of this world. Isaiah 27:1-2 names the enemies that God will defeat as Leviathan, the dragon, and the sea — the very same enemies God defeated before the creation of the world. The vocabulary and imagery about the "last things" result from the transference into the future of the vocabulary and imagery associated with the "first things." In the apocalyptic visions the created order gives way to a new order. Still, both come into existence because God defeats chaotic powers in a great cosmic battle.

When most people think of the Bible's view of creation, they think of Genesis 1. What helps make the Genesis story of creation so attractive is its integrity: it is made up of seven parts whose climax is the creation of the male and female according to God's image and likeness (Gen. 1:26-27). This account of an ordered creation underscores the purposefulness of God's activity and leads to the conclusion that everything in the world is due to the might and generosity of Israel's God. Though the creation of humankind is the centerpiece of the story, Genesis 1 is about God's activity in creating the world and all that is in it. The story begins with a divine wind whirling about above watery, dark, and formless matter. Out of this primal matter God creates the world by the power of the divine word alone. Psalm 33:6 celebrates the creation of the cosmos by the power of God's word:

> By the word of the LORD the heavens were made,
>   and all their host by the breath of his mouth.

The notion of creation by the divine word was not an idea unique to ancient Israel. Egypt already knew of such an idea in the third millennium B.C. The city of Memphis honored Ptah, its patron deity, by asserting that Ptah conceived the idea of the universe, ordered it, and brought it into being by a simple word. This Egyptian notion of creation by the word antedated Genesis 1 by more than two thousand years.

Ancient Israel found the notion of creation by God's word an appropriate way to affirm its beliefs about Yahweh, its patron deity. Creation by word preserves the distance between the creator and the world. The universe is not the result of a type of emanation as it appears to be in some of the earliest of the Egyptian myths. Creation as emanation had its setting in the annual inundation of the Nile Valley. The world began as a formless, watery void — as the Nile Valley appeared during the height of the annual flooding. When the flood subsided, mounds of earth appeared, and so it was when the world began. From the primeval mound the god Atum arose, and from this god all other beings emanated. The Genesis story, while it begins with the same image of a watery void, has God already existing and calling the world and its creatures into existence by the divine word.

A third Israelite pattern of reflection on the origins of the world appears in Israel's Wisdom tradition. Proverbs 8 extols personified Wisdom, and verses 22 to 31, in particular, focus on Wisdom as the "firstborn" of God's ways. Wisdom, then, was with God as the world was called into being, supplying an ordered design for the cosmos and delighting in the final outcome. Psalm 104:24, in praising God for creation, asserts that it was "in wisdom" that God made all that is. The Wisdom tradition looks upon the world and its order with great delight and wonder. This approach to creation also appears in Egypt. There wisdom is personified as the goddess Maat, who accompanies the creator deity. Maat was the first idea that was separated from the primeval nonexistence when the world was created. Maat is the source of the fundamental laws of the cosmos and is responsible for the basic structure of the universe.

The relationship between wisdom and creation takes on a new dimension in the book of Job. The Wisdom tradition affirms that creation is comprehensible because God established an order in creation. Throughout his speeches, however, Job complains that this is difficult to accept. He experiences no divine order or justice in his life. He cries out that a return to the primordial chaos would be better than the so-called divine order in creation (3:3-10). God's reply to Job's complaints describes the grandeur of creation. God's questioning of Job (38–41) implies that Job does not know what he is asking for when he calls for the world to return to chaos. Only divine wisdom can grasp the order with which God has created and sustained the world. It is simply beyond the human mind to comprehend.

The book of Isaiah is the one prophetic text in which the theology of creation is central. The anonymous prophet whose words are found in Isaiah 40–55 has a central role for creation in his oracles. For this prophet the God of Israel was "the creator of the ends of the earth" (40:28) who forms "light and darkness" and creates both "weal and woe" (45:7). This prophet's focus on creation is likely a response to the experience of Judah in exile. In Babylon the exiles became acquainted with the Akkadian creation stories that asserted that Marduk, Babylon's patron deity, was responsible for the creation of the world. The prophet makes it clear that it was Yahweh, Judah's patron deity, who was the world's creator. Isaiah 48 argues that since Yahweh created the world, it must be Yahweh who has empowered Cyrus to defeat Babylon and cause Yahweh's people to return from exile. Because Yahweh alone is the creator and because Yahweh alone raised up Cyrus, Yahweh must be the sole deity. The gods of the nations are no gods. While God's word created the universe, all other gods were silent (41:21-23, 25-26; 44:7). The theology of creation found in Isaiah 40–55 served to support the monotheistic thrust of this prophetic text.

The Old Testament does not offer its readers a single or uniform picture of God's creative activity. The biblical writers were heirs of ancient Near Eastern tradition that offered a variety of explanations of how this world came to be, and they chose to adopt and adapt these traditions in order to affirm that the God of Israel was responsible for the creation of this world. In the process of appropriating the creation traditions from ancient cultures, the biblical writers preserve a good portion of the diversity that is characteristic of ancient Near Eastern cosmogonies. This appropriation of ancient Near Eastern traditions served to express ancient Israel's beliefs about its national deity, Yahweh. It was the God of Israel who was responsible for the creation of the universe. A second Old Testament affirmation about creation is that this world is comprehensible because it was set in order by God. What human beings are to do is to discern that order in creation and live in accordance with it. Ignoring that order is perilous and foolish.

Creation in the New Testament

The New Testament makes far fewer references to the origins of the world than the Old Testament, principally because it simply assumes the essential features of the Old Testament idea of how the world came to be. For example, Paul affirms that there is one God "from whom are all things" (1 Cor. 8:6) but does not expand on this affirmation. There is one Pauline statement that does not appear to reflect Old Testament perspectives. It is his observation that all creation has been "subject to futility" and is waiting for its release (Rom. 8:19-22). Unfortunately Paul does not develop this idea, which may have its origins in gnostic speculation about creation. The Fourth Gospel begins with the first words of Genesis 1, i.e., "In the beginning . . ." But it uses these words not to introduce new affirmations about how the world came to be but to focus on the divine origin of the Word in order to introduce the redemptive function of the Word, who became flesh for the salvation of the world (John 1:14). The book of Revelation appropriates the ancient Near Eastern notion of creation through conflict in describing the creation of the new world it envisions. The visionary describes a great cosmic battle with a dragon (Rev. 12) and a beast that comes out of the sea (Rev. 13). The great harlot Babylon lives near "the many waters" (17:1, 15). The new heaven and new earth come after "the sea was no more" (21:1). Revelation appropriates the imagery of a cosmic battle not to speak about the origins of this world but to encourage believers as they await the creation of a new world.

The hymn to Christ in Colossians 1:15-20 is the best example of the way the New Testament transforms biblical creation traditions. It affirms Christ as the unique mediator of creation (vv. 15-18a) on the model provided in Proverbs 8:22-31. But the universe was created not only through Christ but for Christ. Creation, then, reaches its fullness in Christ. The hymn continues to celebrate Christ as the unique mediator of the world's transformation (vv. 18b-20). It is through Christ that the world was created and is sustained. What began through the Wisdom of God continues because of the Wisdom of God incarnate in Jesus Christ.

Creation in Christian Theology

Almost every religious movement devotes some attention to the issue of beginnings, and of course Christianity is no exception. Following the lead of the Bible, Christianity begins its profession of faith by confessing God to be the creator of the universe. For much of the church's history believers considered

Genesis 1:1–2:4 an accurate account of how the world came to be. Today most Christians, except for fundamentalists, regard the story in Genesis as a theological statement rather than a scientific one. Two developments in the scholarly world have led to that conclusion. First was the emergence of modern science, which has shown that the world is much older than the Bible assumes and that plant, animal, and human life developed into the forms they have today over millions of years. Christians struggled to reconcile their faith with the theory of evolution, which many viewed as undermining the very basis of that faith, i.e., the existence of a God who acted with purpose in the creation of the world. Some Christians, however, sought to harmonize science with the Bible. For example, they suggested that the six days of creation were not twenty-four-hour periods but geological ages which may have spanned millions of years. But most believers regard such attempts as futile since the Bible is not a scientific text. Reading the Bible as if it provided scientific data obscures its theological function.

Some Christians still regard evolution as an unproven hypothesis whose real purpose is to subvert religious faith. They believe it their duty to promote the teaching of Genesis 1 as an alternative to the teaching of evolution. Because the Constitution of the United States prohibits the establishment of religion, the courts have not permitted what are regarded as religious doctrines to be taught in public schools, so the teaching of Genesis 1 has been advanced under the guise of "scientific creationism." Still, what creationism promotes is not *the* biblical teaching on creation but *a* biblical view. No creationist suggests that as a prelude to the creation of the sun and stars God first "broke the heads of the dragons in the waters" and "crushed the heads of Leviathan" as does Psalm 74:12-17.

The second development that led Christians to regard Genesis 1 as theology rather than science was the discovery and analysis of ancient Near Eastern creation stories. Egyptian, Akkadian, and Ugaritic texts help clarify the details of the biblical accounts of and allusions to the process of creation as the people of the ancient Near East envisioned it. While most interpreters do not posit direct literary dependence of the biblical creation stories on specific ancient Near Eastern texts, it is clear that Genesis 1 represents one variant of a cultural pattern that can be easily discerned in the ancient Near Eastern literature that goes back as far as the fourth millennium B.C. Texts such as the Baal cycle from Ugarit and the *Enuma Elish* from Babylon have helped clarify the cultural context from which the Bible's approach to the origins of the cosmos emerged. Analysis of the biblical text against this backdrop helps clarify the main concerns of the Genesis account: the sovereign power of Israel's God as the creator of the universe, the purposefulness of God's creation, and the role of humankind in the world God called into being.

One reason for the neglect of the biblical allusions to a cosmic battle as preceding the creation of the world was that such allusions seem to be incompatible with what became an important Christian affirmation about creation: *creatio ex nihilo,* i.e., that the universe was created from nothing. A careful reading of the Genesis 1 account suggests that ancient Israel's story of creation followed the common ancient Near Eastern pattern without being literarily dependent on an individual text. These ancient traditions begin the story of creation by asserting that before creation a watery void existed in darkness. While it is doubtful that affirming *creatio ex nihilo* was a concern of the biblical texts, this notion does underscore what the Bible affirms: the sovereignty of God over all creation. The notion of ex nihilo creation, then, is a legitimate development from the biblical tradition. Creation belongs to God and not some other being, though experience seems to suggest that evil has some sort of power over creation. Believers wait for the day when God's sovereign power over creation will be revealed finally and definitively.

Following from this emphasis on the sovereignty of God over all creation is the Christian affirmation that the world that God has created is good. This, of course, flows directly from Genesis 1, which affirms the goodness of creation six times. But the notion that creation is "good" flies in the face of the experience of the presence and power of evil in the world. Despite this presence, Christian theological tradition affirms that the world is intrinsically good. Evil entered the world *after* God had created it. The Christian faith, then, considers the world as a gift from God to be cherished and protected.

In Romans 1:20 Paul affirms that God can be known "in what [God] has made." The Catholic theological and philosophical tradition, then, believes that God can be known by the light of unaided natural reason. Creation, then, makes it possible for human beings to know God even apart from the revelation given in the Scriptures. The Catholic tradition understands creation sacramentally, i.e., the universe created by God mirrors God's own glory and testifies to God's presence. Protestant Christianity, however, demurs from such an affirmation because of questions about the capacity of reason unaided by grace.

A sacramental view of creation sees the universe as a dynamic reality. God's power and presence in the world are manifest because creation is a continuing divine activity. The dynamic quality of the universe makes it possible for human beings to perceive the designs of God continuing to unfold. This view of creation is not new. In the patristic era it was known as the *creatio continua,* the continuous act of creation whereby God is not only sustaining but perfecting the world. In the medieval period the Franciscans championed this view of the creation, articulated most forcefully in Duns Scotus's teaching on the primacy of Christ as the "firstborn of creation" (Col. 1:15). Through the incarnation Christ brings to perfection what God has begun in creation. For Scotus, then, the incarnation was the logical outcome of God's movement outside of Godself in the act of creation. Through the incarnation God becomes part of creation itself, making possible the universe's fulfillment of its divinely established destiny. A modern variant of this idea was articulated by the Jesuit paleontologist Teilhard de Chardin (1881-1955). He asserted that as the world continued to evolve, creation was being drawn to what he called its "Omega Point," which he identified as Christ. This evolving universe will "sum up all things in Christ, in heaven and on earth" (Eph. 1:10). Creation was not something that happened in some primordial time. It continues today, for creation is a dynamic force moving to its perfection in Christ.

Creation Theology for Our Time

Understanding the function of the biblical traditions about creation does not necessarily result in making these traditions relevant to contemporary believers. What value are the allusions to the combat myths that probably originated in the alternation of dry and wet seasons in the Levant? While scientific hypotheses about the origins of the universe may be more intellectually satisfying, they are impersonal. They do not deal with the question of purpose — only an explanation that sees creation as a personal act can do this. While the scientific method can illumine the processes of creation, it is not as successful in making creation comprehensible. A theological perspective on creation makes it possible for us to comprehend the interconnectedness of all creatures. It also provides the means to deal with the paradoxes and ambiguities surrounding the human experience of the cosmos by affirming its purposefulness and direction. Creation is heading for its perfection in Jesus Christ. From a theological perspective, creation is not a static reality to be analyzed but a dynamic reality to be celebrated.

A theology of creation that focuses on the dynamism of the universe can inform the contemporary concern for the environment. From such a perspective it is not possible to consider Genesis 1:26 ("Let them have dominion over the fish of the sea . . .") as permission for human beings to use creation without concern for how this use affects the environment and the other creatures with whom human beings share the earth. As those charged with helping to bring creation to its destiny, human beings cannot allow themselves to exploit the earth. They are to care for it. Air and water pollution, the destruction of rain forests, the overdependence on fossil fuels — these are just some examples of the thoughtless exploitation of God's creation. The exploitation and thoughtless misuse of God's creation prevent that creation from achieving its destiny. Again, while such concern for the environment is a recent development, it is not an entirely new idea. Francis of Assisi thought of all creatures as his brothers and sisters. In his *Canticle of Brother Sun,* Francis calls upon all creatures, the sun, moon, stars, and elements to praise God. Francis's attitude toward creation anticipated the contemporary notion that sees the destiny of humankind intimately tied up with the destiny of the planet and all creatures that inhabit it.

Recognizing the integrity of creation cannot limit itself to ecological issues but will necessarily include issues of justice as well. Access to the blessings with which God endowed the earth is a basic human right. The use of most of the earth's resources by a tiny fraction of its population is not responsible stewardship. The earth and its bounty are gifts that God has given to all people, and access to them takes precedence over the right to private property. The amassing of large tracts of private land and driving people into poverty in the face of the great resources with which God has endowed this planet is an injustice that demands redress. Land reform, a more equitable access to natural resources, and justice for the poor are ways that a contemporary theology of creation can have practical effects in people's lives.

The biblical stories of creation have the same function today as they did when they were first written. They make comprehensible what people find mysterious, and they provide a rational basis for human conduct. Though today's reader of the Bible approaches these texts with the background of modern, scientific explanations of how the world came to be, people still marvel at the majesty of the heavens, the grandeur of the earth, and the mystery of life. Astronomers speak about the immensity of the universe and physicists describe the smallest particles of matter. The sun warms a child at play. Rain waters the soil. Seedlings that eventually become acre upon acre of grain emerge from the soil. The Bible attempts to make these phenomena comprehensible by affirming the purposefulness of the universe. The world and all that is in it are the products of a God who chose to move out of the isolation of divinity by expressing a word that brought everything into existence. The Christian sees that this divine purpose is made ever more clear in Christ, the "firstborn of all creation" (Col. 1:15). Christ and creation go together. The universe has been created through Christ and for Christ (Col. 1:16). Christ is the first to come forth through the power of God's Spirit. Christ, the Word of God, the Word of Life, has become flesh — has become part of the created universe — and dwelt among us.

47

Even evolution, which some believers reject, helps us comprehend our world as it unfolds before our eyes. It underscores a biblical truth: creation is not something God has done in some primordial time. Creation is something God continues to do in and through Jesus Christ. God cannot leave creation alone, for if God's creative energies were withdrawn from the universe — even for an instant — nothing of the universe would continue in existence. To affirm God as creator is to affirm that everything depends upon God's sustaining love. But the creator is still active and is now perfecting all things.

Finally, the stories of creation provide a basis for human conduct. People can be awestruck by the sky on a starlit night. But the stars can never see the people marveling at their beauty. There is something that sets humankind apart from the rest of creation. It is at the beginning of a new human life that God's creative power expresses itself in a special way. The creation of a human life is a sacred moment because Christians believe that God has a direct and personal relationship with each person even before it stirs in the womb (see Jer. 1:5). God creates, loves, nourishes, and guides each human life. And human beings can respond to that love. Belief in God, the creator, involves responding to the divine revelation that is creation. A human being cannot remain unmoved and indifferent to creation. Human beings can respond to creation with the language of praise and with a life of commitment to the creator. The Bible affirms that there is a moral coherence to the universe. That is the point of the biblical tradition's emphasis on creation as a divine act that brings order out of chaos. There are ambiguities and paradoxes in life, but faith in God as creator means acting with the assurance that life is worth living because of Christ through whom and for whom all was made (see John 1:3).

The End in the Beginning

Genesis 1:1–2:3

SCOTT E. HOEZEE

Science has long been fascinated with both the cosmic beginning and its ending. Both involve a certain amount of speculation, though at least with the universe's beginning there is real evidence to look at. But since the end has not yet come, there is no data to examine, and so speculation is all science can offer. But in terms of the beginning, there is mounting evidence that at some point about 14 billion years ago all that we now know burst into being in a superhot explosion of unfathomable power. So amazing was the shock wave of that explosion that its effects have yet to die out. Indeed, new evidence suggests that this shock wave of energy essentially never will die out.

The universe continues to expand, hurtling ever deeper into the far reaches of space. For a long time it was an open question whether that expansion from the big bang would continue to push the cosmos outward or whether the universe would reach an outer limit and then, rubber-band-like, snap back on itself. But the Hubble Space Telescope recently took a picture that indicates that such a recollapse may never happen. Instead the tremendous power of that original explosion will continue to drive matter outward. Eventually, however, the universe's energy will become too thin and diffuse to sustain life. Suns will flatten and wink out, space will grow colder and colder until finally the ultimate result of that first big bang will be a cosmos spread too thin. If so, then the seeds of the universe's end were sown already at its explosive beginning.

Of course, even if this scenario were ever to prove true, it is something like a couple trillion years away, so I wouldn't lose much sleep over it. But

49

how curious that science would now say that something of the universe's end could be contained in its beginning. Truth is, the Bible has said the same thing all along, except that from our faith-informed perspective this is good news. Listen: "In the beginning God." You don't need to read much further than that in the Genesis text to discern how the cosmic end is contained in the cosmic origin.

In the Beginning God

So simple, yet so majestic. Because if that is true, then it's very close to being all we need to know. Science is only too happy to affirm that the statement "In the beginning God" is singularly an article of faith. As many of you no doubt know, the Hubble Space Telescope has begun to peer ever deeper into the far reaches of the known universe, but the farther "out" you look in a telescope, the further "back" you look in time. Light travels very fast, somewhere around 186,000 miles per *second,* or just shy of 6 trillion miles in one year. That's very fast, but the universe is very big, and so even at that breakneck speed it takes a given beam of light a long time to get anywhere. So if it were a clear night this evening and you were to look up at the stars, you'd be seeing old light — light that has been traveling years, even centuries, to get here.

So the farther the Hubble sees out, the older the light it is catching sight of. There are some who say that eventually we may invent a telescope so powerful as to see back to nearly the big bang itself. Even were such a trick of virtual time travel possible, the belief that God is the "Creator of heaven and earth" as we affirm it week by week in the Apostles' Creed would be neither validated nor disproved. No matter how far back a telescope sees, it will never snap a picture of God blowing out the match with which he lit the big bang! We Christians know that to say "In the beginning God" is a matter of faith alone.

But what a key piece of our faith it is! Because contained in that little statement is the keynote of faith: namely, God has something to do with everything. "In the beginning God created the heavens and the earth." The Hebrew phrase in Genesis 1:1, "the heavens and the earth" — which is now preserved in also the language of the Apostles' Creed — is known as a merismus. In a merismus two opposites are used to convey the larger whole. In this case God is said to have created the highest point you can imagine and the lowest, which means he created absolutely everything in between, too! "The heavens and the earth" is the ancient equivalent of saying God created everything from A to Z!

A Sermon: The End in the Beginning

In the Beginning God

In the beginning God created. In the beginning God created . . . *everything.*
Throughout Genesis 1 we have a majestic series of repeated phrases: God
commands, and it is done; God sees, and it is good; there is evening, there is
morning, and so another day. There is something soothing about Genesis 1's
predictability. Authors of children's books know that and so construct stories
which can have a similar effect on young children. A classic example is the
story of the three bears wherein first Goldilocks, and then later upon their return also the three bears, methodically move through the house. They proceed from porridge bowls to chairs to bed, and each time from too hot to too
cold, too hard to too soft, until finally something is "just right." Similarly in
the wonderful book *Goodnight, Moon,* young readers systematically work
their way through a young boy's bedroom, noting each item and then, after
each set, saying "Goodnight" to one of the items.

Genesis 1 is like that, though on a much more sophisticated level. But
there is predictability here — you as a reader know what's coming because it
will echo what came before. And you always know that at the end of the day,
no matter how wildly diverse that day's creative activities were, it's going to
turn out just right. God is going to see that it is good — and in the end he will
see that the whole kit and caboodle is "very good." How profoundly comforting it is to know this as you move along.

In the Beginning God

But there are other, more subtle features to this text that are striking once you
see them. Genesis 1 has a bit of an axe to grind. The author was well aware that
this was not the only creation story available in the world. Myths on how the
universe began were a dime a dozen in the ancient world: The Egyptians had
their story about the sun god Ra and his creating of all life. The Babylonians
had their grand epic of *Enuma Elish* in which the goddess Tiamat is responsible for birthing many gods, out of whose warfare eventually the earth was
born. The universe is filled with gods in most such tales, and some of these
gods could be identified with certain portions of this world: so some people
worshiped the sun even as others bowed down before trees, some sought to
honor the spirits of the rivers while others adored the god of the mountain.

Genesis 1 was written, in part at least, to counteract these alternative narratives of creation and the view of the world those stories supported. Repeatedly the true God of Israel is shown as superior to any portion of the natural

51

world by virtue of God being the one not just to make all things but to move them around so they would do precisely what he alone desired. God is shown here as being so grand that he can accomplish great wonders well beyond the "normal" operation of things. Many in the ancient world worshiped the sun and/or the moon as a god in its own right. So Genesis 1 quite literally puts the sun in its place by having God create light — just pure and stunning *light* — three whole creation "days" before the sun and moon. Why worship the sun when the true God doesn't even need it to make the purest of all light!?

As if that were not an amazing enough feat, God even creates green plants on day three also before the sun was made. This is not an example of ignorant science by this author — although ancient people lacked a knowledge of photosynthesis and its relation to the production of chlorophyll, they nevertheless were well aware that without the sun, plants just don't grow. But Genesis 1 shows the whole earth sprouting with every kind of green plant imaginable even *before* a sun was in place. God alone, and not the sun, is to be worshiped. God alone, and not any supposed spirit living inside a plant, is to be honored.

In the Beginning God

Then there is a wonderful dramatic understatement in verse 16 where, in an almost casual manner, this author just happens to mention "He also made the stars." Amazing! Untold billions of nuclear furnaces pierce the darkness of space, spewing forth the heat, radiation, radio waves, and blazing light that result from their hydrogen-helium fission. The ancients maybe didn't know what the stars were precisely, but we now are staggered to know how many of them there are and how great a variety there is, too: yellow suns, red giants, blue stars, and binary systems. Yet God created them all without breaking a sweat!

But that's part of the nature of Genesis 1: to show the enormous power that allowed God to do it all. God is not stingy in his act of creation but wildly lavish. He is profuse, filling the oceans with vast schools of fish, blackening the skies with vast flocks of birds, setting the very ground of the earth in motion with "swarming swarms" of insects and every kind of land animal.

In Stephen Ambrose's book *Undaunted Courage* we read about the journey of Lewis and Clark. Again and again as they pushed west in the early 1800s, these two explorers were stunned to see prairies literally black with herds of buffalo, the thunder of whose hoofbeats reverberated for miles. Some days the sunshine would be blocked from view for long periods due to passing flocks of passenger pigeons. One day the river on which they were traveling became clotted with some white, fluffy substance. Upon rounding a bend in the river they discovered the source: a mind-numbing rookery of white pelicans who were molting.

Something like that is what Genesis 1 shows us as God's original intent: to fill the world up to the brim with swarms of creatures. But no matter how amazing their variety, no matter how huge their flocks, herds, rookeries, or schools, again and again the point comes through loud and clear: the Lord God made them *every one*. All that oft-repeated talk about the various "kinds" is a none-too-subtle way to head off anyone who would say, "Well, maybe your God got things rolling in the universe, but he didn't make *this*, did he? Maybe he made some generic cow, but the specifics of Holsteins, Herefords, and Guernseys developed without God's help, right?"

Genesis 1 is designed to say to such people, "You're not going to win this one! God has all the bases covered: he made all that there is and their every kind and variety, too. In the beginning God. Don't try to cut God out of the picture, or even out of parts of the picture, but instead give God the glory for a universe so vast and so very, very good."

So far we have not even gotten to the part about humanity's creation. So rich is this chapter's presentation of creation that it is difficult even to summarize it. But the wonder of the man and woman's creation is the divine image in which they were fashioned. That image potentially means so very much — it may even define the essence of who we are. There is a procreative component to this image, as Genesis 1:28 indicates. There is a relationship component to the image, as humanity is the only creature not only made by God but *spoken to* by God. There is a divine command to take care of the earth in a way reminiscent of how God himself would tend it. All of that has something to do with being made in the image of God.

But as part of our whirlwind tour of Genesis 1, perhaps one item we can highlight is how being made in God's image allows us to take note of and deepen our understanding of everything *else* God made. There has been a long-standing debate as to the meaning of God's words in verse 28 about the man and woman's "ruling" over the other creatures. I think it is merely obvious that it means we take care of this creation, preserving it in a way that brings God joy. But the point here is that *only* the man and the woman are directed to observe or have anything to do with absolutely every other creature God made. No other creature is told to take care of any other creature. No other species is told to make a study of any other species.

Unlike other creatures, we humans busy ourselves not merely with our own kind and with what it takes to insure our own survival. Instead we seem unable to resist the urge to snap pictures of distant stars, to catalogue the different kinds of grass found on prairies, to fill up libraries with guidebooks detailing the vast array of fish species, bird species, ant species. It is the spark of God in us that leads us to do the same thing God did at the dawn of time: namely, to look at all God made and to recognize once more that it is good, so very, very good.

We said at the outset that science now suspects that the seeds of the cosmic end may be contained in the cosmic beginning, that the big bang that birthed us may ultimately carry us too far and too wide and too deep into space to sustain life. Who knows whether that's right or wrong. But what we believe is most certainly right: "In the beginning God." The seed of whatever future this universe has was indeed present at the beginning: it is the seed of God's own goodness and grace and creative zest. Our end is found at our beginning, and in both cases we can rest assured that we belong to God alone.

Eugene Peterson once noted that according to Genesis 1, Adam and Eve were created on the sixth day. But that means that the first full day of their existence was the next day, which was the Sabbath. Adam and Eve kicked off the human race by getting a day off, a day of rest! We begin with Sabbath, with rest, with a day in which both God and the infant human race simply soaked up creation and reveled in its swarming swarms of variety — it was that restfulness, peace, and enjoyment that sounded the cosmic keynote for what life is all about finally. It is about glorifying God and enjoying God and his works forever.

In the Beginning God

That's good news. Very good. Amen.

CHAPTER 4

And in Jesus Christ, His Only Son, Our Lord

Et in Iesum Christum, filium eius unicum, dominum nostrum

RICHARD A. BURRIDGE

This phrase takes us not just to the heart of the Creed, but to the very center of the Christian faith. It also makes it distinctive, and gives Christianity its very name. The previous statements — regarding faith in God as Father and creator — mark us out as theists, even monotheists, in beliefs shared in some ways with Islam and Judaism. But this article sets out the profoundly Christian dimension of faith, that this creator, father God is revealed in the person of Jesus of Nazareth — and conversely that Jesus is no less than God himself. It contains several key words about Jesus, which take us through biblical pictures and historical snapshots to some reflections for today.

Key Words

I Believe

The Jews were used to reciting a statement of belief, called the Shema, from its opening word in Hebrew: "Hear, O Israel: The LORD is our God, the LORD alone. You shall love the LORD your God with all your heart, and with all your soul, and with all your might" (Deut. 6:4-5). They must recite these words "to your children and talk about them when you are at home and when you are away, when you lie down and when you rise. Bind them as a sign on your hand, fix them as an emblem on your forehead, and write them on the doorposts of your house and on your gates" (6:7-9). Furthermore, they were also to rehearse the story of their ancestors, the exodus, and the entry into the Promised Land when presenting firstfruits to God: "A wandering Aramean was my ancestor. . . . The LORD brought us out of Egypt . . . and gave us this land, a land flowing with milk and honey" (26:5-9). Thus it is not surprising that Jews who believed that Jesus had brought them into a new covenant with God should also learn short accounts about his life, death, and resurrection, which survive quoted in various New Testament letters (e.g., Phil. 2:6-11; 1 Cor. 15:3-7; 1 Tim. 3:16; 1 Pet. 3:18-22). These early creeds may have been recited in worship, and similar words appear in the first baptismal liturgies: candidates are asked three questions about their belief in God the Father, in Jesus Christ, and in the Holy Spirit, and baptized with water after each statement of faith (Hippolytus, *Apostolic Tradition*). Paul similarly combines personal belief and public confession of faith: "If you confess with your lips that Jesus is Lord and believe in your heart that God raised him from the dead, you will be saved" (Rom. 10:9). Thus it is right that each article of the Creed begins with "I believe," for we are making not an individual, public commitment to believing intellectual ideas, but rather an act of trust in a particular person and the events of his life and death, as narrated in the subsequent clauses.

Jesus

The astonishing thing about the story told by the first Christians was that it was not about a distant ancestor like Abraham or Moses — but about someone who had recently lived and died among them. Christianity is inextricably linked to a historical event in a certain time and place, the life and death of Jesus of Nazareth — and this section of the Creed goes on to narrate various facts about what happened to him, his birth, suffering, death, resurrection, and ascension, looking forward to his coming again as judge. Jesus may have been one of the great teachers of the human race, but Christianity is not primarily about his teaching, and still less about philosophical ideas. It is rooted in the story of Jesus, who was born in the time of the Roman emperor Augustus, who exercised a teaching and healing ministry around the ancient eastern provinces and client kingdoms of Judea-Israel-Palestine and was executed under the governor Pontius Pilate in the reign of Tiberius. This makes our faith vulnerable to historical inquiry: if it were shown that Jesus never existed, or did none of these things, then the whole edifice would come crashing down. This is the risk God took in entering history by becoming incarnate in the person of Jesus. Thus it is not surprising that Christians and non-Christians alike have devoted great energy to historical-critical research. Furthermore, his very name is significant for faith: "Jesus" is Greek for the Hebrew "Joshua," a personal noun derived from the word for "to save" and "salvation," as well as "healing" and "wholeness." As Joshua brought the children of Israel into the Promised Land, so Jesus of Nazareth is our "Savior" in whom we are restored to abundant life with God (Matt. 1:21; John 10:10).

Christ

The word "Christ" appears over 500 times in the New Testament, while Jesus' name appears about 950 times. "Christ" is from a Greek past participle, translating the Hebrew "messiah," both from verbs "to anoint," thus meaning "the anointed [one]." In the Old Testament, anointing by a prophet denotes being set apart by God for a particular calling. Those so anointed were usually priests (e.g., Aaron, Exod. 29, and his descendants, Lev. 6:20-22) and kings (e.g., Saul, 1 Sam. 10:1; David, 1 Sam. 16:12-13 and 2 Sam. 5:3; Solomon, 1 Kings 1:34), though Elijah is also told to anoint Elisha as his successor (1 Kings 19:16). Yet Isaiah even calls a foreign ruler like Cyrus "his anointed," as well as describing himself as "anointed . . . to bring good news to the oppressed . . . liberty to the captives, and release to the prisoners" (Isa. 45:1; 61:1). This all forms the background to speculation in the Gospels about an "anointed one" coming from God to save the people (Mark 12:35; Luke 3:15; John 7:26-27). Eventually Peter blurts out at Caesarea Philippi that he believes Jesus is "the Christ" (Mark 8:29). However, Jesus orders the disciples not to tell people and prefers to call himself "the Son of Man," denoting his coming suffering and passion rather than the messianic expectations of kingly rule for God. Yet when he is crucified, it is for being "the Christ, the King of Israel" (Mark 15:32; cf. Luke 23:2). In the rest of the New Testament, early Christian belief that Jesus is the Messiah results in the word "Christ" being used like a (sur)name for Jesus. Thus "Jesus Christ" occurs some 220 times outside the Gospels, including 165 occurrences in Paul, who also uses the name "Christ" on its own nearly 200 times. So when we express our faith in "Jesus Christ," we are saying that the long biblical tradition of prophets, priests, and kings anointed by God has reached its pinnacle in the Anointed One, Jesus himself.

Our Lord

Yet those first Christians went further still in their estimation of Jesus. Our faith is placed not in ideas but in a person, and he is not only a great founder like Abraham or Moses, nor just a savior like Joshua, nor even anointed like priests, kings, or other messianic figures. Perhaps the earliest Christian creed is preserved in Paul's instructions for worship in the church at Corinth: "No one can say 'Jesus is Lord' except by the Holy Spirit" (1 Cor. 12:3). This simple phrase "Jesus is Lord" is the heart of the Christian faith, and the first creedal statement anyone makes on their spiritual journey — yet it carries enormous theological implications. Paul also calls Jesus "Lord" later, when he quotes the simple Aramaic prayer, *maranatha,* meaning "Our Lord, come!" (1 Cor. 16:22). The use of Aramaic is very significant, for it takes us back into the worship of the very early church — and yet it preserves the application of the word *mar,* "Lord," to Jesus. Jews so greatly revered the name of God that they would not pronounce the four letters YHWH (the tetragrammaton) in texts, but rather read the Hebrew *Adonai,* "Lord," instead. In many English Bibles this is represented by "the LORD" in smaller capitals. In reading Aramaic translations, or in speech or prayer, *mar* would be used similarly to refer to God. Yet here that word "Lord" is now being used for Jesus, the historical person who had lived recently among them but was now being worshiped with God and even as God, "the Lord." Further confirmation can be seen in the way some Old Testament passages where "Lord" refers to God are applied to Jesus in the New Testament: thus Isaiah's "every tongue shall swear" (Isa. 45:23) refers to Jesus in Philippians 2:11, "every tongue shall confess that Jesus Christ is Lord," or Psalm 102:25-27's description of God the creator is addressed to Jesus in Hebrews 1:10-12. This is a seismic shift for Jewish monotheists to take words and beliefs which can only refer to the one true God and apply them to Jesus Christ, "the Lord." Yet "the Lord" becomes a standard designation for Jesus: of the six hundred or so uses of "Lord" in the New Testament, the vast majority mean the person of Jesus, often distinguished from, yet placed alongside, God the Father (e.g., 1 Cor. 8:6; Rom. 1:7). Indeed, God is often described as "the God and Father of our Lord Jesus Christ" (Rom. 15:6; 2 Cor. 1:3; Eph. 1:3; 1 Pet. 1:3; cf. Col. 1:3).

His Only Son

This takes us finally to the relationship of Jesus to God the Father. In Psalm 2:7 God says to his anointed king, "You are my son; today I have begotten you," yet this, together with God's promise to David's descendants in 2 Samuel 7:14, is applied to Jesus in Hebrews 1:5. We have just seen how Jesus Christ as "Lord" is placed alongside God as "Father" — with the obvious implication that Jesus is God's Son. John shows this best as he calls God "Father" about one hundred times and Jesus the "Son" some fifty occasions. In particular, John uses the word *monogenes,* "only" or "only-begotten," in the prologue (1:14, 18) and in his famous teaching section (3:16, 18) — which is picked up in the Creed's phrase "only Son." While John uses language about Jesus as Son throughout, the other Gospels tend to reserve it for divine disclosure at key moments such as the voice from heaven at Jesus' baptism or transfiguration (Mark 1:11; 9:7). In Mark, only demons call Jesus "Son of God" (e.g., 3:11) during his lifetime; the first human being to recognize him as God's Son is the centurion at the foot of the cross in the climactic moment of his death (15:39). In Matthew and Luke, Jesus' sonship is first revealed in the birth stories (Matt. 1:18–2:15; Luke 1:31-33; 2:8-21) as well as in the shared "Q" saying, so reminiscent of Johannine theology: "No one knows the Son except the Father, and no one knows the Father except the Son and anyone to whom the Son chooses to reveal him" (Matt. 11:27; cf. Luke 10:22).

Clearly all these passages reveal the influence of early Christian reflection on and worship of Jesus, and yet there are indications in the Gospels that Jesus related himself to God like a son to a father. Most significant is his use of the Abba, "father," for God, especially in prayer (Mark 14:36; Matt. 6:1-9); however, in his parable of the tenants of the vineyard, Jesus differentiates himself from previous prophets through the picture of God sending various servants, followed by his "beloved son" (Mark 12:1-12). Paul brings all our phrases together when he says Jesus "was declared to be Son of God with power according to the spirit of holiness by resurrection from the dead, Jesus Christ our Lord" (Rom. 1:4). Calling Jesus "the Son of God" or simply "the Son" is another of his favorite descriptions. Furthermore, we can enter into this experience through being baptized into Jesus' death (Rom. 6:3-4) and be adopted as sons and daughters, calling on that same "Abba! Father!" (8:14-17). This concept of Jesus as God's Son is further developed in the New Testament as he shares in God's creation, "the image of the invisible God . . . in him all the fullness of God was pleased to dwell" (Col. 1:15-20; see also Heb. 1:1-4).

Thus these few simple expressions of faith and trust in "Jesus Christ, his only Son, our Lord" go deep into the heart of the New Testament's understanding of Jesus and sum up the church's convictions about him from earliest days right through the experience of millions across time and space to our life here and now.

Biblical Pictures

Early Stories

The Creed uses these titles "Christ," "Lord," and "Son of God" to describe Jesus, all of which recur throughout the New Testament. But titles alone cannot do justice to how the early Christians thought about Jesus. Recently narrative approaches to the Bible have demonstrated how much theology is revealed in the first believers' stories. As we saw with *mar,* even early Aramaic-speaking Jews came to think of Jesus as "Lord." They also drew upon the figure of God's Wisdom, described in the Old Testament as having shared in creation with God and coming to dwell among people to teach them (e.g., Prov. 8:1-36). Paul's letters include various passages which suddenly lapse into a more poetic rhythm with unusual vocabulary — he is probably quoting early hymns or creedal fragments, which take us back into very early Christian worship. They tell the story of Jesus as one who came from God, took human form, lived among us, suffered and died, yet rose again and is now exalted with God (e.g., Phil. 2:6-11; Col. 1:15-20; 1 Tim. 3:16).

Paul's Christology

Paul says remarkably little about Jesus' ministry, and rarely quotes his teaching. Instead he sees the whole nexus of Jesus' life, death, and resurrection as a totality. In the "Christ event" God has acted to save men and women — and the whole cosmos. It is the central pivot of the ages. In the Hebrew Scriptures Adam and Eve reject God, lose paradise, and so human beings are ruled by sin and death in "this age"; yet the prophets longed for the new age to come, the "Day of the Lord" when God will bring the world back to himself. Paul's story is that Jesus is God's agent through whom the new age has broken into our world, and all the Jewish hopes are now available through his death and resurrection. The resurrection is the center of Christian faith for Paul (1 Cor. 15:3-19), and it reveals that Jesus is the Son of God (Rom. 1:4). The resurrection breaks the parallel with Adam, whose disobedience brought death, while Christ is the "last Adam" whose obedience gives life to all (1 Cor. 15:20-57; Rom. 5:12-21). This brings about a new humanity, where anyone "in Christ" is a "new creation" (2 Cor. 5:17), with "no condemnation" (Rom. 8:1-2), and where all the barriers of race, sex, and class are broken down in the "body of Christ" (Gal. 3:28; 1 Cor. 12:12-27). It is a truly cosmic story (Col. 1:15-20).

The Gospels' Portraits

The Gospels are examples of ancient biographies, written in medium-length prose narrative, combining stories and speeches with other material within a bare chronological outline to portray the writer's understanding of this person.[1] Because of the limits of space, every verse or passage must focus on the subject and build up the subject's character. Naturally the Gospels tell us about early Christian belief in Jesus as "Christ," "Lord," and "Son of God." But more important is how the Evangelists each tell the same story in different ways, to explain their understanding of Jesus and demonstrate Jesus' importance for their differing audiences. Thus the Gospels are a form of narrative Christology.[2]

Mark's Gospel is the shortest, and probably the earliest, perhaps written in the 60s. It is direct and vivid, composed in primitive Greek by someone whose first language was Aramaic or Hebrew. After the briefest introduction, Jesus arrives fully grown to be baptized by John (Mark 1:9), and then he sets off on a ministry of preaching, healing, and deliverance. During the Gospel's first half he faces rising conflict, both political and spiritual, and even his own family and followers find him hard to understand (3:19-35). When Peter recognizes him as the Christ and God declares him to be his Son (8:29; 9:7), Jesus warns that he is going to Jerusalem to suffer and die (8:31; 9:31; 10:33-34). After the temple incident he is arrested and tried before Pilate, who sends him to be crucified, where he dies in darkness, abandoned by God (15:33-39). Three days later some women find the tomb empty and his body missing, with the challenge to his disciples to see him in Galilee (16:1-8). It is not a comfortable portrait, yet one which has always spoken powerfully to those suffering persecution.

Matthew probably wrote a decade or two later and retells Mark's basic story in a more Jewish way. He begins by tracing Jesus' descent from Abraham and David and with stories about his birth and the visit of wise men (Matt. 1–2). Like Moses, Jesus spends much time on mountains, giving five main sections of teaching, like the Pentateuch (5–7; 10; 13; 18; 24–25). Although his mission is to the "lost sheep of the house of Israel" (10:6), he is increasingly rejected, and forms instead a new community, the church (16:18; 18:17), leaving only "woes" to the religious leaders (23:1-36). Jesus' death is accompanied by earthquakes and signs of God's presence (27:45-54), while the resurrection

1. See Richard A. Burridge, *What Are the Gospels? A Comparison with Graeco-Roman Biography,* Society for New Testament Studies Monograph Series 70 (Cambridge: Cambridge University Press, 1992), for further details and discussion of the genre of the Gospels.

2. See Richard A. Burridge, *Four Gospels, One Jesus? A Symbolic Reading* (Grand Rapids: Eerdmans, 1994), for fuller accounts of each Gospel's story of Jesus.

separates those who tell lies like the soldiers from the new community of faith who are sent out to "all nations" (28:11-15, 16-20). Thus Matthew shapes the story for Jewish believers during the painful years of the separation of church and synagogue in the 80s and 90s.

Luke, however, is written for the Greek and Roman audiences. Jesus' descent is traced back to Adam, and he is the universal Savior (Luke 2:11; 3:23-38). As well as the Twelve, women disciples and enthusiastic crowds also follow him (8:1-3; 10:38-42; 13:17). Throughout, Jesus cares for the lost and poor, the marginalized and unacceptable, women, Samaritans and Gentiles, and he draws his strength from his life of prayer and the Holy Spirit. Even on his way to die he is concerned for the women of Jerusalem, the ordinary soldiers who "do not know what they are doing," and the penitent thief (23:27-31, 34, 43). After his resurrection Jesus again dines with his friends and sends them out from Jerusalem in the power of the Spirit (24:30-31, 35, 43, 47-49).

Lastly, John's Gospel shows the result of years of spiritual contemplation and theological reflection. He begins neither with Jesus' baptism nor his birth, but "in the beginning" where Jesus is the "Word" with God at the creation (John 1:1-18). Instead of pithy sayings or short parables, long debates and discourses are related to his healing "signs" (e.g., the discussion about "true bread" from heaven follows the miraculous feeding in 6:1-15, 22-58). Jesus knows of his own preexistence and that he is the Son of God the Father (6:38, 40, 62). Despite this most divine portrait, Jesus still gets tired, thirsty, and upset (4:6-7; 11:33-38). However, he is always in control, laying down his life of his own volition (10:18) and explaining it all to his disciples (14–17). On the cross he cares for his mother and dies with a shout of triumph (19:26-27, 30) — only to rise in glory to comfort Mary, challenge Thomas, and restore Peter (20:11-17, 24-29; 21:15-19). John's portrait has kept theologians arguing, mystics praying, and ordinary believers having "life in his name" (20:31) ever since!

The Rest of the New Testament

Most of the rest of the New Testament is briefer letters, addressing various situations within the early church. Hebrews is a theological treatise about how Jesus fulfills the Jewish hopes as both high priest and victim in the heavenly sanctuary, thus replacing the temple. James is more concerned with practical Christian living which flows from calling Jesus "Lord" (James 2:1). Peter writes to Christians who are being persecuted, and encourages them to see Jesus' sufferings as an example, while church leaders should revere him as the "chief shepherd" (1 Pet. 2:21-25; 5:4). The letters of John share a similar style with the Fourth Gospel and take the lordship and divinity of Jesus for granted; the crucial issue concerns those who do not accept that he was also human and "came in the flesh" (1 John 4:2; 2 John 7). Finally the Revelation to Saint John the Divine portrays Jesus as the cosmic Christ (Rev. 1:13-18), who is both lord of the church, to whom he sends seven letters (2–3), and lord of the whole world; while human authorities and demonic powers may persecute the church, Jesus is "King of kings and Lord of lords" (19:16) and will defeat them all, bringing the new Jerusalem down from God (21–22). As with Paul and the Gospels, so all these books relate faith in Jesus Christ as Lord to their readers' needs and situations.

Historical Snapshots

Our key words about Jesus as Christ, Lord, and Son of God crystallize various pictures within the New Testament expressing the faith of the earliest Christians. Over the next two thousand years innumerable other stories were told and portraits painted as believers sought to relate their understandings of Jesus to the world around them, of which we can only include a whirlwind tour of snapshots here.[3]

The Early Church

Paul explained the significance of Jesus through his letters, but writing Gospels in the manner of ancient biographies was itself a christological claim, placing a person — Jesus of Nazareth — at the very center and focus where Jews believed only the Law should be. Justin Martyr (ca. 100-165) composed a *Dialogue with Trypho*, a Jew, to argue that Jesus fulfilled Jewish prophecies and hopes; he also used the philosophical idea of the Logos, or divine Word, to explain Jesus as "Christ . . . Son of the true God" to Greeks and Romans (e.g., *Apology* 1.13.3). In his letters Ignatius of Antioch regularly calls Jesus "our God" (*Ephesians* 18.2) and "our Lord . . . Son of God" (*Smyrnaeans* 1.1). In the later decades of the second century both Irenaeus, bishop of Lyons in

---

3. For an excellent guide through this tradition, see J. Pelikan, *Jesus through the Centuries: His Place in the History of Culture* (New Haven: Yale University Press, 1985); his later *The Illustrated Jesus through the Centuries* (New Haven: Yale University Press, 1997), contains many beautiful reproductions.

southern France, and Tertullian, across the sea in North Africa, refer to a "rule of faith" in God and in "Jesus Christ, his Son," who is also "our Lord." They also began to grapple with how such faith in Jesus affects belief in one God, using early ideas about the Trinity. However, it is Origen (ca. 185-251) who really sets the tracks for later debates as he drew upon Platonic ideas for his theology. He stresses that God is one, yet distinguishes Jesus also as God, the Son, "eternally begotten" (e.g., *De principiis* 1.2.4); the Father, the Son, and the Holy Spirit are three "persons," though the latter two are subordinate. Meanwhile, he also suggests "two natures" for Jesus, divine and human, while trying to maintain his personal unity. Explaining all this was not easy, and Origen's thought was later viewed as too sophisticated or even heretical — yet it led inevitably to the great debates which followed.

Creeds and Councils[4]

According to an old legend, the apostles composed the Apostles' Creed together, with some clauses even assigned to various individuals by name! A better explanation of its title is that it contained the main elements of the apostles' teaching — and its phrases echo the New Testament and writings from the first couple of centuries. It is mostly *functional*, about what Jesus *did* and what happened to him. However, as the church debated this, using Greco-Roman philosophical ideas after the apologists and Origen, *ontological* issues about who Jesus *was* or *is* arose. How did he become "Son of God"? Was he "adopted" at his baptism or his birth? If he preexisted, was he created or begotten, and if begotten, was it at the start of creation — or eternally before all time? As to being "Lord," is he of the "same substance" *(homo-ousios)* as God or "similar substance" *(homoi-ousios* — only an iota's difference!)?

In the early years of the fourth century Arius, a priest in Alexandria, disputed with his bishop by arguing that Christ was the first and greatest to be created, subordinating Jesus within his "triad" to safeguard the uniqueness of God the Father. Athanasius argued against Arius that Jesus was of the "same substance" as God the Father, while some Eastern bishops preferred "similar substance." The Council of Nicea in 325 attempted to resolve things, but the argument dragged on to Constantinople in 381. This council agreed to the Nicene-Constantinopolitan Creed, describing Jesus as "eternally begotten of

---

4. See Frances Young, *The Making of the Creeds* (London: SCM Press, 1991); J. N. D. Kelly, *Early Christian Creeds*, 3rd ed. (London: Longman, 1972); Kelly, *Early Christian Doctrines*, 5th ed. (London: A. & C. Black, 1977).

the Father, true God from true God, light from light," with its stress on "of one being," *homo-ousios*. From now on the Trinity was classically defined as three persons in one being, or substance.

That just left the matter of Jesus to resolve! If he was both God and human, were there two persons existing in one body (as the Nestorians suggested), or did the divine replace his human soul or spirit (according to Apollinaris of Laodicaea)? Were his humanity and divinity divided, mixed up — or simply confused? While some of this may seem esoteric, important theological implications were at stake for understanding the incarnation, for the nature of human beings and which aspects of us can be saved. Eventually the Council of Chalcedon in 451 agreed on the classic definition of two natures in one person, describing Jesus as fully God and fully human. This then reached final expression in the so-called Athanasian Creed around 500, the name recognizing the success of his theology, even if Athanasius himself could not have written it.

While these debates were going on at the highest philosophical, ecclesiastical, and increasingly political levels, ordinary Christians were expressing their faith in Jesus Christ, God's only Son, our Lord. During the early persecutions symbols like the Chi-Rho (the first two letters of *Ch-r-istos*) or the fish (*ichthus* in Greek, whose letters were a mnemonic for "Jesus Christ, God's Son, Savior") had to suffice, followed by representations of Jesus as a teacher or the good shepherd. But when Constantine received his vision of conquering in the sign of the cross at the Milvian Bridge in October 312 and became senior emperor, all that changed. The Council of Nicea was held in a town named after his victory (*nike* in Greek), and representations of Jesus began to borrow the emperor's new clothes. After the great debates about Jesus' involvement in creation, the cosmic Christ starts to appear, leading to the great mosaics of the Pantocrator, ruler of all, fixing his gaze on us from the apses of highly decorated churches in the East.

Developing Cultures and Different Churches

Over the next thousand years various churches developed in different cultures, yet all were inspired by faith in Jesus Christ as Lord and Son of God. Constantine's decision to move his capital to Constantinople (Istanbul in modern Turkey) in May 330 set one direction for the Eastern Empire with its beautifully decorated church mosaics and icons. Meanwhile the withdrawal of Roman troops from Britain around 410 left the Celtic church to develop its own culture, expressing faith in Jesus through wonderfully illuminated manuscripts of the Gospels. After a couple of centuries of defeats for Rome, the crowning of Charlemagne in Saint Peter's on Christmas Day 800 demonstrated the growth of a new Western Roman Empire, united through its faith in Christ.

In the East eighth-century iconoclasts, responding to the expansion of Islamic art and faith, argued that the sole "image" (*icon* in Greek) of God was Christ, who could only be represented in the Eucharist. In response those who used icons used the Chalcedonian definition to argue that since Jesus was truly human as well as divine, it was acceptable to display his humanity. The debate about the "true image" *(vera icon)* also fueled the story of "Veronica," the woman who wiped Jesus' face on his way to the cross and found his "true image" on her cloth, which then became the source for many representations of the face of Jesus in the medieval West. This increasing concentration on the humanity of Jesus focused on his physical sufferings and passion, as in writings like Julian of Norwich's *Revelations of Divine Love* and Saint Thomas à Kempis's *Imitation of Christ.* Personal meditation upon Jesus' wounds and the instruments of the passion is also seen in paintings and sculptures, with increasingly realistic representations of the cross by artists like Dürer. This also drew on the experience of people who received the stigmata, such as Saint Francis. An almost erotic devotion to Jesus was encouraged, from Bernard of Clairvaux's commentary on the Song of Songs (ca. 1135) to the works of Saint John of the Cross and Teresa of Ávila (ca. 1575).

The Renaissance continued the stress on humanity, as is seen in both the scientific and artistic works of Leonardo da Vinci. But Jesus remained central as the ultimate model for the universal man. The developing application of scholarship to biblical texts led Erasmus to publish the Greek New Testament in 1516 and Luther to post his Ninety-five Theses in October 1517 — both crucial events for the start of the Reformation. Again this article of the Creed — "I believe in Jesus" — was central in the Reformers' stress on putting personal faith in Jesus as Son of God for salvation, rather than in the church, as is reflected by the Christ-centered spirituality of works like Bach's settings of the Saint Matthew and Saint John passion stories.

Modern and Critical Interpretations

The Enlightenment stress on human reason and a mechanistic understanding of the universe led to an attack on faith and miracles by writers like Hume (1711-76). The so-called quest for the historical Jesus began with H. S. Reimarus's attempt to discover Jesus' authentic teaching in 1778, followed by

D. F. Strauss's *The Life of Jesus Critically Examined* (1835). Each of our key terms, "Christ," "Lord," and "Son of God," was dismissed as a later projection by the church on to the human Jesus. Ernst Renan's *Vie de Jésus* (1863) gave a more romantic view, which is reflected in Victorian painting from William Blake through to Holman Hunt's *The Light of the World* (ca. 1900), with Jesus knocking on the door of the soul, wanting to be admitted. However, such comfortable images were soon shocked by the figure of the Grand Inquisitor in Dostoyevsky's *The Brothers Karamazov* and Albert Schweitzer's reconstruction of Jesus as a wild apocalyptic prophet (*The Quest for the Historical Jesus*, 1906). Jesus as liberator was invoked by Wilberforce and Abraham Lincoln in the campaign against slavery; while Gandhi and Martin Luther King saw in Jesus a pattern for nonviolent protest, other liberation movements brought him into the armed struggle. Between the wars Barth appealed to Jesus as the divine Word in his opposition to Hitler while Bultmann began his project to demythologize him in existentialist terms. Critical scholarship has expanded exponentially with Käsemann starting the "new quest" for the historical Jesus in October 1953, while recent debate has polarized between the "third quest" of scholars like E. P. Sanders and N. T. Wright concentrating on Jesus in his Jewish setting, in contrast to the Californian interpretations of Jesus as a wandering Hellenistic cynic from the Jesus Seminar. Jesus has even been a big hit in Hollywood, from Cecil B. DeMille's *King of Kings* (1927) through postwar blockbusters like *Ben Hur* to Scorsese's *The Last Temptation of Christ* (1988) and Mel Gibson's *The Passion of the Christ* (2004), not to mention stage shows like *Godspell* and *Jesus Christ Superstar*.

Unity and Diversity?

It all seems a long way from the wandering first-century preacher, but belief in Jesus takes different forms in every culture. The phrases "Christ," "Lord," and "Son of God" were all drawn from contemporary Jewish and Greco-Roman society — but have resonated down the centuries and across the globe. Yet every age also reinterprets Jesus afresh for each generation. So, are all titles acceptable and every portrait valid — a kind of Christology à la carte for a consumer society? Even the New Testament contains a plurality of views about Jesus, as we saw earlier. Having four Gospels rather than one *Jesus: The Authorized Biography* has puzzled critics from pagan opponents in the first centuries to Muslims today. And yet the four Gospels and the rest of the New Testament provide a "canon" or rule for the interpretation of Jesus, just as the creeds and councils set out the boundaries for legitimate interpretation of the Christian tradition. Such canonical plurality provides both a stimulus for new images of Jesus and a control, which means that not everything is equally acceptable (e.g., a Nazi Jesus?). Belief in Jesus as "Christ, Son of God, our Lord" is still the motivating factor for hundreds of millions of people around the globe who find him just as relevant and exciting in their lives today as any of the preceding generations did. And the last couple centuries have shown that even those outside the church still find this formally uneducated man and his brief ministry in a provincial backwater of the Roman Empire absolutely fascinating. As Paul put it, "In every way, whether in pretence or in truth, Christ is proclaimed; and in that I rejoice" (Phil. 1:18).

Contemporary Reflections

These snapshots reveal that faith in Jesus Christ has been expressed in stories and pictures in every generation. Finally, in these concluding reflections let us return to some implications of our three key words for today.

Jesus Christ — the Uniting Point for All Christians

Faith that Jesus of Nazareth was "the Christ" led to the original formation and delineation of the church. The first believers were Jews who saw themselves as followers of "the Way" (Acts 9:2; 19:23), but "it was in Antioch that the disciples were first called 'Christians'" (11:26). Antioch was a cosmopolitan Near Eastern city in Syria, long influenced by Hellenistic culture, under Roman control, with a Jewish population — and any of those groups could have named the "Christians." What distinguished the first believers from other Jews was faith that Jesus was Israel's Messiah, or "Christ." Meanwhile the Hellenistic Near East was full of mystery religions and salvation cults, following various leaders — and the early church's devotion to Christ would have made them look like these: according to Pliny, a Roman governor in Asia Minor around 111, "they chant verses in honour of Christ as if to a god" (*Letters* 10.96). But this also meant they could not sacrifice to the emperor as a god, and the choice of "Christ or Caesar?" would lead many to martyrdom.

So too today, in our multicultural and cosmopolitan world, it is faith in Jesus Christ which distinguishes the church, not just being English, or living in some parts of the United States. In a multifaith society with so many religious groups, the church is the community of those living out their baptismal statement, "I believe in Jesus Christ." Such faith defines the boundaries of the Christian church, including all the various denominations, but excluding those like Mormons and Jehovah's Witnesses who do not accept the ecumenical creeds and councils' decisions about Jesus described above. In their subordination of Jesus as merely "a god" or "divine," they follow Arius's attempt to preserve the uniqueness of God the Father. But such ideas belong within the traditions of "unitarian" theology, rather than a full trinitarian acceptance of Jesus Christ, "true God from true God."

The international ecumenical movement and the World Council of Churches have many problems, and the endless commissions and dialogues can seem wearisome. But over and beyond all our differences, what unites all Christians — Orthodox, Catholic, Anglican, Protestant, Pentecostal, independents alike — is faith in Jesus Christ as understood in the creeds and councils. Yet another problem is that the ecumenical creeds and Chalcedonian definition are expressed in technical terms like "person," "nature," and "substance." It was difficult enough in the fourth and fifth centuries to agree which Latin words carried the same meaning as the Greek words for these concepts. It is even more so today when we do not use the same philosophical Platonic framework. Attempts were made through the last few centuries to redefine these ideas in terms of "modern" philosophy — while the outpourings of "postmodernism" have made the task almost impossible! And yet the creeds and the definition continue to have a normative effect; certainly nothing has been found to replace them. There are those who say that reinterpretation of them for today is impossible — and often they end up leaving behind the Christian tradition. Others prefer to stand within a recognizably orthodox continuity with the tradition, but seek to understand it within contemporary terms.[5] In this respect it is the same challenge to work out our faith in Jesus Christ for this generation as has faced the church throughout history. As Bonhoeffer famously put it, "Who is Jesus Christ for us today?"

God's Only Son — Conversations with Other Faiths

As with "Christ," so too "only Son" was important in both directions for early believers. Their Jewish brothers and sisters thought it compromised their passionate monotheism to put Jesus with God as his Son, while the polytheistic Greeks and Romans with their many gods and children of the gods objected to the exclusive claim that Jesus was God's "only" Son. Similarly, this phrase continues to have important implications within our multifaith world today.

Conflicts within families are always the most bitter, and civil wars the

---

5. See, for example, Colin E. Gunton, *Yesterday and Today,* 2nd ed. (London: SPCK, 1997).

hardest fought. The "parting of the ways" between church and synagogue through the first and second centuries was extremely painful. Palestinian Judaism of Jesus' day was very diverse with lots of groups and sects, most of which perished in the Jewish revolt and Roman war of 66-70. Following the destruction of the temple, rabbinic Judaism began to re-form itself around reading the law in the synagogue while Jews who believed in Jesus as Messiah found themselves in an increasingly Gentile church. Unfortunately Jewish persecution of the early Christians through the first couple centuries was repaid many times over in medieval pogroms and the Holocaust. In recent decades Jewish scholars like Geza Vermes and Jacob Neusner have helped New Testament studies recover the essentially Jewish origins of Jesus. Some Jews today do see Jesus not as the "traitor" or "arch-deceiver" described in early rabbinic material, but rather as a teacher or rabbi within that tradition, while for others this is still too difficult and smacks of enforced conversions. And yet the Judeo-Christian traditions are so closely connected that complete separation is never possible, and so sensitive debate around what calling Jesus "his only Son" means within the monotheism inherited from Judaism must continue.

The same is true with the other "people of the book," Muslims. Here too we share a monotheistic faith in the "God of Abraham." Islam sees itself as the culmination of both Judaism and Christianity and has a very high regard for Jesus. The Qur'an describes him as a great prophet, accepting his virgin birth from Mary (sura 19.30-40) and recounting his miracles and teaching ministry. Furthermore, God accepted and vindicated his ministry by receiving him up into heaven; Jesus did not die on the cross, where "only a likeness" was crucified (sura 4.156-59). So this phrase from the Creed is crucial for Christian-Muslim relations too: that God should take human form in the incarnation of Jesus his Son is inconceivable to the followers of the Prophet, and that he should suffer and die is abhorrent — yet for Christians, this is the basis and the glory of our faith. Regrettably the history of violence on all sides, from the Crusades to the contemporary international situation, makes this dialogue very difficult — and all the more necessary.

Further afield, Jesus is highly respected as a great teacher and religious leader by many within the great religious traditions of the East, Hindus, Buddhists, Sikhs, and so forth. Given their more plural view of the Divine, talk of Jesus' Sonship and divinity is less problematic — but like the Greeks and Romans, they find our claim of "only" Son too exclusive. On the other hand, many secularists and agnostics want to "rescue" Jesus from the church: they include him alongside Buddha, Socrates, and modern heroes like Gandhi or Martin Luther King as the great humanists of all time. Here the description of

Jesus' Sonship is meaningless and the exclusivity of "only" seen as arrogance. And yet our world's fascination with him means that this ultimate example of how God intended human beings to be continues to draw all people to himself (John 12:32) — and the task of those who confess him as "God's only Son" must be to facilitate that, not prevent it.

Our Lord — Implications for Both Church and World

The first creed was "Jesus is Lord" (1 Cor. 12:3), and early Christians understood that the Lordship of Christ allowed no other masters — even Caesar himself — and paid for that confession of faith in Jesus with their lives. To claim Jesus as "our Lord" relativizes all other claims to power, even from the leaders of the most powerful nations on earth, as is made clear in the Technicolor visions of the book of Revelation: Jesus is "King of kings and Lord of lords" and will reign forever (Rev. 19:16). Furthermore, it is a universal claim, for nothing can be outside his sovereignty: as the old saying puts it, "If Jesus is Lord *at* all, he must be Lord *of* all" — and this has immense implications for both church and world.

In one of his earliest letters Paul grapples with how Jesus affects the old divisions between Jews and other people, and whether new converts must accept circumcision and the Jewish law. In the midst of his often convoluted argument he suddenly bursts out: "There is no longer Jew or Greek, slave or free, male and female; for all of you are one in Christ Jesus" (Gal. 3:28). In a flash all barriers of race, social class, and gender are dissolved under the Lordship of Christ. Of course, we must immediately admit that the church has been as guilty of oppression in all these areas as any other human organization through history — and yet that is our calling as we live out faith in Jesus Christ our Lord. Because he is the only true "Son of God," only he can bring all his wandering children from every age, race, creed, society, nation, gender, color, orientation, or philosophy to his heavenly Father. Because he alone is "Lord," all human authorities and empires, armies and governments must yield. At the foot of the cross the ground is level, and we can only stand there, shoulder to shoulder, and kneel together before him.

As Hebrews says, "As it is, we do not yet see everything in subjection to him. But we do see Jesus, who for a little while was made lower than the angels, crowned with glory and honour" (Heb. 2:8-9). Thus we wait, groaning in labor pains along with the whole creation until the Lordship of Christ is finally established over all (Rom. 8:18-23; 1 Cor. 15:20-28). Yet we cannot just wait, passively, doing nothing. Those who confess Jesus Christ as "our Lord" are compelled to extend his Lordship into every area of our world and our life. Thus we need to work for peace in the midst of the violence and conflicts of our world; for justice for the oppressed, food for the hungry, and release for those under the heavy burden of debt. Because there were none that Jesus turned away, or refused to heal, or would not hear, then his followers too should be open, accepting and welcoming all. And since Jesus is Lord of all the earth, and not just human beings, Christians must be also concerned for the environment, for the natural world, and for the biodiversity of our fragile spaceship earth.

It is an extremely demanding task, requiring nothing less than everything. Those simple key words about Jesus as "Christ," "his only Son," "our Lord" sum up the wealth of the biblical portraits, stories, and teachings. As the early Christians reflected upon them, they were led by the Holy Spirit to encapsulate that faith and experience in these phrases of the Creed. Every generation since in all parts of the world have found themselves driven to explain and reinterpret that faith afresh in descriptions, art, science, initiatives, and missions, a few snapshots of which we have seen here. And all that rich tradition confronts us now, reflected in the challenges of today, to see how confessing that same faith might change us and the world — forever. Who ever said saying the Creed was easy — or safe?

I Believe in Jesus Christ, God's Only Son, Our Lord

Ecclesiastes 1:1-11; Philippians 2:1-11

CORNELIUS PLANTINGA

In Ecclesiastes everything is old news. Everything's happened before. People get born, they work, they die, and then their children follow suit. The sun rises and sets, and the next day it does it again. The wind blows through the trees, and the streams run out to the sea, but the wind never blows itself out and the streams never fill up the sea. Everything under the sun plays its little tune till it gets to the repeat sign — and then it just does what the sign says.

"What has been is what will be," says the teacher, "and what has been done is what will be done." Then, almost in despair, the teacher asks a single question: "Is there *anything* of which we may say, 'Look, this is new'?"

Is there anything . . . ?

Advent is a four-week answer to that question, and the answer comes to us in paradoxes. It comes in a whole thicket of paradoxes. Of course it does. The answer would *have* to come that way. You can't get heaven and earth together without some clashing of gears. You can't get time and eternity together without a certain amount of metaphysical shifting and grinding. The one thing under the sun that is really new is the incarnation of Jesus Christ, God's only Son, our Lord. The incarnation gives us a union so amazing, so divine that it demands our soul, our life, our all.

"Is there *anything* of which we can say, 'Look, this is new'?"

How about God in the flesh? How about God with a thumbprint and, for all we know, seasonal hay fever. A baby born in a manger whose previous address was in heaven. Son of Mary and also of the Holy Ghost.

73

How can anybody describe someone like this? Bible writers plundered every source they could think of. They plundered Wisdom literature and prophecy; they borrowed from history, poetry, and apocalypse. So Jesus Christ is word and wisdom. He's the second Adam, the end of the law, the light of the world. He's high priest and apostle. He's "the Lion of the tribe of Judah" but also "a Lamb standing as if it had been slaughtered" (Rev. 5:5, 6).

Or, chiming in with the Creed, he's "Jesus," which means Savior even though the Romans crossed him out. He's "God's only Son," which means he's "the exact imprint of God's very being" (Heb. 1:3), but he's also a particular Jew who didn't especially impress the people he grew up with (Mark 6:1-6). He's "our Lord," which means, astonishingly, that even when he was coughing or wheezing his disciples felt like worshiping him — not just God in him, or God through him, but *him*.

How shattering all this is. Exactly one person, Jesus Christ, is simultaneously the second person of the Holy Trinity and also a particular man who learned to cut boards in his stepfather's carpenter shop, and may have cut some of them too short.

In just a few verses Philippians 2 captures some of the drama and some of the wonder:

> Let the same mind be in you that was in Christ Jesus,
> who, though he was in the form of God,
> > did not regard equality with God
> > as something to be exploited,
> but emptied himself,
> > taking the form of a slave,
> > being born in human likeness.
> And being found in human form,
> > he humbled himself
> > and became obedient to the point of death —
> > even death on a cross.
> Therefore God also highly exalted him
> > and gave him the name
> > that is above every name,
> so that at the name of Jesus
> > every knee should bend,
> > in heaven and on earth and under the earth,
> and every tongue should confess
> > that Jesus Christ is Lord,
> > to the glory of God the Father.

Nothing I can say will do justice to the majesty of these words. Here is Holy Scripture in all its splendor. Here is Jesus Christ in all his terrible glory. Here is the whole career of Christ inside a hymn, the whole career of Jesus Christ shaped like a parabola — from preexistent glory through incarnation, and then down to death, all the way down to death on a cross.

Death on a *cross* — a "howling wilderness event," as Moltmann describes it. The men and women who loved Jesus saw him die on a torture instrument that the Romans had invented to terrorize their enemies. They saw the Romans take his life in a public spectacle that was meant to intimidate anybody with an eye to see or an ear to hear or a heart to tremble at state-sponsored terrorism and the awful suffering it brings. The Romans jammed their crosses into the earth like scarecrows, and every one of them proclaimed to the world, "Caesar is Lord, and don't you ever forget it."

Part of the plan was to humiliate victims. If you were spiked to a Roman cross, the Romans wanted your life. Of course they wanted your life, but not until they had taken your dignity. The Romans shredded your dignity in order to send a message to anybody who looked up to you. They made you suffer in public so that others could enjoy your suffering, or else get sick over it, but in any case so that they wouldn't miss the uproar in your central nervous system and the nightmare in your soul.

Obedient to the point of death, even death on a cross.

Then the mighty upturn as God raises Christ; God exalts Christ; God lifts Jesus Christ to universal triumph and acclaim, so that one day every knee might bend and every tongue confess that Jesus Christ is Lord.

You know, we have heard the words so often that we yawn when we hear them: Jesus is Lord.

Right.

But in the first century people gasped when they heard the words. What struck them is that *Jesus* is Lord. Not Caesar! Not Pol Pot, nor Joseph Stalin, nor Idi Amin. Not Stone Cold Steve Austin. Not Hugh Hefner nor the Marquis de Sade. Not anybody who is vicious or fake or addicted to pleasure. *Jesus* is Lord — the one who prayed all night before he called his disciples, and who still got Judas, and then *kept him*. Jesus kept Judas on, and admitted him to the upper room.

Jesus is Lord — one who dignified women by teaching them theology in a time when it wasn't done. *Jesus* is Lord — the one who lived every day with a man like Peter, and still wanted to build his church on him.

Jesus is Lord. Mark tells us that priests plotted against him, that Judas betrayed him, that three disciples fell asleep on him, that witnesses lied about him, and that Peter denied him. Mark tells us that Pilate flogged him, and that soldiers mocked him. And when the soldiers got tired of kneeling in front of Jesus and then belting him in the face, they led him out to crucify him. All these assaults on a human spirit, all these terrible degradations of Jesus' dignity till finally he was led away to the cross. Mark is telling us, I think, that where degradation is concerned, crucifixion is just a way of finishing it off.

Jesus is Lord. I say there is astonishment built into this claim, and trust. We don't look to the cross to get evil explained to us. It's not as if in pondering Calvary we understand cerebral palsy. No, we lift our eyes to the cross in order to see that God shares our lot and can therefore be trusted. In Jesus Christ God doesn't exempt himself. God doesn't insulate himself against suffering and death. The cross of Jesus Christ tells us of a love so fierce that the Son of God is willing to walk down into the abyss to save us.

Someone once observed that if God's love were available only to those who were sure of God's ways, most of us would be priced out of the market. We are short on answers to suffering. We don't understand a lot of what happens in the world.

What we do understand is that we have a suffering Lord, who is the atoning sacrifice for our sins. What we understand is that all the uproar in his central nervous system is "for us," "for many," "for all." What we understand is that Jesus' resurrection means he is loose in the world, and none of us is safe. He is our Lord, and sooner or later he will come for us.

"I believe in Jesus Christ, God's only Son, our Lord." When we say Jesus is Lord, we are talking about God's greatest reversal, and we are saying that we trust not only Jesus, but also his *program of dying and rising*. We trust his redemptive program in which self-expenditure leads to life, and not just to burnout. We trust that in his death Jesus absorbed the world's evil into himself, and cut the loop of vengeance that has wrecked human life down the ages. We trust that in his resurrection Jesus led out all the captives of the world.

"Let the same mind be in you that was in Christ Jesus, who, though he was in the form of God, / did not regard equality with God / as something to be exploited, / but emptied himself." That's the NRSV, and as Gerald Hawthorne writes, it's got to be wrong. The Greek text doesn't say that *although* he was in the form of God he emptied himself. What it says is, "*Being* in the form of God he emptied himself." You might almost read, *because* he was in the form of God he emptied himself. Because he was in the form of God he humbled himself. Because he was in the form of God he took the form of a servant, washing the feet of disciples who would never dream of doing the same thing for each other.

As John Ortberg once put it, we think of Jesus' servanthood as a disguise. We think of servanthood as a king's disguise, the way it is in fairy tales. But Jesus Christ took the form of a servant because he is a person of God. The mind of Christ is the mind of God, as Karl Barth says — the God who loves those who don't love him; the God who sends warm sunshine and refreshing rain on evil people as well as on good people.

The Son of God just does what he sees his father doing. He empties himself and takes the form of a servant because that's the way they do it in his family. And God exalts Jesus Christ and gives him the name above every name because that too is the Godly way — to exalt the humble, to get very enthusiastic about those who spend themselves for others.

"Let the same mind be in you that was in Christ Jesus." That is, take on self-denial, and trust that you won't be a fool to do it. Take on humility, and trust that humility is actually a sign of strength. Take on the form of a servant, and trust that real flourishing consists in causing others to flourish.

In other words, get into the rhythm of God's great reversal and do some dying and rising of your own.

I say, to believe in "Jesus Christ, God's only Son, our Lord" is to believe in his program of dying and rising. I can let my addiction die, and my terrible anger, and my pride, and my despair, and all that has been weighing me down like a third mortgage. I can let these things die — in fact, I can take out a contract on these things and try to kill them. I can do this because Christ is Lord and those who die with Christ will also rise with Christ.

Faith in Jesus Christ is faith that his program works. But let me add a caution. To have the mind of Christ is to have the mind of a servant. But this does not mean that we owe submission to people who simply want to run over us. We do not owe submission to people who want us to kiss their boots in the name of Jesus. Never. We don't help people if we just reinforce their arrogance. We don't serve people if we give them submission when what they really need from us is resistance. Jesus Christ took on the form of a servant, not the form of a doormat, and we who want the mind of Christ will need to know the difference.

That's why we have church. We have church to learn what kind of dying leads to life and what kind just leads to more death. We have to help each other learn the difference. Christ's death was redemptive. Judas Iscariot's death was not. Jesus gave himself away. Judas threw himself away. We have to die and rise with Christ so that what comes out of it is life, and the kind of unity in the church that makes us a power in the world because we have quit fighting with each other and have started dying and rising together.

"I believe in Jesus Christ, God's only Son, our Lord." I believe in the mind of Christ, and the heart of Christ, and the rhythm of Christ. I believe in the grace of Jesus Christ, who though he was rich became poor for our sakes, so that we who were poor might become rich beyond all thinking and all deserving.

Is there *anything* of which we can say, "Look, this is new"?

Anything?

In the name of the Father, and of the Son, and of the Holy Spirit. Amen.

CHAPTER 5

Conceived by the Holy Spirit,
Born of the Virgin Mary

Qui conceptus est de Spiritu sancto, natus ex Maria virgine

ROBIN DARLING YOUNG

The two participial phrases that describe the Lord's double origin — divine
and human — presuppose both the long development of belief about the
Messiah's arrival to Israel and a daring assertion that God and a woman together fulfilled the prophecies of the incarnation so that both the act and the
woman receive a permanent place in Christian devotion and faith. This central Christian antithesis or paradox provides the basis for a rich tradition in
early and medieval Christianity and seems to defeat any attempt to analyze
the unimaginable joining of flesh and spirit to make the incarnate Lord.

In fact, this portion of the Creed is not meant to answer any questions
about the biology of Jesus' conception. Rather, the Creed establishes the an-
tiquity and depth of this particular mystery, by which is meant a secret plan
of God whose results, but not workings, are manifested to human beings.
Both the Holy Spirit and Mary are the original voices of which echoes have
been heard previously in the Old Testament, and now both become mediators
of God to Christians — one as the divine "spirit" of Scripture and the church,
and the other as a preeminent human intercessor whom the later Byzantine
tradition will laud as "Mother of God," "all-Holy," and "higher than the cherubim, and more glorious beyond compare than the Seraphim." Like Christ,
Mary is praised as a human and a heavenly being (reflected, perhaps, in the
symbolism of the woman clothed with the sun), and also approached with
the frankness characteristic of the early Christian and medieval tradition as a
gynecological wonder: *purus pure puram aperiens vulvam,* writes Irenaeus:
"the Pure One purely opening a pure womb."

Along with their introduction of the Holy Spirit and Mary the virgin as Christ's parents, these clauses express the action that brings about the incarnation, literally the enfleshment of the preexistent Son of God, whereby he begins his existence as a true human being. By the time the Apostles' Creed took final form in 753, these clauses could presuppose the Chalcedonian doctrine that Jesus Christ existed in two natures, human and divine, united hypostatically. As such, all his actions had a dual origin in his one person — a person to whom "God-man" is best applied, as it would be in Cyril's "theanthropos." It is true that the Creed is based on the Old Roman Creed, and thus in content dates from the late second century. The final version of the Creed therefore presupposes or at least accommodates all the theological developments of Chalcedonian Christology up through the eighth century, with that specialized terminology that develops consequent to the disputes over whether Christ had one or two natures.

The language of the Creed is much older, however, than the development of the technical vocabulary of conciliar and polemical theology. It is intended not to secure a theological position in a disputed question, but is meant to be recited as a summary of faith when a person is about to be baptized and begin the Christian way of life. It states in narrative form the actions of Jesus' life on earth as they fit into a description of the central beliefs of the Christian. Therefore the Creed also presupposes a harmonized reading of the biblical witness about the Holy Spirit and Jesus' conception from the Spirit, as well as the character of the virgin Mary who gave him birth.

It is common for scholars to write as if this, like the other statements in the Creed, is a bare declaration of the story of Jesus. But as the following makes clear, the Creed has a deeper resonance. When recited by the believer in the context of the baptismal ritual where he or she "puts on Christ," it becomes her or his story, too.

The point of the clauses, then, is to say that Jesus was divine, that he was human, and that these two sources yielded "the [Almighty God's] only Son, our Lord, Jesus Christ." Because Mary was pregnant with a son conceived by the Holy Spirit, she was eventually called "mother of God," an appellation that the final version of the Apostles' Creed also accommodates, since it was both traditional in the third century and made conciliar doctrine in the fifth. The fascination that Mary held for early Christians was far greater and more important than many commentators on the texts would admit: far from being a kind of afterthought in the Gospels, and far from taking her significance from the status of Christ alone, Mary is both lively and complicated. She stimulated some to veneration already in the second century, and Christian writers reckoned that she reverses the disaster of Eve's disobedience. In her free response to the messenger of God, Gabriel, she was the first to initiate the new dispensation of freedom from Satan, sin, and death.

To explore the union of Mary and the Holy Spirit, this essay will treat two items separately: first, Christ's origin from the Holy Spirit, and second, his birth from Mary. All three arise from the early Christian understanding that Old Testament prophecies are fulfilled in Christ. Thus these beliefs are continuations of earlier interest in the Holy Spirit. This essay will thus consider the roots of these beliefs in the Old and New Testaments, and the way the early Christian tradition builds upon the biblical testimonies.

Conceived by the Holy Spirit

Two passages in the New Testament assert Jesus' conception by the Holy Spirit: Matthew 1:20 and Luke 1:35. The former comes in the dialogue between an angel and Joseph, in which the angel speaks to Joseph in a dream: "Do not fear to take Mary your wife, for that which is conceived in her is of the Holy Spirit." The latter is a more ample description. Here the angel Gabriel announces the conception to Mary, and describes the mode of her husbandless pregnancy: "The Holy Spirit will come upon you, and the power of the Most High will overshadow you; therefore the child to be born [of you] will be called holy, the Son of God." In both cases the Gospel has already asserted the virginity of Mary in a reference to Isaiah 7:14.

Neither text, however, gives any further description of how pregnancy in a human being can result from contact with the Holy Spirit, nor does either specify the character of the Holy Spirit, and whether this being is the same as God or is the "spirit" or "wind" of the OT. Yet the Evangelists Matthew and Luke took great interest in the Spirit of God, and since both understood Jesus to be the fulfillment of the ancient prophecies, it is likely that they wish their readers to consider this Spirit to be the same in both covenants.

In the Old Testament, then, the Spirit of God is first and foremost the Spirit of prophecy, as with Saul in 1 Samuel 10:6-11 and the seventy elders of Numbers 11:25. Particularly in the later prophets, the Spirit is the Spirit that leads to prophetic discourse and also is pictured as the Spirit of God, and the source of renewed life. There the "Spirit of the Lord" brings Ezekiel to the valley of dry bones, where he is commanded to command the spirit to "breathe upon these slain, that they may live" (Ezek. 37:9). The prophetic drama promises new life because "these bones are the whole house of Israel" (37:11).

The Spirit also descended on kings for anointing, as in 1 Samuel 10:1-8. Here the prophet Samuel anoints Saul king over Israel, first anointing his head with oil and predicting: "You shall reign over the people of the Lord and you will save them from the hand of their encircling enemies." Samuel gives Saul a series of signs by which he can recognize his anointment as prince, following which "the Spirit of the Lord will come mightily upon you, and you shall prophesy with them and be turned into another man." The next verse clarifies this by saying that "God gave [Saul] another heart." Thus, in addition to making prophets, the Spirit anointed the king as messiah and made him prophet as well.

The Spirit of God, identified in some later Jewish and early Christian tradition with the Spirit that "hovered over the face of the deep" in the creation story, is also to be poured out on all flesh in Isaiah 32:15, in a passage associated with the restoration of Jerusalem. That city will be "deserted" "until the Spirit is poured upon us from on high." The time of the Spirit is marked by the cultivation and civilization of the wilderness and the peaceable civic life of the people of Israel. In the prophet Joel (2:28) the Spirit is connected with the Messiah, as it is in Isaiah 11:2 and 61:1. In the latter the Messiah is anointed with "the Spirit of the Lord God" in view of his coming "to bring good news to the poor," to "proclaim the year of the Lord's favor," to "comfort all who mourn." These latter as a result "shall build up the ancient ruins, raise up the former devastations; they shall repair the ruined cities, the devastations of many generations."

Although in only two places in the OT is the Spirit called "holy" — Psalm 51:11 and Isaiah 63:10-11 — it is clear that inasmuch as the Spirit of God brings about the restoration of the people of Israel and of the city of Jerusalem, it is associated with the holiness of God and the holiness required of God's people. More important than its title, however, is its association with the Messiah and with the messianic age, in which Israel will be restored.

A full, and even violent, political restoration of Israel was expected by some in the first century A.D., and the Gospel writers gather together the previous beliefs about the Spirit's role in this event and associate them not only with the ministry, passion, and resurrection of Jesus, but with his birth. This is because they believe him to be God himself, although they do not specify how he remains eternal and transcendent while at the same time becoming flesh/man as in John 1:14.

One way of speaking about his divinity is to strongly associate the Spirit with Jesus, as the Gospel of John (1:32-33) does when reporting John the Baptist's prophecy: John bore witness, "I saw the Spirit descend as a dove from heaven, and it remained on him . . . he who sent me to baptize with water said to me, 'He on whom you see the Spirit descend and remain, this is he who baptizes with the Holy Spirit.' And I have seen and have borne witness that this is the Son of God." As in the other three Gospels, the Holy Spirit appears, either to Jesus or to others, at Jesus' baptism, and may be understood to be with or in Jesus until his death on the cross. And later in the Gospel, 3:34-35, "For he whom God has sent utters the words of God, for it is not by measure that he gives the Spirit; the Father loves the Son, and has given all things into his hand."

This association of the Spirit with Jesus' Sonship comes up again in 1 John 5:6: "This is he who came by water and blood, Jesus Christ, not with the water only but with the water and the blood. And the Spirit is the witness, because the Spirit is the truth." Here it seems that the Spirit is the link between Jesus' revelation as son at baptism (water) and his crucifixion (blood).

The (Holy) Spirit both conceived and dwelled in Jesus, at least according to 1 John, until Jesus' crucifixion. This is the way those who believe in Jesus similarly receive the Spirit: at baptism they receive the spirit of adoption and re-creation, and that spirit lives in them as God lived in the temple. The reception of the Holy Spirit at Pentecost provides the link between Christ's reception of the Spirit and the Christian's reception: the Spirit's role in the restoration of Israel, envisioned in Ezekiel and Isaiah, has been adopted by the NT authors and applied to Christ and to those who follow him, effectively making up Israel, now reconstituted in the church, with all the changes of meaning that that entails.

It is evident that Mary plays a crucial role in this restoration, but how she does so will be described in the following section. Suffice it to say for now that her virginity plays a much larger role than simply guaranteeing the fact that she did not become pregnant by a mere male human being. Her virginity effects both the reversal of the original human coupling and its ironic frustration and sterility (where the original children of Adam and Eve are ill fated and one is of dubious origin, according to later tradition a child of Satan); she will be the inception of the new paradise, but also the new city, as her role in both the Lukan narrative and the Revelation to John attest. That Ignatius can refer to her birth as one of the "secrets" of God hidden from Satan means that Mary's role in the economy of salvation is pivotal indeed.

As Paraclete, then, the Holy Spirit first "defends" Mary against the charge of adultery that Joseph evidently considers. But the Spirit's role as Paraclete (= advocate, legal counsel) is explicitly outlined in the Gospel of John. There, as Jesus describes his departure to his disciples, he promises that the Holy Spirit (here the "Spirit of truth," i.e., "true spirit") will be sent in response to his prayer: "And I will pray the Father, and he will give you another Counselor, to be with you for ever, even the Spirit of truth, whom the world cannot receive, because it neither sees him nor knows him; you know him, for he dwells with you, and will be in you" (John 14:16-17).

Further, the Paraclete will defend the disciples against the "ruler of this world." "The Counselor, the Holy Spirit, whom the Father will send in my name, he will teach you all things, and bring to your remembrance all that I have said to you" (14:26). Later on in the farewell discourse, Jesus tells his disciples that "it is to your advantage that I go away, for if I do not go away, the Counselor will not come to you; but if I go, I will send him to you." Evidently his role is to persuade the world of truth through them: "And when he comes, he will convince the world of sin and of righteousness and of judgment; of sin, because they do not believe in me; of righteousness, because I go to the Father, and you will see me no more; of judgment, because the ruler of this world is judged" (16:8-11). The three moments of the redemption of Israel are here linked with the presence of the Spirit, as they would be in 1 John 2:1-2; "if any one does sin, we have an advocate with the Father, Jesus Christ the righteous; and he is the expiation for our sins, and not for ours only but also for the sins of the whole world." Again, the Spirit and the temple, particularly here its sacrifices, are linked with Jesus.

The final passages to note, on the entry of the Spirit into human life through Christ, are Acts 2 and Revelation 1. In the first the disciples are gathered when the Spirit is distributed to them: "They were all filled with the Holy Spirit and began to speak in other tongues, as the Spirit gave them utterance." Following the reversal of Babel, Peter prophesies, recalling Joel 2:28-32 with its prediction of the messianic age. This quotation of the prophecy, and the explanation of the meaning of Christ's suffering, results in the conversion and baptism of a large number of early followers and results in a common life deliberately depicted as being like the peaceable civilization envisioned in the other prophets. Finally, John writes in Revelation 1:10, "I was in the Spirit on the Lord's day, and I heard . . . ," which precedes his long account of the eschatological events presaging the return of the Messiah and the creation of the holy city.

In all these the Spirit that conceived Jesus has evidently conceived not only him but the entire community of Israel that now continues Jesus' life on earth and, following him through persecution, joins him in heaven, linking the two in a concert of expiation and righteousness. Although the Spirit is not termed "God" until the later fourth century, it here is a conduit of God, and if considered as the active role of God in the birth of Jesus, may be thought of as divine in itself.

One place a strong link exists between the Holy Spirit in the church and the Holy Spirit in Mary is in Acts 1:12, on Pentecost, where the apostles had returned to Jerusalem to receive the Paraclete. The eleven remaining apostles were in the upper room; "All these with one accord devoted themselves to prayer, together with the women and Mary the mother of Jesus, and his brothers." Once another apostle is chosen to bring the number to twelve as representative of the tribes of Israel, the Holy Spirit filled the entire group. The Spirit who had made Mary conceive a child was present as the church was made a new Israel, paralleling the first birth with the birth of the church.

This insistence on the Holy Spirit's filling the church, or filling each Christian in the church, becomes a pronounced feature of Paul's letters, in Galatians, 1 and 2 Corinthians, and Romans. In Galatians Paul exhorts his readers to "walk by the Spirit, and do not gratify the desires of the flesh" (5:16). In a reinterpretation of the presence of God in the temple that Paul writes in 1 Corinthians 3:16, Paul casts himself as another Solomon building the church up like a temple (3:10) and writes, "Do you not know that you are God's temple, and that God dwells in you? If any one destroys God's temple, God will destroy him. For God's temple is holy, and that temple you are" (3:16-17). Paul writes in 6:19 both to recommend the body and also to discipline it with ascesis: "Do you not know that your body is a temple of the Holy Spirit within you, which you have from God?" (cf. Rom. 8:9, "the spirit of God dwells in you"). Ephesians 2 carries forward Paul's understanding of the church as a temple whose cornerstone is Christ, "in whom you also are built into it for a dwelling place [temple] of God in the Spirit" (2:22).

In the church as altar, building, and body, is precisely where the fathers of the church connect the holiness of Jesus, anticipated in the holiness of the prior temple, with the holiness of the church — the church, and each Christian, possesses the Holy Spirit, the same spirit of prophecy that now is transferred to the apostles. Before the apostles received it, however, the Holy Spirit also came to another group; these were, in the stories of Matthew and Luke, those who prophesied in response to the arrival of Jesus.

Born of the Virgin Mary

Two elements are important here, the first being the virginity of the birth itself, making it a miraculous birth because outside the normal human means of procreation. The second is the person of Mary, who from the first century was evidently regarded as a highly holy woman, a prophetess and a disciple among those who accompanied Jesus and therefore assisted in the restoration of Israel.

Matthew's mention of Mary turns on his interpretation of Isaiah 7:14, "Behold, a virgin shall conceive and bear a son, and his name shall be called Emmanuel." Although, famously, the Greek text is based on the LXX interpre-

tation of Hebrew *almah,* "young woman," as *parthenos,* "virgin," the importance of the birth from the virgin goes far beyond the particular translation.
First, given the odd appearance of Mary in the Matthean genealogy of Jesus
— taking her place among the four women mentioned, none of them virgins
but all giving birth to crucial Israelites by out-of-the-ordinary means — the
following dialogue between Joseph and the angel is of heightened significance. Because before her marriage "she was found to be with child of the
Holy Spirit," Joseph, "a righteous man," was apparently afraid to marry her;
he is told, "Do not fear to take Mary your wife, for that which is conceived in
her is of the Holy Spirit." In Matthew Mary is not specifically called a virgin,
but the quotation from Isaiah makes it evident that she is.

Luke, on the other hand, draws out the account of Mary's virginity by
putting it into her (not Joseph's) dialogue with an angel, whom he names Gabriel. The angel was "sent from God to a city of Galilee named Nazareth, to a
virgin betrothed to a man whose name was Joseph, of the house of David;
and the virgin's name was Mary." The angel announces that the Lord is with
her, and that she has found favor with God, and that she will conceive and
bear. Mary asks the direct question: "How can this be, since I have no husband?"

It is in response to this question that the angel gives the most direct description of the mode of conception: "The Holy Spirit will come upon you,
and the power of the Most High will overshadow you; therefore the child to
be born [of you] will be called holy, the Son of God." The angel cites as a parallel miracle the conception of John the Baptist by Mary's relative Elizabeth, a
woman past menopause.

But the first consequence of the conception by the Holy Spirit is Mary's
long quotation of Hannah's prayer in 1 Samuel 2:1-10, which is inspired
speech that also reinterprets Hannah's inspired speech when she is about to
give birth to the prophet Samuel. In fact, all three figures of Luke 2 are filled
with the Holy Spirit: Elizabeth, Mary, and Zechariah, although Mary is not
directly said to be so — she is filled with the Spirit by virtue of her pregnancy.
In fact, all these examples are gathered to emphasize Mary's virginity — she is
what other mothers of important messianic sons have been, the mother of a
prophet, but she is also a virgin, as emphasized in the text.

Mary's virginity itself has also very likely gained importance not only because the receptacle of the Holy Spirit is undefiled by human semen, and
therefore her spotlessness, accented by the later tradition, is also present here,
and not only because of her analogy to the cultic purity required of Israel for
holiness of worship and legal observance, but because she represents the state
of sexual abstention that was becoming of great interest to Jews of the first

century, most particularly the Jews of the Qumran community, of John the Baptist's sect, and of the early mission of the church. That early Christianity preferred sexual abstinence, whether by virginity or by postsexual continence and chastity, can hardly now be denied. Composed in the first century, the accounts of Mary's conception fit well, then, with a tradition increasingly emphatic about the importance of sexual abstinence as a foundation for devotion to God. That Jesus himself remains unmarried and a virgin from his birth to his death, according to NT writers, is another significant reference to this preference for the holiness of unmarried life — a preference that will gain increasing favor as the tradition of early and medieval Christianity develops.

If Jesus' birth is a remaking of Israel, and if the incarnation of the Logos is also a remaking of the world, as in the prologue to the Gospel of John, then Mary's role was possibly of great interest to the Gospel writers because she, like important mothers in Israel before her, provided not merely a prophet or a patriarch to the nation, but the actual Messiah and Son of God himself, who also was a patriarch in the sense of refounding Israel and a prophet because he is called one in several places. Mary's story is inevitably one, then, of a matriarch and prophetess in Israel, and the later patristic tradition does not de-emphasize this; rather, it heightens it. The important qualifier here is that Mary now, in a church largely Gentile, becomes a kind of mother of the church and eventually someone who is venerated alongside her son Jesus. The very qualities that, for the first-century writers, made Mary a matriarch and prophetess now make her Theotokos and New Eve, and most estimable among women, until finally the Byzantine liturgy refers to her as "higher than the cherubim / more worthy beyond compare than the seraphim" and the *Panagia,* "all holy [woman]."

The beginnings of this tradition may be seen in the writings of Paul, who states that Jesus is "born of a woman" (Gal. 4:4) and "descended from David according to the flesh" (Rom. 1:3). In the first, Paul links Jesus' being "born of a woman, born under the law" with the arrival of the messianic age, "when the time had fully come." Being born of a woman is linked with Jesus' redemption, "so that we might receive adoption as sons."

The second place, part of the prologue to the letter to the Romans, is the first appearance of a narrative about Jesus' birth expressed in the form of an antithesis. Paul here describes himself as set apart for that gospel "concerning [God's] Son, who was descended from David according to the flesh and designated Son of God in power according to the Spirit of holiness by his resurrection from the dead, Jesus Christ our Lord" (1:3-4). On the one side of Jesus' ancestry is the Davidic line, and on the other side is his designation as Son according to the Holy Spirit — an antithesis that expresses his double descent and also the incommensurability, inequality, and utter distinction of the two lines: the natural and human on the one side and the supernatural and divine on the other.

Although Mary is mentioned in only one of these passages, and not by name, something like a narrative elongation of the antithesis of Romans appears in the Gospels of Matthew and John. Likewise Galatians's brief statement of the divine economy where the age of law is succeeded by the messianic age also prepares the way for the Gospels' narrative, as does, of course, Philippians 2:6-11, where the *kenosis* and exaltation of Jesus Christ are described in terms of the natural and supernatural realms.

The Evangelists know, or choose to tell, fuller traditions about Mary, which may be why she is not merely indicated by the designation "woman," as in Paul, but becomes a pivotal figure in the two Gospels that describe her part in the life of her son. Apart from his announcement of her virginal conception, Matthew in describing Herod's efforts to find and kill Jesus, a rival king, makes Mary and Jesus a pair requiring Joseph's defense. Matthew speaks of "the child with Mary his mother" and "the child and his mother," heightening a sense that she is in danger as well. Just as she was protected by an angel, an angel saves Mary and Jesus by coming to Joseph in a dream to instruct him to leave Palestine, and in another, later, telling him to return.

In Luke Mary's obedience to Gabriel is stressed, from her first response: "Here am I, the servant of the Lord" (1:38). Her encounter with the angel Gabriel is, as noted above, described in detail, and her own meditation on the birth of Jesus also receives attention. Likewise, with Joseph Mary continues her faithfulness to the Law. They have Jesus circumcised and consecrate him in the temple as a newborn (2:21-35). In addition, they go to Jerusalem for the annual Passover festival (2:41-52), which is the occasion for Jesus' first revelation of the difference between himself and his parents. Luke continues to refer to Mary; she is the occasion for Jesus' referring to the ones obedient to him as his true "mother and brothers" (8:19-21), and she is also present in Jerusalem after Jesus' death, waiting with the other disciples at Pentecost (Acts 1:14).

Finally, in the Gospel of John, which (as noted above) omits a story of Jesus' birth and so omits an account of Mary's reaction, there is a reference twice to "the mother of Jesus." The first one is at the wedding in Cana (2:1-12), where she and Jesus engage in a dialogue about the significance of the failure of wine; she acts as his intermediary to the servants, and therefore as a catalyst for the miracle there. In John's account of the crucifixion, she is given by Jesus to the beloved disciple as a mother (19:25-27).

The Johannine tradition preserves one more account of Mary, as a symbol who appears in the prophecy of Revelation. The "woman clothed with the sun" seems to be Mary herself as both Israel and the church. That she "brought forth a male child, one who is to rule all the nations with a rod of iron," suggests that this identifying line of the Son of Man makes her the mother of Jesus. Yet when the child ascends to the heavenly throne, she goes to the wilderness to escape the dragon/Satan and stays in "a place prepared by God, in which to be nourished for 1,260 days" (Rev. 12:1-6). It is important that this entire scene takes place in front of "God's temple in heaven" where the ark of his covenant was visible, in the midst of a thunderstorm. This woman later is given wings to "fly from the serpent into the wilderness," and though pursued by the dragon, is never killed by it.

This association of Mary with the temple will receive much more attention in the second-century *Protoevangelion of James.* In fact, this passage in Revelation is the narrative basis for the elaborated attention to Mary that develops from the second century onward, just as the antithesis in Paul is the basis for the linkage of Mary as natural mother and the Holy Spirit as supernatural father that continues, in various forms, throughout the history of early Christianity. It is with this double tradition of Mary that this essay now concludes.

In the second century, the period of the compilation of the New Testament by the church, numerous Christian writers began to think further about the virgin Mary, and for a number of possible reasons. The first reason is that she herself was the first human being in the generation of Jesus to alert the Jewish people that the Messiah had arrived. Second, she has all the marks of a prophet. Third, she signifies the church, now being understood as the true Israel. Her prophetic status has been explored already; she is directly involved, though, in the origins of the church, as depicted in Acts. In the second century a famous inscription describes her in ecclesiastical terms: "Faith led me everywhere and offered me a fish of the spring, very large and pure, which a holy virgin had caught. And this she gave her friends to eat always." With its reference to Christ as the ichthus monogram, this inscription makes Mary as virgin-church also the one who offers the eucharistic food to "her friends," combining her role with that of her son.

Fourth, Mary is the "New Eve," according to Justin and Irenaeus. Thus she becomes along with Christ the new parent of the human race, beginning with those enrolled in the church. This enhances her status as mother, doubtless allowing cultural symbols of motherhood divine and human to be associated with her.

Finally, if Christ is God — as the Evangelists indicate and the second-century authors plainly state — then Mary is the mother of God, although the title is not articulated until the writings of Origen in the early third century. As mother of God she seems to participate in the exchange of qualities between her son and herself — giving her son her own humanity through his gestation and growth in her womb and her giving birth to him painlessly but in the normal human way (tradition of the midwives requiring her to undergo an examination for virginity) — and is in some ways godlike herself, although early Christians are cautious about the way they discuss the blending of these qualities. But the way the Virgin is depicted in Christian art makes her clearly the queen of earth and heaven — consider only the triumphal arch of the Church of Santa Maria Maggiore in Rome, where Mary wears imperial purple, studded with jewels, and sits upon a throne, all images plundered from the Romans and reapplied to an Israelite.

Ignatius, then, in his *Letter to the Ephesians* 7, writes of the "one Physician," that he comes "from Mary and from God, first passible and then impassible, Jesus Christ our Lord." In 18, "Our God, Jesus the Messiah, was of Mary according to the economy of God, on the one hand from the seed of David, and on the other from the Holy Spirit." In 19 the fullest expression: "And the virginity of Mary, and her childbirth, were concealed from the Prince of this world, as was also the death of the Lord. Three mysteries which were wrought in the stillness of God." Justin's *Dialogue with Trypho* dwells on the family of the Virgin in a long section on the incarnation that wants to associate the Messiah with "Jacob and Israel." But Justin also makes her parallel to Eve, who was disobedient: "Eve, who was a virgin and undefiled, having conceived the word of the serpent, brought forth disobedience and death. But the Virgin Mary received faith and joy, when the Angel Gabriel announced the good tidings to her that the Spirit of the Lord. . . . And by her has He been born."

The most extensive treatment of the Virgin in the second century is in the *Protoevangelion of James,* a work that seeks to associate Mary and her child with the temple and the priesthood, and to tighten the connection between the old covenant and the new. An expanded interpretation of Luke and Matthew, the *Protoevangelion* claims to come from James, therefore from the family of Jesus. It dwells upon the parents of Mary, associating them both with the barren women of the Old Testament and also with the temple, where Joachim makes an offering; then insists that Mary is raised undefiled, first in a room of her mother and then in the temple, from her third year. As a three-year-old she was placed on the third step of the altar; she lived in the temple and was fed by angels until her twelfth year, that is, her menarche and nobility. She was removed lest she defile the temple. A clear account of her labor is given; she has to stop because her baby is about to be born; and later, after she has given birth, a midwife named Salome disbelieves in her virginity, gives her an internal examination, and for her unbelief her right hand is burned up. The fiery body of the Virgin does no permanent damage, however, because Salome's hand is restored miraculously.

Ode of Solomon 19 is the first to speculate on the exact nature of the conception:

> it was by milk from the "two breasts of the Father"
> The womb of the Virgin took and received conception and gave birth
> So the Virgin became a mother with great love
> And she labored and bore the Son but without pain
> Because it did not happen fruitlessly
> And she did not seek a midwife
> Because he caused her to give life
> Like a hero, she gave birth willingly
> And she gave birth according to the testimony
> And she got [a son] with great might
> And she loved with salvation, and kept with sweetness,
>   and testified with greatness (the magnificat): Hallelujah.

If the Father is understood to have begotten the Son, then the image of the Father as having a breast and womb is not as startling; it is recalled as well by Clement of Alexandria and by Ephrem the Syrian a century and a half later.

Once Mary had been recognized as Theotokos by Clement and Origen, and once Christians began to combine the two major stories of her in Matthew and Luke with other references, as described above, it is not hard to see how Mary would play a role in Christianity not unlike that of the matriarchs of Genesis or the prophets of the later biblical books. With the exception of Nestorius's objection to the great veneration given her by Christians, the early church merely continued to expand devotion to her, speculation about her life, feasts dedicated to her, and images of her as the mother of God. Numerous sermons exist that consider her conception, her role in the lives of Christians, and her conception of Jesus "through the ear" (i.e., through obedient hearing). Only in the West, and in the Reformation, was the reaction against virginity and against prayer and devotion to the saints strong enough to create a form of Christianity in which she not only did not play a large role, but in which devotion to her was considered a sign of idolatry. The mainstream of Christianity considers honor to her a part of the honor given to Christ, and finds her a fulfillment of certain types central to the life and devotion of Israel. In the past twenty years there has been renewed interest in her among Protestant theologians, as ecumenical dialogues have explored her significance as a disciple of Christ, as an example of a strong female prophet, or as a model for Christian believers.

These newer appreciations among contemporary Christian thinkers might be seen as additions to the expansive veneration accorded Mary in, for example, the Byzantine rite in the Liturgy of Saint Basil, which names Mary the object of heavenly and earthly praise, and as a figure of Eden, the temple, and even as an antithesis in herself — a woman who was "wider than the heavens." The Irmos of that liturgy says, "In you, O woman full of grace, all creation exults, the hierarchy of angels together with the race of men: in you, sanctified Temple, spiritual Paradise, Glory of virgins of whom God took flesh — from whom our God who exists before the world, became a child! For he has made your womb his throne, making it more spacious than the heavens. In you, O Woman full of grace, all creation exults: glory to you!"

A Christmas Eve Sermon

Luke 1:1-20

ROBERT LOUIS WILKEN

After weeks of being bombarded by the incessant repetition of "Rudolph the Red-Nosed Reindeer," "Frosty the Snowman," and "I Saw Mommy Kissing Santa Claus," it is a relief this evening finally to sing real Christmas carols like "Silent Night," "O Little Town of Bethlehem," and "It Came upon the Midnight Clear," hymns that celebrate the birth of Christ and meditate on the helpless infant who is God among us. It is customary during Advent and Christmas for preachers to rail against the secularization and commercialization of one of the church's most holy festivals. Yet the effort to return Christ to Christmas in the department stores and malls is as futile as trying to turn back the coming of the snows of winter.

It is better to let the world go its way and turn within, to hear again the ancient and stirring words of the Scripture, to let the rhythm of the church's calendar order our celebration, and to make the most of the disjunction between the shopping frenzy that goes on around us and the church's festival. The disconnectedness between the two is almost complete. For the world Christmas is the end of something, for the church it is a beginning. Each December I am astonished that on the radio and in the stores Christmas music ceases immediately the day after Christmas, and already on the morning of December 26 the disc jockeys begin talking about Christmas in the past tense. Yet on the second day of Christmas the church has just begun her celebration and will continue to sing "Gloria in excelsis Deo" until Epiphany. Many Christians, and I hope you are among them, do not take down the Christmas tree and "break up Christmas," to use a nice southern expression, until January 6.

To be sure, according to the church's calendar Christmas is the culmination of a period of anticipation we know as Advent. As in life, so in history and in faith, anything of great worth arrives only over time, after preparation, waiting, even yearning. And in that sense Christmas is the fulfillment, the end toward which the four weeks of Advent were heading. But the most important thing about Christmas is not that it is the end of something, but that it is a beginning, *the* beginning that bears in it another kind of ending. In the words of the book of Revelation and the medieval carol, "He is Alpha and Omega, He the Source, the Ending He." One way, then, to enter more deeply into the mystery of Christ's Nativity is to consider the ways Christmas is a beginning, for Christ, for each one of us, for his people the church.

Let us begin on the human level. On this holy day a new human being came into the world. Birth is always a matter of astonishment. A few months back one of my nieces gave birth to a son. Several days after the birth she said that on the way to the hospital she was overcome with this thought: when I return home from the hospital, I will have in my arms a new human being, someone who is wholly unique, unlike every other newborn, a person with distinctive eyes and mouth and personality. And so it was with Jesus. A new human being came into the world, and all wondered at him, as parents and grandparents and aunts and uncles and brothers and sisters and neighbors and friends marvel at every new baby. No doubt, like all parents, they also imagined what he would be like when he was grown.

The Scriptures tell us that Jesus was Mary's first child. "And she gave birth to her firstborn son and wrapped him in swaddling cloths, and laid him in a manger." The birth of Jesus was a beginning for Mary. It was her first pregnancy, and at an early age. In the ancient world women married young, and she probably gave birth while still a teenager, sixteen or seventeen years old. For Mary, as for any young woman, the birth of her first child was a beginning with consequences beyond imagining. In a revealing aside, Luke says that shortly after Jesus' birth, after the shepherds came to the inn to worship Jesus, "Mary kept all these things, pondering them in her heart." Though she could not know what the future would bring, for Mary everything would be different, her hopes and her fears, her relation with her family, her loves, and of course, what her son's life would hold for her.

God's coming to us is an affair of very human things. As the epistle to Hebrews has it, "It is not with angels that he is concerned," but with human beings. The gospel does not arrive as a thunderclap from the heavens or a mysterious voice within; it takes form among us in the concreteness of life, in a family, among persons we can recognize. Recall the touching scene when Mary visited her kinswoman Elizabeth, who was pregnant with John. When

Elizabeth heard the greeting of Mary, the "babe leaped in her womb." Or the very human gesture one often finds in icons of the nativity. Off to the side of the central scene of Mary and the child is a small tub for washing, and the midwife touches the water with her finger to make certain it is not too hot for the newborn.

But the account in the Gospels is of course not the report of a conventional birth. The beginning the Scripture speaks of is of a different sort. For one thing, from the time of his conception the Holy Spirit is present with Christ. This is made clear in the announcement of the angel to Mary: "The Holy Spirit will come upon you, and the power of the Most High will overshadow you; therefore the child to be born will be called holy, the Son of God" (Luke 1:35).

The Old Testament is filled with stories of remarkable men and women who were set aside by God from birth to serve God in extraordinary ways. Recall the story of Samuel, who was born only after Hannah his mother, who was childless, had beseeched God day and night in the temple to bless her with a child. When Samuel was born, she dedicated him to the Lord and sang a beautiful hymn: "My heart exults in the Lord; my strength is exalted in the Lord." Though Samuel went forth to do great things in Israel, nowhere is it said that his birth was the work of the Holy Spirit.

In the case of Jesus, however, the Spirit is not only present at the beginning or as a momentary source of inspiration but accompanies Jesus throughout his life. When he is baptized, the Spirit descends on him as a dove from heaven. After his baptism he is "led up by the Spirit into the wilderness to be tempted" (Matt. 4:1). When he works miracles the Spirit is present (Matt. 12:28). But perhaps most revealing, according to the Gospel of John, at his baptism the Spirit descended on Jesus and "remained" on him. What began in Christ will endure. That is why his birth is a beginning unlike any other. It is not a temporary eruption into our world, but a permanent presence.

In the Old Testament the Spirit is often associated with the prophets. When the Israelites were in the desert, Moses gathered seventy elders of the people to serve as prophets, and as he spoke to them the Spirit came upon them, and when it "rested" on them they were able to prophesy. Ezekiel the prophet was brought to the valley of dry bones "by the Spirit of the Lord." And when kings were anointed the Spirit descended on them.

But the visitation of the Spirit on prophets and kings was short-lived and for a specific purpose. With Jesus the Holy Spirit came to rest among human beings for good. The word in the Gospel of John, "remain," found a place deep within the soul of early Christian commentators. Some said it was the

descent of the Spirit on Christ that set him apart from all other human beings. By his disobedience the first Adam did not preserve the gift of the Holy
Spirit, and as a consequence his descendants were overcome by sin and death.
Christ was the first human being in whom the Holy Spirit could again take up
residence among human beings. Among human beings Christ was unique in
that he achieved for others the stability that had been lost in Adam's fall. For
this reason he is called the second Adam, and in him the human race rises up
again to a second beginning, reformed to newness of life, in the words of an
early Christian.

In Christ's birth we see for the first time what human life can be. That is
no small gift. Here was someone who was like us in every respect, yet he lived
a life that was unlike any other human life, one that none of us is able to live
no matter how determined we may be or how mightily we strive. Christ was
fully human, born of a woman, flesh of our flesh, limited as any human being
is limited, yet he was singular. Unlike the first Adam, he did not drive the
Spirit away by what he did or failed to do; he did all things right and made it
possible for the Spirit to enter into other men and women. As another early
Christian writer put it: Christ's life was "strange and wondrous," for it was
imprinted with the "power of a person who lived life in a new way."

In some Christmas carols the wonder of Christ's life is projected back into
his childhood, albeit in a somewhat charmingly didactic way. Stanza 3 of the
carol "Once in Royal David's City" reads:

And through all his wondrous childhood
   He would honour and obey
Love and watch the lowly maiden
   In whose gentle arms he lay.
Christian children all must be
   Mild, obedient, good as he.

The celebration of the Nativity of Christ is also a beginning for each one
of us. In a sermon preached on the feast of the Nativity centuries ago, Leo the
Great said: "Today's festival renews for us the holy childhood of Jesus born of
the Virgin Mary. And in adoring the birth of our Savior, we find we are celebrating the commencement of our own life. For the birth of Christ is the
source of life for Christian folk and the birthday of the head is the birthday of
the body."

With the New Year only a week away, some of you may already be making
your list of New Year's resolutions. But for Christians the time for new resolutions is not New Year's Day but the festival of the Nativity. Today is a day of

new beginnings, of possibilities that far exceed the trivial matters that fill up the lists of New Year's resolutions.

Christmas is not, however, about resolutions, and Christian life is not a matter of willing to do something. It is about being given something, about receiving new life. Leo says Christ is the *source* of life for the Christian people. The biggest hindrance to growth in Christian life is to go it alone and to depend only on ourselves. Christ is the source of our life, Christ is the living water that nourishes our souls, Christ is our strength. "When I am weak, then I am strong," said Saint Paul. Welcome the Christ child into your life. Take him to yourself as a newborn babe. Hold him and love him and hug him and kiss him and let the radiance that beams from his face lighten your face.

The words of the Epistle for this holy night put it clearly. "The grace of God has appeared." In the church's language no sound is more beautiful than "grace," no word more pleasing or more welcome. Christ comes to us, we do not come to him. Christ finds us even when we are not looking for him. Christ is born in us even as we allow all sorts of alien growths to take root and flourish within us. Grace means that we are vessels waiting to be filled and that in the little beginnings we undertake, Christ is ahead of us beckoning, alongside of us guiding our steps, and behind us pushing.

That is why the celebration of the beginning of Christ's life as a human being is a beginning for each one of us. Christ is Immanuel, "God with us." Because he is with us and in us, the life he lived becomes our life.

Saint Leo said the birth of Christ is the source of life for the Christian folk. He did not say for the individual Christian, but for the Christian people. When the Holy Spirit was poured out on Pentecost, the church came into being. Those who followed Christ and believed in him were made into a fellowship, a community unlike any other, defined not by race or ethnicity or geography, but by the head, the living Christ. Christianity is not a religion of individuals who just happen to gather together to worship and pray or to pool resources for the service of others. When you were baptized you were baptized into Christ. He is the "source and ending" of all, and we are all one in him.

This has very practical consequences. For one thing, we know that the same people — or at least most of them — who are gathered here this evening to celebrate Christ's Nativity will also be receiving ashes at the beginning of Lent and will venerate the holy cross on Good Friday and sing alleluias at Easter. It is as God's people, the church, that we live through the great events of Christ's life in the course of the year. It is as God's people, the church, that we serve those who live near us and are in need or want.

And it is as members of God's people, not as solitary individuals, that we grow in faith and love. For the fellowship of the church is a vehicle of God's grace. The Christian people no less than Christ are a gift. We learn by example, by the lives of those who have gone before, the saints of old and the good and holy men and women who are in our midst today. Without the witness of others, without the example of parents and grandparents, aunts and uncles, neighbors and friends, we would be far less prepared to embark on the new beginning that Christmas offers. From the beginning the birth of Christ brought people together. When the shepherds heard the angels singing "Glory to God in the Highest," they said, "Let *us* go over to Bethlehem and see this thing that has happened which the Lord made known to us." And when the wise men came from the East, they came not singly but as a company of three.

Let the world then bid good-bye to its Christmas tomorrow morning. Let the silly carols cease, let the artificial trees be put back in their boxes, let the tinsel and garlands be thrown into the trash, and let tomorrow, the day after Christmas, be just like any other day. For the church celebrates another festival, a Christmas that is old yet always new, a celebration that recalls a day long ago but delights in the presence of Christ who is alive still. He is here among us in his holy body and blood, and he will go from this place with us to whatever beginnings we face tomorrow and in the weeks and months to come. Christmas is a day of hope, the promise that only life can give. Today Christ is born, today we are born anew, today the church is filled with new life. *Gloria in excelsis Deo.* Glory to God in the Highest.

CHAPTER 6

He Suffered under Pontius Pilate,
Was Crucified, Died, and Was Buried

Passus sub Pontio Pilato, crucifixus, mortuus et sepultus

FRANCES M. YOUNG

There are two striking things about this article of the Creed: (1) nothing is said which attempts to elucidate the meaning of the events summarized — they are just part of a catalogue of statements about Jesus Christ; (2) the reality of these events was contested at a very early date, and indeed are still contested in Islam, which, while acknowledging the prophetic status of Jesus, believes it was not Jesus himself who was crucified.

By the time of Ignatius (bishop of Antioch in the early second century), the reality of the crucifixion clearly needed defending. Already the stereotyped phrase "under Pontius Pilate" was well established in connection with the "persecution" and crucifixion of Jesus,[1] and in the creedlike passages where this occurs, there is always a polemical edge:

Be deaf when everyone speaks to you apart from Jesus Christ . . . who was truly born, ate and drank, was truly persecuted under Pontius Pilate, was truly crucified and died. (*Trallians* 9)

. . . being fully persuaded as regards our Lord, that he was . . . truly nailed in the flesh on our behalf under Pontius Pilate and Herod the Tetrarch. (*Smyrnaeans* 1.1-2)

---

1. In the New Testament the phrase "under Pontius Pilate" is linked with Christ's testimony, when he made the "good confession," in 1 Tim. 6:13; otherwise it does not appear in the same manner as in the creeds.

Clearly some were suggesting that in Jesus an angelic visitant had only appeared to be human and to die a human death (Docetism), or that the Christ, remaining impassible as a spiritual being, had descended on the human Jesus at the baptism and withdrawn before the crucifixion — a view already attributed to Cerinthus, with whom, according to legend, the aged John the Apostle had disputed in the baths in Ephesus. For a supernatural being, a real human birth and a real death were highly problematical. Hence the need to keep asserting these things, and so their presence in the Creed. Indeed, the prominence of the passion narratives in the Gospels, and the emphasis given the suffering and death of Christ in the Pauline Epistles, may itself reflect the need to assert the reality of these events.

Eventually it would not be their reality that was contested but their meaning, and in particular the Reformation would focus attention on how the Pauline texts were to be interpreted, given the fact that it is there in the New Testament that explicit statements purport to interpret the death of Christ rather than describe it. The Creed did not preempt the discussion.

The Pauline Epistles

In the earliest Christian writings we possess, the centrality of the cross is clear. Even if we acknowledge that there were factors in the controversies in which Paul was engaged which shaped what he has to say, it is evident that the death of Jesus Christ is crucial to Pauline theology.[2] Not that Paul ever gives an account of the events — for that we have to await the Gospels. Rather, the reality of Christ crucified undergirds almost all his argumentation.

In 1 Corinthians 15:3-4[3] Paul recites what was probably already a stereotyped confession: "I handed on to you as of first importance what I in turn had received: that Christ died for our sins in accordance with the scriptures, and that he was buried. . . ."

Of course, this recital goes on to speak of the resurrection, and in the Pauline texts that is almost invariably the case. Death and resurrection go together. The other constant is the assertion that Christ died for our sins (Gal. 1:4; Rom. 5:6-9; Eph. 1:7; cf. 1 Cor. 8:11 and Rom. 14:15, where Paul speaks of the need to respect the brother "for whom Christ died"). There are clues to Paul's

---

2. This remains true whether we confine our attention to the four Pauline epistles universally accepted as genuine, namely, Romans, 1 and 2 Corinthians, and Galatians, or take the other Paulines into account, as the following discussion does.

3. All quotations from Scripture are given in the NRSV.

underlying understanding of these events: Galatians 1:4 states that he "gave himself for our sins to set us free from the present evil age"; and Romans 5 suggests that, justified by his blood, we will be saved through him "from the wrath of God." Putting these statements into the wider context of Paul's argumentation, especially in Romans, we may outline his perspective as fundamentally eschatological. No one expected the resurrection of an individual — resurrection was associated with the end time when God would raise everyone up to face the final judgment. What Paul apparently believes is that in Christ's death and resurrection the end time is already anticipated. The wrath of God is already being revealed, and the creation is groaning in labor pains to give birth to the new creation (cf. Rom. 1 and 8). The "gone-wrong-ness" of the old order is dealt with as Christ offers his body as a sacrifice on the cross; through the resurrection the new creation is begun, and a new covenant established. Christians are currently living "between the times," since in one sense this is accomplished, in another sense it is still being realized.

Later interpretations of Paul will focus on ways the death of Christ brings about atonement, emphasizing the metaphors of redemption, sacrifice, and reconciliation. But reading Paul against the background already sketched, we can see that the death of Christ is hardly conceived in juridical terms. As in much apocalyptic-eschatological thought, there is an underlying typology at work: as God rescued his people from Pharaoh and slavery in Egypt, so in Christ God has rescued humankind from its slavery to the forces of evil and idolatry, and believers need to live this out in lives that are transformed. "Clean out the old yeast so that you may be a new batch, as you really are unleavened. For our paschal lamb, Christ, has been sacrificed. Therefore, let us celebrate the festival, not with the old yeast, the yeast of malice and evil, but with the unleavened bread of sincerity and truth" (1 Cor. 5:7-8). Romans, if read in the light of this, makes the same kind of sense. "All have sinned and fall short of the glory of God" (Rom. 3:23) — for all live in the present evil age which God is now subjecting to judgment. But God has provided the sin offering to end all sin offerings (Rom. 3:25), so that through God's gracious gift escape is possible — redemption from slavery to journey to the Promised Land. As in Adam all die because of sin, so in Christ will all be made alive (Rom. 5:12ff.; 1 Cor. 15:21-22). We are baptized into Christ's death — our old self being buried with him, "so that, just as Christ was raised from the dead by the glory of the Father, so we too might walk in newness of life" (Rom. 6:4). In Paul's mind the blood of Christ is significant because it has the power of the blood of the sin offering which God gave to his people to make atonement on the altar (Lev. 17:11), and the power of the blood of the Passover lamb which protected God's people from the angel of death. The memorial of this Passover sacrifice, which dealt with sin and established the new covenant, is not to be defiled, instituted as it was "on the night in which he was betrayed" by Christ himself (1 Cor. 11:20-34).

For Paul believers are in the process of making the transition from the old order to the new. This is possible because Christ has already gone that way. "I have been crucified with Christ; and it is no longer I who live, but it is Christ who lives in me" (Gal. 2:19b-20). A kind of exchange has taken place: "For our sake he made him to be sin [or perhaps, a sin offering] who knew no sin, so that in him we might become the righteousness of God" (2 Cor. 5:21). So it is not surprising that, as the present evil age continues, Christians share in the woes of the end time. Suffering not only conforms to the way of Christ (and even completes "what is lacking in Christ's afflictions for the sake of his body, that is, the church" — Col. 1:24), but produces endurance. The resurrection and the new creation will come, but only after struggle, only after the birth pains, which are experienced both individually and cosmically.

Some of Paul's opponents in Corinth would appear not to have grasped the inevitability of suffering in the "between times," and rather believed the resurrection had already happened for them, spiritually rather than literally. Hence his categorical assertions in 1 Corinthians 15. Hence too his emphasis on the cross at the beginning of the epistle. In the first chapter Paul speaks ironically of the message of the cross being foolishness, suggesting that God's foolishness is wiser than human wisdom. In the second chapter he reminds the Corinthians that he did not come proclaiming the mystery of God in lofty words or wisdom, for he decided to "know nothing among you except Jesus Christ, and him crucified" (cf. Gal. 3:1 — "Jesus Christ was publicly exhibited as crucified"). By contrast with their riches and their boasting of wisdom, he sketches his own poverty, foolishness, weakness, persecution, hardship, and suffering for the sake of the gospel. This kind of refrain climaxes in 2 Corinthians, where the crucifixion of Christ becomes a model or "type," conformity to which guarantees the genuineness of his apostleship:

We are afflicted in every way, but not crushed; perplexed, but not driven to despair; persecuted, but not forsaken; struck down, but not destroyed; always carrying in the body the death of Jesus, so that the life of Jesus may also be made visible in our bodies. (4:8-10)

Therefore I am content with weaknesses, insults, hardships, persecutions, and calamities for the sake of Christ; for whenever I am weak, then I am strong. (12:10)

For he was crucified in weakness, but lives by the power of God. (13:4)

Maybe this emphasis on the cross betrays the fact that already people had difficulty taking its reality seriously. It was a disgrace, a stumbling block, and a
"curse." But for Paul, by bearing the curse Jesus had removed the power of the
curse for all those who believe (Gal. 3:10-14). He had also provided an example:

> Let the same mind be in you that was in Christ Jesus,
> who, though he was in the form of God,
>> did not regard equality with God
>> as something to be exploited,
> but emptied himself,
>> taking the form of a slave,
>> being born in human likeness.
> And being found in human form,
>> he humbled himself
>> and became obedient to the point of death —
>> even death on a cross.

(Phil. 2:5-8)

The Passion Narratives of the Gospels

All four Gospel accounts of the passion are shaped by a sense of destiny. If
scholarship is right to identify Mark as the first Gospel to be written, we may
justifiably see the dramatic shape of the story in this Gospel as establishing
enduring features of the church's memory of the events. More than a third of
Mark's Gospel is devoted to the passion narrative, confirming the Pauline
perspective that the crucifixion of Christ is the key to his significance, and re-
ducing the ministry almost to an extended prologue. From the moment of
Peter's confession (Mark 8:27ff.), the suffering and death of Jesus is depicted
as inevitable. "It is necessary *(dei)* that the Son of Man must undergo great
suffering, . . . and be killed" (8:31). Peter's refusal to accept this is treated as a
satanic temptation. From there the narrative is punctuated with passion pre-
dictions (9:31-32; 10:33-34), culminating in the parable of the vineyard
(12:1ff.), which is clearly intended as an allegory of the rejection of the prophets, and then the killing of the Son of God.

The sense of a fulfilled destiny is reinforced by the use of scriptural quotations and allusions in the telling of the story, beginning[4] with the quotation
attached to the parable —

---

4. I mention in the text only those quotations referring to the suffering under Pontius Pilate

The stone that the builders rejected
   has become the cornerstone;
this was the Lord's doing,
   and it is amazing in our eyes.

(12:10-11; cf. Ps. 118:22-23)

Others include: "I will strike the shepherd, / and the sheep will be scattered" (Mark 14:27; cf. Zech. 13:7); the silence of Jesus at his trial (cf. Isa. 53:7); the mocking (cf. Pss. 22:7; 69:19-20); the dividing of the clothes and casting lots for his raiment (cf. Ps. 22:18); the sponge of vinegar (cf. Ps. 69:21); and the final cry of dereliction, "My God, my God, why have you forsaken me?" (Mark 15:34; cf. Ps. 22:1).

This cry is the climax to another feature of the Markan narrative, namely, the progressive isolation of the central character in the drama, which proceeds somewhat like a Greek tragedy. Things might seem to be going his way at the triumphal entry, as he is acknowledged as the one who comes in the name of the Lord (Mark 11:1ff.), but Jesus is soon the center of controversy and dispute, the leaders of the people turn them against him, a disciple plots betrayal, other followers fail to support him in Gethsemane, Peter denies him thrice, and the crowds bay for his blood, "Crucify him." He is mocked, taunted, and challenged to save himself, and finally cries out, "My God, my God, why have you forsaken me?" It is as though Mark needs to bring out the absolute depths of desolation he had to plumb. Apart from indicating that it was not a tragic accident but within the providence of God, the only hint Mark gives as to its meaning is the suggestion that Jesus gave his life a ransom for many (10:45). It seems that Mark, like Paul, needed to counter emphasis on the resurrection with a story focused on the reality of the crucifixion — indeed, it is possible that his entire Gospel ends on a note of fear rather than triumph, as the women, on being told that he has been raised, are overcome with terror and amazement.[5]

Matthew's Gospel fills out the ending more positively, and reduces the dramatic tension of Mark while essentially developing the Markan pattern.

---

and the crucifixion. Others reinforce this sense of destiny, such as the obvious background of the triumphal entry in Zech. 9:9, the quotation from Isa. 56:7 at the cleansing of the temple, the background to Israel as vineyard in Isa. 5, the dispute over Ps. 110:1 in Mark 12:35ff., the biblical language and allusions of the Little Apocalypse in Mark 13, the covenant language at the Last Supper, the rending of the temple veil, etc. The story is set on a cosmic canvas by these features.

5. There are two different endings appended to Mark's Gospel in the manuscript tradition. Both seem to be secondary. Was the original ending lost? Or did scribes seek to conclude what seemed an unfinished story, given the failure to record any resurrection appearances, etc.?

There are anticipations of opposition and rejection in his additional material, such as the slaughter of the innocents (Matt. 2:16ff.), his warnings about persecution (e.g., at the end of the Beatitudes [5:10ff.] and in the Mission Discourse [10:16ff.]), and his interpretation of the sign of Jonah (12:40). Furthermore, the fulfillment of prophecy is made far more explicit throughout his Gospel, with many additional quotations.[6] It is evident also that Matthew's Gospel has a far deeper anti-Jewish streak, with its chapter of woes on the scribes and Pharisees (23); its lament over Jerusalem, the city which kills the prophets (23:37); and its heightening of blame for their killing of their King-Messiah. Pilate, recognizing that the Jewish authorities had handed over Jesus out of jealousy, and encouraged by his wife's dream to think Jesus is innocent, washes his hands, saying, "I am innocent of this man's blood; see to it yourselves" (27:24). The people as a whole answer, "His blood be on us and on our children!" (27:25). This episode runs counter to the character of Pilate found in all other ancient sources, and the summary statement of the Creed, "under Pontius Pilate," captures the reality that crucifixion was a Roman punishment and Jesus must have been put to death under Roman procedures. There is some justice in twentieth-century questioning of Gospel accounts that sought to put *all* the blame on the Jews and fostered anti-Semitism down the centuries.

The passion narratives of Luke and John are in various ways distinctive, though each in its own way also works out the destiny theme. In the mission speeches in Acts, his second volume, Luke spells out the fact that the crucifixion happened "according to the definite plan and foreknowledge of God" (2:23) — for "in this way God fulfilled what he had foretold through all the prophets, that his Messiah would suffer" (3:18). Indeed, in Acts he quotes Isaiah 53 (Acts 8:32ff.) to explain what happened, and also Psalm 2:1 (Acts 4:25-26), commenting on the latter that "in this city . . . both Herod and Pontius Pilate, with the Gentiles and the peoples of Israel, gathered together against your holy servant Jesus, whom you anointed." This statement (in the context of a Christian prayer) may throw light on why Luke alone has a trial before Herod in his passion narrative — it showed how this Psalm text was fulfilled. Otherwise in the passion narrative, Luke largely follows Mark, but it is not just Psalm 22 (with some drawing on Ps. 69) that shapes the crucifixion scene: the casting of lots for the clothing, the vinegar, and the mocking are retained, but instead of "My God, my God, why have you forsaken me?" Je-

---

6. Often quotations are introduced with a formula indicating that this was to fulfill such and such a prophecy — e.g., 1:22; 2:5, 17; 3:3; etc. In the passion narrative this occurs at 21:4, introducing the Zechariah text at the triumphal entry.

sus dies saying, "Father, into your hands I commit my spirit" (Luke 23:46; cf. Ps. 31:5).

Also, the two bandits enter into conversation with Jesus, who assures one, "Truly I tell you, today you will be with me in Paradise" (Luke 23:43). And in Luke alone (although even here this is lacking in some manuscripts) the famous saying, "Father, forgive them; for they do not know what they are doing" (23:34), appears on the lips of Jesus when he is crucified. Thus the whole atmosphere is fundamentally different from that in Mark. Rather than tasting utter desolation, Jesus continues to act in character with the teaching about forgiveness and loving enemies attributed to him earlier, and to die trusting entirely in the Father who sent him. Luke would seem to treat the manner of Jesus' death as exemplary, the way of forgiving humility to be followed by those who believe in him and take up their cross daily (9:23; 14:27). Although in Acts there are references to his dying for the forgiveness of sins (a formula established early, as we have seen in the Pauline material), in the Gospel Luke omits the Markan saying about a ransom for many and provides no alternative explanation. In Luke it seems Jesus simply goes through suffering to his enthronement, along the way long prepared for him, a destiny revealed by the prophets.

The sense of destiny in John's Gospel is reinforced by certain features which again provide a radically different perspective from that of Mark. In Mark Jesus is a victim handed over and dealt with by others; in John he remains in control throughout, deliberately ensuring that he fulfills all that is destined for him. At Gethsemane (John 18:1ff.) the authorities are unable to arrest Jesus until he allows it. He asks the group of Roman soldiers and temple guards whom they are looking for. They reply, "Jesus of Nazareth." On hearing him say, "I am he," they immediately draw back and fall to the ground! Jesus insists they let everyone else go and arrest him alone. Subsequently, when the high priest questions Jesus, it is Jesus who takes charge (18:19-21), and when Pilate sits on the judgment seat (19:13), there is a strong sense that the roles are reversed: in 19:11 Jesus had already stated, "You would have no power over me unless it had been given you from above," having earlier argued with Pilate about the nature of his kingdom and of truth. Pilate is thus reduced, and indeed, as in Matthew, blame is redirected to the Jews. Even in the crucifixion scene Jesus continues to take the initiative: he speaks to his mother and entrusts her to the beloved disciple; he says, "I thirst," in order to ensure that Scripture is fulfilled; and he then says, "It is finished," before bowing his head and dying. The latter is usually interpreted as a cry of triumph at fulfilling all he had to do. Already in chapter 10 it has been made clear that, as the Good Shepherd, he chooses to give up his life ("No one takes [my life] from me, but I lay it down of my own accord. I have power to lay it down, and I have power to take it up again" [10:18]), and in chapter 11 it appears that he deliberately endangers his life in order to give life to Lazarus (11:8-16). Jesus ensures that his destiny is fulfilled.

This sense of Jesus fulfilling his destiny is long prepared for in the Gospel of John. From as early as the wedding at Cana Jesus is saying, "My hour has not yet come" (2:4; cf. 7:6-8, 30). As the passion narrative approaches, so does the hour — indeed, after the triumphal entry Jesus says, "The hour has come for the Son of Man to be glorified" (12:23), and a parable is used to explain the significance of what is to happen: "Very truly, I tell you, unless a grain of wheat falls into the earth and dies, it remains just a single grain; but if it dies, it bears much fruit" (12:24). There follows a passage often taken to be John's equivalent to Gethsemane, an incident omitted from the later narrative: "'Now my soul is troubled. And what should I say — "Father, save me from this hour"? No, it is for this reason that I have come to this hour. Father, glorify your name.' Then a voice came from heaven, 'I have glorified it, and I will glorify it again.' The crowd standing there heard it and said that it was thunder" (12:27ff.). Notably Jesus does not pray for the cup to pass; rather he proclaims this as the moment when "the ruler of this world will be driven out" (12:31). In a reflective summary of the many interrelated themes of this very different "spiritual" Gospel, the author now sets the whole thing in a cosmic context — the struggle between light and darkness already sketched in the prologue. In fact, the rejection of Jesus and the judgment of those who fail to respond are themes which run all through this Gospel, with frustrated attempts to stone him and plots to kill him, together with talk of him being lifted up and giving his life, constantly punctuating the narrative. The hour of glory is when the life is laid down. The picture seems to be one of God's Word/Son confronting, entering into, and transforming ultimate darkness into the light of the divine glory: "Now the Son of Man has been glorified," Jesus says, "and God has been glorified in him. If God has been glorified in him, God will also glorify him in himself and will glorify him at once" (13:31-32).

Thus, through the death of Jesus Christ, light and life are imparted to believers, in accordance with God's plan. Overall the Gospel writer would seem to associate the passion with rescue from spiritual powers of evil, their judgment and defeat. This is reinforced by the Passover symbolism that pervades the Gospel. Jesus dies on the Day of Preparation, at the very moment the Passover lambs were being killed in the temple (19:31); thus the story embodies the Pauline idea that "our paschal lamb, Christ, has been sacrificed" (1 Cor. 5:7), and differs from the other Gospels, which present the Last Supper as the Passover meal. Because of the approaching Passover, the Jews did not want the bodies left on the crosses — so soldiers came to break their legs. For Jesus they did not need to since he was already dead. This happened so that the Scripture might be fulfilled, "None of his bones shall be broken" (John 19:36). The quoted text is a statement about the Passover lamb (Exod. 12:46). Already John the Baptist had greeted Jesus with the words, "Here is the Lamb of God who takes away the sin of the world!" (John 1:29). Also, the exodus associations are clear in the discourse on the manna and the bread of life in John 6. As God's people were redeemed from the clutches of Pharaoh at the exodus, so again God provides redemption through the blood of the Lamb, so imparting eternal life to all those who believe.

From the New Testament to the Traditions of Christian Theology

The Passover theme seems to underlie other New Testament treatments of the passion (e.g., 1 Pet. 1:19), and it became a major motif in the subsequent centuries. It is true that the Eucharist was celebrated frequently (daily or weekly), but clearly an annual "Christian Passover" quickly established itself as a commemoration of the passion. One second-century controversy was concerned with this celebration: the Roman church objected to the practice of the so-called Quartodecimans in Asia Minor, who were given the name because they celebrated the death of Christ on 14th Nisan, following the Johannine chronology and developing a counter–Jewish Passover Haggadah. This may well be preserved for us in what is known as the Paschal Homily of Melito of Sardis. Even when the Jewish calendar was abandoned, paschal homilies continued to develop the ways in which salvation in Christ was anticipated in the Passover, with ever more allegorical detail.

The prefiguration of the cross in what became for Christians the Old Testament was elaborated by all kinds of other associations, largely because apologetic proof required the demonstration that the (unexpected) death of the Messiah had been prophesied. The Epistle to the Hebrews had already worked out an elaborate typological scheme whereby the sacrificial rituals described in the Scriptures all found their fulfillment in the sacrifice of Christ. The Day of Atonement, the daily sin offerings, the sacrifice which established the covenant — all were drawn into the collage, and so the obedient self-offering of Christ gave meaning to what had gone before, even as the old provisions shed light on the meaning of his death. Quickly Abraham's offering of Isaac became another prefiguration, as did the story of the Israelites prevailing over the Amalekites as long as Moses held up his arms in the "type" of the cross. The fulfillment of prophecy was the major theme of early Christian preaching on the crucifixion. Undoubtedly this was fed by the Gospels' emphasis on the fulfillment of a destiny long prepared.

A welter of biblical imagery thus clustered around the story of the passion, and the prevailing view that held this together seems to have been that through the incarnation, death, and resurrection of God's Son the forces of evil were outwitted and conquered — *Christus Victor!* The devil was offered a ransom price but was unable to hold on to it — Christ descended to the underworld, and on the third day burst forth again, dragging up Adam and Eve with him — this is graphically depicted in the traditional icon of the anastasis. There is a tension between this picture of a ransom offered to the devil and the notion of a sacrifice of total obedience offered to God, which no one thought to question before the fourth century. Even then the Eastern tradition avoids juridical theories of atonement. Gregory of Nazianzus spoke of the mystery of God's economy (*Orationes* 45.22). In his *De incarnatione* Athanasius developed the notion of the "the divine dilemma": God had said disobedience would lead to death, so Adam was drifting back to the nothingness out of which he had been created. God could not compromise his integrity, yet in his mercy and love he could not allow his creature to be lost. So God reendowed humanity with the life and reason of the divine Logos (Word) through the incarnation, and Christ bore the death Adam should have died.

For the Eastern tradition sin is a mortal disease, and what is needed is healing. Only God can effect this "re-creation" or "divinization" *(theopoiesis)*. For the Western tradition, however, sin seemed to require recompense. It was Anselm (1033-1109) who developed a theory of atonement, arguing (in *Cur Deus Homo?*) that justice requires that sin be punished. Human creatures owe satisfaction for the sin committed but can never compensate for it, however much they performed penance, did good deeds, and offered God worship — they should be doing all that anyway! Man owed the debt, but only God could pay it. So God arranged for the debt to be paid by the God-man, who suffered the punishment due. Later treatments of this theory drew Pauline imagery into the picture, suggesting that God's wrath against sin needed to be propitiated by the sacrifice of Christ. This potentially sets Son against Father, dividing the Trinity, as well as subjecting God to abstract principles outside himself, though more subtle expositions speak of God's justice and God's mercy being implicated in the saving solution. Anselm's near contemporary, Abelard (1079-1142), suggested a view that avoided some of these difficulties, namely, that the cross was simply a demonstration of the lengths to which God's love would go, and "liberals" have emphasized this against the "conservative" atonement theory held by both Roman Catholics and Protestants.

Christians have been united, however, in placing the cross at the center of their devotions, and in art and icon believers have been drawn into the story, making the sufferings of Christ their own, seeing their own sufferings as taken up into the sufferings of Christ.

Reflection

Evangelical preaching has tended to focus on the guilt of individuals, and the Christian tradition as a whole has tended to focus on the moral aspects of sin, seeing the cross as the saving solution. Modernity, however, has posed the problem of suffering and evil as the principal argument for atheism. Natural disasters challenge the notion that this is the creation of a good God and drive believers to engage with theodicy rather than atonement. Racism challenges the idea that sin is simply to be described in terms of wrong moral choices. But self-serving attitudes, which people defend or even feel proud of, may well represent a deeper moral malaise which afflicts the human race corporately.

In this context I would suggest that a return to the New Testament and early Christian sources, undistorted by later atonement theories, may give us deeper insight into the meaning of the passion for our day. This alone provides a genuinely Christian theodicy: for what the Bible consistently shows is God engaging with what is wrong so as to bring good out of evil, liberate from enslavement, heal and restore. Indeed, the sacrificial metaphors are about God's provision of a way to restore purity where all is polluted (Lev. 17:11; Heb. 9:22), pollution being another way of describing the corporate sin that has tainted the planet and engendered conflict within the human family. The narratives of Mark and John suggest that on the cross Jesus entered into all the "gone-wrong-ness" of the creation — its suffering, sin, and evil. The Fathers loved the paradoxes — the impassible suffers, the immortal dies! God the Son tasted "Godforsakenness" — the absence and presence of God thus being most supremely evident on the cross. So our experience of God's abandonment of us is transfigured. Through the dying and rising of Jesus Christ, humanity itself dies and rises into God's new creation — for we are baptized into his death.

"He suffered under Pontius Pilate, was crucified, died and was buried." These, the Creed affirms, were real events. And the tradition of the church affirms that they were no accident — they do not constitute a sign of the failure of Christ's mission. Rather this was God's way of reclaiming his "gone-wrong" creation.

The Call of the Crucified

Matthew 16:24

RALPH C. WOOD

The declaration that Jesus Christ "suffered under Pontius Pilate, was cruci-fied, died, and was buried" comes right at the center of the Apostles' Creed. This is altogether appropriate, because the cross is also the center of the Christian faith. The call to take up our cross and to follow the Lord all the way to death is the very heart of the gospel. It is the summons to suffer as Christ suffered, to be crucified with Jesus, to die and to be buried with him. Far from a dour and forbidding summons, this is the highest and gladdest of all privi-leges. The call to suffering and death and burial is not a summons that we grimly answer by our own unaided effort. Rather is it the new and glorious life that Christ himself grants to us as the gift of faith. Jesus is no heroic exam-ple, however noble, whom we are called to emulate. He is the crucified Son of God who atones for our sin and enables our redemption through our suffer-ing for his sake and the kingdom's.

*   *   *

When we confess that our Lord "suffered under Pontius Pilate," we are deal-ing with concrete, visible reality. No other claim in the entire Creed can be historically attested. Every other article concerns truth that is either invisible or undemonstrable. There is no proof, for example, that Christ was spiritually conceived and virginally born. We affirm these things by faith, and we cannot convince anyone to believe them who has not been granted the blessing of faith. About one matter, however, there is no doubt at all — that Christ "suffered under Pontius Pilate." Even the Roman historian Tacitus confirms that the crucifixion was the ultimate public event of Christ's life and ministry.

There is no denying that our Lord experienced other kinds of suffering. He suffered the sorrows and disappointments that mortal flesh is heir to. He suffered the shame and scorn that good people always meet in evil times. He suffered the incomprehension of his own disciples, none of whom truly grasped the gospel that he called them to follow. Yet not one of these torments is mentioned in the Creed. Jesus' real suffering was at the hands of the Roman prefect of Judea, Pontius Pilate, who colluded with the Jewish establishment to have Christ killed. Jesus' real pain was outward and public, and we do violence to his cross if we concentrate primarily on his inward and private suffering. The hard fact is that Christ ran afoul of Jewish and Roman authority, and that he suffered a cruel death for it.

Why was the rabbi from Nazareth such a severe threat to Pontius Pilate, and to those Sadducees and Pharisees the local prefect dared not defy? And why should we Christians pose a real peril to the cultural authorities of our own time? The answer has to do with Pentecost and the birthing of the church. Once the early Christians had been filled with the Holy Spirit, their cross-centered faith revolutionized the world. They became unabashedly clear in their conviction that Christ's death had taken away the sin of the world, and that they participated in God's own life through baptism and Eucharist. They astonished the pagans by their love for each other. They showed hospitality even to aliens and strangers. They cared for the poor and the needy, the prostitutes and lepers. They forgave not only their friends but also their enemies. They refused to abort their babies or abandon them to death. They gave themselves over to a disciplined life of prayer and fasting — and often celibacy as well. Above all else, they were willing to die rather than renounce their Lord and his gospel of redemption.

The Romans assumed they could readily suppress the followers of this Lord whose crucifixion Pontius Pilate had engineered. They mocked the Christians as "atheists" because they had only a single God. To the Romans, with their many gods, worshiping only one God was tantamount to worshiping none. When the Christians refused also to offer sacrifices to Caesar himself, they were threatened with death. The Romans believed such persecution would put an end to these "Christers," as they were derisively called at Antioch. In fact, the Romans were already defeated when Christians fell to their knees in the Coliseum, praying for the forgiveness of those who burned them to death or fed them to savage beasts.

No oppressive religious or political establishment can withstand such freedom — such strange liberty and power to become utterly alive, and thus to be utterly unpanicked by suffering and death. This is the one King whose kingdom runs athwart every nation and state, every demonic principality and power, every ethnic group and voting bloc, every worldly authority that claims final authority. It matters not whether the demand for absolute allegiance occurs under the tyranny of a Roman emperor or the republican rule of a popularly elected president. The Southern novelist Flannery O'Connor made exactly this point when she said that the death camps of Germany and Poland could also have been erected in her native state of Georgia.

I learned this unwelcome lesson when my family and I visited Dachau, the concentration camp located near Munich. With good cause the Germans have not made it an easy place to find. Having finally located the train for Dachau, we discovered that it was loaded with American college students enjoying their European spring vacation. They, too, were traveling to Dachau. It was the weekend of the NCAA basketball championship, and the train was full of raucous talk about the tournament. We might as well have been at Wendy's or McDonald's. It was not a proud moment to be an American or a Christian — traveling to a Nazi death camp as if to a sporting event.

Yet something surpassingly strange happened when we Americans entered the camp gates adorned with their mocking slogan, *Arbeit Macht Frei* (Work Makes Free). Silence fell over us. Everything became eerily quiet. As we walked through the dormitories and past the crematoria, no one clucked confidently about the terrible thing that the Germans had done to the Jews. We all seemed to sense, in a subterranean and unconfessed way, that we also could commit such unspeakable crimes. I had no desire to shout, "*They* did this," but rather, "*We* did this" — we human beings who killed the ultimate Jew named Jesus the Christ.

In slaying him, Pontius Pilate — together with the Pharisees and the Sadducees who persuaded him that Christ must be killed — serves as our representative. The killing of Jesus reveals the horrible heart of sin. Sin, said Luther, is not lying and cheating; it is not slander and adultery; it is not even murder. These dreadful sins, plural, are the ugly manifestations of sin singular. It is the rejection of God's mercy and grace. It is the refusal to entrust ourselves into Christ's keeping. It is the denial that the triune and incarnate God took upon himself the sins of the world — bearing the massive burden of evil, atoning for it by himself alone — that we might be released from the yoke of our bondage. Hence the call of the Crucified for us to take up our cross and follow him, to lose our lives for his sake and the kingdom's, to die in order that we might truly live.

The Crucified calls us to take up our own cross, to follow him, to suffer for the world's redemption as he suffered. I once believed, quite mistakenly, that our cross is to be found in the special burdens that, patiently and faithfully, we are called to bear — perhaps an incurable illness, a mentally ill child, an unhappy marriage, a miserable work situation, a wretched old age. Such afflictions are real and often terrible, and we are in fact summoned to shoulder them without self-pity or despair. But Jesus' audience would not have pondered these mortal ills when they heard him command them to take up their cross and follow him. What they knew is what we must learn: that our cross is our witness — our public testimony, even unto death, that we belong to the community of the Crucified, to the church of the suffering Savior, to this singular body that has been branded with the mark of the Nazarene.

It is no happenstance that the root meaning of the word "martyr" is "witness." Nor is it surprising that the early church identified those who had been killed for their faith as its most important witnesses. In fact, the church took the words of the second-century theologian Tertullian and formulated a motto to describe the effect of their deaths. "The blood of the martyrs is the seed of the church." The slaying of the faithful is, ironically, the worst way to silence their witness. Far from stamping out the faith, martyrdom gives it an odd kind of vibrancy. A persecuted church is, paradoxically, an honored church. Alexandr Solzhenitsyn once said the Communists paid Christianity the ultimate tribute when they tried to exterminate it. He added, ever so harshly but ever so truly, that we Americans offer Christ the ultimate insult by seeking to domesticate him.

The sayings of Tertullian and Solzhenitsyn are truer for our time than ever before. It is a staggering, a chilling fact that more Christians were killed for their faith during the twentieth century than in all the previous centuries combined. Nearly 40 million were martyred during the past one hundred years, compared to roughly 27 million in the prior nineteen hundred years. Approximately 12 million Christians perished in the Soviet Union alone. Though such martyrdom may seem to be a remote likelihood for American Christians, we should be prepared to suffer under modern Herods and Pilates — even as we must also be prepared to reject their violence. To be the friends of God is, alas, to have adversaries in the world. As G. K. Chesterton wittily and aptly observed, "Our Lord commanded us to forgive our enemies — not to have none."

Christians whose souls and bodies have been transformed by a Messiah who himself could not be turned back from his cross will make enemies. Yet it is important to remember that we are called to suffer not primarily as individuals but as a Christian community. A church that does not bow down to our contemporary idols will be persecuted. It will not be allowed freely to follow its Lord. The community of the Crucified will inevitably clash with a culture that despises suffering and worships what it calls "freedom of choice" — whether in amassing untold wealth or in aborting unwanted babies. A church that refuses to offer sacrifices to these and our other gods of comfort and convenience will surely incur the wrath of the cultural police force — whether from public pressure or governmental power, whether from the educational establishment or the therapeutic priests of our time. If we refuse to participate in our culture of death, as Pope John Paul II rightly calls our deadly moral climate, we must be prepared to suffer as members of Christ's crucified body.

Allow a single illustration to suffice, even if it requires a necessary verbal violence, lest we sanitize sin. The Watts Street Baptist Church in Durham, North Carolina, served as a powerful Christian voice during the racial crisis of the 1950s and 1960s. Its minister, Warren Carr, was not ashamed of the gospel. He had the courage to proclaim its good news that, in the atoning life and death and resurrection of Jesus Christ, we have all been reconciled to God. Having one Lord and one faith and one baptism, we are brothers and sisters without regard to skin color or social class. In the midst of a rigidly segregated society, this Baptist congregation stood with its minister in extending these claims to the race question. As a result, the church came under periodic attack. On a certain Thursday morning, after the gospel of reconciliation had been announced the previous day, there appeared on the doors of the church an ugly slogan: "Go to hell, Warren Carr." The minister ordered this crude insult to be scrubbed off immediately. On Friday there was another racist slur scrawled on the church entrance: "Go to hell, you nigger-loving Warren Carr." Again the minister ordered that it be quickly removed.

On Saturday, still more racist invective had been sprayed across the front of the church. Yet the vilifiers had slightly shifted their attack: "This church loves niggers." Reverend Carr ordered that the accusatory sentence be left visible for a few days. Despite their odious slur word, the hatemongers had advertised the church's real business. In their blind fury they had at last got the gospel right. It is not about a courageous individual defying an unjust social order and being attacked for his keen social conscience — although a firebomb was in fact thrown against the front window of the Carr parsonage. The call of the Crucified concerns the witness of the entire church. Jesus summons us to live as a redeeming and atoning community. We are to invite everyone — young and old, rich and poor, divorced and married, gay and straight, red and yellow, black and white — to receive forgiveness of sin, to suffer and die and be buried with Christ. There alone lies the Way to abundant, joyful, lasting eternal life.

Stanley Hauerwas rightly observes that our culture has only a single fundamental belief — namely, that we are to fear death above all else. So fully have even we Christians lost sight of the cross that we have become terrified of dying. Yet there is a subtler dread also at work here: we are afraid of being raised from the dead by the risen Christ. We fear our own transformation, knowing that its blessings will cost us no less than everything — our souls, our lives, our all. *Blessed are the dead who die in the Lord. If we have died with Christ, we shall also live with him.* Such unfathomably simple claims explain why the church commemorates its saints, not on the day of their birth, but rather on the day of their death. Our coming into the world matters far less than our going from it — our passage into eternal life. In our death, our lives are meant to reach their completion and fulfillment in Christ. Hence these final words of Dietrich Bonhoeffer as he was hanged at Flossenbürg prison just a few days before it was liberated by the Allies in 1945: "This is the end — for me, the beginning of life."

*   *   *

Whether our witness brings us suffering great or small, our death is the one thing that no one can take from us. Though Jesus suffered and was crucified under Pontius Pilate, he was no unwilling victim: Christ gave up his life freely, if also amidst agony. Even if we are never called to suffer "unto blood," as the author of Hebrews says, we remain Christ's witnesses in both our living and our dying. We are called to testify that because in our baptism we have been buried with him, so in our death will we rise with him. "It is not the suffering," said Saint Augustine, "that makes genuine martyrs; it is the cause." So it is with us who are called to be living rather than dead witnesses of the gospel. We have the right cause and the right Man on our side — the kingdom and the Crucified. Amen.

CHAPTER 7

He Descended into Hell

Descendit ad inferna

JAMES F. KAY

No other clause of the Apostles' Creed elicits more unease among Christians today than the affirmation that Jesus Christ "descended into hell." Its late entrance into the Creed, its allegedly weak scriptural support, its intricate history of interpretation, and its mythical cosmology all conspire to unite both conservatives and liberals in a perennial and common cause to excise this claim from the Creed. At the time of the Reformation, when nearly everything was up for grabs in the church, John Calvin cautioned, "If any persons have scruples about admitting this article into the Creed, it will soon be made plain how important it is to the sum of our redemption: if it is left out, much of the benefit of Christ's death will be lost."[1] In this vein, the following essay argues that the descent into hell plumbs the depths of our Redeemer's vocation and destiny, and thereby that of the redeemed as well. What remains at stake is nothing less than "the sum of our redemption."

Preliminary Observations

Hell belongs not only to doctrines of eschatology and to preaching on the "last things," but more fundamentally to the church's "rule of faith," that summary of the gospel known as the Apostles' Creed. Handed over through baptismal catechesis, the Creed regulates the church's teaching and preaching. It provides

---

1. John Calvin, *Institutes of the Christian Religion*, trans. Ford Lewis Battles, ed. John T. McNeill (Philadelphia: Westminster, 1960), 1:513 (2.16.8), hereafter *Inst.*

the lens through which Christians read the scriptural witness to Jesus Christ, a witness out of which the Creed arises and to which it remains bound. This is not to say that the affirmations of the Creed, including the one about hell, are either self-evident or beyond the need for interpretation. The gospel is not simply reducible to a reiterated mantra or to print on a page, but it comes to us as a word on target, spoken and heard in ever new situations. As is the case with the Holy Scriptures, so likewise the liturgical and catechetical use of the Creed requires interpretation and, hence, theological reflection.

We begin our own theological reflection by observing that the Creed speaks of hell with reference to Jesus Christ. Hell only appears in relation to him. Whatever hell may turn out to be, and whatever metaphors we may use to speak of it, from "fire and brimstone" to "outer darkness," it cannot be confessed independently of Jesus Christ. It is inextricably linked to his name. He did not evade hell. He entered into it.

Our Lord's destiny also includes his conception, birth, suffering, crucifixion, death, and burial. After declaring "He descended into hell," the Creed further recounts his resurrection, ascension, session, and promised coming to judge the living and the dead. Hell therefore could be taken as one of the discrete scenes in the drama of redemption; or, by contrast, it could serve as an interpretive gloss on the other scenes in this drama. For example, "hell" could characterize what befell Jesus Christ in his crucifixion, or it could portray more deeply the victory over sin and death wrought by his resurrection. Both approaches are known to the history of interpretation. Whether taken as an episode in the drama of redemption or as a theological commentary on another aspect of it, the entire "second article" of the Creed, by acknowledging hell, becomes more textured with interpretive possibilities. While we are not able to explore all these possibilities here, focusing instead on the main streams of interpretation, we can say that excision of the clause risks flattening the apocalyptic reality of salvation into a purely historical process, thereby shrinking back from the cosmic depths of divine redemption.

One of the difficulties interpreters face in grappling with "hell" is the wide semantic range of this term (from the Old English, *helan*, "to conceal"). It is found in an Old English version of the Creed from around 1125 to render the *descendit ad inferna* (from *infernus*, "that which is below") in the standard text of the Apostles' Creed that had jelled by the eighth century.[2] Neverthe-

---

2. On the received text, see J. N. D. Kelly, *Early Christian Creeds*, 3rd ed. (New York: Longman, 1972), pp. 368-78. For an Old English version see Nicholas Ayo, trans. and ed., *The Sermon-Conferences of St. Thomas Aquinas on the Apostles' Creed* (Notre Dame, Ind.: University of Notre Dame Press, 1988), pp. 197-98.

less, *ad inferos* (from *inferus*, "of the lower world") was also employed instead of *ad inferna* in some other early Christian creeds and in the text of the Apostles' Creed commented upon by Thomas Aquinas in 1273, John Calvin in 1559, and Karl Barth in 1935.[3] While *infernus* may suggest to our ears a place of punishment for the damned, as in Dante's *Inferno*, it is used in the theological tradition interchangeably with *inferos*, thereby indicating they are simply Latin synonyms for the "inferior" or lower world. Moreover, "hell" is used over fifty times in the Authorized Version (AV) of the Bible (1611) to render Hebrew and Greek terms (*Sheol, Hades, Gehenna*, and in one instance, *Tartarus*), each with its own semantic shading. Thus the meaning of "hell" is largely determined by its use in particular contexts.

Hell Enters the Creed

The ancient baptismal creed of the church in Rome is the basis for the text now known as the Apostles' Creed. For centuries it made no mention of the "descent into hell," but neither, to take one other example, did it name the Father Almighty as "Creator of heaven and earth."[4] The baptismal creeds of other local churches in the Western Empire largely followed that of Rome, both in their triadic structure and even wording, but variant readings of the typical clauses did emerge in different geographical locations. In the Roman West our first evidence for a creedal *descendit ad inferna*, as distinct from the teaching of individual church fathers, comes from the creed used in Aquileia and taken up by Rufinus (ca. 345-410) in his *Commentary on the Apostles' Creed* (ca. 404).[5] Here are found several recurring themes and motifs on the descent into hell that remain influential to this day.

First, Rufinus notes that "its meaning . . . appears to be precisely the same as that contained in the affirmation BURIED."[6] In defense of this view Rufinus appeals especially to Psalms 16:10; 22:15; 30:3, 9; and 69:2. By a christological reading, they are heard as the Lord's prophecies regarding his

---

3. Cf. Ayo, pp. 78-85; Joannis Calvini, *Opera Selecta*, 5 vols., ed. Peter Barth and Wilhelm Niesel (Munich: C. Kaiser, 1926-62), 3: 492-98 (*Inst*. 2.16.8-12); and Karl Barth, *Credo: A Presentation of the Chief Problems of Dogmatics with Reference to the Apostles' Creed*, trans. J. Strathearn McNab (London: Hodder and Stoughton, 1936).

4. Kelly, *Early Christian Creeds* (1972), pp. 369-70.

5. Rufinus, *A Commentary on the Apostles' Creed*, trans. and ed. J. N. D. Kelly (New York: Newman Press, 1978). For patristic background and developments, see Kelly, *Early Christian Creeds* (1972), pp. 378-83.

6. Rufinus, p. 52.

own death.[7] Taking two for closer examination, the NRSV rendering of Psalm 16:10 simply transliterates the Hebrew word *Sheol:*

> For you do not give me up to Sheol,
>   or let your faithful one see the Pit.

The AV renders this *Sheol* as "hell," while the Old Latin text used by Rufinus employs the term *inferna*. The pattern of Sheol being rendered by the Old Latin as *inferna* also holds with Psalm 30:3, which the NRSV again translates by transliterating *Sheol:*

> O Lord, you brought up my soul from Sheol,
>   restored me to life from among those gone down to the Pit.

As the Hebrew parallelism suggests, *Sheol* can denote a "grave," and is so rendered here by the AV, as it is in one other context by the NRSV (Song 8:6). At the most literal level, then, the descent *ad inferna* means that Jesus Christ went to his grave like any other child of Israel. Thus the descent into hell, in reinforcing the creedal "was buried," underscores that Jesus Christ was truly dead.

Nevertheless, hell becomes more than a gloss on the burial of Jesus Christ, expanding into a scene of its own in the drama of salvation. This takes place because *Sheol* represents in Hebrew and Jewish traditions "the place of the dead." It is cryptically and variously depicted in the Old Testament as a dark, lower world where the dead linger as shadows of their former selves, cut off from the living, and oblivious to (the praise of) God (Ps. 88). As such, it functions analogously to the *Hades* of Hellenistic mythology. Indeed, *Hades* is frequently used in the Greek Septuagint and New Testament (e.g., Acts 2:27, 31) as a synonym for *Sheol*. So Rufinus can allude to 1 Peter 3:18-20 to characterize the activity of Jesus Christ in this netherworld, namely, *"to preach to those spirits which were shut up in prison, who had been incredulous in the days of Noe."*[8]

Significantly this saving scene sketched by Rufinus expands as elsewhere he portrays the activity of Jesus Christ among the dead not only in terms of proclamation — but in terms of liberation:

> It was in order to accomplish salvation through the weakness of flesh that His divine nature went down to death in the flesh. The intention

---

7. Rufinus, p. 61.
8. Rufinus, p. 61, Kelly's emphasis.

was, not that He might be held fast by death according to the law governing mortals, but that, assured of rising again by His own power, He might open the gates of death. It was as if a king were to go to a dungeon and, entering it, were to fling open its doors, loosen the fetters, break the chains, bolts, and bars in pieces, conduct the captives forth to freedom, and restore *such as sat in darkness and in the shadow of death* [cf. Ps. 107:10] to light and life. In a case like this the king is, of course, said to have been in the dungeon, but not under the same circumstances as the prisoners confined within it. They were there to discharge their penalties, but he to secure their discharge from punishment.[9]

Here the descent into hell is transposed by Rufinus from a gloss on the burial of Jesus Christ to a thematic scene of his resurrection — and in direct relation to human redemption. Jesus Christ follows humanity's descent into death and the grave, so that humanity may then follow his lead in rising up to freedom, light, and life. He is not only the victim of death; he is the victor over death.

Thus several lines of patristic interpretation converge in Rufinus: The affirmation of hell refers to Jesus Christ as "dead and buried." He went to *Sheol*, both in going to his grave and going to the place of the dead. In this realm Jesus Christ savingly acts both as proclaimer and as liberator. Thus the descent into hell can also be read as an interpretation of what it means to confess that Jesus Christ "rose from the dead." Rather than the final act of the passion, the descent into hell can be taken as the first act of the resurrection. With the vivid imagery of loosened fetters, broken chains, and captives led to their freedom, we find in Rufinus the familiar features of the "harrowing of hell," so prominent in later Western art, literature, and hymnody. While Rufinus clearly associates these images with liberation from *Sheol,* insofar as they also suggest the subjugation of the place of *punishment,* they intimate aspects of *Gehenna.*

Originally a geographical term, *Gehenna* literally referred to what in Hebrew was called the Valley of Hinnom, a ravine south of Jerusalem. Here fiery human sacrifices were once offered under Judah's apostate monarchs (2 Chron. 28:3; 33:6; Jer. 7:31; 32:35), leading Jeremiah to prophesy the divine wrath in store for that site (Jer. 7:30-34; 19). These associations of Hinnom with fire, divine judgment, and destruction coalesced so that, by metaphoric extension, *Gehenna* commonly came to refer to "the eternal fire prepared for the devil and his angels" (Matt. 25:41). Here is where the final punishment of

9. Rufinus, pp. 51-52, Kelly's emphasis; cf. pp. 49, 62-63.

the wicked takes place (e.g., Matt. 5:22, 29, 30; 10:28; 18:9; 23:15, 33; Mark 9:43, 45, 47; Luke 12:5).

Thus the perennial challenge for the church's teaching about the descent into hell is how to relate the respective scriptural traditions about *Sheol*, as the abode of the dead, to those about *Gehenna*, as the place of divine punishment, and to connect them to the saving work of Jesus Christ. One of the most systematic and comprehensive attempts to do so was that of Thomas Aquinas (1225?-1274).

Thomas Aquinas on the Descent into Hell[10]

In his Lenten sermons on the Apostles' Creed, Thomas introduces the descent into hell by defining death as the separation of the soul from the body. This destiny holds true for Jesus Christ as it does for all human beings. What distinguishes his death from all others is that in him humanity and divinity are so "indissolubly united" that his divinity remains "perfectly present both to the soul and the body." Thus "the Son of God was both in the tomb with the body and descended into hell with the soul." But to what end? Thomas offers four reasons.

First, the divine punishment for sin was the death of the body *and,* before the coming of Christ, the confinement of every soul to hell. Thus, desirous "to shoulder the full punishment of sin, and so expiate all of its guilt," Jesus Christ "wished not only to die, but also to descend into hell as a soul" (cf. Ps. 88:4). Whereas the patriarchs of Israel "were conducted and detained there from necessity . . . Christ went down in power and on his own initiative" (cf. Ps. 88:5, Jerusalem Bible, note c). Here Thomas has in mind hell in the sense of *Sheol*, what he also terms in the *Summa Theologiae*, "the hell of the Fathers," "the hell of the just," or "Abraham's bosom" (Luke 16:22-23), that "limbo" where the souls of the faithful departed, who died prior to Christ, were confined and "punished," but only in the sense of exclusion from the beatific vision of God. The Son of God thus comes to them, onto the scene of their privation, but without divesting his deity, and therefore in active, saving power.

Thomas develops this soteriological aspect in his second explanation for the descent into hell. The vocation of Jesus Christ was not to rescue the damned or the wicked, but rather "all good people" who died in the past, "such as Abraham, Isaac, Jacob, and David, and other just and virtuous men,

---

10. For what follows, see Ayo, pp. 78-81, and St. Thomas Aquinas, *Summa Theologiae,* 60 vols. (New York: McGraw-Hill, 1964-66), 54: 153-79 (3a.52), hereafter ST.

who departed with faith and charity in the One who was to come." Along with these saints, the Son of God also rescued his "friends," that is, "his own," who died during his lifetime. Thus the descent into hell extends the salvation effected by the cross and resurrection backward in time to those who could only greet it from afar in anticipation of the fulfillment to come. In this sense the affirmation of hell teaches that "the communion of saints" embraces all the faithful departed, including those who lived before the first Easter.

The third reason for the descent into hell was that the Son of God "might completely triumph over the devil." The triumph of our Lord extends to "the capture of the devil's kingdom." The power of Jesus Christ enters the domain of the devil "to bind him in his own house, which was hell" (cf. Mark 3:27; Matt. 12:28-29). Here Thomas thinks of hell along the lines of *Gehenna,* the headquarters of evil itself, which his *Summa Theologiae* terms "the hell of the damned." The "harrowing" or plundering of this lower domain of the damned is not to rescue the wicked, but to strip the devil of his power. In this way our Savior becomes sovereign not only in heaven and on earth, but over the lowest depths of hell itself (cf. Phil. 2:10-11).[11]

Finally, lest this victory over the diabolical power opposing God's saving work be misinterpreted in terms of universal salvation, Thomas concludes by noting that "although Christ completely destroyed death, nonetheless he did not altogether destroy hell." Hell (in what varied senses is not specifically stated here) remains the final destination for those who die uncleansed by circumcision or baptism from "the original sin of Adam," or who die in mortal sin, or who die as unbaptized children.

This exposition of the descent into hell by Thomas Aquinas, in its main contentions that Jesus Christ "did really die and through his death for us conquered death and the devil," and that "in his human soul united to his divine person, the dead Christ went down to the realm of the dead [and] opened

---

11. In his *Summa Theologiae* Thomas stresses that the Son of God descends essentially only to the hell of the just and not to the hell of the damned, since there is no fellowship of light with darkness (2 Cor. 6:14). When we say Jesus Christ descended to the hell of the damned, what is meant is that his saving influence extended and operated there from the higher hell of the just, but only as a subjecting, and judging, power. For this reason Jesus Christ did not preach to the unbelieving and wicked in hell the good news of salvation. Thomas follows Augustine in interpreting 1 Pet. 3:18-20 as referring to Christ's preaching to the unbelievers of Noah's time in the "prison-house" of their mortal flesh through "inward inspirations," as well as by the "outward admonitions" of the righteous. The scriptural referent is to the saving work of Jesus Christ, but in the antediluvian period "in the spirit of his godhead" and not by his subsequent descent into hell. *ST,* 54: 156-61 (3a.52.2).

heaven's gates for the just who had gone before him," remains standard teaching in the Roman Catholic Church to this day.[12]

John Calvin and the Descent into Hell

As a theologian trained in the humanist learning of the Renaissance, John Calvin (1509-64) well knew that the "descent into hell" only gradually became customarily used in the churches. Nevertheless, he also holds the affirmation as scriptural and essential to a proper understanding of salvation.[13] His *Institutes* (1559) argues on different grounds from those embedded in Rufinus and Thomas Aquinas.

For example, Calvin disagrees with the contention of Rufinus that this clause "repeats in other words what had previously been said of his [Christ's] burial." He is aware, as we have noted, that *infernus* can be used "in Scripture to denote a grave." But Calvin finds it unlikely and unconvincing that the obscure clause "he descended into hell" would have entered the Creed to explain the rather straightforward affirmation that Jesus Christ "was buried." On the other hand, given the linguistic compression of the Creed, why would this clause have been added if it did not contribute something essential to the understanding of our faith?[14]

This leads him to examine the view of Aquinas that Jesus Christ descended to the limbo of the Fathers. Calvin finds allegorical appeals, such as those to Psalm 107:16 and Zechariah 9:11 about liberation from bondage, to misread their historical referents. Therefore he regards as "childish" the notion that "the souls of the dead" were enclosed "in a prison." This is simply a tall tale. Nevertheless, taking up 1 Peter 3:19, Calvin reads this text in its context as indicating that "Peter extols the power of Christ's death in that it penetrated even to the dead; while godly souls enjoyed the present sight of that visitation which they had anxiously awaited. On the other hand, the wicked realized more clearly that they were excluded from all salvation." While rejecting the colorful mythology of "the descent into hell" as a distinct scene of salvation history, Calvin does retain here the symbolic interpretation given to it by Thomas, if on opposite exegetical grounds.[15]

More momentous for the history of Christian doctrine was Calvin's view

---

12. *Catechism of the Catholic Church* (Mahwah, N.J.: Paulist, 1994), p. 165.
13. *Inst.*, 1:513 (2.16.8).
14. *Inst.*, 1:513-14 (2.16.8).
15. *Inst.*, 1:514-15 (2.16.9).

that the real referent for the "descent into hell" is not a mythical netherworld, but the sufferings of Christ on the cross: "The point is that the Creed sets forth what Christ suffered in the sight of men, and then appositely speaks of that invisible and incomprehensible judgment which he underwent in the sight of God in order that we might know not only that Christ's body was given as the price of our redemption, but that he paid a greater and more excellent price in suffering in his soul the terrible torments of a condemned and forsaken man."[16] Hell is a theological gloss on the cross, not a mythological scene that follows after the crucifixion.

Christ died in the place of sinners (Isa. 53:4-6). As such, he suffered in body and soul the torments of damnation, of God's severity, wrath, and judgment. "No wonder, then, if he is said to have descended into hell, for he suffered the death that God in his wrath had inflicted upon the wicked!" In this sense the imagery of *Gehenna* replaces that of *Sheol* as more adequate in describing the depths of anguish that the Son of God endured for the sake of sinners. This atoning work, framed in terms of substitution of the sinless Son of God in our sinful place (2 Cor. 5:21), brings its own "incomprehensible judgment" into the very heart of God. This is shown in the "cry of dereliction" from the cross: "My God, my God, why have you forsaken me?" (Ps. 22:1; Matt. 27:46; Mark 15:34). Calvin comments, "And surely no more terrible abyss can be conceived than to feel yourself forsaken and estranged from God, and when you call upon him, not to be heard." In other words, hell in the Creed is defined by the cross of Jesus Christ. Hell is godforsakenness. To enter into this state is what it means to descend into hell.[17]

Since hell is now defined by our Savior's cross, Calvin also proceeds to demythologize the "harrowing of hell" by transferring its traditional and picturesque language of plundering the devil's kingdom to the victory that took place in the struggle at Golgotha (cf. Col. 2:15). Here we step on to the apocalyptic battlefield and in the person of Jesus Christ discover not only its first casualty, but its decisive victory. For it is here that our Savior grappled "hand to hand with the armies of hell and the dread of everlasting death." On the cross Jesus Christ faced down "the fear of death" that subjects everyone to

---

16. *Inst.,* 1:516 (2.16.10). Paul Althaus contends that Luther anticipates Calvin's understanding of Christ's descent into hell as his bearing of God's eternal wrath toward sin in his passion culminating with the cross. Yet Luther also retains the descent as a discrete scene following the death of Christ in which the unjustly held are freed and the devil is bound. It is this latter theme, codified in the Formula of Concord, that became standard in Lutheran orthodoxy. See Althaus, *The Theology of Martin Luther,* trans. Robert C. Schultz (Philadelphia: Fortress, 1966), pp. 204-8.

17. *Inst.,* 1:515-17 (2.16.10-11).

"lifelong bondage," and on the cross "death has been overcome." Its "pangs," Calvin declares with reference to Acts 2:24, were real, but they could not hold him: "For feeling himself, as it were, forsaken by God, he did not waver in the least from trust in his goodness. . . . For even though he suffered beyond measure, he did not cease to call him his God, by whom he cried out that he had been forsaken." As a cry from hell, this terrifying lament uttered by Jesus is simultaneously his cry of victory. On the cross he kept faith with God unto the very end.[18]

The Sum of Our Redemption

As our forays into the history of interpretation suggest, the descent into hell is the place in the Creed where the cross and the resurrection rendezvous in their significance for salvation. It is also the place in the Creed where the dead and the damned encounter their Savior and Lord. Here we see that the salvation occurrence is not simply a linear progression moving step by step, or scene by scene, toward the consummation of all things, but it is also the vertical, eschatological event breaking into human history and constituting a new state of affairs that is cosmic in its scope and reach. We now conclude by offering some lines of interpretation to guide the preaching and teaching of the church. They focus on three themes entailed by the belief that Jesus Christ descended into hell. They are: the universal scope of salvation; the solidarity of God with a suffering and sinful humanity; and the subjection by God of sin, death, and evil.

The Scope of Salvation

In the patristic and medieval periods, we have seen by reference to Rufinus and Thomas Aquinas that the descent into hell was primarily understood as the journey of Jesus Christ to *Sheol* or *Hades* as "the place of the dead."[19]

18. *Inst.*, 1:517-20 (2.16.11-12); cf. *Inst.*, 1:511 (2.16.6).

19. The rendering of *ad inferna* or *ad inferos* in recent English translations as descended "to the dead" results in a somewhat sanitized version of the clause, guaranteeing that amid the innumerable "hells" of this world the term need no longer embarrass us in church. This change in the wording of the Creed, a product of the International Consultation on English Texts (ICET), has now been adopted in the service books of denominations influenced by the liturgical reforms of Vatican II. See *The Daily Office*, Prayer Book Studies 22 (New York: Church Hymnal Corporation, 1970), pp. 38-41.

While this is only one thread in the tapestry of interpretation, it is rich with significance for the preaching and teaching of the church.

If death were an impenetrable barrier for God's redeeming grace, then death would be God. Death would have the final word, and death would have the final victory over life. Christ's descent into hell, as descent to the dead, disputes this claim of death to absolute lordship. "For to this end Christ died and lived again, so that he might be Lord of both the dead and the living" (Rom. 14:9). In Jesus Christ there is constituted "the communion of saints" by virtue of his descent to the dead. The church is not simply defined by its empirical existence in the world, but it also exists eschatologically as a community embracing both the living and the dead.[20]

Moreover, in confessing that Jesus Christ "descended to the dead," the church simultaneously disavows that Jesus Christ and his gospel are confined to the realm of the empirical church. Since the efficacy of his cross and resurrection extends far beyond the bounds of any particular historical period or geographical place, it also extends far beyond the confines of what is called "Christianity" or "Western civilization." By breaking the monopoly of the visible church on the gospel of Jesus Christ, the affirmation of the descent into hell frees its members from either triumphalism or defensiveness in mission. The gospel has already gone ahead of its earthly witnesses, so that the reality of Jesus Christ and his salvation reach far beyond those who knowingly give thanks for them.

Solidarity in Suffering and Sin

What is the death of one man by crucifixion? Many Jews were so executed by the Romans, perhaps more than one named Jesus. This is not to say that crucifixion was not a ghastly affair. As an instrument of torture, the practice of crucifixion meant for its victims almost unimaginable agony, for which the word "hell" is not too strong. What makes the suffering of this one man by crucifixion significant for "all" is that this Jesus, this broken one, without ceasing to be fully human, was also the eternal Son of God. However we understand the atonement accomplished on the cross of Jesus Christ, the reconciliation of the world was only wrought through a complete identification by God with a suffering humanity in the grips and clutches of hell.

And here is where matters become even more shocking. For though he

---

20. See further Jürgen Moltmann, *The Way of Jesus Christ: Christology in Messianic Dimensions*, trans. Margaret Kohl (San Francisco: Harper Collins, 1990), pp. 189-92.

died as an innocent victim of torture, Jesus Christ died the death worthy of the godless, of those who themselves torture the helpless and the innocent, or who otherwise stoke the fires of hell. "God made him to be sin, who knew no sin" (2 Cor. 5:21), so that the solidarity with sinners we find in Jesus Christ is not only with those who are victims of the power of sin, but also with those who are in its grips as victimizers, as the perpetrators of evil. Jesus Christ took upon himself freely this vocation, to become what he was not, and in so becoming entered into that abysmal experience of rejection by God.[21]

Here we stand before an incomprehensible mystery where the Father and the Son, joined by a mutual Spirit of love and freedom, take into the very dynamics of their relationship the ravages of sin in order to destroy its dominion over the human creature. In the cry of the Crucified we are compelled to rethink the usual notions of God's "almightiness" as arbitrary or tyrannical power. In light of the cross, divine power is now seen as that which comes all the way down in suffering love to the depths of depravity and estrangement to bring forth eternal life. By descending into hell, God in the person of Jesus Christ places the worst that can befall human beings within the redeeming embrace of the cross.

The Subjection of Sin, Death, and Evil

As we have seen in the history of its interpretation, the descent into hell has been a way for the Creed to speak of the work of Jesus Christ in terms of "God's ultimate rejections."[22] The descent into hell has been understood as subjecting the devil and his kingdom, and thereby similarly sealing the fate of the eternally lost. This rhetoric of rejection, historically prominent in revivalism as a strategy for conversion, is often eschewed in today's churches as incompatible with a loving God. The question thus arises how the church can speak of God's ultimate rejections of evil in ways consistent with God's unfathomable love.

One way to adjudicate the conflicting scriptural evidence on election and reprobation is to place the testimony of individual damnation into a wider,

21. "To be excluded from God's nearness in spite of clear consciousness of it would be hell. This element agrees remarkably with the situation of Jesus' death: as the one who proclaimed and lived the eschatological nearness of God, Jesus died the death of one rejected." Wolfhart Pannenberg, *Jesus — God and Man*, trans. Lewis L. Wilkins and Duane A. Priebe, 2nd ed. (Philadelphia: Westminster, 1977), p. 271.

22. Christopher Morse, *Not Every Spirit: A Dogmatics of Christian Disbelief* (Valley Forge, Pa.: Trinity Press International, 1994), p. 335.

cosmic and apocalyptic framework within which Christ subjects every enemy power in a universal victory of life over death. In this way eternal rejection becomes understood as "subject to the eternal life that is in Christ," who will come, in the words of the Creed, "to judge the living and the dead" (cf. 1 Cor. 15:20-28). "What the coming judgment eternally rejects may be said to be not the creature 'made in the likeness of God' [James 3:9] . . ., but the creature as cursed or accursed by all that stands in opposition, including self-opposition, to the creature's own good."[23]

In this sense the message of the gospel is that our real life and true destiny are to be found only in Jesus Christ, so that what became of him will become of us: "For as all die in Adam, so all will be made alive in Christ" (1 Cor. 15:22). Therefore this coming subjection of death to eternal life calls into judgment and subjects every future that is projected apart from the will and way of Jesus Christ. Every future projected apart from him is doomed and it is damned. It is in fact this hellish "future" of opposition to the love and freedom of God that Jesus Christ overcame on his cross, storming into it, eradicating its power, and ending its reign. The "harrowing of hell" is nothing less than the subjection of every power in us and in our world that "denies, betrays, and crucifies the love that comes to set us free."[24] This harrowing is the symbol of that final judgment by which our true freedom will be ratified.

That Jesus Christ "descended into hell" is therefore "the sum of our redemption." There is absolutely no possibility for us and for all creation that is beyond the reach of the triune God's unfathomable, unquenchable, and irresistible love.

---

23. Morse, p. 340.
24. Morse, p. 340.

Harrowing

Isaiah 52:13–53:12; Psalm 22; 1 Peter 3:17–4:6; John 18:1–19:42

SCOTT BLACK JOHNSTON

This afternoon, like so many Good Fridays before it, the faithful gather to re-flect on the public humiliation and savage execution of Jesus. It is not an easy thing. In fact, we may wish to look away, even as we sing hymns that place us in the vicinity of the cross — ("Were you there when they crucified my Lord?"). We may want to avert our gaze, even as John's account of the passion unfolds, with each verse taking us closer to the scene on Calvary's summit. On this most solemn of Christian days, it is difficult to look without blinking at the brutal death of our Savior.

There are many reasons Christians wince at the sights and sounds of Je-sus' death. Certainly there are those of us whose Good Friday resolve wavers as the liturgy bends the laws of space and time to place us among the blood-thirsty crowds — to invest us with a sense of responsibility for the crucifix-ion. It is a daunting thing to observe the passion if you are convinced you had something to do with it. Others of us find it difficult to stare intently at the scene of Jesus' death, because the sight of the broken body being carried to the tomb brings to mind all the beloved bodies we have carried to the cemetery, the ever growing list of those dear ones we have placed in the

This sermon was delivered at a Good Friday service held in the Robert M. Shelton Chapel at Austin Presbyterian Theological Seminary on April 18, 2003, during the final active days of the Iraq war. The liturgy (taken from the Presbyterian Book of Common Worship) includes the reading of the entire passion account in John's Gospel interspersed with hymns appropriate to the day.

grave. Beyond that, as if freshly awakened grief is not bad enough, the crucified Jesus also evokes broader images of suffering and dying. Somehow, for many of us, this singular death calls to mind all the bloody newspaper and magazine pictures we have seen in our lives. Somehow this ancient act of violence reminds us of all the violence that surrounds us. There are many reasons, good reasons, that this afternoon's liturgy has us holding tight to the pews, fighting the urge to bolt from the sanctuary and seek out some humdrum place where our psyches and our faith can be sheltered from the stark pictures of Golgotha.

Perhaps then, during the Gospel reading today, you felt, as I did, some relief at hearing Jesus murmur the words "It is finished." Finished. Once again Jesus has traversed the path from the garden to the graveyard. Dutifully we have followed along, witnessing each stage: the trials, the flogging, the taunting, and finally those gasped words . . . "It is finished." "He suffered under Pontius Pilate; was crucified, died, and was buried." Finished. At least we can take comfort that the terrible ordeal is over. Jesus is done suffering. He is dead, and now, for three days, even God will be silent. "Now," we tell ourselves, "we can enter the solemn intermission of the liturgical year, a time when our faith can safely retreat from the trauma of the crucifixion to that numb, postfuneral state that Christians inhabit while we await the dawn of the resurrection."

But before we settle into such a postpassion anesthesia, it may be worth noting that this is not where the Christian tradition intends to leave us at the conclusion of Good Friday worship. Our ancestors in the church did not want us to put our faith *on pause* simply because Jesus has breathed his last. For as Alan Lewis, former professor of theology here, claims in his book *Between Cross and Resurrection,* our tradition clearly states that there is something going on in the life of God between Good Friday and Easter Sunday.[1] We are asked to attend to that "something going on in the life of God" by confessing, in the words of the Apostles' Creed, that (after the suffering, the dying, and the burial) Christ descended to hell.

The descent into hell — it is easily the most controversial clause in the confession. Many Christian denominations choose to replace it with the less daunting phrase "descended to the dead." And others choose to leave the phrase out of the Creed altogether. Why?

Recently a white-haired man approached me at the end of a Sunday school class and reminded me of the vigor behind such confessional aversion.

---

1. Alan E. Lewis, *Between Cross and Resurrection: A Theology of Holy Saturday* (Grand Rapids: Eerdmans, 2001).

Looking me straight in the eye, he declared, "My Jesus did *not* descend to hell." He went on to explain that while he was indeed a member of a church that used the "descent into hell" in its version of the Apostles' Creed, he had, for the past forty years, remained silent when the congregation got to that point in their confession of faith. His rationale for these four decades of silence was straightforward. God, he asserted, would not send Jesus to the torment reserved for the Adolf Hitlers of the world.

In many ways it is difficult to argue with this response. For if we Good Friday travelers have trouble with visions of the crucified Jesus, how can we possibly imagine Christ subject to the white-hot flames of hell? Or if hell, for you, is not so much a literal place, not some Dante-like, fiery realm filled with torture devices and demonic inquisitors — if hell, for you, is simply the worst thing you can imagine on earth — you still might ask, what good can come of picturing Christ there?

Talking about Christ's descent at the present time might bring to mind the phrase "War is hell." However much a cliché it may be to connect combat with hell, somehow it still seems to express an important truth — so much so that even when soldiers have been certain that their cause is just, they will still describe the bloody fury of battle as hell. The danger, the fear, the eruptions of fire, the hailstorm of bullets and shrapnel, and (in the quiet that follows) the terrible sight of what explosive steel can do to the bodies of friends, enemies, and civilians.

From time to time artists (playwrights and poets, photographers and painters) have tried to capture these scenes for those of us who have never been in the inferno of combat. Easily one of the most famous artistic attempts to render the horrors of war for those who have not experienced them firsthand is Picasso's mural *Guernica*.

On April 27, 1937, Adolf Hitler did a "favor" for his friend Francisco Franco, a general who was leading a rebellion against the Spanish Republic. For almost four hours the German air force "practiced" dropping incendiary bombs on a source of resistance to General Franco, a little Basque village in northern Spain. The stark black-and-white photographs that witnessed to the aftermath of the bombed village of Guernica prompted Pablo Picasso to paint perhaps his most disturbing work. In the mural *Guernica*, viewers are assaulted by a jumble of tortured images. The entire village in the painting has been twisted by the explosions; buildings, animals, and people have been deformed by the violence. Frightening as it is, we can still pick out recognizable images: an agonized woman holding a dead child, a mutilated horse bleating in pain, a severed arm clutching a shattered sword. It is as stark an image of hell as I can imagine.

If I correctly heard my white-haired friend, the one who skips the "descent into hell" when he says the Creed, I find myself sympathizing. I do not want to paste "my Jesus" into this scene. Perhaps our Christian forerunners made a mistake when they insisted on including the "descent to hell" in their creed back in the eighth century. Is this really something that contemporary Christians ought to confess?

Over time many Christian thinkers have argued that "the descent" is (while very difficult) an essential part of a vital faith. Curiously, however, there is considerable disagreement among these theological luminaries as to what we should have in mind when we say together, "he descended to hell."

The reformer John Calvin saw great significance in the "descent into hell," referring to the clause as a "not-to-be-despised mystery."[2] In grappling with this mystery Calvin concluded that the descent was not a trip to a netherworld, but a description of the spiritual torment that Christ suffered on the cross. Calvin claimed that Christ's death was not just any death, but the kind of demise that God reserved for the truly wicked. As such, Christ "descended to hell" by suffering the full weight of God's curse as he died. God's "curse"? What does that mean? Well, for the Reformer it meant that Christ experienced real dread as his own death approached. For Christ, dying on the cross was not a simple matter of dutifully following God's instructions. Instead it was an agonizing struggle that culminated in Jesus feeling utterly abandoned by God above. So, in effect, Christ has "descended to hell" when we hear him cry out using the words of the lament psalm, "My God, my God, why have you forsaken me?" Those of us who have howled similar questions at the cold, empty sky may agree with Calvin. For it is hard to imagine something worse than such moments of utter aloneness. If they are not hell, then we do not know what hell is.

Still, other Reformers, like Luther's student Philipp Melanchthon, took a different approach in embracing Christ's descent to hell. For Melanchthon, and indeed for many of his Catholic contemporaries, Christ's descent into hell was really the first activity of the one who was now victorious over death. This meant that "the descent" was a way to express a vision of Christ eradicating the power of Satan and the forces of hell. It was not a further humiliation of the cross, as it was for Calvin, but really the first bold, life-affirming act of the resurrection. For those of us who found the agony of the crucifixion difficult to endure, this interpretation of the descent may come as a relief. For on this trip to hell, Christ defeats the very powers that worked for his destruction. Christ breaks down the gates of hell and routes Satan and all his min-

---

2. Calvin, *Inst.* 2.16.8-12.

ions. This interpretation of the Creed would have confessing believers understand the descent as the opening trumpet blast in a triumphal Easter celebration.

In many ways Melanchthon's perspective on the descent into hell is a modification of the medieval tradition known as the "harrowing of hell" — a confessional belief that likened Christ's trip to the inferno to an agricultural practice that still endures today. A harrow is a farm implement, something like a rake, that when dragged through a field will pick up stones and clods of earth, sweeping the field clean. Christ, in the minds of many medieval Christians, traveled to hell to harrow it. He swooped through the halls of the underworld not to battle Satan (as Melanchthon argued), for that was left to the last battle, but to gather up all the faithful souls who had not had a chance to hear the gospel in the time before Christ came. So Abraham and Sarah, Jacob and Samuel, Ruth and Jonah were all gathered up in Christ's rescue mission to Limbo — a suburb of hell where the saints of God who had lived before the Messiah's arrival were awaiting deliverance. No doubt this understanding of the descent provided comfort to those who worried that somehow good people who had not heard the message of Jesus, who had not had a chance to confess faith in him, might be consigned to an eternity of torment.

These different perspectives on Christ's "descent to hell" have theological merit. We would do well to meditate on them as we move from Good Friday to Holy Saturday. Surprisingly, however, these doctrinal options do not rely on the biblical passage that early theologians most frequently cited as scriptural evidence for this part of the Creed — 1 Peter 3.[3] Maybe that is because 1 Peter offers the least satisfying option of all. In explaining Christ's purpose for descending to the underworld, 1 Peter tells us that after Jesus' death in the flesh he descended in spirit to make proclamation to the spirits in prison — specifically to the wicked from the time of Noah — those who did not obey God and were destroyed in the flood.

1 Peter does not, à la Calvin, see the descent as another way of looking at the crucifixion, although clearly it is the crucified one who descends. Nor does it, following Melanchthon, have a victorious, kick-down-the-gates Messiah, who conquers hell and its inhabitants in an easy three-day battle. And finally, it does not tell of the harrowing of hell in which Jesus descends purely for the sake of those former saints, those worthy individuals whose only crime was being born prior to the babe of Bethlehem. Instead, 1 Peter tells us that Christ descended to preach the gospel to those who were so wicked that an aggrieved God once thought them worthy of destruction.

---

3. See J. N. D. Kelly, *Early Christian Creeds* (London: Longman, 1950), pp. 378-83.

So the startling answer 1 Peter gives to our question — Why did Christ descend to hell? — is: Christ "descended" to preach the good news to those we would place beyond hope. Or as James F. Kay puts it, the descent is "the place in the Creed where the dead and the damned encounter their Savior and Lord." It is a powerful statement; but do we dare risk proclaiming Christ among "the dead and the damned"? Do we taint our faith and our Redeemer by picturing him on a preaching junket in hell?

On January 27 of this year, as the United Nations was preparing to debate a possible war in Iraq, the copy of Picasso's *Guernica* that hangs at the entrance to the chambers of the U.N. Security Council was covered with a blue cloth. At first the U.N. press secretary explained that the blue cloth provided a better color for the television cameras that would film interviews in that space. But later, another diplomat owned up to the fact that if an ambassador was giving an interview about possible conflict in the Middle East, it would not be appropriate to show him or her in front of a background of screaming animals, men, women, and children.

Hmm. Not appropriate? I wonder. Do images of hell really distract from our ability to tell the truth? Maybe it is the other way around. Could it be that the presence of hell actually tests the resolve of the speaker and the truth of the speaker's message? In other words, the gospel spoken by the one who descended to proclaim the truth of God's grace is not incinerated by the furnace of the inferno, but is thrown into even sharper relief by the proximity of hell's flames. Perhaps that image is at the heart of a creed that locates our Savior after his death with those we would consider hopeless. In the end, at the very moment when God seems the most silent — "crucified, dead and buried" — the Creed tells us that the proclamation of the gospel goes on.

All of which leaves contemporary Christians with an important challenge this Good Friday. Do we need a simple blue curtain behind us when we speak? Or will we risk the prodding of a creed that would have us proclaim the good news against the backdrop of hell's fires?

According to Dante, the gates of hell have an inscription above them that reads: "Abandon all hope, ye who enter here." "Not so!" says the community of 1 Peter. "Not so!" states the Apostles' Creed. "Not so!" say Christians this day, as we boldly confess our faith, a faith which compels us to stand with our Lord in the most hopeless of places, still speaking the good news of God's grace and love, and allowing the truth of our words to be tested by the fires of hell, even as we await the glorious coming of Easter's light. Amen.

CHAPTER 8

The Third Day He Rose Again from the Dead

Tertia die resurrexit a mortuis

GEORGE HUNSINGER

The Daybreak of the New Creation:
Christ's Resurrection in Recent Theology

"The third day," states the Creed, "he rose again from the dead." We may certainly wonder: What kind of event is being affirmed here? How are we supposed to know about it? And what might it mean for us today? While these are the basic questions, they do not always receive equal attention. In particular the first is often overshadowed by questions about knowledge or meaningfulness. If we are trying to understand the church's faith, however, based on the apostolic testimony as set forth in the Creed, then the first question must not be given short shrift. The apostolic witness confronts us as the proclamation of something extraordinary, so extraordinary that many dismiss it, not surprisingly, as absurd. Largely for that reason, modern discussion has often tried to explain Christ's resurrection in terms of ordinary, critical methods of knowledge and generally familiar forms of religious experience.

The position to be taken here is that an event extraordinary in kind will, of necessity, involve modes of knowledge and significance that are also extraordinary. From the standpoint of the church's faith, although ordinary ways of knowing, including modern critical methods, need not be ruled out, they cannot be allowed to control the discussion, nor can their relevance be more than secondary. Likewise, Christ's resurrection is necessarily of uncommon significance. While its revelation may overlap with other, more familiar forms of religious experience, it will necessarily displace and transcend them by its own singularity. In short, the church's faith in Christ's resurrection, as attested by the apostles and affirmed by the Creed, cannot be understood if the resurrection's uniqueness is not allowed to determine the modes of knowledge and significance appropriate to it. Otherwise the nature of the resurrection will be determined in advance by resort to inapplicable categories.

The Nature of the Event: Three Views

Christ's resurrection has been understood in at least three ways. For lack of better terms, these will be called the "spiritual," the "historical," and the "eschatological." The spiritual view, in deference to modern skepticism, attempted to relocate the resurrection. It was no longer a bodily event that happened to Jesus but a spiritual event that happened to the disciples. The question of religious meaning, we might say, was given priority over questions about knowledge and uniqueness. Prominent representatives of this view included Schleiermacher, Bultmann, and Tillich.

The historical view, for its part, fell into two types. Both granted preeminence to the question of knowledge, and both worked primarily with modern critical methods. However, whereas the one type attempted to take the very definition of history and integrate divine transcendence into it, so that the resurrection event became paradigmatic of history itself, the other more or less deferred the question of transcendence so that it appeared only on the margins of discussion. Both types were notable in their insistence, however, that by nature the event was somehow "historical." The first type was represented by Pannenberg; the second by Wright.

Finally, the eschatological view took its bearings from the question of uniqueness. Unlike the first view, it did not restrict the encounter with transcendence to experiences of religious interiority. It affirmed that Jesus was raised bodily from the dead. Unlike the second view, however, it was less confident that the category "history" was adequate for describing the nature of the event. It was therefore considerably more reticent about the relevance of modern critical methods of investigation. The transcendent mystery of Christ's bodily resurrection, being sui generis, brought history to its categorical limit. This was the view associated, among others, with Moltmann, Frei, and Barth.

The Spiritual View

In his great work *Christian Faith,* Friedrich Schleiermacher took the position that belief in Christ's resurrection was logically unnecessary for experiencing his religious significance. In a postscript he went on to concede that belief in the resurrection, though expendable, should nonetheless be acknowledged as "the general faith of Christians."[1] The important thing about Christ, however, was not his resurrection. It was "the spiritual presence that he promised" along with the "enduring influence" that he had on his followers. Influence and spiritual presence were all that really mattered. They did not depend on his being raised from the dead. "The disciples recognized in him the Son of God without having the faintest premonition of his resurrection and ascension, *and we too may say the same of ourselves*" (p. 418, emphasis added). The idea that Christ's "redeeming efficacy" — his presence and influence — bore no relation to his being raised bodily from the dead was one of Schleiermacher's legacies to modern theology, though it also posed a quandary for that theology if it wished to remain recognizably Christian (p. 418).

Two other legacies are worthy of note. First, accepting historical claims like that of Christ's resurrection from the dead could not be made to rest on apostolic testimony, it was felt, but only on critical investigation. "All that can be required of any Protestant," wrote Schleiermacher, "is that he shall believe in [such matters as Christ's resurrection] in so far as they seem to him to be adequately [i.e., critically] attested" (p. 420). Articles of belief had to be revised or abandoned if they could not pass critical muster. Second, Christ's spiritual presence and influence continued to be mediated to the church through the vehicle of the Word. "His original influence was purely spiritual, and . . . even now his spiritual influence is mediated through the written Word and the picture it contains of his being and influence" (p. 467). The important thing about Jesus was, above all, his spirituality — his "God-consciousness." While the (dubious) historicity of his resurrection remained a matter for critical assessment, the (salutary) transmission of his spirituality depended chiefly on his depiction in the Word.

The basic lineaments of this position would reappear as time went on. Like Schleiermacher, for example, Rudolf Bultmann continued to concentrate, in some sense, on the "spirituality" of Jesus. But where the former theologian had spoken typically in terms of "God-consciousness," "spiritual presence," and "enduring influence," Bultmann spoke more simply of "faith." Faith, he ex-

---

1. Friedrich Schleiermacher, *Christian Faith* (Edinburgh: T. & T. Clark, 1928), p. 421. Page references in the following text are to this work.

plained, was a spiritual way of understanding existence in its deepest vulnera-
bilities, culpabilities, and potentialities. Unlike Schleiermacher, however, Bultmann did not approach the question of Jesus' resurrection merely by discarding
it as irrelevant. Instead he sought to reinterpret it along existentialist and modernist lines. He focused on four points: the significance of the resurrection for
the disciples, its significance for Jesus, its impossibility as a "historical" event,
and its mediation to the present by the Word. By refusing to consider the person
of Jesus apart from his cross and resurrection, Bultmann differed from
Schleiermacher. But he followed him by emphasizing Christ's resurrection as a
matter of interiority and religious significance.

One of Bultmann's more famous remarks was that Christ's resurrection
should be regarded as "the rise of faith" in the disciples.[2] According to
Bultmann, this faith was more nearly a subjective disposition than a matter of
beliefs with propositional content. Faith, for the disciples, was a reversal of
the crisis generated by their master's capture and public execution. As expressed by Paul, it meant "that in the cross of Christ God has pronounced
judgment on the world and precisely by so doing has also opened up the way
of salvation. Because a crucified one is proclaimed as Lord of the world, it is
demanded of [humankind] that [it] subject [itself] to God's judgment, i.e., to
the judgment that all [human] desires and strivings and standards of value
are nothing before God, that they are all subject to death. . . . All [human] ac-
complishments and boasting are at an end; they are condemned as nothing
by the cross."[3]

The rise of faith in the disciples was identical with this austere view of
judgment and salvation. Yet in effect the cross had only taught the disciples to
see and accept what Jesus had proclaimed by his Word. Jesus had required a
decision for God and detachment from the world; he had urged repentance
from all guilty, this-worldly entanglements, while offering hope for fulfillment beyond the grave. For the disciples his resurrection was not an event in
the external world (according to modern hindsight). It was an acceptance of
Jesus' understanding of existence in light of the cross, an understanding identical with faith.

Nevertheless, although not widely noted, it seems that Jesus' resurrection,
as interpreted by Bultmann, was not restricted only to a change in the disciples' consciousness. It also meant something for Jesus, who was "raised" or

2. Rudolf Bultmann, "The New Testament and Mythology," in *Kerygma and Myth*, ed. H. W.
Bartsch, vol. 1 (New York: Harper and Row, 1953), pp. 1-44, on p. 42.

3. *Existence and Faith: Shorter Writings of Rudolf Bultmann*, ed. Schubert M. Ogden (Cleve-
land and New York: World Publishing, Meridian Books, a Living Age Book, 1960), p. 197.

exalted to eternal life. "That he who was dead is alive," wrote Bultmann, "is the message of Easter and the core of the Christian kerygma, and this life is indeed an eternal, indestructible one."[4] No longer bound by the limitations of time, Jesus could be seen as the Lord who became present again and again through proclamation. However, it was one thing to claim that Jesus was raised to eternal life, but quite another that he became present as the Lord. Was it really Jesus who became present, or merely the experience of his faith? It remained as ambiguous in Bultmann as in Schleiermacher whether Jesus was present to faith in any more than a manner of speaking.[5]

Bultmann was emphatic that the raising of Jesus to eternal life, whatever else it may have involved, was not a bodily event. "For the resurrection, of course, simply cannot be a visible fact in the realm of human history."[6] "An historical fact," Bultmann explained, "which involves a resurrection from the dead is utterly inconceivable!"[7] This was so, because "all our thinking today is shaped irrevocably by natural science."[8] "Man's knowledge and mastery of the world have advanced to such an extent through science and technology that it is no longer possible for anyone seriously to hold the New Testament picture of the world — in fact, there is no one who does." To affirm the bodily reality of something like Jesus' resurrection "would involve a sacrifice of the intellect which could have only one result — a curious form of schizophrenia and insincerity. It would mean accepting a view of the world which we should deny in our everyday life."[9]

The resurrection as a "spiritual" event — in one way for Jesus, in another for the disciples — allowed "Jesus" to be mediated to the present by the Word. As Bultmann again famously remarked: "Jesus is risen in the kerygma."[10] What this rather cryptic remark meant was apparently something functional: the kerygma (the proclamation of the Word) functioned now for the church as Jesus had once functioned for the disciples. Just as Jesus was the bearer of the Word who called forth the disciples' faith, so now the Word that pro-

---

4. Bultmann, in Rudolf Bultmann and Artur Weiser, "Faith," in *Theologisches Wörterbuch zum Neuen Testament,* by Gerhard Kittel (London: A. & C. Black, 1961), p. 63.

5. See R. H. Fuller, "Some Reflections on *Heilsgeschichte,*" *Union Seminary Quarterly Review* 22 (1967): 94.

6. Bultmann, *Theology of the New Testament,* vol. 1 (New York: Charles Scribner's Sons, 1951), p. 295.

7. Bultmann, *Kerygma and Myth,* p. 39.

8. Bultmann, *Kerygma and Myth,* p. 3.

9. Bultmann, *Kerygma and Myth,* p. 4.

10. Bultmann, "The Primitive Christian Kerygma and the Historical Jesus," in *The Historical Jesus and the Kerygmatic Christ,* ed. Carl E. Braaten and Roy A. Harrisville (New York and Nashville: Abingdon, 1964), p. 42.

claimed Jesus fulfilled the same function in the church, namely, that of elicit-ing faith. It was in this functional (and minimalist) sense, it seems, that "Je-sus" was risen in the kerygma. (This function also seemed to be his "presence" as the risen Lord.) To put it another way, through the church's proclamation of the crucified Jesus, the eternal God became present to those who suffered the dissolutions of time, offering the prospect of hope. "Christian faith in the resurrection believes that death is not a sinking into nothing, but that the same God that is always coming to us also meets us in our death."[11]

To sum up: What made Jesus significant for salvation was not so much his resurrection as his understanding of existence in faith (though for the disci-ples the two were finally one). The same faith that was in Jesus, and that he sought to elicit in his disciples, was reduplicated through the kerygma in the church.[12] Jesus was more the source than the object of this faith, and the hope that faith brought seemed closer to immortality than to resurrection. As pre-sented by Bultmann, resurrection hope meant not that time was redeemed but that it would be left behind; not that death was destroyed, but that it would be surpassed; not that evil was defeated, but that it would be escaped. It was not a hope that God would transform the old creation into a new cre-ation, but that he would allow the believer to transcend the old creation through an immortality beyond the grave. As with Schleiermacher, so also with Bultmann, emulating Jesus' disposition did not require believing in his bodily resurrection. Everything depended on the existence of a verbal me-dium that allowed Jesus' spirituality (whether called "God-consciousness" or "faith") to be perpetuated here and now in the church.

Where Schleiermacher had posited the dispensability of Jesus' resurrec-tion, Paul Tillich seemed to draw the ultimate consequence by positing the dispensability of Jesus. Jesus, for Tillich, was the bearer of the New Being (just as for Schleiermacher he had been the bearer of God-consciousness, and for Bultmann the bearer of the Word). Jesus represented the highest possibility of human life: the actualization of the New Being under the estranged condi-tions of existence. He was therefore materially decisive, but not logically in-dispensable. Having spiritually conquered estrangement, his "concrete indi-vidual life" was "raised above transitoriness into the eternal presence of God

---

11. "An Interview with Rudolf Bultmann," *Christianity and Crisis,* November 14, 1966, p. 254.

12. Bultmann, of course, denied that there is any continuity between the church's christological affirmation of Jesus and Jesus' own understanding of himself. The two cases were quite different. Whereas Jesus proclaimed the coming kingdom, the kerygma proclaimed Jesus as the Christ. Nevertheless, this point should not be allowed to obscure the continuity that Bultmann posited between the faith of Jesus and that of the church, when faith is taken as an understanding of existence before God.

as Spirit."[13] This elevation into God's eternal presence was the "factual" side of his resurrection (p. 156).

For his disciples a more "religious" or "spiritual" side then corresponded to it: "In an ecstatic experience the concrete picture of Jesus of Nazareth became indissolubly united with the reality of the New Being. He is present wherever the New Being is present. . . . But this presence does not have the character of a revived (and transmuted) body . . . it has the character of a spiritual presence" (p. 157).

For Christians the picture of Jesus as the Christ now functioned in exactly the same way as Jesus had once functioned for the disciples. The picture served as a verbal icon. It conveyed to Christians the experience of the New Being. Jesus was the source of this experience for them, but the experience was possible without him. "The New Being is not dependent on the special symbols in which it is expressed. It has the power to be free from every form in which it appears" (p. 165). With Tillich the train of thought initiated by Schleiermacher thus seemed to reach its conclusion. If resurrection meant no more than spiritual regeneration (first in time, then in eternity), and this experience was all that made Jesus savingly significant (along with the hope for immortality), then regeneration was logically possible first without reference to his bodily resurrection and finally without reference to him.

The Historical View

In sharp contrast with the spiritual view, representatives of the historical view saw Christ's resurrection as a bodily event in the external world. To substantiate this claim they worked as vigorously as possible with modern critical methods of investigation. Reliance on these methods was indispensable, they believed, under the conditions of modernity. They disagreed among themselves, however, on other ways that modernity needed to be taken into account. These internal differences were well exemplified by two prominent figures, Wolfhart Pannenberg and N. T. Wright.

With the spiritual view Pannenberg shared certain modernist assumptions. Like Schleiermacher, Bultmann, and Tillich, he rejected any resort to supernatural explanation. He also agreed with them that belief in Christ's resurrection could be warranted only if critically substantiated. Unlike them,

---

13. Paul Tillich, *Systematic Theology,* vol. 2 (Chicago: University of Chicago Press, 1957), p. 157. Page references in the following text are to this work.

however, he insisted that Christ's resurrection could meet these conditions precisely as a bodily event.

In rejecting supernatural explanation, Pannenberg appealed directly to Schleiermacher's statement that every event was a "miracle" when seen in relation to God.[14] "God's activity in both natural events and human history," he explained, "does not have to be seen as in competition with the operation of creaturely factors" (*ST,* 3:501-2). When all history was understood as revealing God, as Pannenberg proposed, "the historical self-demonstration of God" no longer needed to be restricted "to exceptional miraculous events" (*ST,* 1:229). Supernatural explanation was, in any case, "unacceptable to the critical reason of the historian, since by asserting transcendental incursions it would cut short historical research into inner-worldly causes and analogies."[15] Theology should not "supplant detailed historical investigation by supranaturalistic hypotheses" (*BQT,* 1:79).[16]

While Pannenberg allowed that Christ's resurrection involved an element of "radical transformation,"[17] he insisted nonetheless that the event was "historical" so that it did not differ, in essence, from any other historical event. All historical events would ultimately reveal the power of God that operated, in a hidden way, through (and only through) created structures. At the same time, all historical events shared the property of contingency (*JGM,* p. 98), which, Pannenberg suggested, was simply a philosophical term for "the creative action of God." "Contingency" applied "to all events and therefore to the world as a whole" (*ST,* 2:69). The creative divine power at work in Christ's resurrection was, from this standpoint, no more than an anticipatory realization of what would finally be revealed as obtaining in all events and in history as a whole. The event of Christ's resurrection should be seen as the paradigmatic historical event, not as a miraculous exception. It represented "the ordinary, and in no way supernatural, truth of God's revelation in the fate of Jesus."[18] As a historical event it was special in function, not in kind.

---

14. Wolfhart Pannenberg, *Systematic Theology,* 3 vols. (Grand Rapids: Eerdmans, 1991-98), 2:46, hereafter cited in the text as *ST,* followed by the volume number and page reference.

15. Pannenberg, *Basic Questions in Theology,* 2 vols. (Philadelphia: Fortress, 1970-71), 1:76, hereafter cited in the text as *BQT,* followed by the volume number and page reference.

16. Similarly, Tillich stated that "God's presence and power should not be sought in supranatural interference in the ordinary course of events," but only in the saving power that works "in and through the created structures of reality" (*Systematic Theology,* 2:161).

17. Pannenberg, *Jesus — God and Man* (Philadelphia: Westminster, 1974), pp. 76-77, hereafter cited in the text as *JGM.*

18. Pannenberg, "Dogmatic Theses on the Doctrine of Revelation," in *Revelation as History,* ed. Wolfhart Pannenberg (New York: Macmillan, 1968), pp. 136-37.

That death was overcome in the resurrection by new eschatological life was a "factual statement about a past event." It was not a theological claim open only to faith, but "a historical claim" open to critical investigation (*ST*, 2:362). Pannenberg engaged in this investigation himself. He argued that the probabilities supported such assertions as these: that the traditions about Jesus' resurrection appearances and about his empty tomb were originally separate, that they mutually supported one another, that in Jerusalem the earliest Christian community could not have proclaimed Jesus' bodily resurrection if the tomb had not been empty, and that the appearance tradition, which increasingly took on materialistic aspects, grew out of original visions of light accompanied by auditions and interpreted by apocalyptic metaphors (*JGM*, pp. 53-114; *ST*, 2:343-96).

What relevance did Pannenberg think this kind of historical investigation had for faith? The short answer was that faith's certainty depended on it. "Every theological statement must prove itself on the field of reason," he explained, "and can no longer be argued on the basis of unquestioned presuppositions of faith" (*BQT*, 2:54 n). Because faith depended on claims about history, and because critical investigation was the only mode of access to past events, "the burden of proof" fell "upon the historian" (*BQT*, 1:66). He did not shrink from the full consequences of this view: "Whether or not a particular event happened two thousand years ago is not made certain by faith but only by historical research, to the extent that certainty can be attained at all about questions of this kind" (*JGM*, p. 99). With respect to Christ's resurrection, faith had no certainty that did not rest on historical investigation. Since this investigation could obtain no more than "approximate certainty," only approximate certainty could be assigned to faith (*JGM*, p. 99). Like all human knowledge, Pannenberg concluded, faith's certainty about Christ's resurrection was "at best . . . a matter of probability" (*ST*, 3:153). The resurrection would not receive final confirmation until history's end, which it had anticipated and actualized in advance.

Two objections to this position may be mentioned, one about "contingency," the other about "certainty." As Jürgen Moltmann would observe, Pannenberg did not properly distinguish historical contingency from radical contingency. The resurrection's contingency, however, was more radical than that of other events. "For the raising of Christ involves not the category of the accidentally new, but the expectational category of the eschatologically new. The eschatologically new event of the resurrection of Christ, however, proves to be a *novum ultimum* both as against the similarity in ever-recurring reality and also as against the comparative dissimilarity of new possibilities emerging in history. To expand the historical approach to the extent of taking account of the contingent does not as yet bring the reality of the resurrection into view."[19] The raising of Christ was comparable, in radical contingency, only to the world's creation ex nihilo, not to ordinary historical events. Resurrection faith presupposed creation faith, or faith in God as creator, in a way that mere "historical contingency" did not.

Many have objected, moreover, that Christian faith was more than a matter of mere probabilities or approximate certainties. The faith of the prophets, the apostles, and, not least, the martyrs seemed, for example, to exhibit more than "at least approximate certainty." It seemed to rest on some other, more secure foundation. Faith could not be made to depend so completely on the vicissitudes of historical research without ceasing to be faith. While Pannenberg was not necessarily wrong to submit claims about Christ's resurrection to critical scrutiny, he was wrong to insist that "only by historical research" could faith be made certain.

Just how was historical research related to the certainty of faith? This question was unfortunately not greatly advanced, despite his distinguished contribution, by the work of N. T. Wright. Unlike Pannenberg, he assumed, no doubt correctly, that he could engage in historical inquiry without proposing a metaphysic of revelation and history. Nevertheless, despite producing an enormously learned and significant body of work, Wright not only exaggerated his historical conclusions but also left obscure how they were actually related to faith.[20]

In some ways Wright proceeded, as he acknowledged, in a manner reminiscent of C. F. D. Moule.[21] Yet what distinguished Wright from Moule, in part, was that the latter remained noticeably more circumspect. Wright, of course, published a landmark tome of more than 700 tightly argued pages that went well beyond the small essays Moule had devoted to the subject of Christ's resurrection. Yet what Moule lacked in quantity he perhaps made up for in wisdom. Wright was prone to make excessive statements like this: "The *only* possible reason why early Christianity began and took the shape it did is that the tomb really was empty and that people really did meet Jesus, alive again." "I regard this conclusion as coming in the same category, of historical

---

19. Jürgen Moltmann, *Theology of Hope* (New York: Harper and Row, 1967), p. 179, hereafter cited in the text as *TH*.

20. Wright's essay "Why I Believe in Jesus," *Stimulus* 4 (1996): 2-3, was written at a popular level, but included a statement to the effect that while faith had to tackle the hardest intellectual challenges, it did not depend on scholarship.

21. N. T. Wright, "Jesus and the Resurrection," in *Jesus: Then and Now*, ed. Marvin Meyer and Charles Hughes (Harrisburg, Pa.: Trinity Press International, 2001), pp. 54-71, on p. 58. This essay is an excellent summary of Wright's argument.

probability so high as to be virtually certain, as the death of Augustus in AD 14 or the fall of Jerusalem in AD 70."[22] Contrast this rhetoric with Moule's more measured way of making essentially the same point: "The birth and rapid rise of the Christian Church . . . *remain an unsolved enigma for any historian who refuses to take seriously the only explanation offered by the Church itself.*"[23] "If the coming into existence of the Nazarenes, a phenomenon undeniably attested by the New Testament, rips a great hole in history, a hole the size and shape of the Resurrection, what does the secular historian propose to stop it up with?" (*PNT*, p. 3).

Leaving the matter as an unsolved enigma and a challenging question for wary historians who might still disagree was arguably more consonant with both the state of the evidence and the oddity of the claim than untoward assertions of virtual certainty. "Equally clear," wrote Moule, "is the fact that what the Christians alleged of Jesus is something which cannot be confined within historical terms. It transcends history; but, for all that, it is rooted in history" (*PNT*, p. 20). Unlike Pannenberg, Wright did not attempt to historicize the radical transcendence presupposed in the church's witness to Christ's resurrection. Yet he focused so single-mindedly on historicity that he relegated the question of transcendence to the margins, or at least to another day.

The Eschatological View

An attempt to do justice to the question of radical transcendence without diminishing that of real historicity was what distinguished the final view to be considered. Jürgen Moltmann was especially forceful in explaining that Christ's resurrection was, by definition, unique in kind: "The resurrection of Christ is without parallel in the history known to us. But it can for that very reason be regarded as a 'history-making event' in the light of which all other history is illumined, called in question and transformed" (*TH*, p. 180). For Moltmann Christ's resurrection was more nearly the end and fulfillment than the exemplification of history. It foretold not only God's absolute judgment on the evils of world history, but also the transfiguration of history itself. "Anyone who describes Christ's resurrection as 'historical,' in just the same

---

22. Wright, *The Resurrection of the Son of God* (Minneapolis: Fortress, 2003), p. 8, Wright's emphasis, and p. 710.

23. C. F. D. Moule, *The Phenomenon of the New Testament* (London: SCM Press, 1967), p. 13, Moule's emphasis; hereafter cited as *PNT* in the text.

way as his death on the cross, is overlooking the new creation with which the resurrection begins, and is falling short of the eschatological hope. The cross and the resurrection stand in the same relation to one another as death and eternal life. . . . Since resurrection brings the dead into eternal life and means the annihilation of death, it breaks the power of history and is itself the end of history."[24] Whereas Christ's death on the cross was a historical fact, his resurrection was "an apocalyptic happening" (*WJC*, p. 214).[25] It was the daybreak of the new creation, holding out the promise that all things would be made new (Rev. 21:5).

Although Moltmann welcomed critical inquiry into the events recounted by the resurrection narratives, and although he accepted many of the same results as Pannenberg and Wright, he did not base faith on these results. "Judgments of faith," wrote Moltmann, "cannot be founded on historical judgments based on probability" (*WJC*, p. 243). Certainly the risen Christ himself could not be known by means of historical research. "The risen Christ," wrote Moltmann, "is known in the present energies of the Spirit and is perceived through them. . . . Faith in the resurrection is based on the present 'proof of the Spirit and of power' (Lessing's phrase)" (*WJC*, pp. 241, 243). The actual mode of knowledge corresponded to the uniqueness of the event.

The meaning of resurrection hope, Moltmann realized, was likewise determined by the nature of the event. As the event was essentially holistic, so the hope was no less holistic. "Christ's resurrection," Moltmann noted, "is bodily resurrection, or it is not a resurrection at all. . . . It is not merely his spirit which continues to be efficacious and his cause which goes on" (*WJC*, pp. 256-57). Because the whole Christ in person was raised from the dead, body and soul, the hope was all-encompassing in its scope. "Resurrection hope is a hope for the transformation of this world, not a hope for escape from it. It is the hope that evil in all its forms will be utterly eradicated, that past history will be redeemed, and that all the things that ever were will be made new. It is the hope of a new creation, a new heaven and a new earth, in which God is really honored as God, human beings are truly loving, and peace and justice reign on earth."[26] "With the raising of Christ," Moltmann

---

24. Moltmann, *The Way of Jesus Christ* (San Francisco: Harper Collins, 1990), p. 214, hereafter cited in the text as *WJC*.

25. It is not easy to see how Moltmann's stress on Christ's resurrection as apocalyptic, transcendent, and radically unique can be squared with his idea that an "immanent power" of resurrection inheres in the nature of things. See *WJC*, p. 261.

26. *The Study Catechism*, ed. Presbyterian Church (U.S.A.) (Louisville: Witherspoon Press, 1998), p. 54. This statement, though not written by Moltmann, would seem to capture the essence of his position.

commented, "the vulnerable and mortal human nature we experience here is raised and transformed into the eternally living, immortal human nature of the new creation; and with vulnerable human nature the non-human nature of the earth is transformed as well" (*WJC*, p. 258).

In short, by doing justice to the uniqueness of the event, Moltmann was in a strong position to do justice also to the questions of knowledge and significance. One point, in passing, may be singled out for critique. Moltmann saw hope for the new creation as a hope for "the future of Jesus Christ" (*TH*, pp. 202-3). It was never entirely clear, however, where the accent was meant to fall. Was it a hope for the future of *Jesus Christ* or the *future* of Jesus Christ? The question is whether the risen Christ was more, for Moltmann, than merely a prototype of the promised future. While the issue is subtle and the evidence mixed, it is a question of how Christ and his benefits were related. It would be one thing for Christ to be only the firstfruits of some benefit other than himself (in this case, of the new creation), but quite another for the benefits to be inseparable from his person. In that case, union and communion with Christ would be eternal life itself, and *participatio Christi* would involve more than participation in a future of which he was merely the first instance. In the symbolic language of the Revelation to John, was Christ really the victorious Lamb who would reign over the new creation and be worshiped and praised by all (Rev. 7:9-17)? It seems fair to say that in Moltmann's theology it remained uncertain whether the risen Christ was really the center or merely the prototype of the new creation.

Among those taking the eschatological view, it was perhaps Hans W. Frei who shed the most light on how faith might be related to historical inquiry. If Moule was correct that Christ's resurrection, by nature, could not be confined within historical terms, then Frei concluded that neither could it be historically confirmed. In principle, he argued, historical inquiry might indeed disconfirm the claim that Christ had risen from the dead, but it could not possibly validate it. If the claim were true, the transcendence of the object would elude historical grasp.

The "fact claim" about the risen Christ, Frei explained, was inseparable from the affirmation of his "actual living presence."[27] According to the Gospel narratives, Christ's identity as the Savior was "inseparable from the fact that he is" (p. 147), and in particular from the mystery of his ongoing presence by Word and sacrament (p. 158). The narratives were pointing to a "self-warranting fact" (p. 143), a fact to which there was no direct access apart from

---

27. Hans W. Frei, *The Identity of Jesus Christ* (Philadelphia: Fortress, 1975), p. 147. Page references in the following text are to this work.

the narratives themselves. Why some accepted this "self-warranting fact" (i.e., the self-attestation of the risen Christ) while others did not was "impossible for the Christian to explain" (p. 152).

In any case, Frei noted, "the logic of religious discourse . . . is odd," because it has a "self-involving quality" (p. xiii). No neutral or detached affirmation of Christ's resurrection would be possible. "Unlike other cases of factual assertion, the resurrection of Christ shapes a new life" (p. xiii). "Concerning Christ and him alone," Frei commented, "factual affirmation is completely one with faith and trust of the heart, with love of him, and love of the neighbors for whom he gave himself so completely" (p. 175). Therefore Frei agreed with Moltmann that "actual belief in the resurrection is a matter of faith and not of arguments from probability or evidence" (p. 152).

Although the resurrection fact-claim was neither simple nor simply historical, Frei believed critical inquiry was not completely irrelevant. "Because it is more nearly factlike than not, reliable historical evidence *against* the resurrection would be decisive. In other words, if the resurrection is true, it is unique, but if false, it is like any other purported fact that has been proved false: there is nothing unique about it in that case" (p. 152). Therefore, while the church did not need the kind of strong historical validation championed by Pannenberg and Wright, it did need to know whether the historical aspect of its faith had been disconfirmed. Here a further consideration needed to be taken seriously. The limited and fragmentary state of the historical evidence, Frei argued, was simply not sufficient, one way or the other, to command general agreement. "It is not likely that successive generations of critics will agree on what is probable fact in the Gospel accounts. The criteria for historical reliability in regard to the Gospel story will — in the absence of external corroborations — always rest on shifting grounds" (p. 141).

On the basis of modern critical inquiry, several outcomes are possible. Affirming the factuality of Christ's resurrection might be (i) the *only* plausible historical judgment, all others being implausible (Wright's position). Or it might be that a judgment of factuality was (ii) *relatively* more plausible than any other historical conclusion (apparently Pannenberg's position). Or it might be that factuality was (iii) just *one* among several plausible historical assessments (perhaps Moltmann's position). Or, finally, it might be that the evidence at hand was (iv) actually insufficient to generate a widespread and lasting consensus (Frei's position). Frei's point was that none of these outcomes would be unsatisfactory to faith, though he did not want the discussion to get bogged down in sterile debates about historical factuality. Since faith did not depend on the results of historical research, it needed only to make sure it had not been disconfirmed, as arguably was manifestly the case.[28]

Frei, it may be noted in passing, also advanced a less successful argument. Just as Pannenberg had failed to distinguish between two types of contingency, so Frei failed to distinguish between two types of necessity. Disbelief in Christ's resurrection was, Frei claimed, "rationally impossible" (p. 151). According to the inner logic of faith, Christ's identity "is such that he cannot be conceived as not present" (p. 155). "How can he who constitutes the very definition of life be conceived of as the opposite of what he defines? To think of him as dead is the equivalent of not thinking of him at all" (p. 148). To grasp the identity of Jesus Christ is to see that his nonresurrection is inconceivable (p. 145).

This "Anselmian" argument for the resurrection fails to distinguish clearly between strict and conditional necessity. In Anselm's famous (and famously vexing) ontological argument, the formulation "that than which no greater can be conceived" cannot be denied to the definition of "God" without lapsing into logical incoherence. The conclusion (that "therefore God necessarily exists") takes the form of strict necessity (regardless of whether one decides the inference is valid or not). The same cannot be said of Frei's proposal, which might be rephrased as follows: "If the identity of Jesus Christ is what the Gospel narratives depict it to be, then he cannot be conceived as not risen from the dead." In this case the conditional clause can be denied without incoherence. Hence, while the conclusion follows logically from the premise, its necessity is still conditional, because the premise is merely conditional. A careful reading suggests that Frei saw the difference between these two types of necessity without ever making it clear. His point was more limited than may have appeared at first glance. Anyone who had accepted the conditional clause, he wanted to say, was logically committed to the stated conclusion — a point of some pastoral (and perhaps polemical) significance (p. 152).

Like Frei and Moltmann, Karl Barth believed that Christ's resurrection was unique in kind, and that this uniqueness determined the questions of knowl-

---

28. Both Pannenberg and Wright, it should be noted, sometimes expressed themselves more judiciously than their other statements might lead one to expect. *Pannenberg:* Faith in Christ's resurrection "will remain a matter of dispute in this world. But it is neither confuted, nor does it lack for evidence" (see Pannenberg, *The Apostles' Creed* [Philadelphia: Westminster, 1976], p. 114). *Wright:* "Historical argument alone cannot force anyone to believe that Jesus was raised from the dead; but historical argument is remarkably good at clearing away the undergrowth behind which scepticisms of various sorts have been hiding" (*Resurrection*, p. 718). Both statements approximate Frei's standard of "not disconfirmed." "It is always possible," Frei observed dryly, "that the degree of a claim's credibility is proportional to its modesty" (*Identity of Jesus Christ*, p. 48).

edge and significance. How he differed from them, it will come as no surprise, was that, if possible, he was more thoroughly christocentric at each point.

Barth agreed that Christ's resurrection was complex in nature, involving aspects of historicity and transcendence. Being in but not of the world, it was a singular event. It could not be denied that the event took place in time and space, if the New Testament witness were taken seriously. "However different it may be in other respects, as history it must be like all other history in regard to its historicity."[29] "It is impossible to erase the bodily character of the resurrection of Jesus and his existence as the Resurrected" (III/2, p. 448). The appearances were not, as modernist exegesis sometimes suggested, originally visions of light (and perhaps audition) that only later were clothed in bodily terms.[30] The resurrection, wrote Barth, "involves a definite seeing with the eyes and hearing with the ears and handling with the hands, as the Easter stories say so unmistakably and emphatically. . . . It involves real eating and drinking, speaking and answering, reasoning . . . and doubting and then, believing" (IV/2, p. 143). In short, Jesus Christ was "risen — bodily, visibly, audibly, perceptibly in the same concrete sense in which he died" (IV/1, p. 351).

Transcendence, however, was the aspect that greatly interested Barth, and he paid it particular attention. The bodily resurrection, he argued, affected Jesus Christ as a whole person — not only as a psychosomatic unity, but also as a spatiotemporal unity. The body was the vehicle of one's identity through time, so that one's embodied identity was inseparable from one's life history. Though without referring to Barth, Moltmann here makes Barth's point nicely: "If the whole human being is going to rise, he will rise with his whole life history, and be simultaneous in all his temporal Gestalts, and recognize himself in them. What is spread out and split up into its component parts in a person's lifetime comes together and coincides in eternity, and becomes one" (*WJC*, pp. 267-68). This transcendent aspect of bodily resurrection meant that the person of Jesus Christ — in (and not without) his life history and his saving work — had been elevated into eternity. It meant that he had been made "the Contemporary of all human beings" (III/2, p. 440, rev.). "As the Crucified 'he lives and reigns to all eternity' (Luther). . . . As the One who was in this time, he became and is the Lord of all time, eternal as God himself is eternal, and therefore present in all time" (IV/1, p. 313).[31]

---

29. Karl Barth, *Church Dogmatics*, 4 vols. (Edinburgh: T. & T. Clark, 1936-77), vol. IV, part 1, p. 298; hereafter cited in the text by volume and part, e.g., IV/1.

30. Wright argued the same point on historical-critical grounds (*Resurrection*, pp. 375-98).

31. Barth therefore allowed for miracle: "God is free to be and operate in the created world either as unconditioned or as conditioned. God is free to perform his work within the framework of what we call the laws of nature or outside it in the shape of miracle" (II/1, p. 314).

In his treatment of the question of knowledge, Barth did not keep the same balance between historicity and transcendence. He focused almost entirely on the transcendent aspect while denying any significance to modern historical inquiry (IV/2, pp. 149-50). The possibility of disconfirmation, as explored by Frei, apparently did not interest him; consequently Frei's thoughtful emendation of Barth's position was arguably more nuanced and satisfying. Nevertheless, Barth richly developed the transcendent aspect in a way that remains unsurpassed. He was untiring in his stress that if Christ was risen from the dead, so as to be present as the risen Lord, then his own self-witness as the one who lives was always necessarily decisive. Faith depended not on historical investigation but on an encounter with the living Christ. "This faith did not consist in a reassessment and reinterpretation *in meliorem partem* [in some better sense] of the picture of the Crucified [e.g., through critical inquiry], but in an objective encounter with the Crucified and Risen One, who himself not only made himself credible to them, but maintained himself as the 'author of their salvation' (Heb. 2:10) and therefore the 'author and perfecter of their faith' (Heb. 12:2)" (III/2, p. 449, rev.). The living Christ made himself present, Barth stressed, by the power of the Holy Spirit, "giving himself to be known . . . as the One he is" (IV/2, p. 131). His resurrection was either affirmed on the basis of such an encounter or not at all.

Barth also treated the question of significance in distinctively christocentric terms. The tenor of his view, as of course developed at enormous length, can be gained from this summation:

> The relevance of the self-manifestation of the risen Christ is to be found always in the demonstration of his identity with the One who had lived and taught and acted and gone to his death. It is true that this One in his history and existence is the reconciliation of the world with God and therefore the new human being, the daybreak of the new creation, the beginning of the new world. But it is not only in his resurrection that he is this. He became and was and is it in his life and death. The point about his resurrection is that in it he reveals himself as the One who was and is and will be this in his life and death. (IV/2, p. 145, rev.)

From this standpoint there could be no doubt that the *future* of Jesus Christ was indeed the future of *Jesus Christ*. As Barth had said in another connection: "He is *the* substance of the whole" (IV/2, p. 156) — the center by which all things cohered, the Lord whom all joyfully served, and the Savior by whom they were made new.

In conclusion, each of the three major views had a different way of negotiating between the historical and transcendent aspects of the apostolic testimony. By rejecting the historicity of Christ's bodily resurrection, the "spiritual view" was left with a conception of transcendence that was anchored in religious inwardness, and for which Jesus himself, though materially decisive, was not logically indispensable. The "historical view," for its part, retrieved a robust interest in historicity but only at the expense of transcendence. The transcendent aspect of Christ's resurrection was either overly historicized (Pannenberg) or deferred (Wright). Finally, the "eschatological view" found its most satisfactory representative in Barth, though only as later emended by Frei and Moltmann. All three grasped that the ineluctable conjunction of historicity and transcendence made Christ's resurrection unique in kind. While Barth then rightly stressed the active self-witness of the living Christ more forcefully than any of the others, his blanket dismissal of modern critical inquiry was thoughtfully revisited by Frei. Finally, Barth's unambiguous conception that resurrection hope concerned the future of *Jesus Christ* offered a framework within which almost everything could be critically appropriated that Moltmann had expressed about the *future* of Jesus Christ. Moltmann thus sketched out that "complete theology of the resurrection" which Barth had planned but never developed (III/2, p. 447).

The Third Day He Rose Again from the Dead

Isaiah 25:6-9; 1 Corinthians 15:1-11; John 20:1-18

DAVID F. FORD

"The third day he rose again from the dead." That is what we celebrate today. "Christ is risen!"

A Day of Superabundance

This is a day of superabundance, celebrating an event so big, so multidimensional, so all-embracing in its meaning for our world and for our past, our present, and our future, so endless in its implications for our understanding and for the ways we shape our attitudes, our imaginations, our hopes, our worship, our relationships, our living, that we can hardly begin to do justice to it.

In the accounts of the resurrection of Jesus that were written down many years later in the Gospels, you still get a sense of that first amazement, of being overwhelmed by something that does not fit any of the available categories and ideas. This was, and is, a day of astonishment, of overflowing joy, dazzling light, life that is no longer subject to death; and at the heart of it all is the crucified and risen Jesus Christ, the one who is in person the resurrection and the life, the light of the world.

Sermon preached at Holy Trinity Church, Cambridge, Easter Sunday, April 20, 2003.

Paul on Resurrection

Our New Testament readings, from Paul's first letter to the Corinthians and from Saint John's Gospel, give us two wonderful ways into this inexhaustible event and to the person at its heart. So let us try to savor each in turn.

Paul in his first letter to the Corinthians serves the best wine last, in chapter 15. Before that there has already been some pretty strong drink: he began the letter by wrestling with the depth and mystery of the cross, Christ crucified as "the power of God and the wisdom of God" (1:24) — the extraordinary revelation that Christ crucified — out of love for us — is the deepest secret of our universe and of our creator. Paul had gone on to deal with all sorts of problems in the church in the light of that wisdom. Then in the middle of his treatment of the gifts of the Holy Spirit (with its vision of the church as a body of closely interrelated members in which "if one member suffers, all suffer with it; if one member is honoured, all rejoice together with it" (12:26), Paul embeds chapter 13, that most famous of all passages on love — the love without which everything else is worth nothing, and which "bears all things, believes all things, hopes all things, endures all things" (13:7).

But there is more to come, and our reading from chapter 15 sets out in summary form the reality that Paul says bluntly is the basis for everything else. He sums up the essence of the message he had brought to the Corinthians when they became Christians as being the good news of the resurrection of the crucified Jesus Christ:

> For I handed on to you as of first importance what I in turn had received: that Christ died for our sins in accordance with the scriptures, and that he was buried, and that he was raised on the third day in accordance with the scriptures, and that he appeared to Cephas, then to the twelve. Then he appeared to more than five hundred brothers and sisters at one time, most of whom are still alive, though some have died. Then he appeared to James, then to all the apostles. Last of all, as to one untimely born, he appeared also to me. (15:3-8)

Here and in the rest of chapter 15 Paul makes it perfectly clear how utterly vital to Christian faith the resurrection is. If we take this chapter together with what he says elsewhere about the resurrection in his letters, the picture we get is something like this: the God who created all things has, through his Holy Spirit, raised Jesus Christ, the Messiah, bodily from the dead; the risen Jesus Christ is the same person as the one who was crucified, but now transformed, with what Paul calls a "spiritual body," alive with a new kind of life;

this resurrection with transformation is promised to us too in the future; and this will be part of a transformation of the whole of creation which will, as he says in Romans 8 in an extraordinary passage, "be set free from its bondage to decay and will obtain the freedom of the glory of the children of God" (8:21); and in the meantime, between the resurrection of Jesus and our resurrection, the reality of the resurrection and the gift of the Spirit of Jesus Christ are the secret of Christian living now. Baptism, the core sign of Christian identity, identifies us with the death and resurrection of Jesus Christ — this is what defines who we are most fundamentally; and our whole life is marked by the fact that a new creation has begun in the midst of the old, inspiring us to have confidence — whatever our situation, whatever our sufferings, whatever our sins — in the God who raises the dead, and enabling us above all to love with a new freedom and risk taking. The Spirit of Jesus Christ crucified and risen is the secret of the love that "bears all things, believes all things, hopes all things, endures all things" (1 Cor. 13:7) — and, one might add, transforms all things, people, marriages, families, communities, and even, as Romans 8 says, the cosmos itself.

Scope of Resurrection, Scope of God

So, that is the scope of what we celebrate today, and it can be summed up very simply: the scope of the resurrection is nothing less than the scope of God. When the New Testament writers try to express the reality of this event, the parallels they find least inadequate are the great acts initiated by God alone — creation, life, covenant: the resurrection of the crucified Jesus initiates a new creation, new life, a new covenant. And the resurrection is the vital clue to why Christians came to affirm that God is Father, Son, and Holy Spirit: the Trinity. In this event God the Creator and Father acts; and when God acts it is Jesus who appears, as the full content of the activity and reality of God; and this comprehensive act of new creation and revelation is done through the Holy Spirit and generates the outpouring of the Holy Spirit, who is God's own life and self being shared without limit. So God as Trinity is best understood through Easter. The resurrection is God's initiative as Creator and Father — the transcendent God; it is the climax of God's embodiment in Jesus Christ — God the Son made flesh in history; and it is the action of God the Spirit, the life-giver — God in self-giving and abundant self-distribution.

John on the Resurrection of Jesus

When we turn to the Gospel of John, we find, right from the start, the same concern with God the Creator, God in person in history, and God's life shared in the Spirit. All through this Gospel there are pointers to the resurrection as its culmination. Then at last we reach today's reading in chapter 20: the vivid, literally breathless account of the discovery of the empty tomb, as Peter and the disciple Jesus loved run to it after Mary has run to tell them the stone has been removed; and then there is Mary's meeting with the risen Jesus. These eighteen verses are packed with meaning. I want to make just two points.

Belief and Trust

First there are the different reactions in the tomb of Peter and the other disciple. Peter simply sees the linen wrappings there and the cloth that had covered Jesus' head rolled up separately. The other disciple sees exactly the same things, but, it says, "he saw and believed" (20:8). John's Gospel is fascinated by the different ways people come to believe and also by the ways they resist belief or refuse to believe. By believing (the verb is *pisteuein*) is meant something much more than just believing that something is the case, though the truth issue is included and is important. It is also about a relationship of trust, what or who we trust ourselves to, where we place our reliance. And John knows that in the really big matters to do with trust, we can never have neutral proof about what is right — whether it is to do with who to marry, how far to rely on a friend, what career to follow, or whether to say yes to the call of Jesus Christ to follow him. Especially in his resurrection chapters John gives all sorts of ways in which people come to believe and trust in the risen Jesus. The beloved disciple sees the sign of the tomb and graveclothes and believes. Mary meets Jesus incognito, looking like a gardener, and recognizes Jesus' voice. The gathered disciples find Jesus standing among them, and he shows them his wounds. Thomas doubts and refuses to believe their report. He believes when Jesus appears to him, but is also told: "Blessed are those who have not seen and yet have come to believe" (20:29). That covers most of us, and it is perfectly clear from what he goes on to write what John sees as the normal way to faith: through reading or hearing Scripture and people who teach what Scripture teaches. As he says: "These are written so that you may come to believe that Jesus is the Messiah, the Son of God, and that through believing you may have life in his name" (20:31).

There are, of course, all sorts of arguments and discussions to be had about what John and others say about the resurrection of Jesus — we theologians spend a great deal of time on them. If I were to choose just one recent work that engages with all that discussion and comes to clear and well-argued conclusions, I would choose Tom (N. T.) Wright's recent book, *The Resurrection of the Son of God* (London: SPCK, 2003). It is a good read, and in eight hundred pages he covers a good deal of the scholarship and the historical and theological discussion. But in the end there is no getting away from trust. History cannot be rerun. It is a one-off set of events, and there is no avoiding dependence on witnesses. We can rigorously cross-examine the witnesses, but there is finally no alternative to trusting or distrusting them. The church is the community of those who trust (with, as Wright shows, good reason) the testimony of John, Paul, and the others who say: the tomb was empty; Jesus appeared to us; he is risen indeed!

Mary!

The second point is just to savor that meeting of Mary with Jesus. Jesus calls Mary by name. The risen Lord Jesus Christ is still doing this. He calls each one of us here by name too. Those of us who have not been baptized he invites to be named in his name in baptism, identifying with his death and resurrection and becoming one of those who call him, like Mary, "Rabboni, Teacher!" and, like Thomas, "My Lord and my God!" Those of us who have been baptized he invites to remember our baptism, especially today. The early church used to have most of its baptisms at Easter, and some churches today follow this tradition.

Last night in Ely Cathedral many hundreds of people from this diocese gathered for a powerful Easter vigil that included the baptism and confirmation of sixty people. One thing was especially striking. It took what seemed like ages for Bishop John to address each candidate as he or she was presented to him one by one: "Olivia, Melanie, Mark, Frances, Caroline, John, Richard, Chad, Louise, Markus, Adam, Hermione, [and so on]: God has called you by name and made you his own. Confirm, O Lord, your servant Olivia, Melanie, Mark . . . with your Holy Spirit. Receive the seal of the Spirit." Yet there seemed to be no impatience. The congregation, even the children, seemed to recognize that this name after name after name is of the greatest importance.

So Easter is a time to renew our trust in Jesus Christ, who not only calls us by name but also knows us more intimately than we know ourselves, who loves us to the point of laying down his life for us, and who calls us to become not only his servants but his friends.

Conclusion and Collect

So let this Easter Day be a time for us to stretch our imaginations, our minds, and our hearts to try to appreciate more adequately something of the scope of this God-sized, superabundant event.

As we grow in appreciation of it, let it also transform our hoping, our living, and especially our loving.

And above all, let us hear in faith our name being called, let us trust ourselves completely, in life and in death, to the one who calls us by name, and find, in following him and in friendship with him, our resurrection life and joy.

As so often, Isaiah offers us the best words. In our first lesson he evokes the ultimate in celebration:

> On this mountain the LORD of hosts will make for all peoples
> > a feast of rich food, a feast of well-aged wines,
> > of rich food filled with marrow, of well-aged wines strained clear.
> And he will destroy on this mountain
> > the shroud that is cast over all peoples,
> > the sheet that is spread over all nations;
> > he will swallow up death for ever.
>
> > > > > > > > (Isa. 25:6-8)

And the culmination of the celebration of the fact that death does not have the last word is recognition of the one who has and is the ultimate word:

> It will be said on that day,
> > Lo, this is our God; we have waited for him, so that he might save us.
> > This is the LORD for whom we have waited;
> > let us be glad and rejoice in his salvation.
>
> > > > > > > > (Isa. 25:9)

He is risen indeed. Alleluia!

Let us now close by praying again together the great collect for Easter Sunday. I sometimes think that if we were to pray the weekly collects with full attention through the year, meditating on them and letting them shape not only our prayer but also our thought, imagination, and action, we would be well on the way to having a rich, balanced, and deep theology and spirituality for all seasons. This Easter collect is the climax of a wonderful series through the Sundays of Lent, and it is worth taking with us through the next forty days that the church has traditionally observed as the time to celebrate Easter. Let us pray:

> Lord of all life and power,
> who through the mighty resurrection of your Son
> overcame the old order of sin and death
> to make all things new in him:
> grant that we, being dead to sin
> and alive to you in Jesus Christ,
> may reign with him in glory;
> to whom with you and the Holy Spirit
> be praise and honour, glory and might,
> now and in all eternity.
> Amen.

CHAPTER 9

He Ascended into Heaven and Is Seated at the Right Hand of God the Father Almighty

Ascendit ad coelos, sedet ad dexteram dei patris omnipotentis

LOIS MALCOLM

The doctrine of ascension has not received much attention in the history of Christian theology, but its importance must not be underestimated.[1] Between the resurrection and the final parousia, it depicts how the crucified Jesus of Nazareth was raised from the dead and now reigns at the right hand of God, filling all in all with his fullness. It also depicts how Jesus promises to send the Spirit after he ascends to empower his disciples in their witness to "all nations." In this witness Christians make the eschatological claim that the ascended humanity of this crucified Messiah discloses not only who God truly is but who we as human beings truly are. What is most poignant about this claim is that it affirms — in the face of historical evidence that often appears to contradict it — that ultimate reality is defined not by egoistic grasping and exploitation but by the wisdom and power — the kenotic abundance — that inheres in this Lord's crucified humanity.

---

1. For comprehensive historical and theological studies of the ascension, see Douglas Farrow, *Ascension and Ecclesia: On the Significance of the Doctrine of Ascension for Ecclesiology and Christian Cosmology* (Grand Rapids: Eerdmans, 1999), and J. G. Davies, *He Ascended into Heaven* (London: Lutterworth, 1958). Among short articles, see Joseph Ratzinger, "Ascension of Christ," in *Encyclopedia of Theology,* ed. Karl Rahner (London: Burns and Oates, 1975); J. M. Robinson, "Ascension," in *The Interpreter's Dictionary of the Bible* (New York: Abingdon, 1962); and Rowan Williams, "Ascension of Christ," in *A New Dictionary of Christian Theology,* ed. Alan Richardson and John Bowden (London: SCM Press, 1983).

A Biblical Context

Although the NT interpretation of Jesus' ascension has roots in Jewish interest in the ascent of OT figures (especially Enoch, Gen. 5:24, and Elijah, 2 Kings 2:1-12),[2] the most important theological context for interpreting Jesus' ascent is the way the motif of ascent/descent is used to depict the Hebrew understanding of how God promises blessing and judgment to a people in actual historical events.[3] Adam and Eve are commanded to descend from the mountain-garden Eden after their sin. The Tower of Babel, as a false attempt to ascend to the heavens, is destroyed. Noah and his family are saved by ascending Mount Ararat after the great flood. Moses ascends Mount Sinai to receive the instructions for the holy tabernacle in which the high priest was to ascend for the people. The tabernacle, in turn, with its holy of holies, is lifted up on Mount Zion where it is aligned with David's throne. And finally, significant for the image of Jesus' ascent is the way the glory of the Lord takes the form of a cloud as it follows the tabernacle from Sinai to Zion.

Two additional motifs emerged after the exile in Babylon, when hope for the restoration of the Davidic monarchy was transferred to an eschatological future. On the one hand, he is the apocalyptic "Son of Man" who sits at God's right hand restoring the Davidic reign of justice and peace (drawing especially on Ps. 110:1, but also on Pss. 2 and 8) in an everlasting dominion that includes all peoples, nations, and languages (Dan. 7:13-14). On the other hand, he is the "Suffering Servant" (e.g., Isa. 52:13–53:12) and righteous sufferer (e.g., Ps. 22) whose sacrificial death undoes the priestly sacrificial system, making him the eternal high priest who opens up a "new and living way" through the "curtain" of his flesh (Heb. 10:19).

Although Matthew's depiction of Jesus' final appearance in Galilee contains the theme of the ascension, that "all authority in heaven and on earth has been given to me" (Matt. 28:18), and Matthew and Mark do speak of the "Son of Man" coming in the clouds (Matt. 16:27; 24:30; 26:64; Mark 8:38; 13:26), Luke is the only Gospel with an actual depiction of the ascension. (There is an ascension scene in the longer ending of Mark [16:9-21], but biblical scholarship has concluded that it is a later insertion.)

Drawing on the Son of Man motif, Luke depicts the ascension as occurring after two incidents. First, Jesus meets with two disciples who are on their way to the village Emmaus, talking with each other about Jesus' crucifixion

2. See Martha Himmelfarb, *Ascent to Heaven in Jewish and Christian Apocalypses* (London: Oxford University Press, 1993).

3. See Farrow, pp. 26-29 and 278.

(Luke 24:13-49). While they are talking, Jesus appears and walks with them — but they do not recognize him. He listens to their disappointment about his failure to be the leader who would restore Israel and then discloses who he is by interpreting the scriptures. They then urge him to stay with them. He does, and while eating with them he takes bread, blesses it, breaks it, and gives it to them. As he does this, their eyes are "opened" and they recognize him. Then Jesus vanishes, and they recall their experience with him on the road to Emmaus and observe that their hearts "burned within" when he "opened the scriptures" (v. 32).

The second incident occurs when Jesus appears again to all the disciples. They think he is a ghost, but he has them touch his hands and feet and even eats a piece of broiled fish in their presence. Again he "opens their minds" to understand what had happened to him by interpreting scriptures, that the Messiah was to suffer and rise from the dead on the third day, and that repentance and the forgiveness of sins were to be proclaimed in his name to all people, beginning in Jerusalem. He then tells them that he will send what his Father has promised (which, we find out in Acts, is the Holy Spirit); they are to stay in Jerusalem until they have been "clothed with power from on high" (24:49).

He then takes his disciples out to Bethany, lifts up his hands, blesses them, and while blessing them withdraws and is carried into heaven (24:50-51).

The other NT book with an ascension scene is Acts. Its account differs from that in Luke's Gospel in significant ways, although it makes similar theological points. Occurring after forty days of Jesus' appearing to his disciples and speaking to them about the kingdom of God, it comes right after Jesus promises that the Holy Spirit will come upon them and they will be his witnesses in Jerusalem, Judea, and Samaria, and to "the ends of the earth." As he says this, he is lifted up and a cloud takes him out of their sight. Two men in white robes appear and tell the disciples that Jesus has been taken up into heaven and will return in the same way that he left.

In the same way that Luke in the Gospel and in Acts portrays the "ascension" as the pivot around which the Spirit's activity shifts from Jesus' life and ministry to that of the early Christian communities, so Paul relates the exaltation of Jesus to the new age of the Spirit ushered in by his incarnation, crucifixion, and exaltation. In the famous hymn of Philippians 2:6-11, Christ Jesus is the one who, though in the "form of God," did not regard his "equality with God as something to be exploited, but emptied himself," taking the form of a slave and humbling himself to the point of death, even death on a cross. Now exalted, he has been given by God the name above every name. His humiliation and exaltation are the basis for Paul's exhortation for sharing in the life of the Spirit (2:1) by having "the same mind in you that was in Christ Jesus" (2:5). Here again the exaltation of Christ signals the shift in the Spirit's activity from the person and ministry of Jesus to the life of the church.

In 1 Corinthians 15 Christ's exaltation subjects both history and cosmos to the risen Lord. He will, at the end, destroy every authority and power and God will "put all things in subjection under his feet" (vv. 24-28; see Pss. 8:6 and 110:1). In Romans 8:34 this Christ Jesus is the one who died, was raised, and "is at the right hand of God," interceding for us. Because of this, nothing can separate us from God's love in Christ Jesus — not death/life, angels/rulers/powers, things present/things to come, height/depth, or anything else in all creation (8:38-39).

Colossians and Ephesians stress the way Christ has not only been raised from the dead but is seated at God's "right hand in the heavenly places" and placed above all rule, authority, power, and dominion — above every name. God has "put all things under his feet" and has made him the "head over all things for the church" — indeed, the "fullness" of God, which "fills all in all," now fills him and the church, which is his "body" (Eph. 1:20-23; cf. Col. 1:18b-20). Those who are baptized have been raised with Christ and seated with him in the heavenly places (Eph. 2:6; see also Col. 2:12; 3:1).[4] For this reason they too "set their mind on things that are above" where their life is "hidden with Christ in God" (Col. 3:2-3). They put to death, strip themselves of, and get rid of such things as "anger, wrath, malice, slander, and abusive language" (3:8), and instead "clothe themselves" with "compassion, kindness, humility, meekness, and patience" (3:12). They have been renewed in the image of their Creator, and distinctions among them between Greek/Jew, barbarians/nonbarbarians, and slave/free no longer hold (3:11; cf. Gal. 3:28; 1 Cor. 12:13).

John's depiction of the exaltation centers on reference to the motif of the "descending and ascending Son of Man." In 1:51 Jesus tells Nathanael that he will see "heaven opened and the angels of God ascending and descending upon the Son of Man" (cf. Gen. 28:12). In 3:13, after telling Nicodemus that "no one has ascended into heaven except the one who descended from heaven, the Son of Man," Jesus compares the Son of Man being "lifted up" to Moses lifting up the serpent in the wilderness (Num. 21:9). As elsewhere in John (8:28; 12:32-34; cf. Isa. 52:13), "lifted up" refers both to Jesus' glorification and his crucifixion. Finally, the ascending of the Son of Man is mentioned in 6:61-63 in Jesus' discourse on the "bread of life" where Jesus relates his words to the "Spirit that gives life."

---

4. Although in the undisputedly Pauline letters, Paul speaks of the believer's resurrection as occurring in the future (Rom. 6:5; 1 Cor. 15:21-23; Phil. 3:10-11).

Although John does not have an explicit account of the ascension like those found in Luke and Acts, he does have Jesus speak about going away or departing to his Father. Although Jesus' glorification begins with the cross, it will not be complete until his return to his Father (7:39; 12:16, 23; 13:31, 32; 17:5). After he returns to the Father, those who believe in him will do greater works than he has done. Indeed, he will do whatever is asked in his name. He will send an Advocate, the "Spirit of truth," whom the world cannot receive, see, or know, but who will "abide" and "be in" Jesus' followers, teaching them every-thing and reminding them of what Jesus said to them. This Advocate will con-vict them of "sin, righteousness, and judgment"; guide them into all truth; and speak not his own words but the truth revealed in Jesus (John 14–16).

Finally, there is the dramatic scene in John 20:17 where Mary Magdalene weeps beside the empty tomb and mistakes Jesus, who appears standing be-side her, for a gardener. She recognizes him when he calls her by name, but when she tries to touch him he admonishes her, "Do not hold on to me, be-cause I have not yet ascended to the Father," and tells her to announce to the disciples that he will ascend to "my Father and your Father, to my God and your God." He then appears to the disciples and, after breathing on them and saying, "Receive the Holy Spirit," gives them authority to forgive and retain sins (vv. 19-23).

In Hebrews Jesus is the "purification for sins" as sacrifice and high priest who now sits down "at the right hand of the Majesty on high" and, having a name superior to that of the angels, waits "until his enemies would be made a footstool for his feet" (1:1-4; 8:1; 10:12; 12:2; cf. Ps. 110:1). He has entered a very different kind of sanctuary not made by human hands where he appears in God's presence on our behalf (Heb. 9:24; see also 4:14; 8:1-2; 9:11-12). His sacri-fice is precisely that of becoming like us, his brothers and sisters, "in every re-spect," being tested by what they suffered so that he could make a "sacrifice of atonement" for their sins and thereby destroy not only death (which in the NT is the consequence of sin), but the one with the power of death, the devil (2:14-18; 4:14-16). Because he was tested "in every respect" — but without sin — we can have the confidence to approach his throne and receive mercy and grace in time of need; he is able to sympathize with our weakness (4:14-16). His sacrifice undoes the sacrificial system based on the blood of goats and calves. Like the Hebrew prophets who criticized the sacrificial system, the writer of Hebrews stresses how Christ's sacrifice "purifies our conscience from dead works to worship the living God" by opening a "new and living way" through the "curtain" of his flesh (9:11-14; see Ps. 50:13; Isa. 1:11). We can therefore approach his sanctuary in the presence of God with full assurance of faith, hold fast without wavering to our confession of hope, and attend to how we might best "provoke one another to love and good deeds" (Heb. 10:19-25).

Among the other texts on the ascension in the NT, 1 Timothy 3:16 contains a reference to Christ Jesus being "taken up in glory" in a hymn fragment on the "mystery of our religion." In turn, 1 Peter contains a reference to it in a larger section on suffering for doing what is right. Unlike Jewish and Greek heroes who suffer for the law or worthy persons, Christ suffered *for sins* (2:21; cf. 2 Macc. 6:28; see also Rom. 5:7-8). His death prefigures the baptism that saves — not merely "as the removal of dirt from the body," but "as an appeal to God for a good conscience, through the resurrection of Jesus Christ, who has gone into heaven and is at the right hand of God, with angels, authorities, and powers made subject to him" (1 Pet. 3:18-22).

Finally, in Revelation the ascension is identified with the heavenly enthronement of the resurrected Christ, but this enthronement is one that he shares with those who "conquer." To those who "hear my voice and open the door," he says, "I will come in to you and eat with you, and you with me." Indeed, Jesus declares, "I will give a place with me on my throne, just as I myself conquered and sat down with my Father on his throne" (3:20-22; cf. Ps. 110:1).

A Brief History of the Doctrine

Belief in the ascension, as articulated in the Apostles' Creed — *ascendit ad coelos, sedet ad dexteram dei patris omnipotentis* (he ascended into heaven, and is seated at the right hand of God the Father almighty) — soon became normative for the theology of the Western churches. By the fourth century it was celebrated in liturgy. Most of what is written about it in the first few centuries of Christianity, however, comes in passing references — a reference to it in the *Epistle to Barnabas* and Melito of Sardis's paschal homily, and more numerous references in Justin Martyr's *Apology* and *Dialogue,* and in more than one of Tertullian's writings. It is a theme in the sermons of John Chrysostom, who speaks of Christ's glorification as the firstfruits of a deified humanity.

Nonetheless, by the second century Irenaeus of Lyons gave it a central role in his doctrine of recapitulation, which describes how Christ restores the image and likeness of God that was destroyed by Adam's fall, a restoration that reaches its completion when Christ is "ascended on high." According to Irenaeus, Christ is the second Adam who "recapitulates" ("repeats" and "sums up") what the first Adam experienced and was tempted by, but who does so in a fashion that reverses the consequences of the first Adam's disobedience. If one was disobedient by grasping for godlike power, leading to sin and death for all, the other was obedient by emptying his deity for the sake of human beings, leading to righteousness and life for all *(Against the Heresies)*.

After Irenaeus, two influential interpretations of the ascension were offered by Origen (ca. 185–ca. 254) and Augustine (354-430). Origen is best known for his controversial contention that Jesus' ascension was an "ascension of the mind rather than the body" *(On Prayer* 23.2). Further, he argued that Jesus' admonition to Mary Magdalene not to "touch him" should be interpreted mystically and not literally *(Commentary on Saint John)*. By contrast Augustine argued for the bodily ascension of Christ, relating it, following Ephesians, to a doctrine of the "whole Christ" *(totus Christus)* consisting of Head and members which stressed the way the latter (the church) participated in the former's (Christ's) ascension by an intrinsic "bodily" unity between them.[5]

On the whole, however, most patristic and medieval writers were interested in describing how the ascended Christ perfected — or, better, glorified — the whole person (body and soul) in the humanity of the ascended Lord. This theme is depicted in the matins on Ascension Day *(Aeterne Rex)* probably originating from the fifth century: *Peccat caro, mundat caro, Regnat Deus Dei caro* (flesh hath purged what flesh had stained, and God, the Flesh of God, hath reigned). Athanasius (290-373) played an important role in defining this theology. He contended that Christ's "exaltation" pertained to his humanity and not his "essence" as the Word, since the Word was already equal with God (John 5:18). Because Christ, who bore our flesh, has now entered heaven and opened it for us, appearing in God's presence as our advocate, we too are exalted in him *(Apology against the Arians;* cf. Heb. 6:20; 9:24). This theme was further developed in Leontius of Byzantium's (d. 543) doctrine of the *enhypostasia*, which argued, further refining Cyril of Alexandria's views (378-444), that the human element in the incarnation entailed the assumption of all humanity in the second person of the Trinity. Later it was influential in the Eastern theology in the writings of Maximus Confessor (580-662) and John of Damascus (676-749?).

The Reformers shifted attention to the Lord's Supper.[6] In his argument against Ulrich Zwingli, Martin Luther argued for the "real presence" of Christ in the Lord's Supper, buttressing his claim with an understanding of the ubiquitous omnipresence of his humanity.[7] Later Lutheran orthodoxy would argue that Christ's glorified body is neither "everywhere" *(ubique)* nor "no-

---

5. See William Marrevee, *The Ascension of Christ in the Works of St. Augustine* (Ottawa: University of Ottawa Press, 1967).

6. James Benjamin Wagner, *Ascendit ad Coelos: The Doctrine of the Ascension in the Reformed and Lutheran Theology of the Period of Orthodoxy* (Winterthur: Keller, 1964).

7. Luther, *Luther's Works*, Weimarer Ausgabe (edition) (1527), 23:133.

where" *(nullibi)* but free from all external circumscription, and that the Son of God could will to be present bodily in his humanity whenever and wherever he will. By contrast, John Calvin argued that Christ had ascended to God's throne as a localized bodily presence and had a spiritual, not bodily, presence in the church and sacrament.[8] He also stressed Christ's work, not merely his person, as prophet, priest, and king, and emphasized how the Holy Spirit raises the believer to be with Christ in the heavenly realm in holy communion and in the life of sanctification.

Liberal theologians in the nineteenth century criticized the Reformation debates over the Lord's Supper for being overly mythological. Most "lives of Jesus" written in that century rejected belief in the ascension because it relied on an outmoded cosmology. Friedrich Schleiermacher did so in *The Christian Faith* ([1830] 2.99), as did Adolf von Harnack in "The Apostles' Creed" (1892). In the twentieth century Karl Barth revitalized the doctrine — although he rejected visualizing it as a literal event, like going up in a balloon. He argued that Jesus Christ's risen humanity within the inner trinitarian life of God and the assumption of all human flesh within that humanity is, as an eschatological repetition and expectation of Christ's resurrection, the condition for the possibility of our knowledge of God in time (*Church Dogmatics* [1955] IV/2).

Most notable since Barth are the following. T. F. Torrance argued for a way of thinking about the ascension within a contemporary scientific worldview.[9] By way of a retrieval of Irenaeus's understanding of "recapitulation," Gustaf Wingren sought to relate the ascension to the church's mission of preaching and sacraments and the vocation of the baptized in the world.[10] In very different ways — as a Roman Catholic and a Reformed theologian, respectively — Hans Urs von Balthasar and Jürgen Moltmann have written vividly about humanity's eschatological participation in Christ's crucified and raised humanity within the trinitarian life of God.[11]

---

8. Calvin, *Institutes of the Christian Religion* (1559), 4.17.12.

9. See T. F. Torrance, *Space, Time, and Resurrection* (Grand Rapids: Eerdmans, 1976).

10. See Gustaf Wingren, *Gospel and Church,* trans. Ross MacKenzie (Edinburgh and London: Oliver and Boyd, 1964).

11. See, e.g., Hans Urs von Balthasar's *Mysterium Paschale: The Mystery of Easter* (Ignatius, 2000) and Jürgen Moltmann's *The Spirit of Life: A Universal Affirmation* (Minneapolis: Fortress, 2001).

What Does the Ascension Mean for Us Today?

What does ascension mean? What difference does it make for how we perceive and respond to life? First, it has to do with Jesus' departure not as the Messiah his disciples had anticipated but as one who comes and goes as he wills, and as one who keeps them from recognizing him and only opens their eyes to his identity in the breaking of bread (Luke 24). Even Mary Magdalene is told not to hold on to him but to announce his resurrection to the other disciples (John 20:11-18).

Second, it has to do with his sending the Holy Spirit to empower his disciples' missionary vocation to "all nations." In John Jesus breathes the Holy Spirit on the disciples, giving them the power to forgive and retain sins (20:22-23). In Matthew Jesus tells the disciples to baptize and teach, and make disciples of "all nations" (28:18-20). Most importantly, Luke depicts how the same Spirit active in Jesus' ministry is now poured out on "all flesh." This Spirit empowers Jesus' disciples to carry their witness to all that come in his name — repentance, forgiveness, baptism, and experience of the Spirit. As they do this — from Jerusalem to Judea and Samaria to the "ends of the earth" — radical Spirit-led transformations cause the disciples to rethink what it means to be Christian as the new Gentile converts are brought into their initially Jewish-Christian community.

Given Jesus' promise before his ascent, it is not insignificant that the rest of the book of Acts is organized around the movement of the Spirit's activity from Jerusalem (2:14–8:13) to Judea and Samaria (8:26-40) and finally to the "ends of the earth" (9:1–28:14). Even in Jerusalem the Spirit falls upon the disciples, enabling the Jews from the diaspora to hear them speak in their own native languages. Occurring on the Jewish festival of Pentecost, this event appears to overturn the human attempt to "ascend" to heavens with the Tower of Babel and its one language and culture. In his speech after this event, Peter quotes the Septuagint version of the apocalyptic vision in Joel 2:28-32, where "in the last days" God pours out his Spirit on all flesh — sons/daughters, young/old, male/female slaves (Acts 2:14-21). All that occurred in Jesus' proclamation of God's reign — bringing good news to the poor, releasing captives, giving sight to the blind and freedom for the oppressed — is now identified with the church's preaching about Jesus (Luke 4:18-19; cf. Isa. 61:1-11). In addition to its teaching, fellowship, breaking of bread and prayer, the early Christian community is characterized by "signs and wonders," sharing "all things in common," distributing to all as any has need, and "eating with glad and generous hearts" (Acts 2:37-46; 4:32-37; 6:1-6).

What is most important, however, for understanding precisely who this exalted Lord is, and what the Spirit and mission he commissions are about, is related to what his disciples found most troubling after his death, namely, his humiliating crucifixion. In John his crucifixion is linked with his exaltation, and in the Pauline letters his *kenosis* and cross cannot be divorced from his "dominion" above every cosmic and mundane power, a dominion that encompasses life/death, things present/things to come, height/depth, and indeed, the very fullness of God (Eph. 1:21; Rom. 8:38; 1 Cor. 15:24; Col. 1:16; 1 Pet. 3:22). At issue in Christ's ruling at the right hand of God precisely in the fullness of his crucified humanity is not the empirical question of how he might be everywhere and yet still fully a human body. At issue rather — for him and for us — is the more profound question of temptation and faith.

Following Paul and Irenaeus, we can observe that Jesus did not succumb to the temptation of rejecting his "cup" of suffering even though he had every right, in his innocence, to protest this unjust verdict. Instead of exploiting and grasping at his divinity by justifying himself or proving his righteousness, he emptied himself, becoming fully human, even to the point not only of death but of experiencing the sting of that death, God's wrath against sin. As the second Adam, Jesus reversed the consequences of the first Adam and Eve's grasp at being godlike, thereby bringing sin and death, by enacting the very opposite, self-giving love. In doing this he bestowed on the rest of humanity righteousness and life and restored its birthright of being created in the image of God, freeing it to robustly enact its proper human "dominion" or stewardship of creation.

But if this *kenosis* enacts the full humanity of the one who shared equality with God, then it also reflects God's nature. It indicates that God is revealed precisely in the humiliation of Christ's humanity and that the depth of God's being is characterized by love, a kenotic abundance that does not grasp at or exploit what it possesses but gives of itself in order to liberate others.

This, then, is what it means to say that Christ rules precisely in the fullness of his crucified humanity. His *kenosis* is not a simple negation of power. Indeed, it cannot be divorced from his resurrection, which frees human beings from the power of sin and death and enables them to assert confidently that nothing can separate them from God's love, neither life nor death, past, present, nor future because in Paul's words, "all is yours" (1 Cor. 3:22; cf. Rom. 8:38-39). Jesus' resurrection and exaltation are the "firstfruits" of our resurrection and exaltation. The same Spirit who raised him from the dead enables us to live out of the "spiritual" *(pneumatikos)* — as opposed merely to "empirical" or "prudential" *(psychikos)* — power of his resurrected body (1 Cor. 15). With this spiritual power, which brings life out of death, Christ restores the image of God in us, our created birthright, and frees us to live our human lives as stewards of our responsibilities in truly wise and powerful ways. We too now, through Christ's cross and resurrection, have been given the "mind of Christ," a mind that can afford to be kenotic precisely because it is already "above scrutiny" and able to "discern all things" and not because it needs to grasp at or achieve these powers (1 Cor. 2:14-16).

Indeed, we have been baptized into Christ's death and freed to live out of his resurrected life — a life empowered by the Spirit's abundant love, joy, and peace. Our old life in Adam — our false ego — has died. We are now freed to be our true selves in Christ. In this baptism we no longer see one another in the same way. We are now a new creation, a new humanity, freed not only from sin and death but from the very distinctions we use to secure or grasp at our identities — distinctions not only between wisdom/foolishness, power/weakness, but even more basic distinctions between what is law/not-law, male/female, Jew/Greek, slave/free, barbarian/nonbarbarian. We no longer need to exploit one another with our false self's tactics (anger, wrath, malice, slander, abusive language — or, to draw from another list, idolatry, enmities, strife, jealousy, anger, quarrels, dissensions, factions, envy, drunkenness [Gal. 5:19-21]). As those who have been raised with Christ, we can now "clothe" ourselves with his humanity — compassion, kindness, meekness, patience, bearing with one another, and when we have complaints about others, forgiving them (Col. 3:1-17; Ephesians).

We renew this baptism by worshiping with one another, hearing the preaching of the forgiveness of sins that comes in Jesus' name, and "proclaiming his death" by eating his "bread" (his "body") and drinking his "cup" (his "blood") (1 Cor. 11:23-26). As 1 Corinthians indicates, we discern this "body" precisely in the midst of life's messy complexity, in actual conflicts over sex and marriage, lawsuits, social status, syncretistic religious practices, abuses at the Lord's Supper, the use of spiritual gifts, conflicts over worship, the role of women, belief in the resurrection, and so on. Our baptism is renewed daily, not in some ethereal spiritual sphere but in the prosaic circumstances of our lives at home and at work, as those who participate in families, communities, institutions, and as citizens of nations. The Spirit converts us, annihilating the grasping "old Adam or Eve" in us and raising us to our true selves in Christ precisely as we seek to discriminate and sift among the multifarious demands made upon us by those among whom we live and work, and discern our own fears and desires in the face of them.[12]

Indeed, the *koinonia* (fellowship) of the church flourishes in its purest form when it, like Christ, empties itself for others out of the abundance and

12. See Wingren, *Gospel and Church*.

fullness of the Spirit's life. Our sacrifice of praise takes on an eschatological form in the face of real human need, in the face of Christ in the "least of these" of "all the nations" — the hungry, the thirsty, the stranger, the naked, the sick and the imprisoned (Matt. 25:31-46). We have been given access to the intimacy Jesus shares with his Father, an intimacy that enables us to be fully united with one another, not so we can hoard or contain it but so we can, like Christ, be sent, in this time between his ascension and his final return, as ambassadors for reconciliation in the world (John 17; 2 Cor. 5:20). The metaphor of the pangs of childbirth characterizes the eschatological sorrow and joy we experience as we, empowered by the Spirit, witness to the fact that humanity — indeed, crucified humanity — is with the Christ exalted in glory at God's right hand. The power to live in the fullness of that resurrected life in every moment of our prosaic lives is received in the forgiveness and healing that comes in the name of this crucified Messiah whose fullness fills all in all.

God Has Gone Up with a Shout!

Acts 1:6-11

RICHARD A. LISCHER

We say it every Sunday, not because we understand it but because it is in the script: "He ascended into heaven and is seated at the right hand of the Father." The idea behind reciting a creed is reasonably simple. If you do not say the right lines, you *may* not be in the right story. For example, if you don't hear the lines, "To be or not to be, that is the question," chances are you are not watching a performance of *Hamlet*. If you find yourself telling the story of Jesus but omitting his ascension, the account of his life is incomplete.

The story of the ascension follows a familiar pattern in Luke's script. It is the pattern of Jesus' withdrawal from his friends in order to commune with his Father. It begins early in the Gospel. After his first sermon in Nazareth, Jesus is taken by his parishioners to the edge of a cliff where they plan to push him off, but he passes through them and, Luke says, he "went away." Later, at his transfiguration a cloud overshadowed them, and the scene appears to be set for yet another fadeaway, but when he could have gone away he chose to descend the mountain and head toward the cross. At Emmaus, after he opens the scripture and blesses the bread, he disappears. Finally, at Bethany he preaches to them essentially the same sermon he had preached in the synagogue at Nazareth about fulfilling everything written in the law, the Prophets, and the Psalms, and then he fades from the scene. This time he really is *gone*. As he blessed them, Luke says, "he parted from them." The end.

Like any writer, Luke faced the problem of how to end his story. He had no idea his first book would be so successful that its readers would demand a sequel. As with any sequel, a little overlap is inevitable and perhaps desirable. In volume 1, the Gospel of Luke, the ascending Jesus is the *end*. His ascension represents the triumphant, Hollywood-style end of a life in which nothing further can take place. In volume 2, the Acts of the Apostles, the ascending Jesus is the *beginning* of an exciting movement, one that will see its share of triumphs, to be sure, but also persecution, internal conflicts, suffering, and many tattered endings. But the *ascending* — the ascending is so important that it serves as the linchpin that connects two scripts — the life of Jesus and the mission of the Christian community.

Yet the ascension is oddly missing from most preachers' story of Jesus. When I was serving a church, we celebrated Ascension Day every year with a choral concert and an ice-cream social. I never preached on those occasions, preferring to let the music and the ice cream convey the message. Like most pastors, I was grateful that Jesus had ascended on a Thursday and not a Sunday, which meant that I never had to make sense of the ascending Christ who is triumphantly ending one ministry in the flesh and beginning another in the spirit.

But if you have to make sense of death — and we all do — then you have to reckon with the ascension. For death *and* the hope of triumph are written in *our* script, for when you make a confession you are saying as much about yourself as you are about God.

We read stories about death every day in the newspaper. Death's "script" appears often unexpectedly on the front page, but more predictably in the obituaries, which, you may have noticed, have been changing. In our local newspaper the obituaries used to be strictly boilerplate. Each was written with the same tone of factual objectivity, as if the most fascinating news about a person's life was his or her place of birth, degrees attained, or Masonic affiliation. But now the obits have become interesting, because our newspaper has invited surviving friends and relatives to write *spiritual* accounts of their loved ones' lives.

For example, the parents of a boy named Ray wrote that Ray has graduated from this school to a higher form of knowledge. Another said a chap named Wallace has moved up to a higher stage of development. Most of the obituary writers, however, use traditional religious language: George has fought the good fight, kept the faith, and therefore a crown of righteousness awaits him. Bessie has loved the Lord her whole life long, and has now gone home to be with Jesus.

It is about time the newspapers allow us to tell the world what our lives *really* mean. How much imagination does it take to absorb the brutal facts and conditions that attend a young woman dying of cancer, a child struck by an automobile, or an old man breathing his last in a nursing home? Is this all we have to report?

Those of you who have attended the dying — and the dead — have entered fully into the chaos and finality of the event. Then, at the very end, when all you are left with is a corpse and a tableau of grief, you have absorbed the scene into your soul and reframed it. You have added something. Depending on your tradition, you have made the sign of the cross upon the forehead, eyes, and breast; you have anointed the body with oil, recited a psalm, made a blessing, said a prayer. You have added something, which is a way of saying, "There is more to this story than meets the eye."

More than three decades ago Martin Luther King, Jr., was murdered in a seedy Memphis motel. He bled to death on the balcony with one leg protruding through the rail at an awkward angle as his friends wept and dabbed at his wounds. May none of us meet such an ending.

Today, when you walk into the undercroft of King's old church in Montgomery, Alabama, the first thing you see is a startling piece of religious art. It is a mural depicting a life-sized Martin Luther King in a cream-colored robe and cincture, arms extended in benediction, as he ascends into the clouds surrounded by the mothers and fathers of the African American church. They are on their way to heaven. If you've seen the photographs from the Lorraine Motel, you have every right to ask, Which is the true ending of Martin Luther King — the scene on the balcony or the scene in the mural?

Which is the true end of each of our lives? You thought you saw your loved one die gasping in an emergency room or on the freeway in an accident. You think you have caught sight of your own mortal end, and you do not like what you see because not only does it not look pretty, it does not look finished, and certainly not triumphant. Most of us conclude our lives in the descendant rather than the ascendant mode.

But no. The script says more and other. It says, "He ascended." And when you make that confession, you say as much about your own destiny as you do your Lord's: He ascended. He moved on to his own higher plane. He graduated. He fought the good fight. He went home. I know many preachers "read" the ascension as a prelude to modern humanity's alienation in a world from which God is absent. But the church has chosen another lens, that of Psalm 47:5, through which to read the event, and it is not forlorn or tragic but triumphant:

God has gone up with a shout!
   the LORD with the sound of a trumpet.

The ascension marks Jesus' entry into heaven. When I was a boy I loved the poem by Vachel Lindsay about the founder of the Salvation Army, titled "General William Booth Enters into Heaven," except I imagined the poet was not speaking of Booth but Jesus:

> *Jesus* led boldly with his big bass drum.
>   *Are you washed in the blood of the Lamb?*
> The Saints smiled gravely, and they said, "He's come."
>   *Are you washed in the blood of the Lamb?*

I suppose it would be too much to expect the church to celebrate Christ's triumph as boisterously as it deserves to be celebrated, and let it go at that. But Christians have long made a *problem* of the ascension and Christ's postresurrection state. They have debated the exact *location* of the heaven to which he ascended. *Where* exactly does he sit at the right hand of God? In what place? In a bold interpretation of this passage, Luther said famously, "The right hand of God is everywhere." Jesus had to leave one place so he could be *everywhere* in heaven and earth, so that his fullness could fill all in all.

In his lectures on homiletics, Karl Barth said the preacher stands between two Advents, the first and second comings of the Lord. That means that the preacher is free to look for Jesus in all the wrong places, for he is coming toward us from more than one direction. *Everywhere* means that the object of our hope is not always receding into the murky past (as all things strictly historical must) but is waiting to meet up with our confessions of faith and to confirm them in ordinary experience. Our job is not to retrieve him from his *Sitz im Leben* but to meet him where he promised to be: among those who suffer and seek redemption, in the neighborhoods, hospitals, cemeteries, and lost causes where the risen one is coming into the world.

Last Easter Sunday my wife and I were driving through eastern North Carolina at twilight, through some of the poorest and most depressed communities in our state. We passed a cottage where someone had taken a piece of poster board and made a little sign and planted it at the end of the driveway where everybody on the main road would have to confront it. Written in Magic Marker, it said, "The grave could not hold him."

This roadside poetry sounds almost conspiratorial, does it not, like the underground slogan that circulated in France before the revolution: "The bread is rising." "Psst. The grave could not hold him. Pass it on." Because he is risen and now ascended, he rules. The Lord is now free to be "everywhere."

Every great text in the Bible has what one homiletician calls a performance-response, something it wants you to *do*. For example, when Jesus says, "Go, tell your friends what great things God has done for you," it is not hard to guess the appropriate response. Every text suggests an action: to do, strive, think, give, grow, love.

For those who believe they control their own destiny, and that includes most of us, the story of the ascension demands the most difficult response imaginable: wait. Wait for the Spirit to be poured out. Wait for God to come into your lives. Go to Jerusalem, get a room, and wait. They were to wait for the Holy Spirit. And even though the Holy Spirit has been given to the church, the command to wait has not been rescinded. When a congregation or an individual loses this sense of receptivity characterized by the power to wait, spiritual death is sure to follow. It will be a death marked by enormous outlays of activity to be sure, but death it will be. Only those with a risen and ascended Lord can wait. For he comes to us, not we to him.

Because the grave could not hold him,
   wait for him.
Because he comes to us in the final descent, at the loose and
     fraying ends of life,
   wait for him.
Because he will sneak up on you like a conspirator of love,
   wait for him.
Because his victory belongs to our script too,
   wait for him.
Because there is more to our stories than meets the eye,
   wait for him.
Because the grave could not hold him,
   wait for him.

CHAPTER 10

From There He Will Come to Judge the Living and the Dead

Inde venturus est iudicare vivus et mortuos

DANIEL L. MIGLIORE

In the concluding affirmation of the second article of the Creed, the church looks to the future coming of Christ. It confesses that the drama of salvation, begun at creation and centered in the ministry, crucifixion, resurrection, and ascension of Christ, is unfinished. A final act of the drama remains. The Christ who has come, and who now reigns in heaven, will come again to judge the living and the dead.

How are we to understand this affirmation? Is it good or terrifying news? Does it have any practical significance? As perhaps no other affirmation of the Creed, confession that Christ will come to judge the world causes deep uncertainty. For many Christians it may bring to mind great works of art like Michelangelo's *Last Judgment,* in the Sistine Chapel, or the thundering "Dies Irae" of Verdi's *Requiem Mass.* Under the influence of such portrayals, Christians are likely to confess the coming of Christ in judgment more with gnawing fear than with expectant joy.

With this, as with all the articles of the Creed, the primary task of theological reflection is to discover how each fits within the larger pattern of truth attested in Scripture and proclaimed in the church as the gospel of Jesus Christ. Seen as part of this pattern, Christ's coming as judge is not to be equated with vengeance and punishment. At the same time, a responsible interpretation will have to avoid a superficial dismissal of this least-loved statement of the Creed as a piece of mythology that enlightened Christians have outgrown. There is, in fact, no salvation without judgment. The grace of God does not leave things just as they are. The fundamental questions, however, are, Who is our judge? and What is the purpose of his judgment? We begin with a brief summary of the answers of Scripture and the theological tradition to these questions.

Biblical Roots of the Doctrine

The conviction that God is judge is an integral element in every genre and in every layer of the scriptural tradition. Contrary to popular assumptions, however, the distinctive meaning of God's actions as judge is not the distribution of rewards and punishments but the making and renewing of just order. God's judgments aim to create and restore justice and peace among the people of God and throughout the creation. In this sense God's activity as judge and savior is inseparable.[1]

According to the Old Testament, God is the "judge of all the earth" (Gen. 18:25). The righteous judgments of God are recounted in many stories: the loss of Eden (Gen. 3:14-19), the great flood (7–9), the fall of the Tower of Babel (11:1-9), the destruction of Sodom and Gomorrah (19:24-25), the plagues in Egypt (Exod. 7–12), the multiple occasions when God's chosen people stray from God's commandments.

But this activity of divine judgment is never an end in itself. The Psalms testify to the intimate connection between the judging and saving work of God in both personal and communal life. If God's judgment is necessary for the salvation of individuals (Ps. 51:2, 7, 10), the saving purpose of God's judgment is also seen in the communal sphere in God's activity on behalf of the poor, the fatherless, and the widow (Pss. 10:18; 68:5; 72:4). Hence the psalmist can speak of God's coming judgment as a cause for joy.

> Let the floods clap their hands;
> let the hills sing together for joy
> at the presence of the LORD, for he is coming
> to judge the earth.
> He will judge the world with righteousness,
> and the peoples with equity.
>
> (Ps. 98:8-9)

---

1. See Bernd Janowski, "Gericht Gottes, II. Altes Testament," in *Religion in Geschichte und Gegenwart*, 4th ed. (Tübingen: Mohr Siebeck, 2000), 3:733; also Klaus Seybold, "Gericht Gottes, I. Altes Testament," in *Theologische Realenzyklopaedie* (Berlin and New York: Walter de Gruyter, 1984), 12:460-66.

The link between divine judgment and salvation is expressed in different ways in the Old Testament witness. Sometimes God shows mercy *after* judgment (Gen. 6–8), sometimes *instead of* judgment (Hos. 11:9), sometimes *through* judgment (Pss. 76:9; 146:5-7).[2] In whatever form, judgment is not isolated from God's redemptive purpose. This is especially clear in God's activity as judge on behalf of the poor and the defenseless, a recurrent theme of the prophets (Isa. 42:1-4; Jer. 7:5-7; Amos 5:11).

According to the prophets, the activity of God as judge will be realized fully only at the end of history. The prophets warn of the coming "day of the Lord," when God will come to judge the nations (Isa. 13:6; Jer. 46:10; Joel 1:15; 2:1; Mal. 4:5). Whereas some prophets see the coming day of judgment as one of sheer darkness and doom, others understand it as integral to the coming of God's salvation, justice, and peace. When God judges between the nations, "they shall beat their swords into plowshares" (Isa. 2:4).

> With righteousness he shall judge the poor,
>   and decide with equity for the meek of the earth.
>
> (Isa. 11:4)

> I am God and no mortal,
>   the Holy One in your midst,
>   and I will not come in wrath.
>
> (Hos. 11:9)

Like the Old Testament, the New Testament offers multiple traditions of God's activity as judge rather than a simple, uniform description.[3] Jesus preaches the good news of the dawn of the reign of God in his message and ministry. He calls people to repent, to trust in God alone, to love God and neighbor, and to forgive their enemies. Jesus' message also includes a warning of a coming day of judgment (Matt. 11:22). According to the "little apocalypse" of the Gospel of Mark, the coming of the Lord will be sudden, and it is necessary to keep awake (Mark 13:37). Jesus' familiar depiction of the coming judgment of the nations underscores the surprise of both the blessed and the accursed (Matt. 25:31-46).

When we turn to the place of the divine judgment in the preaching of the apostles, four things stand out. First, all are sinners who stand under God's

---

2. Janowski, 3:733.

3. See Egon Brandenburger, "Gericht Gottes, II. Neues Testament," in *Theologische Realenzyklopaedie*, 12:469-83.

judgment (Rom. 1–3). Second, Christ has borne the judgment sinners deserved. "Christ redeemed us from the curse of the law by becoming a curse for us" (Gal. 3:13). Christ died for our sins (1 Cor. 15:3); there is therefore no condemnation of those who are in Christ (Rom. 8:1). Christians have already been judged and crucified with Christ (Gal. 2:19). Third, the very same Christ who died and was raised for us will be our judge in the last day. Paul speaks not simply of "the day of the Lord" but of "the day of our Lord Jesus Christ" (1 Cor. 1:8; Phil. 1:6, 10), and Paul prays fervently for the coming of this day: *Maranatha,* "Our Lord, come!" (1 Cor. 16:22). It is Christ who will sit on the judgment seat (2 Cor. 5:10; Rom. 14:9). Fourth, Christians are called to a holy life that they may be "pure and blameless" on the day of Jesus Christ (Phil. 1:10).

Is Paul's belief in a coming judgment of Christ at odds with his doctrine of justification by grace through faith alone? Paul is everywhere emphatic that salvation is by God's grace and not by our works (Rom. 3:28). Nevertheless, he does not preach "cheap grace." He wants Christians to produce a "harvest of righteousness" that comes through faith in Christ for the glory and praise of God (Phil. 1:11). Paul speaks of the coming day of judgment as a day when everything other than what has been built on the foundation of Jesus Christ will be burned up (1 Cor. 3:11-15).

Peter also preaches that Christ is the one ordained by God as judge of the living and the dead (Acts 10:42; 1 Pet. 4:5; cf. 2 Tim. 4:1). He calls his readers to holy living so that their deeds may glorify God "when he comes to judge" (1 Pet. 2:12). While not denying a future judgment (John 12:46ff.), John's distinctive emphasis among the New Testament witnesses is that the judgment of God is already present in the decision for or against Christ (3:16-19; 5:24). Christ is the judge here and now. John's Gospel also includes the saying of Jesus, "I came not to judge the world, but to save the world" (12:47; cf. 3:17). This saying does not exclude all judgment but only a "crude misinterpretation" of judgment that divorces it from salvation.[4]

Although there is diversity in its witness, the apostolic church awaits the coming of Christ with confidence and joy. Written in the midst of persecution, the book of Revelation reminds the church of the promise of its Lord, "Surely, I am coming soon." To this the church responds, not in fear but in hope, "Amen. Come, Lord Jesus!" (Rev. 22:20-21).

---

4. See C. H. Dodd, *The Interpretation of the Fourth Gospel* (Cambridge: Cambridge University Press, 1963), p. 209.

Doctrinal Development

That Christ is coming to judge the living and the dead was widely affirmed in the church long before its formal inclusion in the Nicene and Apostles' Creeds.[5] Written early in the second century, 2 Clement says, "Brethren, we must think of Jesus Christ, as we do of God, as the judge of the living and the dead."[6] Christ's coming to judge the world is clearly an integral part of Irenaeus's formulations of the early church's rule of faith.[7] By the early fifth century Augustine can say it is a "belief held by the whole church of the true God" that Christ is to come from heaven to judge the living and the dead.[8]

One important use of this affirmation by the patristic theologians is to urge fellow Christians to a disciplined and upright life. According to Origen, "The preaching of the church includes a belief in a future and just judgment of God, which belief incites and persuades men to a good and virtuous life, and to an avoidance of sin by all possible means."[9] If we detect in the patristic writers a certain moralistic drift — the loss of a firm hold on the primacy of grace and a tendency to portray God as the judge who distributes rewards and punishments according to works — Kelly cautions that this criticism can be overdrawn. The real concern of these writers, like that of the apostles before them and sound preachers of every age, is to say that the grace of God by which we are saved calls for a life of obedience and service.[10]

In addition to their hortatory use of the doctrine of Christ's coming judgment, the patristic writers also employ it for apologetic purposes. Irenaeus appeals to the coming judgment of Christ to counter the Marcionite division between the merciful God of the New Testament and the judging God of the Old. "In both Testaments," he contends, "there is the same righteousness of God."[11] With his insistence on the coming judgment, Irenaeus also counters the general gnostic view of God as indifferent to human actions.[12]

For the Alexandrian theologians, the work of the Logos is essentially that of a teacher instructing students, or a physician caring for the sick. Judgment

---

5. See Helmut Merkel, "Gericht Gottes, IV. Altes Kirche bis Reformationszeit," in *Theologische Realenzyklopaedie,* 12:483-92.

6. 2 Clement 1.1.

7. Irenaeus, *Against Heresies* 1.10.1; 3.4.2.

8. Augustine, *City of God* 20.1.

9. Origen, *On First Principles* 3.1.1.

10. J. N. D. Kelly, *Early Christian Doctrines* (New York: Harper and Brothers, 1958), pp. 460-61.

11. Irenaeus, *Against Heresies* 4.28.1.

12. Irenaeus, *Against Heresies* 5.27.1.

thus means something very different from retribution. The discipline of the divine pedagogue is for the sake of edification, never for the sake of punishment in itself. As "the physician of our souls," God's punishment by fire is "applied with the object of healing," says Origen.[13] "We say that God brings fire upon the world, not like a cook, but like a God, who is the benefactor of them who stand in need of the discipline of fire."[14]

In the West the tendency toward a legalistic interpretation of God's coming judgment becomes increasingly strong. According to Tertullian, we do well to fear God's anger.[15] God has given us "the rules . . . for securing his favor, as well as the retribution in store for the ignoring (of) . . . them."[16] While Augustine has a very robust doctrine of grace, this does not diminish his emphasis on the divine righteousness and the corresponding seriousness of the coming judgment. He argues that eternal punishment is both possible and appropriate for unbelievers.[17]

Thomas Aquinas and other medieval theologians add two themes to the interpretation of the final judgment. They distinguish between a first judgment of the individual soul immediately upon death and a second, universal judgment at the general resurrection. They also teach, in agreement with ancient tradition, that the apostles and the saints will have an active part with Christ in the final judgment.[18]

The Reformers hold firmly to Scripture and creed in their interpretation of the final judgment. Their primary emphasis is that the very same Christ who is our savior is the coming judge. At least for believers, this is a cause for joy and not terror. According to Luther, "I have been baptized and believe in Christ who has suffered for me, and I do not fear the judgment because Christ sits next to the Father and is my guardian and advocate."[19] Calvin, always interested in the benefits to be derived from the doctrines of the church, writes, "No mean assurance, this, that we shall be brought before no other judgment seat than that of our Redeemer, to whom we must look for our salvation! . . . By giving all judgment to the Son (John 5:22), the Father has honored him to the end that he may care for the consciences of his people, who tremble in dread of judgment."[20]

13. Origen, *On First Principles* 10.6.6.
14. Origen, *Against Celsus* 5.15.
15. Tertullian, *The Soul's Testimony* 2.
16. Tertullian, *Apology* 18.
17. Augustine, *City of God* 22.
18. Aquinas, *On the Truth of the Catholic Faith* 4.96.
19. *Luthers Werke* (Weimar), 37:150.
20. Calvin, *Institutes of the Christian Religion* 2.16.18.

A Contemporary Interpretation

During the theological resurgence of the twentieth century, Roman Catholic and Protestant churches reclaimed the centrality of the creedal affirmations of the incarnation, cross, and resurrection of Jesus Christ. His "second coming," however, has remained for the most part the domain of fundamentalist and sectarian groups. This has been to the impoverishment of the life and witness of the ecumenical church. Without the affirmation of Christ's coming to bring God's purposes to fulfillment, the plot of the biblical story is severely truncated and the Christian message badly distorted. When Christ the savior is no longer expected as ruler and judge of the earth, the church is tempted to make triumphalist claims to be ruler and judge in its own right. It also relaxes its prophetic criticism of all forms of injustice, including the abusive exercise of state power. Karl Barth is right: "If Christianity is not altogether thoroughgoing eschatology, there remains in it no relation whatever with Christ."[21]

Because the coming of Christ to judge the living and the dead is expressed with striking economy in the Apostles' Creed, each phrase deserves our attention.

"From There"

Unlike the false prophets who set dates for the Lord's arrival, the Creed says not a word about *when* this event will occur. It respects the limitations of our knowledge and is mindful of the word of Jesus that "about that day or hour no one knows, neither the angels in heaven, nor the Son, but only the Father" (Mark 13:32). As for the *how,* whereas the Nicene Creed describes the event as a coming "in glory," the Apostles' Creed is again silent. The absence of the phrase "in glory" in the Apostles' Creed tends to emphasize the identity of the crucified and risen Lord and the coming judge. Not that the distinction between Christ's coming in humility and his coming in glory is unimportant. On the contrary, there is solid biblical support for it. However, the distinction should not be understood to mean that while Christ came first as a lowly prince of peace, when he comes again it will be as a mighty potentate with armies to coerce obedience to his rule.

Although the Creed remains silent about the when and the how, it does refer to the *origin* of the coming judge, the place from which Christ will come. He will come "from there." This is not explained as meaning "from the clouds" or

---

21. Barth, *The Epistle to the Romans* (London: Oxford University Press, 1933), p. 314.

even "from heaven." But if not from the clouds or from heaven, from where? The implied answer is: from the whole history of God's saving work in Christ that has been recounted in all the previous declarations of the Creed. Still more directly, "from there" refers to the Father's "right hand," where, according to the immediately preceding affirmation, the ascended Son now sits. "Seated at the right hand of the Father" is a symbol for participating in the power and authority of God. Christ comes "from there," from God the Father, and even more specifically, from the sovereign love of God the Father. It is "from there," from all that the Father is and eternally gives to the Son and through the Son to us, that Christ has already come and will come. "From there" Christ now rules the church by his Spirit, and "from there" he will come to rule the whole world. As Hans Urs von Balthasar puts it, Christ will come as he always comes, from the almighty Father's love. "Fundamentally, the Son always comes from the Father."[22] Only-begotten of the Father's love, Jesus Christ will come to judge the world "from there," from the eternal, sovereign love of God.

That Christ will come "from there," from the omnipotent love of God, means, negatively, that he will not come from the anger and wrath of God as so many contemporary preachers of apocalyptic horrors tell us. Nor will Christ come from the resources of the church, from the treasures of personal religious experience, or from the vitalities and movements of history. All these may bear witness to his coming, but they are not the origin of it. Christ will come from where only God himself can come. Christians are not to expect his coming as the inevitable result of the unfolding processes of nature, or as the consummation of political or ecclesiastical empires, or as the result of revolutionary movements against these empires. They are, therefore, not to be fooled by reports, "'Look, here it is!' or 'There it is!'" (Luke 17:21). Because Christ will come "from there," from the all-powerful and all-transforming love of God, Christians are free to participate critically, responsibly, and constructively in the struggles for greater justice, freedom, and peace on earth this side of the eschaton, without falling into despair or yielding to false hopes.

"He Will Come"

The basic question now and always is, Who is the coming one? "Are you the one who is to come, or are we to wait for another?" (Matt. 11:3). The unequivocal answer of Scripture and creed is that the coming one is none other than

---

22. Hans Urs von Balthasar, *Credo: Meditations on the Apostles' Creed* (New York: Crossroad, 1990), p. 69.

the one who has come in the flesh, Jesus Christ the Redeemer. The very one who, according to the Creed, suffered under Pontius Pilate, was crucified, and rose from the dead is the one who is coming. According to the faith of the church, the coming one is not an unknown *x*, nor is he different from the one who blessed the children and hung from the cross. When Christ comes, he will not have changed his identity or altered his purpose. He will be the very Christ who is proclaimed in the gospel. There are not two different Christs, one who comes in grace and mercy and one who comes in wrath and vengeance. There is only one Christ, and he will come in merciful judgment, for he is "the same yesterday and today and forever" (Heb. 13:8).

Christ has come, continues to come, and will come. He *has come* decisively in his incarnation, ministry, passion, and crucifixion. He has come in his resurrection from the dead and in the gift of the Holy Spirit at Pentecost. And he *continues to come* in the preaching and hearing of the Word, in the celebration of the sacraments, and in a still more hidden way, in the cries of the hungry and the abandoned. In all these different ways God in Christ continues to come to us. But, as the Creed declares, he also *will come* in a definitive, open, and conclusive way to judge the living and the dead.

Christ is appropriately named the one "who is to come" (Rev. 1:8) because God is ever and again the coming God. In the Christian theological tradition God has often been described as the one "necessary being." But God is more than "being,"[23] even "more than necessary being."[24] God is the living God, the acting God, the gifting God, the coming God. As such, God can never be exhaustively comprehended by us or treated as one of our possessions. God always comes to us in incomprehensible freedom and inexhaustible love. God's coming is always a gift, always new, always surprising. When Christ comes again, it too will be a coming far beyond our calculation and our merit.

When the church confesses "he will come," it does not comfort itself with a vague hope of an open future whose content is uncertain. Christians do not hope for *something*, perhaps the realization of a noble ideal or the fulfillment of a precious dream; instead, they hope in a very particular and concrete *someone*. Jesus Christ will come. It is for the coming of Christ and his reign that we stay awake, pray, and labor in love.

Knowledge that Jesus Christ is the coming one keeps our life in motion, prevents us from making peace with injustices of the present, makes us restless, reminds us that we seek a better homeland, prompts us to pray,

23. See Jean-Luc Marion, *God without Being* (Chicago: University of Chicago Press, 1991).
24. See Eberhard Jüngel, *God as the Mystery of the World* (Grand Rapids: Eerdmans, 1983), p. 24.

Your kingdom come.
Your will be done,
   on earth as it is in heaven.

(Matt. 6:10)

This restless expectancy of Christian life is not the same as mere activism or just keeping busy. Because it is directed to Christ, our hope can be patient as well as restless. It is a hope based not on our ability to move toward him but on his promise to come to us. Only he can bring us to our final goal, and only he can bring God's reign of justice, peace, and joy to all creation.

"To Judge"

We are now at the point where the gospel is found or lost in the interpretation of this affirmation of the Creed. We are also at the point where church divisions have occurred. Are we accepted by the astonishing grace of God that is received by faith, or must we prove ourselves acceptable by our works? Is our judge Christ the redeemer who has graciously taken the judgment we deserve upon himself, or is Christ our redeemer only up to the point when we must stand before him as judge on our own merits?

We have said that the exercise of God's judgment, as seen in Scripture, is fundamentally different from an act of retaliation and revenge. God's judgment establishes order and restores peace. God's judgment sets things right, serves the divine purpose of justice, reconciliation, and life in communion with God and with all the people of God. Just as God's thoughts and ways are not our thoughts and ways, so God's judgment is different from human judgment. In the words of Karl Barth, the one who will come to judge is the very one who has already given himself for the salvation of the world as "the judge judged in our place."[25] The coming of this judge does not inaugurate a reign of terror. Instead, his cross and resurrection have opened to all a new world of justice and reconciliation. When he comes to judge, he will make known to all the justice and peace established by his cross and resurrection. He will come to reign over all things and to confirm the final victory of justice over injustice, peace over war, and life over death. Because Christ is the coming judge, we can, as the Heidelberg Catechism says, expect his coming "with head held high."[26]

---

25. Barth, *Church Dogmatics* IV/1 (Edinburgh: T. & T. Clark, 1956), pp. 211-83.

26. Heidelberg Catechism, q. 52; see Barth, *Dogmatics in Outline* (London: SCM Press, 1949), p. 134.

Does this mean that the coming judgment is no longer real or serious? By no means. Judgment, we have emphasized, is an integral part of the work of salvation. That fact is writ large in the gospel story and is experienced to some extent in the life of every Christian. The question is only, what is the nature and purpose of this judgment? Is it only to condemn and destroy? Or is it to purify and prepare for the fulfillment of life in eternal communion with the triune God?

We are surely in line with the witness of Scripture and the spirit of the Creed if we think of the final judgment of Christ as the conclusive and universal shining of the light of Christ on us and the whole world. In the light of this universal revelation, this unobstructed radiance of the crucified and risen Christ, we will finally see and judge ourselves as we really are, sinners who are unworthy, utterly dependent on the grace of God embodied in Jesus Christ. The coming judgment of Christ will be this universal and definitive revelation of his and our own true identity.

We think further in line with Scripture and creed if we speak of the coming judgment that Christ will render as being according to the "law of Christ" (Gal. 6:2). By what judgment will he judge? His self-giving love to God and to others, consummated on the cross, is the measure of judgment than which there is none higher. His sacrificial love is the concrete fulfillment of the law, the ultimate basis of all justice and peace. In Christ our lives are renewed and gifted by that love, but we are also, as the judgment scene of Matthew 25:31-46 makes clear, judged by that love.

Finally, we are in line with the witness of Scripture and the spirit of the Creed when we say that the judgment of Christ is like a cleansing fire. Fire is, of course, a metaphor, as are all words about the end of time. But the metaphor points to a profound reality. There is much, both in our individual and our communal life, that needs to be exposed as empty and worthless. There is much that must simply be left behind. There are terrible injustices in every human life and in human history as a whole which must be exposed and to which a divine No must be said. They must be consigned to the fire. We are saved by grace alone, but the grace alone that saves is a strong and purifying grace.

According to Oliver O'Donovan, "Society cannot live without judgment."[27] That is true not only of every earthly society; it is also true of the society of God's people graciously chosen to participate in God's own eternal life. Our savior is also our judge who will bring final clarification of what can endure in our life and relationships, as individuals, as communities, as na-

27. Oliver O'Donovan, *The Desire of Nations: Rediscovering the Roots of Political Theology* (Cambridge: Cambridge University Press, 1996), p. 256.

tions, and what must be cast into utter darkness. Who can properly judge our violations and betrayals of God, of each other, and of ourselves; who can rightly judge what is "good" and well done but the one supreme judge who is also our merciful savior?

When the judge separates the wheat and the chaff, "Where will we stand, left or right?" asks Balthasar. "From what we know of ourselves, we can assume: most probably on both sides."[28] Does this mean that we are finally judged by our works? Is the doctrine of salvation by grace rather than by the works of the law turned upside down at the end? No, but the grace of God awaits our thankful response. God gives us gifts and opportunities for service, and we will be held accountable for our use of them.

"The Living and the Dead"

This phrase simply means everyone and everything. No one will be exempt. Men and women of every age, past, present, and future, good and bad, believers and unbelievers — all will be judged by Christ. So too will all nations, societies, cultures, and institutions, the church most certainly included. Jesus Christ will come to judge all, to reveal to all what remains hidden to the world, save as this is made known in the proclamation of Jesus Christ as Lord. As truly God, he unmasks our idols as illusions. As truly human, he shows to all what it means to be human as God intended.

Judgment means yes and no. But God's yes and no are not equally balanced. God does say no as well as yes, but he says no for the sake of his yes. Does this mean universal salvation *(apokatastasis)*? Origen apparently thought so. But Origen went too far, and his view was censored by the church. The Creed is silent on the question of universal salvation, and wisely so. Some passages of Scripture appear to teach a double outcome of history (e.g., Matt. 24:36-42). Other passages give reason to hope for the salvation of all (e.g., 1 Cor. 15:22). Scripture gives us a stern warning and a great hope.

As Barth contends, we have no right to offer guarantees of universal salvation. "No such postulate can be made even though we appeal to the cross and resurrection of Jesus Christ. Even though theological consistency might seem to lead our thoughts and utterances most clearly in this direction, we must not arrogate to ourselves that which can be given and received only as a free gift."[29]

---

28. Balthasar, *Credo*, p. 71.

29. Barth, *Church Dogmatics* IV/3/1, p. 477; Barth, *The Humanity of God* (Richmond: John Knox, 1960), pp. 61-62.

On the other hand, as Barth also teaches, we have no right to limit the free and sovereign grace of God. We may therefore hope and pray for the salvation of all.[30]

Confession that Christ will come to judge the living and the dead is of great practical significance for Christian life and the mission of the church. Christ is head of the church, and all its structures and practices must be subordinate to him. He is also ruler and judge of the world, even if now only in hidden form. The church's commitment to justice falters when the church is no longer convinced that the crucified and risen Christ is judge of the world; its commitment to peace becomes ambiguous when the church is uncertain whether the judge of the earth is the prince of peace or a vindictive warrior; its commitment to care for the earth diminishes when the church lacks conviction that the earth truly belongs to the Lord, who wills to share his wealth with all.

With "head held high" and with joy, we confess that Christ will come to judge the living and the dead. We know that nothing can separate us from the love of God in Christ Jesus our Lord. We must not disregard or toy with the warnings of Scripture and its serious calls to love God above all else and our neighbor as ourselves (Mark 12:28-31), to do justice, to love mercy, and to walk humbly with God (Mic. 6:8). But we fearlessly place our trust in the grace of Christ. In our prayer and hope we embrace all people and yearn for the renewal of all creation. For if the coming judge is none other than Jesus Christ, we may be sure that all will be judged in a manner far different, far more surprising, and far more merciful than we dare to believe or are able to imagine. The weight of sin is exceedingly great; the power of grace is greater still (cf. Rom. 5:20). "From there," from the sovereign grace of God, "he will come to judge the living and the dead."

---

30. *Church Dogmatics* IV/3/1, p. 478; cf. Hans Urs von Balthasar, *Theo-Drama: Theological Dramatic Theory,* vol. 5, *The Last Act* (San Francisco: Ignatius, 1998), pp. 316-21.

From There He Will Come to Judge the Living and the Dead

Romans 10:14

WILLIAM M. SHAND III

The story is a bit shopworn by now, but it bears another telling. A cardinal dashed into the pope's study and breathlessly announced, "Holy Father, I have good news and bad." The Holy Father looked up from his desk and asked for the good news first. "Our Lord has returned, and he wishes to speak with you on the phone right now." The pope was elated, but then remembered the cardinal's caveat about bad news. "What could possibly be bad news on such a day?" Came the cardinal's reply: "He's calling from Salt Lake City."

The gentle humor of this old story underscores the Christian's ambivalence about the great question of our Lord's return. We have lived through the end of the twentieth century and are making our way into the twenty-first. We smile at reports of people waiting in the desert somewhere in anticipation of our Lord's return, and yet week by week as we recite the creeds, we say we expect precisely the same thing.

Christians encounter this same ambivalence every year in the holy time of Advent. That season's themes of Scripture, hymns, and prayers point to the Lord's return. Only as a secondary theme are we called to prepare for Christmas. Meanwhile, the secular impulses all point in the direction of Yuletide, not the Lord's return, and come the twenty-sixth of December the world moves quickly on. It is not sleigh bells that we hear in December, but rather the summons to repentance, to watchfulness, and to preparation for that day "when he shall come again in his glorious majesty to judge both the quick

191

and the dead."[1] It is ironic, at the least, to note the disparity between the "solemn warnings" of Advent and the forced, seasonal gaiety of the secular world. The church is saying that we do expect our Lord's return, and that it is serious business getting ready for his return.

II

This raises a question: If this is indeed such serious business, why don't we do a better job of getting on with it? Is it because we don't really put much credence in this article of the faith any longer? We know that early Christians had to settle down for the "long haul," and perhaps in that accommodation were sown the seeds of embarrassment that Christ had not returned as he said. The "cooler" expectations between 1 Thessalonians and Romans suggest that even Saint Paul was not immune from this, although he is quite clear in the latter that "we will all stand before the judgment seat of God" (Rom. 14:10). Could it be that this article of the Creed is just impossible to affirm in our day and time?

Consider the history of the church's appropriation of this article. In the ancient cathedrals of Europe it was not uncommon to find scenes of the last judgment represented in sculpture and glass. The scenes depicted were often horrific, and fear was one of the primary reactions to the notion of judgment. Indeed, the last judgment was seen more as a threat than as good news of any kind. The passage of time made the reaction inevitable: fear subsided, to be replaced by neglect, tinged with embarrassment about an archaic doctrine. Go to the Cathedral of Saints Peter and Paul in Washington, D.C. The message is clear: Rather than a tympanum representing anything like a scene of judgment to put the visitor on notice, as it were, a splendidly wrought sculpture of the creation of Adam greets the visitor. High above the main altar Christ is shown in glory, but without a note of judgment. It is all very moving and majestic, but the message is not the same. It is as though the story of creation has no sequel.

To be honest, the church often sends a mixed message. While we affirm our belief in the Lord's return every time we say the Creed, we tend often to hide from the implications of those words, as though we are embarrassed by what his return would mean. And so we adopt a watered-down approach, talking about how Christ returns every time Christians pray together, or break bread together, or offer a cup of water in his name. To be sure, these are all blessings of the disciple's life, but the Creed asserts more.

1. The collect for the first Sunday of Advent, from the *Book of Common Prayer* (1979), p. 159.

Moreover, the world in which we live does not much like this kind of story. It is not just that there is talk of matters of faith; one would not expect the world to think much about those. Rather it is the spirit of our age, the idea of a "postmodern world," in which there are no universal truths, no "old verities," to borrow William Faulkner's great phrase. No story binds us together, and if no story, then no criteria on which any judgment can be made. We may lament the growing lack of biblical literacy in our culture — and lament it we should — but then we have to ask ourselves if we take seriously what the Bible tells us and the world. In the mountains of western North Carolina is an old highway used for years by people driving to their summer homes in the cooler climes. At one point a sharp and dangerous curve presents itself as the road wraps around a steep hill. On a rock is painted the one word "Repent." It is impossible to miss the warning, but one doubts that many on their way to their summer vacations bother to heed the warning. That is for those same types who sit out in the desert. The world won on that curve.

So neither the church nor the world seems to take seriously our Lord's return and our need to be ready to greet him. And yet . . . yet, we say these words week after week. Where is the good news in affirming that our Lord will return again? Is there something in this ancient truth that offers a word to the contemporary believer?

III

The key insight into discovering anew the meaning of this ancient hope lies in the opening words: "From there he shall come . . ." *From there:* From the heart and mind and eternal purposes of God. From the same source which called creation into being, the same source which caused Miriam to dance and sing on the safe eastern shores of the Red Sea, the same source which filled the night skies with the songs of angels, the same source which called a fearful Mary Magdalene by her name in a garden early on the first day of the week, the same source which set heads and hearts aflame in Jerusalem and then turned the world upside down. The promise and the hope that the Lord shall come again to judge us comes from that selfsame source, the heart and mind of God.

The very strangeness of the notion of our Lord's return forces us to re-think his role as judge. In recent years it has been fashionable to think in terms of "what would Jesus do?" That popular formula has found its way even onto key chains to hang around one's neck. While it is salutary to keep that sort of thing in mind, we have to admit it is presumptuous to think we would always — if ever — know the answer. One thing about our Lord was that he constantly surprised even those who thought they knew him best. "What manner of man is this?" they must have asked themselves more than just on the storm-tossed sea. So one ought to tread lightly in laying claim to knowledge of what Jesus would do. And nowhere is that more important than in the matter of judgment.

The old gospel hymn puts it best: "There is no place where earth's sorrows are more felt than up in heaven; there is no place where earth's failings have such kindly judgment given."[2] If this be true now, then does it not follow that at the last judgment, when he returns from the heart and mind of God, our Lord's judgment upon us will be on this same order? To be sure, we may be mixing metaphors a bit with this hymn, but the point is clear: God's judgment differs from ours as widely as the wideness of the sea. If an anthropomorphic image could be pressed, God sees things differently than do we. Is it not wise to assume that God's judgment, just as God's justice itself, is different both in quality and in substance from our own imperfect judgment? That is especially good news: the Lord who returns to judge us is the one who already understands, and understanding, has lived and died among us.

Call to mind *who* will come to be our judge. It is the Lord. There was once a state judge in a small, rural county in Maryland. He was a highly respected member of the community, and exerted no small amount of influence on the course of life there. At one and the same time he was called upon to render legal judgments in a court of law and also offer informal advice on the routine problems of life. People knew him and trusted him, in part because his family had been in that same county for three centuries. His own character was sterling, but it was probably because of the strong identity the residents could feel for him that their trust was so high. A "foreign" judge from another county might have been every bit as well versed in the law, but it is doubtful he would have been so highly regarded in that small county. Identifying with the judge himself made all the difference. The unknown author of Hebrews understood this: the one who is our judge is also our great high priest, and he is not "unable to sympathize with our weaknesses" (Heb. 4:15). So it is with the one who is our judge. It is not a matter just of divine jurisprudence, as it were, but of a judge who knows us better than we know ourselves.

So with the one who is to come from the heart and mind of God — he brings us promise and hope. The promise is written bold and consistently in every verse of the great symphony of Holy Scripture. Like the movements of that symphony, the Lord's return is treated with variations on that one great

---

2. Hymn 470, in *Hymnal 1982*, of the Episcopal Church.

theme, but always the same theme. In the time of Jesus himself, the people were on the "tiptoe of expectation," and sometimes their way of describing the Lord's return made it seem something not to be wished: "Pray that it may not be in winter!" Saint Mark warns. And yet these images and urgings are all set in the greater symphony of God's deliverance of the entire created order. That is the promise, and as a powerful hymn puts it, "God is working his purpose out as year succeeds to year."[3]

The church has failed to hold out the hope that our Lord's return portends as well. In the older burial liturgies the final commendation included this affirmation. At the powerfully symbolic moment at which earth is cast on the coffin, the officiating minister would commend the soul of the departed to almighty God "in sure and certain hope of the Resurrection of our Lord Jesus Christ, *at whose coming in glorious majesty to judge the world, the earth and the sea shall give up their dead; and the corruptible bodies of those who sleep in him shall be changed, and made like unto his own glorious body.*"[4] Those words are absent in newer burial liturgies. Whatever else may have changed, there is surely no sense of God's judgment and the hopeful changes it will create. Perhaps we are less confident of God's ability to change us than we were in generations past.

William Frey, the sometime Episcopal bishop of Colorado, is fond of saying that we have more future with God than we do past. We live "in sure and certain hope" of many things, one of which is that the Lord will return. Our future is secure in God, even as we await the Lord's return in judgment. It is not our own vindication that we seek, but rather the completion of that process which began in the heart of God and caused the morning stars to sing together at creation's dawn.

That process has not gone uninterrupted, however, and we Christians have an old-fashioned name for that interruption: the fall. Part of our hope for our Lord's return is the completion of that glorious process of the restoration of all of creation. Judgment reveals how far creation has to go. In fact, it is more accurate to say, judgment reveals the extraordinary lengths to which God's grace will flow for that re-creation to begin afresh. We can begin to measure the full extent of grace only when we begin to measure the depth of the fall.

As the nineteenth century yielded to the twentieth, the myth of progress dominated the thought of many intellectuals. And then came the bloody trenches of World War I, and progress was exposed as a false idol. Two de-

3. Hymn 534, in *Hymnal 1982*, of the Episcopal Church.
4. *Book of Common Prayer* (1928), p. 333.

cades later came the horrors of World War II, and evil took a human and obscene face. The century limped to its sorry conclusion with the killing fields of Cambodia and the gruesome tribal warfare of Africa. Then, not long into the new century, came the shocks of September 11, 2001. Where is the judgment of the wise and virtuous? Where is the judgment of the naive or the self-deluded? It is not just the existence of the fallen state of the natural order that reveals things are amiss; humanity has contributed to the story in myriad ways.

A patient goes to the doctor with a "fever of unknown origin." The doctor performs an examination and runs a few tests. When the data are all available, a diagnosis can be rendered, and a course of medical treatment can begin. Without the examination, however, little can be done for the patient. The Lord's return is akin to that examination, when what is wrong will be fully and definitively revealed. The fallen weakness of the whole creation and all God's creatures can then be addressed, and the restored creation will be more glorious than the first.

No one understood this more fully than Charles Wesley. Often overshadowed in the history books by his brother John, Charles was not only a faithful pastor, but a prodigious author of hymn texts. Among his most beloved is "Love Divine, All Loves Excelling." In the final stanza Wesley wrote of the sequel to judgment:

> Finish then thy new creation; pure and spotless let us be;
> let us see thy great salvation perfectly restored in thee:
> changed from glory into glory, till in heaven we take our place,
> till we cast our crowns before thee, lost in wonder, love, and praise.[5]

Wesley's understanding is just right: the new creation we are in Christ is finished, made perfect, but only in God's time. A bumper sticker on an old pickup truck read, "I ain't perfect! God ain't done with me yet." Deliberately quaint language hides profound good news — the promise and the hope that God will finish the new creation even in the likes of us. The Lord shall return not to judge us into condemnation, but to judge us into eternal life by his grace. It is God's judgment that finishes the new creation.

5. Hymn 657, in *Hymnal 1982*, of the Episcopal Church.

CHAPTER 11

I Believe in the Holy Spirit

Credo in Spiritum sanctum

WALTER R. BOUMAN

When the Spirit of truth comes, he will guide you into all the truth;
for he will not speak on his own, but will speak whatever he hears,
and he will declare to you the things that are to come. (John 16:13)

1. The doctrine of the Holy Spirit received modest attention in the history of the church.

Giving doctrinal attention to the topic of the Holy Spirit is challenging for at least two reasons. First, the frequent mention of the Holy Spirit in the textbooks of theology does not provide theologians with a model or tradition of topics and issues to address.[1] Second, this topic in the Apostles' Creed intersects almost all the other topics. Thus to speak about the Holy Spirit means that doctrinal organization will always be somewhat idiosyncratic, and that one must necessarily refer to nearly all the topics in the Creed.

The creeds themselves are of little assistance. The chief doctrinal controversy regarding the Holy Spirit has been the addition of the phrase "and the Son" *(filioque)* to procession "from the Father" in the text of the Nicene Creed by the Western Church. The proposal to add the phrase originated in Spain in the fifth century. It was strongly supported by Charlemagne; and ultimately

---

1. Carl Braaten and Robert Jenson called attention to the novelty of including a separate locus on "the Holy Spirit" in the preface of their *Christian Dogmatics*, vol. 1 (Philadelphia: Fortress, 1984), p. xix.

in 1014 it received papal approval to be officially included in the Creed.[2] It thereby became both occasion and cause of the great schism between the Eastern and Western Churches in 1054.

The Eastern Church resisted its inclusion because of its conviction that a creed formulated by an ecumenical council cannot be amended except by a subsequent ecumenical council. Most churches today agree with this concern.[3] Ted Peters argues that the addition of the *filioque* makes theological sense because it is an evangelical explication of the doctrine of the Holy Spirit; and it ties the Holy Spirit more closely to Christ.[4] Jürgen Moltmann insists that it is superfluous and probably tends toward subordinating the Spirit rather than confessing the Spirit as an equally reciprocal entity in the Trinity.[5] The argument does not affect the Apostles' Creed.[6]

Attention to the Holy Spirit has occurred chiefly in the many "charismatic movements" in Christian history. The first such movement precipitated one of the earliest schisms. Montanus, a Phrygian presbyter of the middle of the second century, sought to revive the intensity of the early church's experience of the Holy Spirit in the context of strong apocalyptic expectations of the return of Christ. Montanus opposed "both the decline in the [church's] eschatological hope and the rise of the monarchical episcopate."[7]

In the thirteenth century Joachim of Fiore awaited a dramatic outpouring of the Holy Spirit. He looked for an "age of the Holy Spirit" to follow the "age of the Father" which lasted forty-two generations from creation to the incarnation, and an "age of the Son" which lasted an equal number of generations from the birth of Jesus to Joachim's own time. Joachim believed the age of the Holy Spirit was about to come upon the church and give it a new (renewed) spiritual quality, a "resurrection" to new life.[8]

---

2. *Die Religion in Geschichte und Gegenwart*, 3rd ed., 4:1454.

3. Ted Peters, *God — the World's Future* (Minneapolis: Fortress, 2000), p. 261.

4. Peters, p. 262.

5. Jürgen Moltmann, *The Spirit of Life* (Minneapolis: Fortress, 1992), p. 306.

6. The brief discussion in J. N. D. Kelly, *Early Christian Creeds* (New York: David McKay Co., 1960), pp. 358-67, indicates why the addition was attractive to the Western Church. It arose because Augustine does not begin his doctrine of the Trinity with the Father but with the idea of the one simple essence of divinity with the three persons as derivative inner-trinitarian distinctions. Catherine Mowry LaCugna has argued that this has had the consequence of making the external or "economic" Trinity largely irrelevant to us (*God for Us: The Trinity and the Christian Life* [San Francisco: Harper Collins, 1991], pp. 4-17).

7. Jaroslav Pelikan, *The Emergence of the Catholic Tradition (100-600)*, vol. 1 of *The Christian Tradition* (Chicago: University of Chicago Press, 1971), p. 98.

8. Jaroslav Pelikan, *The Growth of Medieval Theology (600-1300)*, vol. 3 of *The Christian Tradition* (Chicago: University of Chicago Press, 1978), pp. 301-3.

The sixteenth century witnessed a fresh outburst of apocalyptic and charismatic fervor. Martin Luther's Wittenberg experienced the arrival of prophets from Zwickau in 1522. They claimed direct revelation from the Holy Spirit, a claim Luther resisted.[9] Luther called them *Schwärmer* (roughly translated, "enthusiasts") and saw them as dangerously linked with the movement led by Thomas Müntzer and the bloody Peasants' War.[10]

The charismatic movement of the twentieth century had three phases. An early phase began with revivals among the very poor in the black and white populations of the United States and led to the formation of Pentecostal denominations. A second phase, originating in 1960, took place in the middle and upper classes of most mainline denominations in the United States but did not result in the formation of any new denominations. The primary feature of both phases was attention to the gifts of the Holy Spirit, especially glossolalia and miraculous healing.[11] A third phase produced the rapid spread of Pentecostal churches in Latin America and Africa.[12] The main controversial issue in charismatic and Pentecostal movements has been whether, in contrast to giving new *insights*, the Holy Spirit continues to give individuals and the church new revelation. This controversy is not addressed in the Apostles' Creed, nor has it resulted in new creeds. Article V of the Lutheran Augsburg Confession responded to its sixteenth-century encounter by linking the Holy Spirit exclusively to the "means" of "the gospel and the sacraments."[13] The most fateful theological factor concerning the Holy Spirit occurred in the transition from the church's Jewish matrix to its Hellenistic context. It involved the church's growing surrender to Platonism, especially in the clash with gnosticism. This has been succinctly described by Moltmann.

> In the degree to which Christianity cut itself off from its Hebrew roots and acquired Hellenistic and Roman form, it lost its eschatological hope and surrendered its apocalyptic alternative to "this world" of violence and death. It merged into late antiquity's gnostic religion of redemption. . . . God's eternity now took the place of God's future, heaven re-

---

9. Regin Prenter, *Spiritus Creator* (Philadelphia: Muhlenberg, 1953), pp. 247-302.

10. Eric Gritsch, *Reformer without a Church: Thomas Muentzer* (Philadelphia: Fortress, 1967), pp. 185-89. Gritsch protests that Luther's condemnation was unfair.

11. Michael Hamilton, ed., *The Charismatic Movement* (Grand Rapids: Eerdmans, 1975), pp. 15-32 and 145-71.

12. Walter Hollenweger, *The Pentecostals* (Minneapolis: Augsburg, 1972), pp. 75-175.

13. *The Book of Concord*, ed. Robert Kolb and Timothy J. Wengert (Minneapolis: Fortress, 2000), pp. 40-41.

placed the coming kingdom, the spirit that redeems the soul from the body supplanted the Spirit as "the well of life," the immortality of the soul displaced the resurrection of the body, and the yearning for another world became a substitute for changing this one.[14]

Many of the issues raised by Moltmann must be addressed in any account of the doctrine of the Holy Spirit.

2. The Holy Spirit is confessed simply in the Apostles' Creed.

The Apostles' Creed does not identify the Spirit with more than the adjective "Holy," and that twice. The Holy Spirit is the power associated with the conception of Jesus; and faith in the Holy Spirit is confessed in the first phrase of the third article. The Nicene Creed has a modest paragraph about the Holy Spirit. The Holy Spirit is "the Lord and Life-giver, who proceeds from the Father [and the Son], who with the Father and the Son is worshiped and glorified, who has spoken by the prophets."[15]

The Holy Spirit is identified as "life-giver" (*zōopoion*), empowering human life (Gen. 2:7) as well as the resurrected life of Israel (Ezek. 37:7-14) and of Jesus (Rom. 1:4). The Holy Spirit is differentiated from the Father as one who proceeds (*ekporeuomenon*) from the Father. In the New Testament the Holy Spirit is also differentiated from Jesus, who both promises the Spirit (John 14:26) and is raised by the Spirit (Rom. 1:4). The Holy Spirit is not regarded as a creature because "to proceed from" is not the same as "to be created by," and because the Holy Spirit is worshiped (*sunproskunoumenon*) and glorified (*sundoxazomenon*) together with the Father and the Son.[16]

Finally, the Holy Spirit "has spoken through the prophets." The preexilic prophets of Israel do not claim to have been speaking under the impact of the *ruach* of YHWH.[17] But the exilic and postexilic prophets are replete with references to the Spirit. Here the words of the prophets are words of promise, God's promised future, including the words of Isaiah 61:1-2, which Jesus read in the Nazareth synagogue (Luke 4:17-19). The prophets do not predict

14. Moltmann, *The Spirit of Life*, p. 89.

15. This translation, based on the Greek text, is from *The Book of Concord*, p. 23; various other contemporary translations are identified on p. 21 n. 2.

16. The Western creed ascribed to Athanasius emphasizes the divinity of the Holy Spirit in the context of the Holy Trinity, but adds nothing else to the doctrinal teaching about the Holy Spirit.

17. Alasdair I. C. Heron, *The Holy Spirit* (Philadelphia: Westminster, 1983), pp. 14-17.

the future. They announce the future, and in so doing their word "*creates* the future."[18]

But none of this is in the Apostles' Creed. "It is obvious that we must not attempt to squeeze out of [this] creed the developed theology of the Spirit which commended itself to fourth-century orthodoxy."[19] We must, however, remember that behind this very simple formula, "I believe in the Holy Spirit," lies the trinitarian "ground plan" which Kelly says is "obstinately" present in the entire New Testament.[20]

The simple confession of faith in the Holy Spirit received no further elaboration. The only phrases added to the third article of the old Roman creed are *sanctorum communionem* ("communion of saints" or "communion of holy things")[21] and *et vitam aeternam* (and the life everlasting).[22] It is worth noting that the apparently random sequence of phrases which continue and complete the Creed — church, forgiveness of sins, resurrection of the body, and life eternal — are appropriately identified with the Holy Spirit.

The remainder of this chapter seeks to explicate the doctrine of the Holy Spirit in terms of six theses.

3. The Holy Spirit is the presence and harbinger of the eschaton.

"He will declare to you the things that are to come" (John 16:13). The chief task of a doctrine of the Holy Spirit is to recover the experience of the Holy Spirit as essentially eschatological in character in terms of the Jewish roots and eschatology of early Christianity. "Eschaton" means "end" in the sense of the goal or outcome or consummation of history. The earliest disciples of Jesus were convinced that this outcome of history had been disclosed proleptically in the resurrection of Jesus, that the hidden victory of God was already on the scene, that the messianic age had already begun, and that it would most certainly be consummated in the final revelation of the victory of God. Arland Hultgren states that from "the beginning of the Christian

---

18. Robert W. Jenson, "The Holy Spirit," in *Christian Dogmatics,* ed. Carl E. Braaten and Robert W. Jenson, vol. 2 (Philadelphia: Fortress, 1984), p. 112.

19. Kelly, p. 154.

20. Kelly, pp. 23-24.

21. The argument for the latter translation is made both by Werner Elert, *Abendmahl und Kirchengemeinschaft in der alten Kirche hauptsächlich des Ostens* (Berlin: Lutherisches Verlagshaus, 1954), pp. 5-16, and Stephen Benko, *The Meaning of Sanctorum Communio* (London: SCM Press, 1964), pp. 69-90.

22. Kelly, p. 369.

movement the presence and power of the Spirit were a matter of experience."
This signified "that a new age had dawned, the era of eschatological redemption, and that the old age had passed away."[23] The Pentecost narrative of Acts
2 is central.[24]

In the Pentecost narrative Peter quotes the words of Joel 2:28-32 to explain
the phenomenon of the multitude of languages which "amazed and astonished" the crowd that had gathered. There is one significant change in the
quotation. Joel begins the second section of his oracle with the phrase "then
afterward," that is, after the plague of locusts is gone, after the famine has
ended, after the return of fertility and the removal of shame, then follows the
promise of the Spirit. Peter introduces the quotation by substituting an eschatological phrase: "*In the last days* it will be, God declares, that I will pour
out my Spirit upon all flesh, and your sons and your daughters shall prophesy, and your young men shall see visions, and your old men shall dream
dreams. Even upon my slaves, both men and women, in those days I will pour
out my Spirit; and they shall prophesy." This is in anticipation "of the Lord's
great and glorious day" (Acts 2:17-20). Something radical and decisive has
happened. The last chapter of history has dawned.

This radical event comes to expression in 2 Corinthians 1:22, where Paul
states that God has given "his Spirit in our hearts as a *first installment*." The
Greek term is *arrabon*, and "first installment" as a translation gets it just
about right. It is like our term "down payment." Less helpful is the translation
"guarantee" in 2 Corinthians 5:5, and the translation "pledge of our inheritance" in Ephesians 1:13-14. "First installment" or "down payment" suggests
that one is to live as if one is already in possession of something. Having paid
the first installment, one gets title to the car and can drive it as if it were already owned, even though the final payment on the loan is forty-eight
months away. Having made the down payment, one can move into the house
and live as if it were already owned, even if the final payment on the loan is
twenty-five years in the future.

All of this has come about in the resurrection of Jesus, of which the disciples are witnesses. In the resurrection "God has made him both Lord and
Messiah, this Jesus whom you crucified" (Acts 2:36). This is Paul's "gospel,"
described in Romans 1:2-4: "concerning his Son, who was descended from
David according to the flesh and was declared to be Son of God with power

---

23. Arland Hultgren, *Christ and His Benefits* (Philadelphia: Fortress, 1987), pp. 32-36.

24. There is an excellent critical discussion of the Pentecost narrative in James D. G. Dunn,
Baptism in the Holy Spirit (London: SCM Press, 1970), chap. 4, pp. 38-54. See also James D. G.
Dunn, *Jesus and the Spirit* (Grand Rapids: Eerdmans, 1997), chap. 6, pp. 135-56.

according to the Spirit of holiness by resurrection from the dead, Jesus Christ our Lord." The resurrection of Jesus is not a resuscitation, which his contemporaries would have understood as the vindication of a righteous sufferer. Rather it is a profound eschatological event, the dawning of the messianic age. The disciples have been let in on the great "secret" of history. They know the identity of the Messiah, that is, the identity of the final judge. It is Jesus of Nazareth, the crucified Jew. What is more, they know the verdict. It is God's great "YES." "For the Son of God, Jesus Christ, whom we proclaimed among you, Silvanus and Timothy and I, was not 'Yes and No'; but in him it is always 'Yes.' For in him every one of God's promises is a 'Yes.' For this reason it is through him that we say the 'Amen,' to the glory of God" (2 Cor. 1:19-20). Of this eschatological YES the Holy Spirit is the down payment (1:22).

The old age is characterized by its bondage to the power of death. Its fear of the power of death drives it to be self-protective, and just so, oppressive. But if Christ, and not death, has the final say, then the new age, the messianic age, has indeed come; and the Holy Spirit is the down payment. "But if Christ is in you, though the body is dead because of sin, the Spirit is life because of righteousness. If the Spirit of him who raised Jesus from the dead dwells in you, he who raised Christ from the dead will give life to your mortal bodies also through his Spirit that dwells in you" (Rom. 8:10-11). There is more to do with life than to protect it. It can be offered into the service of God (12:1-2). For "we do not live to ourselves, and we do not die to ourselves. If we live, we live to the Lord, and if we die, we die to the Lord; so that, whether we live or whether we die, we are the Lord's" (14:7-8). All of this has to do with the eschatological reign of God "in the Holy Spirit" (14:17).

4. The historical Jesus is under the aegis of the Holy Spirit
as the eschatological Messiah.

All four Gospels signal that the Holy Spirit is the agent and sign of the new reality that has come in Jesus, the Messiah. This is the way in which the early church told the story of Jesus. The birth narratives in Matthew and Luke are told in terms of Jewish eschatology. The Holy Spirit is not "father" of Jesus. The narratives simply state that the conception and birth of Jesus are under the aegis of the Holy Spirit. Jesus' baptism is told as a messianic commissioning. The coming one proclaimed by John the Baptist will baptize with "the Holy Spirit and fire," symbols that are eschatological because they are messianic, and vice versa. The Holy Spirit accompanies/leads Jesus into the wilderness temptation of his messianic mission.

Jesus' mission is the announcement and embodiment of the reign of God. He engages in this mission anointed by the Spirit (Luke 4:18). In the power of the Spirit Jesus casts out the demons (Matt. 12:28). Jesus promises the Holy Spirit as the Father's answer to eschatological prayer (Luke 11:13) in a sequence of sayings which begins with the messianic prayer known as "the Lord's Prayer." "Jesus thought of himself as God's son and as anointed by the eschatological Spirit, because in prayer he experienced God as Father and in ministry he experienced a power to heal which he could only understand as the power of the end-time and an inspiration to proclaim a message which he could only understand as the gospel of the end-time."[25] Jesus instructs his disciples "through the Holy Spirit" in the postresurrection appearance narrated in Acts 1:2. He promises that the disciples "will be baptized with [or by] the Holy Spirit not many days from now" (1:5). They will be empowered by the Holy Spirit for their witness (1:8).

In the Gospel of John the Holy Spirit is another "advocate" (paraklētos), "to be with you forever" (John 14:16), the "Spirit of Truth" in contrast to the devil, who is "murderer" and "father of lies" (8:44). The promise of the Spirit is dependent upon Jesus' "going to the Father," a reference to the cross (16:7-11). The Spirit will lead them into all truth. This has a double significance. The Holy Spirit will be the "aha!" of insight as they remember and recall all that has taken place. And the Holy Spirit will keep them focused on the last chapter of history as they thread their way through the maze of unfolding history. Led by the Holy Spirit, they will participate in history differently and thus change the course of history. They will understand the cross and resurrection as eschatological salvation (16:13-15). The promise of the Spirit is fulfilled in the resurrection appearances and is associated with the forgiveness of sins, that is, the new eschatological possibilities grounded in the resurrection (20:19-23). The empowering Spirit is the way Jesus is present to the disciples after the ascension. He does not ascend out of the world, but ahead of the world.[26]

5. As the Lord and giver of life, the Holy Spirit confers authentic freedom.

The Holy Spirit confers on the church the freedom of the gospel. "Where the Spirit of the Lord is, there is freedom" (2 Cor. 3:17). As the harbinger of the

---

25. Dunn, *Jesus and the Spirit*, p. 67.

26. Jürgen Moltmann, *The Trinity and the Kingdom* (San Francisco: Harper and Row, 1981), pp. 88-90.

eschaton, the Holy Spirit is confessed as the "Lord and giver of life" in the Nicene Creed. Life is about the power of the future. "Only he who has a future is in possession of power."[27] Because of his resurrection from death to life, Jesus not only has the absolute power of the future. He confers that power of the future on the church in the gift of the Holy Spirit. The Holy Spirit means life, that is, the possibility of the future, and therefore the Holy Spirit means authentic freedom. "A spirit is simply a person, insofar as the person is present in other lives to open new possibilities there; thus a synonym for 'spirit' is 'freedom.' God the Spirit is God's freeing Presence, for and in himself and around and among us."[28]

Paul understood both gospel and church in terms of the blessing of and covenant with Abraham (Rom. 4). The blessing and promise to Abraham was that "in you all the families of the earth shall be blessed" (Gen. 12:3; cf. 22:18), a blessing that was universal in its vision. In terms of the Abrahamic covenant the confession of Jesus as Messiah meant that this universal vision had come to fruition, that Gentiles were to be grafted on to the "olive tree" of Israel (Rom. 11:17). In the gospel the Gentiles experienced a freedom described by Paul as freedom from the Law. "But if you are led by the Spirit, you are not subject to the law" (Gal. 5:18). The freedom from the Law, that is, freedom from obedience to the commandments of the Torah and especially from the requirement of circumcision for male converts, was the most controversial and far-reaching decision of the early church (Acts 15:1-35; cf. Galatians).

But the freedom of the Holy Spirit is not the freedom of autonomy, in which we are a law unto ourselves. Nor is it the freedom of solitude, in which we want nothing so much as to be left alone by others. Rather, it is the freedom experienced and expressed in terms of what Moltmann calls "sociality." "I am free and feel free when I am respected and accepted by other people, and when I for my part respect and accept other people too. . . . Then the other person is no longer the limitation of my freedom, but its extension."[29] Thus the freedom conferred by the Holy Spirit is the freedom of the church to be for the world as God in Christ is free for the world. This alone is authentic freedom. This is the freedom Martin Luther describes in his great Reformation treatise, *On the Freedom of the Christian,* which explicated two paradoxical theses: "The Christian is a perfectly free lord of all, subject to none." "The

27. Wolfhart Pannenberg, *Theology and the Kingdom of God* (Philadelphia: Westminster, 1969), p. 56.

28. Robert Jenson, *A Large Catechism* (Delhi, N.Y.: American Lutheran Publicity Bureau, 1991), p. 28.

29. Moltmann, *The Spirit of Life,* p. 118.

Christian is a perfectly dutiful servant of all, subject to all."[30] Only one who receives authentic freedom from the Holy Spirit is able to express that freedom in authentic servanthood.

6. The Holy Spirit is the dynamic of the church
which is called to anticipate the reign of God.

The term "Holy" as the sole descriptive term for the Spirit is itself theologically significant. In contemporary culture the term "spirit" is used to describe the dynamic of a community. We recognize the presence or absence of "team spirit" and the menace of "mob spirit." The focus in such a way of speaking and thinking is on the *quality* of the community, on whether the "spirit" displayed is good or evil, holy or unholy. The "spirit" is operative in and through the community. What Christians mean by saying that the "holy" Spirit is operative in and through a community has at least minimally to do with whether the impact and the dynamic of a community is constructive or destructive, deadly or life-giving.

"Holy" thus identifies the divine in contrast to and in conflict with the demonic. It means being set apart for God's purposes instead of being in the service of the powers of death. This takes us directly into the thought world of Paul. His "alternative realms of reality" have been often noted.[31] Among others, they include light and darkness, faith and works, life and death, and for this topic, flesh and Spirit (Rom. 8:11-27).[32] "Flesh" in Paul's antithesis is existence that refuses to acknowledge or even rejects the new reality present in Jesus, the Christ. "Spirit" is life in that new reality.

The church is the continued mission of Jesus. Luke's Acts and the epistles do not understand the church as the community *after* Jesus, but as the community *of and under* Jesus, the community in and through which Jesus continues to be present and to engage in his mission. Jesus is experienced not in the diminishing presence as a memory, but as the intensified presence of one who comes in the eschatological Spirit, as the one who comes not from the past but from the final future of the victory of God.[33] The risen Jesus sends his disciples "as the Father has sent [him]" (John 20:21). When Jesus confers the Holy Spirit, it empowers the church to enact the eschatological verdict of

---

30. Martin Luther, "The Freedom of the Christian," in *Luther's Works*, American ed., vol. 31 (Philadelphia: Muhlenberg, 1957), p. 344.

31. Heron, p. 45.

32. See the excellent analysis of Rom. 8 in Jenson, "The Holy Spirit," p. 118.

33. Jenson, "The Holy Spirit," p. 145.

Jesus as the forgiveness of sins (John 20:22-23; Acts 2:38). When the church is persecuted, it is Jesus who is persecuted (Acts 9:5). The church is the "body of Christ" and is set apart by the eschatological meal to embody Jesus' own mission to the poor (1 Cor. 11:17-26, esp. v. 22).

This calling and mission of the church means that the Holy Spirit of Christ is at the same time the Holy Spirit of the church. The church's consciousness of being community is always associated with the Holy Spirit (Acts 2:42; 1 Cor. 12:12-13). The unity of the church, the unity to which the church is called, is "the unity of the Spirit in the bond of peace. There is one body and one Spirit" (Eph. 4:3-4).

7. The Holy Spirit gives the church its institutional structures and ethic.

Because the Holy Spirit is the "down payment" on the reign of God, the Holy Spirit animates the church as the community that anticipates the coming reign of God in its membership, its rituals, its leadership, its life, and its witness. Under the dynamic of the Holy Spirit the church is called to anticipate the reign of God by its openness to the full variety of human being. The Spirit-given oneness of the church is to be a sign of the eventual oneness of all of humanity. The church as the anticipation of the reign of God includes persons of every race, nation, ethnic group, of every time in human history, of every age group and intellectual ability, of every economic and social class. "There is no longer Jew or Greek, there is no longer slave or free, there is no longer male and female; for all of you are one in Christ Jesus. And if you belong to Christ, then you are Abraham's offspring, heirs according to the promise" (Gal. 3:28-29; cf. Col. 3:11). "For in the one Spirit we were all baptized into one body — Jews or Greeks, slaves or free — and we were all made to drink of one Spirit" (1 Cor. 12:13). When death, the last enemy, is destroyed, then God will be everything in everyone, "all in all" (15:26-28).

Like Israel in the wilderness, all the church is to eat "the same *spiritual* food" and drink "the same *spiritual* drink" (10:3-4). The church's Eucharist is the meal which anticipates the eschatological messianic banquet. The prophets of the exile, especially Deutero-Isaiah, link food and drink with God's future salvation (Isa. 48:21 and 49:9-10). The Isaianic apocalypse is especially important. "It speaks of a future feast for *all peoples,* in a context of the *abolition of death* and *a day of salvation and rejoicing.*"[34] Following the exile, the meal motif in relation to messianic expectation intensifies. Jesus' parables

---

34. Geoffrey Wainwright, *Eucharist and Eschatology* (London: Epworth, 1971), p. 21.

and sayings, his table collegiality with "sinners" and his feeding of the multitudes play into this expectation. It culminates in his promise at the last meal before his crucifixion. "I tell you, I will never again drink of the fruit of the vine until that day when I drink it new in the kingdom of God" (Mark 14:25 and par.). In the wake of the resurrection meals, the "breaking of bread" becomes the ritual by which the disciples of Jesus are identified as the eschatological messianic community because they are anticipating the eschatological messianic banquet.[35] Jesus comes to the meal from the eschatological *future*, and therefore his coming is through and by means of the invocation of the eschatological Holy Spirit.[36]

The leadership of the church is given by the Spirit (1 Cor. 12:4-11). Women are to share equally with men in leadership as a sign of the Holy Spirit's eschatological presence. The Pentecost narrative states that in the outpouring of the Holy Spirit women as well as men will be prophets (Acts 2:17-18), and that is how they functioned (Acts 21:9; 1 Cor. 11:5). Junia was one of the apostles (Rom. 16:7) who shared Paul's imprisonment and was a disciple before Paul himself became one. Phoebe was a deacon (16:1). Prisca was a missionary leader and coleader with her husband of "the church in their house" (1 Cor. 16:19). Euodia and Syntyche are leaders in the church of Philippi and may be among the "bishops and deacons" who are addressed in Philippians 1:1. When women and men share leadership in the church, the church is both obedient in receiving the gifts of the Holy Spirit and faithful to its calling to anticipate the eschatological reign of God.[37]

Because Jesus' mission was to announce, embody, and enact the reign of God, the church is called to serve the reign of God in its ethic.[38] The same eschatological Spirit at work in the historical Jesus is now at work in the church. The life of the disciples is described as the "fruit of the Spirit." "Live by the Spirit, I say, and do not gratify the desires of the flesh. . . . The fruit of the Spirit is love, joy, peace, patience, kindness, generosity, faithfulness, gentleness, and self-control. . . . If we live by the Spirit, let us also be guided by the Spirit. Let us not become conceited, competing against one another, envying one another.

---

35. Joachim Jeremias, *The Eucharistic Words of Jesus* (Philadelphia: Fortress, 1966), p. 120. See also Robert Jenson, "The Means of Grace," in *Christian Dogmatics*, 2:344-49.

36. John Calvin, *Institutes of the Christian Religion* (1559) (London: James Clarke and Co., 1953), 4.17.10, pp. 563-64.

37. Ute E. Eisen, *Women Officeholders in Early Christianity* (Collegeville, Minn.: Liturgical Press, 2000), pp. 47-49, 116-42, 199-216; Antoinette Clark Wire, *The Corinthian Women Prophets: A Reconstruction through Paul's Rhetoric* (Minneapolis: Fortress, 1990), pp. 135-58.

38. Paul Jersild, *Spirit Ethics: Scripture and the Moral Life* (Minneapolis: Fortress, 2000), pp. 85-106.

My friends, if anyone is detected in a transgression, you who have received the Spirit should restore such a one in a spirit of gentleness" (Gal. 5:16–6:1).

Paul affirms the authenticity of the Spirit's more spectacular gifts, the "gifts of healing," "the working of miracles," "various kinds of tongues," and "the interpretation of tongues" (1 Cor. 12:9-10). But these are not to be regarded as greater than other gifts of the Spirit. And indeed, the point of Paul's whole discussion is to show "a still more excellent way" (12:31), the way of that love which "bears all things, believes all things, hopes all things, endures all things" (13:7). Paul urges the Corinthians to "pursue love and strive for the spiritual gifts," and especially the gift of intelligible proclamation (14:1-33). The presence of the Holy Spirit is thus evident in the lives which engage in mutual care and commitment. The Spirit is also evident in the church's concern for the good of the world. "A primary task of the church in relation to the social order is to articulate its vision concerning the purposes of God and what those purposes mean for human life and destiny."[39] This vision comes to expression in Jesus' message of the reign of God, a message that belongs essentially to an ethics of the Spirit.

8. The Holy Spirit is one of the "persons" of the Holy Trinity together with Jesus and his Father.

The Holy Spirit is the bond of unity in the Holy Trinity. The Holy Spirit animates the creation of the Father and encompasses the messianic mission of the Son. The Holy Spirit drives the reign of God, the will of the Father embodied in the history of the Son, toward its consummation. The Holy Spirit gives power and quality to the church, the community created by the Father's covenant and called to be the body of the Messiah Son. There are two trinitarian issues. The first is how the Spirit participates in the vulnerable suffering of the Trinity. The second is the personhood of the Spirit.

The Father suffers as the one who gives the Son (Rom. 8:32), and the Son suffers in giving himself into obedience to the mission he shares with the Father (John 18:11). But there is no mention of the Holy Spirit's participation in the suffering and self-offering of Jesus. It can be conceived in this way. The Spirit is life and freedom. The cross is the "hour" of the powers of death and sin (Luke 22:53). The Spirit suffers because this "hour" which negates life and freedom must be endured. But in enduring death, the Life-giver overcomes it and gives Jesus the victory.

39. Jersild, p. 101.

We have no difficulty conceiving of the personhood of Jesus, the Christ, who is identified as the "son" of the Father in the Apostles' Creed. His historical personhood receives ample content in the Gospels of the New Testament. We have little difficulty conceiving of the personhood of the one whom Jesus addressed as "Abba," Father, whose mission Jesus shares, whose will Jesus articulates and obeys. But we have difficulty conceiving of the personhood of the Holy Spirit.[40]

Jürgen Moltmann argues that we must not bring our conceptions of personhood to the Holy Spirit. Rather we must ask what qualities and actions are identified with the Holy Spirit and derive our confession of the Spirit's personhood from these qualities and actions. Moltmann believes personhood for the Holy Spirit derives from the Spirit's capacity for self-communication, the Spirit's sociality in relationships, and the Spirit's giving of life to all created being. He proposes the following definition of the Spirit's personhood: "The personhood of God the Holy Spirit is the loving, self-communicating, out-streaming and out-pouring presence of the eternal divine life of the triune God."[41]

The Latin terms, *substantia* for the divinity the persons share and *persona* for the individuality of the Father, the Son, and the Holy Spirit, seem to have been supplied by Tertullian. But the term *persona* came from the world of the theater, where it meant the "role" or "identity" assumed by an actor. It led easily to the modalism against which Western theology has always had to struggle. The equivalent Greek terms were *ousia* and *hypostasis*. Pelikan claims it was actually Tertullian's contending for the divinity of the Holy Spirit that was the most influential impetus for the eventual definition of the trinitarian dogma.[42]

The Augsburg Confession of 1530, claiming patristic warrant, defines "person" as *das selbs bestehet* (that which exists by itself) in the German text, and *quod proprie subsistit* (that which subsists in itself) in the Latin text.[43] Both definitions conceive of "person" in terms of what we today mean by a being capable of functioning as the independent intentional subject of an action. This is helpful because it is an expression of the "Rahner Rule" that is influential in contemporary trinitarian theological thinking. Karl Rahner was the Jesuit theologian who stated that the actions of the "persons" in the universe (the "economic" Trinity) are what allow us to posit the distinctions of

---

40. Joseph Haroutunian, "Spirit, Holy Spirit, Spiritism," in *Dictionary of Christian Theology,* ed. Alan Richardson (Philadelphia: Westminster, 1969), p. 319.

41. Moltmann, *The Spirit of Life,* p. 289.

42. Pelikan, *Emergence,* pp. 211-18.

43. *The Book of Concord,* pp. 36-37.

the "persons" within the divine being in which the actions are grounded (the "immanent" Trinity). Moltmann, Catherine Mowry LaCugna, and Robert Jenson are the most consistent in applying the "rule." Jenson refers to the "persons" as "identities," so that there are distinguishable "identities" in the triune God, but a single subject of the actions, a position he shares with Eberhard Jüngel and Wolfhart Pannenberg.[44]

A more helpful definition of "person" is "the intentional subject of an action." In the life of the Trinity the persons are *interdependent* instead of independent. This yields the following trinitarian formula: Jesus is the fully intentional subject of his eschatological messianic mission in mutual interdependence with his Father and the Holy Spirit. The Father of Jesus is the fully intentional subject of unoriginate creativity which will be consummated in the eschatological "new heavens and new earth" in mutual interdependence with the Son and the Holy Spirit. The eschatological Holy Spirit is the fully intentional subject of the life which animates the universe, which functions in history as the reign of God, and which will triumph in the outcome of history, in mutual interdependence with the Son and his Father.

The oneness of God is a reference to God's uniqueness. That is the meaning of Israel's Shema, "Hear, O Israel, the Lord our God, the Lord is one" (Deut. 6:4). This uniqueness is unconditionally evangelical because the revelation of God in the history of Israel and in its messiah, Jesus, is that God is uniquely forgiving, merciful, compassionate (Hos. 11:8-9; Rom. 11:33-36; Matt. 20:1-11). This uniqueness is identical with the uniqueness of the gospel. The Trinity is the story we must tell about God because the gospel is true.

---

44. All these views are ably described by Ted Peters, *God as Trinity* (Louisville: Westminster/John Knox, 1993), pp. 90-142.

I Believe in the Holy Spirit

Acts 2:1, 4; 2 Corinthians 3:17-18

WM. C. TURNER

On the Day of Pentecost the Jews commemorated the giving of the law at Sinai. There God constituted them as a people. They stood before the mountain as the Lord thundered from the flames, entering into covenant with them, making them a peculiar treasure, a kingdom of priests, and a holy nation. At Pentecost, fifty days following the resurrection of Jesus, that same God created a new Israel, baptizing those gathered in the upper room with the Holy Ghost and fire, seizing their tongues to reverse the curse of Babel, and making them witnesses who could go into all the world.

What a day, what an event, what a marvelous manifestation of power! This is the birthday of the church! The disciples could never be the same: their fear gave way to faith; their disunity dissolved into unity; their cowardice passed over into courage. By a great, powerful, and mysterious working, they were transformed, given new hearts, and their spirits were made obedient to the risen Christ.

Peter emerged as the chief spokesman, and with John by his side many mighty works were done. But at the center of the saga was the divine person who supplied the power for new speech, bold witness, and faithfulness in the face of death. This divine person is none other than the Holy Ghost, the Spirit of the living God, the Spirit of holiness who raised Jesus from the dead, the Spirit of Christ. And so I put the question on this occasion, who is this divine person? Who is the Spirit?

By words of the ancient creeds, by speech so technical our tongues could become tied, we make the good confession concerning the Spirit, who is the

Lord and Giver of life, who proceeds from the Father, and who with the Father and Son is to be worshiped and glorified, who spoke by the prophets. All who have been moved to confess that Jesus is Lord know the presence of this divine person to some degree. Except by the Spirit no one can confess that Jesus is Lord.

It is utterly important that we ask and ponder this question. So easily we can fasten upon a particular work of the Spirit and assume we know the person. Indeed, countless battles in the church rage to this day over this mistake. As divine person the Spirit is author of and in possession of all the Spirit's works.

Who opened your ears so that after countless times of indifferent listening you finally heard the good news of salvation? Who persuaded you after years of shallow living that there is a deeper knowledge of God and a richer, more intimate communion available to believers? Who supplied grace for your last trial, the consolation for the deepest heartache, the assurance in your weakest hour? Any who have communion with God do so by the Spirit's power. Indeed, to be a child of God we must be led by the Spirit. Accordingly, we do well to ask and seek for knowledge concerning this marvelous and mysterious person.

The Spirit is at once so familiar and so strange. The Spirit is as close to us as our breath, and as mysterious as life itself; as near as our walking, as far removed as the knowledge of bodily mobility. Intimately part of all we do yet utterly defiant of our ability to make precise description, the Spirit is as real as our body yet resistant to attempts to make our knowledge rational.

Because we cannot reduce the Spirit to our rational frames, some are sometimes a bit "standoffish" when it comes to this divine person on whom we utterly rely. I mean, when the Spirit moves upon us and works within us, we just may not be in control. But that is the purpose of God precisely: to take us out of control. As a race (the human race) we have proved our inability to produce worthwhile results when we are in control. Do we need more evidence than recorded history? Look at the societies we control, the lives we rule and ruin, the arrangements we determine. Thank God for the Spirit, who is given to take control.

Failing to speak fluently concerning the Spirit, we resort to hints and stammers. You have heard it: while they were singing that song I felt something run all up and down my back . . . or when the altar call was made it felt like something was yanking me from my seat. Recall the song "Something got a hold of . . . I went to the meeting one night and my heart was not right. . . ." No, it wasn't something. A divine person made a visit. That person is the Holy Spirit coming to take control, and to make us obedient to Christ.

213

Who is the Spirit? The Spirit is the very breath of God, proceeding from the depths of the Eternal One who exists before creation. Mysterious like the wind that comes and goes, the Spirit's very nature is to move. Unlike stale air, the Spirit is constantly in motion. Unlike stagnant water, the Spirit gives purity through ceaseless motion. The Spirit gives life, vitality, refreshment. Where the Spirit is present the dull moments do not last, the cloudy day passes away, and the gloom gives way to joy. Where the Spirit abides, shackles are loosed, broken chords vibrate, burdened hearts are lifted, battered bodies are healed, the perishing ones are rescued, and liberty becomes the law.

Not limited to merely psychological projections, the Spirit moves us out of ourselves into the communion God is creating, and connects us with one another as joints bring the members of the body into its unity. The Spirit is not in every feeling we can't explain, in every dream we remember, in every impulse for which we want authority.

The Spirit is not to be turned into a cipher (a category with no substance) that we use to mask our mistakes, to tidy up our ignorance, to cover our fears. No, the Spirit brings us into the unity of the faith, the full stature of who we are in Christ, the perfect obedience God has willed for us. By the Spirit we live in communion with God and all others who are in God.

The Spirit is not "part of God" — as though God could be divided into segments. No, with the Spirit we have come full face and been apprehended by the depth of the mystery. In some ways the Spirit is more difficult to apprehend than the Father or the Son; then again, we are fully dependent on revelation for all knowledge of God. If we are not careful we think the mystery of the Father and the Son has been disclosed because we are familiar with the corresponding social roles. But God's ways are as far above us as the heavens are above the earth, and we completely miss the depth of the revelation if all we can see is the earthly counterpart. With the Spirit, however, there is no shortcut: we must utterly rely on the revelation for our knowledge.

As the Spirit is not part of God, neither is the Spirit third in rank. No, the Spirit is the breath, the life, going forth within God. The Spirit is God going forth giving life to the creation, filling the human creature with the divine image and the capacity to return glory to the Father. Since God is without parts, the Spirit is fully divine, and because of that the Spirit can restore us to communion with the Creator. Like wind and running water, the Spirit is ever moving us out of our self into communion with others in whom the Spirit dwells. Like fire, the Spirit keeps us purified, empowered, and energized. Possessing all knowledge, the Spirit keeps us from being ignorant in the things of God. It is by the Spirit that we are led into the truth — all truth.

See the work of the Spirit in the Son! Within the womb of Mary the Spirit fashioned the body of obedience. At the waters of Jordan the Spirit descended like a dove, to give divine approbation, while the Father spoke approval. In the Spirit the ministry of the Lord Jesus was unfolded. Through the eternal Spirit the Son offered himself without spot unto God. This shows what the Spirit desires to do within us.

The Spirit is the author of worship, and without divine authorship the human effort is feeble at best, and obnoxious at worst. When the heavenly dove is not fluttering in the congregation, everything is a drag: you have to beg for praise, cajole those present into meaningful involvement, and barricade the door to prevent exiting. But when the dove is present, we enter the gates with thanksgiving and come into the courts with praise. Time is nothing but a number or the movement of the hands on the clock. Without the Spirit singing is merely noise; with the Spirit it is a joyful noise. Without the Spirit preaching is a boring talk; with the Spirit it is the life-giving word.

Remove the Spirit and salvation is no more than self-improvement, human willpower, positive thinking, humanistic optimism. In Holiness, Pentecostal, and charismatic circles much emphasis is placed on Spirit baptism and the Spirit's gifts. This arose in large measure to the neglect of the Spirit's work to impart power and gifts to believers and to the church. But another form of neglect can arise when excessive attention is drawn to the work or the gift without adequate attention to the divine person.

The Spirit regenerates, creating a new person in Christ; the Spirit sanctifies, teaching our members to obey the new law of our renewed mind. In baptism the Spirit who regenerates and sanctifies is released in the believer — without resistance or impediment — to take control and perform all that is within the will of God. This is the summary of true liberty: it is the procession of the Spirit through the believer, into the body of Christ that is sent forth into the world that is being transfigured as the home of God.

For the ministry of the Messiah and those he called, the Spirit is the one who leads and empowers the assault against the principalities and the strongholds. As the Lord promised, the Spirit is the one who prosecutes to seek the conviction and execute the sentence against those found in rebellion against God. The tension is abundantly manifest within the ministry of Christ. Immediately following his baptism and anointing, the challenge comes in the wilderness. Not an emissary but Satan the prince comes to sidetrack the mission. With these temptations failing, the demon host arranges itself in lines of battle. The testimony of the Gospels is that they recognize in the one anointed with the Spirit a superior foe, and they cry foul, suggesting that their torment has begun before time.

Jesus insists that the kingdom has come in power, in that by the Spirit of

God the demons are cast out. What's more, he sternly warns those who would discredit this mighty work, saying it is by the power of the devil rather than by the power of the Spirit. The mighty acts show that the strong man has been bound that his kingdom may be plundered. When the disciples went forth to anoint and heal the sick and preach the gospel of the kingdom, their reports of victory were met with the Lord's response that he saw Satan fall like lightning from heaven.

In setting the oppressed free the Spirit leads the attack. The struggle is not against flesh and blood. Figures move to and fro in the scenes of the Gospel to tempt the master. Pharisees, Sadducees, and Roman soldiers appear to be the culprits, but the witnesses would have us know that is the principalities who arrayed themselves against the Lord of glory. In their view their kingdom had come under attack. This attitude is made clear where the demons are dislodged from their abode in the man who is possessed by a legion of them, and they request permission to enter the swine. Even more telling is the lesson concerning how the house is cleared of one demon and left empty. Returning to the house he calls his, the demon goes out to find seven other companions. When they all possess the house, the later condition is worse than the former.

The battle waged for the liberation of persons and communities is spiritual. Evidence of the battle appears in the objective realm in social, economic, cultural, and political manifestations. We are not wrestling against flesh and blood, but against powers, principalities, against the rulers of this present darkness, according to the witness of Ephesians. Drugs, sex, violence, warfare, racism, sexism, and a host of other isms take on a historical (a human) face. But we underestimate the battle and do ourselves and our generation a disservice if we attack only the faces or the persons we see involved; they are victims too. We need the whole armor of God and to pray in the power of the Spirit.

A word is in order here, lest we take on the mean spirit of some political and religious radicals. The church can ill afford to embrace callous and fascist attitudes in the wake of present cultural upheavals. Disgusted though we may be at the violence among us, believers must resist vigilante justice. Fearful though we may be of AIDS, we must see in victims those on whom the Lord has compassion, knowing what we do to the least among us we do to the Lord. Our moral preferences notwithstanding, we must recall whom Jesus befriended. Those we are inclined to fear or regard as enemies are victims — sometimes in the worst sense of the term.

Here is the genius of the Spirit as giver of liberty: the Spirit attacks the principle of evil — the principalities and the strongholds. They know the Spirit and those in whom the Spirit dwells as their mortal enemy. The root of evil is the deliberating will that ponders whether to obey God or to attempt to be God. It is rebellion in the cosmos and the creation that exchanges the place of the creature with that of the Creator, and the consequence is throwing the whole creation into chaos. Specific forms of evil from which we need liberation (deliverance) are manifestations of this primary disorientation.

The work of the Spirit in unleashing the work of liberation, which shall transfigure all creation, initiates inward movement toward God. The nature of this work corresponds to a maternal dimension captured in the Johannine and Pauline image of creation groaning with the pains of labor. Here it is most helpful to reflect on the Spirit with feminine gender images. In this image we see God the Spirit operating umbilically within the creation to apply corrective, restorative virtue gained through the atoning work of Christ.

Like a cosmic intravenous supply, the Spirit inserts medicine into an ailing creation. Not a lethal but a healing injection is supplied. The resurrection of Jesus from the dead was the first convulsion of the sick creation receiving its cure. The gift of the Spirit in the establishment of the church soon followed. The flow and the responses continue with every soul that is regenerated, sanctified, filled with the Spirit, healed, delivered, or sent forth into ministry. The healing, the liberation of creation is the end to which the Spirit is bringing all who are caught in this pneumatological flow. Satan, we're going to tear your kingdom down.

It is no accident that the church is experiencing a fresh outpouring of the Spirit in our day. Where the Spirit of the Lord is, there is liberty; where there is freedom and welcome for the Spirit, shackles are broken. Churches bound by racism and sexism are cured when diseased hearts and minds are treated by the Spirit's powerful flow. Incorrigible lives wrecked and warped by the deadly venom of this culture are resurrected as were bones in the valley of Ezekiel's vision.

To use another image from Ezekiel: it is like healing water flowing from under the throne of God in the temple. In a vision he saw water flowing, into which he was invited to enter. It first reached his ankles, then his knees and waist. Finally it became a river in which a man could swim. The river moved through the desert, on its way to the sea. But wherever the river made contact with the desert, the land was healed. Alongside the river, wasteland was turned into fertile fields.

The Spirit as intravenous flow touches the person inwardly. That is, the Spirit works to restore the image given by God in creation. This involves reconnection between the soul and the one in whose light it glows. Identity streams from the divine light rather than the tarnished valuations of the culture or the circumstances. This is the first movement in liberty: breaking the grip on the mind that institutes the lies of false consciousness, without which a human being cannot be victimized by the vices that plague the culture. The flaw upon which the forces of oppression and possession depend is healed, enabling persons to say no to the lies of racists, drug lords, and all others who rely on the oppressed for their gain.

The apostle likens the scene of this great work of liberty to turning to the Lord and having a veil removed. The similitude is that of the children of Israel awaiting the return of Moses from the mountain where the law was given. They played in the darkness of the valley, creating an image of Baal. When Moses descended with the tables of the law, the glory upon him was so great they shielded their faces, and their minds were blinded. The image is of turning full face to behold the Lord of glory and being transformed by the Spirit who is the author of liberty (2 Cor. 3:17).

The Spirit authors liberty in souls and communities who then resist oppression of every form and become agents of that liberty. This is a radical form of liberty the church has always known and exercised where the Spirit is free. Slave mothers and fathers knew and sang of this liberty. So did leaders like Allen, Garnett, Fisher, and King. This is a liberty that keeps us out of the pockets of the Republicans and Democrats, the conservatives and the liberals. It enables the church to stay focused with an agenda of liberation regardless of the party in power. It utterly defies the notion of opposition between holiness, spiritual empowerment, and prophetic social consciousness.

The orientation toward the Spirit must always be epicletic. That is, there must be continual invocation or calling down of the Spirit in daily affairs. It is not that the Spirit is not present. Rather, it is acknowledgment of need and utter dependence on the Spirit in every moment. Also, such an invocation of the Spirit acknowledges that the Spirit is not ours, in the sense of being a genie, a charm, an amulet, or a domesticated dove to do with as we please. No, for grieving or resisting the Spirit, the heavenly dove is known to have taken flight.

Who is the Spirit? The Spirit is the Lord who gives life, love, salvation, every spiritual blessing. Where the Spirit of the Lord is, there is liberty.

Our prayer should be a contemporary reiteration of the epiclesis sung by sainted mothers and fathers who intoned, "Send it on down. . . . Lord, let the Holy Ghost come on down. . . ."

CHAPTER 12

The Holy Catholic Church,
the Communion of Saints

Sanctam ecclesiam catholicam, sanctorum communionem

SUSAN K. WOOD

The Apostles' Creed along with the Nicene-Constantinopolitan Creed are the two creeds which occur most frequently in liturgical prayer in Christian churches. The article of the Apostles' Creed confessing belief in "the holy catholic church, the communion of saints" names two of the four marks of the church confessed in the Nicene-Constantinopolitan Creed: holy and catholic. The latter adds "one" and "apostolic." The phrase "communion of saints" does not occur in the Nicene-Constantinopolitan Creed and is a latter addition of the Apostles' Creed.

Biblical Sources

Holy

In the New Testament holiness is overwhelmingly an attribute of the Spirit. Nevertheless, this attribute is also a goal of Christians. Jesus prayed for the sanctification of his disciples: "Sanctify them in the truth; your word is truth" (John 17:17). His work of reconciliation in his death was that we might be presented holy and blameless before God (Col. 1:22). Holiness is one of the results of God's election. We were chosen in Christ before the foundation of the world to be holy and blameless before God in love (Eph. 1:4). As God's chosen ones, we are exhorted to be holy and beloved, clothed with compassion, kindness, humility, meekness, and patience (Col. 3:12). We should "pursue peace with everyone, and the holiness without which no one will see the Lord" (Heb. 12:14). This holiness is not a result of our works but is according to God's own purpose and grace (2 Tim. 1:9).

Holiness represents the new state of Christians which distinguishes them from the Gentiles. In contrast to darkness in understanding and the futility of their minds, Christians are to be renewed in the spirit of their minds and to clothe themselves "with the new self, created according to the likeness of God in true righteousness and holiness" (Eph. 4:23-24). As a result of God's promise to be their God and his claim on them as his people, Christians are to come out from among unbelievers, cleanse themselves from every defilement of God and of spirit, "making holiness perfect in the fear of God" (2 Cor. 7:1). Holiness is what we are called to by God (1 Thess. 4:7) and manifests a way of life (2 Pet. 3:11).

The New Testament contains numerous texts identifying the church as a holy community. Christ gave himself up for the church "in order to make her holy by cleansing her with the washing of water by the word, so as to present the church to himself in splendor, without a spot or wrinkle or anything of the kind . . . so that she may be holy and without blemish" (Eph. 5:26-27). As a group Christians are to be a spiritual house, a holy priesthood, to offer spiritual sacrifices acceptable to God through Jesus Christ (1 Pet. 2:5). They are "a chosen race, a royal priesthood, a holy nation, God's own people" (2:9). Christians are "built together spiritually into a dwelling place for God," a "holy temple in the Lord" (Eph. 2:21).

Catholic

The term "catholic" is never applied to the church in Scripture. The church as it appears in the New Testament consists of a number of churches or communities.[1] The picture we have is one of local churches linked by their common belief in Jesus Christ rather than a universal church. The exception is the account of Pentecost in Acts 2, where the diversity of language and the presence of "devout Jews from every nation under heaven living in Jerusalem" witness to the universality of the Christian experience.

---

1. Raymond E. Brown, *The Churches the Apostles Left Behind* (New York: Paulist, 1984); Frederick J. Cwiekowski, *The Beginnings of the Church* (New York: Paulist, 1988).

Communion of Saints

The term "communion of saints" also does not occur in Scripture, although both *koinōnia* and "saints" occur frequently. The noun *koinōnia* and related verbs and adjectives occur thirty-eight times in the New Testament. *Koinōnia* is preeminently a Pauline term, with thirteen of the nineteen New Testament examples occurring in the apostle's acknowledged letters. This terminology in the New Testament originates in the Greek world. There is no counterpart term in Hebrew and little significant use of *koinōnia* in the Greek Old Testament. There is no recorded usage by Jesus. The earliest use of *koinōnia* in Christian documents occurs in 1 Corinthians.[2]

The noun *koinōnia* has a considerable range of meanings in the New Testament. It can mean (1) close association involving mutual interests and sharing, translated as "association," "communion," "fellowship," "close relationship" (Phil. 1:5; Rom. 15:26); (2) an attitude of good will that manifests an interest in a close relationship translated as generosity (2 Cor. 9:13); (3) an abstract term for the concrete "sign of fellowship, proof of brotherly unity, or gift or contribution" (Rom. 15:26; 1 Cor. 10:16); or (4) participation or sharing in something: Christ's sufferings (Phil. 3:10), the body and blood of Christ (1 Cor. 10:16), the Holy Spirit (2 Cor. 13:13), faith (Philem. 6).

Koinōnia, as Reumann notes, refers to the call to believers to "fellowship with Christ and the Spirit, participating in the blessings of Jesus' death and fellowship with Christ and the Spirit, participating in the blessings of Jesus' death and being a part of Christ's body, through faith, with responsibilities for mission, care of the saints locally and in Jerusalem, and hospitality and benevolence." *Koinōnia,* strictly speaking, is not a synonym for "church" except through interpretations of 1 Corinthians 10:16 (we as one body partake of one bread) and 2 Corinthians 13:13 as "the community created by the Holy Spirit."[3]

Members of the churches are often called "saints": "To the church of God which is at Corinth, to those sanctified in Christ Jesus, called to be saints together with all those who in every place call on the name of our Lord Jesus Christ, both their Lord and ours" (1 Cor. 1:2). The closest biblical equivalent of the phrase may be "cloud of witnesses": "Therefore, since we are surrounded by so great a cloud of witnesses, let us also lay aside every weight, and sin which clings so closely, and let us run with perseverance the race that

---

2. See John Reumann, "Koinonia in Scripture: Survey of Biblical Texts," in *On the Way to Fuller Koinonia,* ed. Thomas Best and Gunther Gassmann, Official Report of the Fifth World Conference on Faith and Order (Geneva: WCC Publications, 1994), pp. 37-69.

3. Reumann, p. 51.

is set before us" (Heb. 12:1). The term refers to those persons in the Old Testament who bore witness to their faith. Consequently, both the "saints" and "witnesses" are those who profess faith.

Historical Interpretations

The Holy Church

"Holy" was the first "mark" attributed to the church. In the second century Saint Justin's *Dialogue* describes the people redeemed by the Lord as holy: "We are not only a people, but we are a holy people, as we have already showed — 'And they shall call them the holy people, redeemed by the Lord'" (Isa. 62:12).[4] The phrase "the holy Church" occurs in the baptismal creed in the *Apostolic Tradition* formerly attributed to Hippolytus (ca. 215). A Greek text of the creed including the phrase was included in the apologia which Marcellus, bishop of Ancyra in Cappadocia, submitted to Pope Julius I at the synod held in Rome in 340.[5] It occurs in its Latin form in the treatise *Commentarius in symbolum apostolorum,* which the Aquileian priest Tyrannius Rufinus wrote around 404.[6]

Belief in the holiness of the church has led at times to restricting who was considered to be a member of the church. In the time of Saint Augustine the Donatists believed sinners would not be tolerated as members of it. Augustine responded with the parables about the weeds sown among the wheat.[7] His point was that the church contained both saints and sinners, and that the separation of the two was to take place only at the final judgment. This teaching led Richard Hooker in 1594 to assert that a "mark" or defining characteristic of the church is not perfect holiness of life but rather the church's doctrine and sacraments.[8] On the other hand, the Puritan John Owen considered the church to be a body which has separated from the world and whose members are distinguished by their profession of faith and their holiness of life.[9] For him both right faith and personal discipline are marks of both a true Christian believer and a true Christian church.

4. Justin, *Dialogue* 119, cited by J. N. D. Kelly, *Early Christian Creeds,* 3rd ed. (London: Longman, 1972), p. 159.

5. Kelly, p. 102.

6. Kelly, p. 101.

7. Augustine, *On Baptism against the Donatists* 4.9.13; 5.17.23; 6.25.48.

8. Richard Hooker, *Laws of Ecclesiastical Polity* 3.1.7-8; in Richard Hooker, *Works,* ed. J. Keble, vol. 1, 3rd ed. (Oxford: Oxford University Press, 1845), pp. 342-43.

9. John Owen, *The True Nature of a Gospel Church,* in *Works,* ed. W. H. Goold, vol. 16 (London: Johnstone & Hunter, 1853), pp. 11-15.

Yet others affirmed holiness as a mark of the church, yet distinguish the visible church, which includes the reprobate, from the church in the proper sense, which is the assembly of saints who truly believe the gospel of Christ and who have the Holy Spirit.[10] For example, the Apology of the Augsburg Confession (1531) comments on the repetition of Ephesians 5:25-27 in the confession at the same time it asserts that "certainly the wicked are not a holy Church!"[11] Evil people and hypocrites are mingled with the church and are members of the church according to the outward associations of the church's marks, namely, Word, confession, and sacraments, especially if they have not been excommunicated. They belong to the outward fellowship of the church, and the sacraments they administer are efficacious. However, the Apology adds that "the church is not merely an association of outward ties," but is mainly "an association of faith and of the Holy Spirit in men's hearts."[12] Consequently, "this church alone is called the body of Christ."[13]

John Calvin, in the *Institutes of the Christian Religion* (1559), distinguishes between a visible church and an invisible church. The visible church is composed of a mixture of the adopted sons of God, who are by the sanctification of the Spirit true members of Christ, and hypocrites, who have nothing of Christ but the name and outward appearance. The invisible church of the sanctified is manifest only to the eye of God.[14] He affirms the holiness of the church based on Ephesians 5:25-27, but notes that its holiness makes daily progress but is not yet perfect. He places the holiness of the church in an eschatological framework by using a typological interpretation of the prophets: "Then shall Jerusalem be holy, and there shall no strangers pass through her any more"; "It shall be called, The way of holiness; the unclean shall not pass over it" (Joel 3:17; Isa. 35:8). Calvin cautions that holiness is not to be understood "as if no blemish remained in the members of the Church; but only that with their whole heart they aspire after holiness and perfect purity: and hence, that purity which they have not yet fully attained is, by the kindness of God, attributed to them."[15]

Within Roman Catholicism the *Catechism of the Catholic Church* teaches: "The Church . . . is held, as a matter of faith, to be unfailingly holy. This is because Christ, the Son of God, who with the Father and the Spirit is hailed as 'alone holy,' loved the Church as his Bride, giving himself up for her so as to

10. Apology of the Augsburg Confession, art. 7.28, in *The Book of Concord*, trans. Theodore G. Tappert (Philadelphia: Fortress, 1959), p. 173.

11. Apology, art. 7.8.

12. Apology, art. 7.3.

13. Apology, art. 7.5.

14. John Calvin, *Institutes of the Christian Religion* 4.1.7.

15. Calvin, *Institutes* 4.1.17.

sanctify her; he joined her to himself as his body and endowed her with the gift of the Holy Spirit for the glory of God. The Church, then, is 'the holy People of God,' and her members are called 'saints.'"[16] The holiness of the church enables the church to be sanctifying through its union with Christ. All its activities are directed toward the sanctification of people in Christ and the glorification of God.[17] The *Catechism* situates the holiness of the church within a realized eschatology: "the Church on earth is endowed already with a sanctity that is real though imperfect. In her members perfect holiness is something yet to be acquired."[18] The church lives in the paradox of being "at once holy and always in need of purification," and "follows constantly the path of penance and renewal."[19] The *Catechism* applies the parable of the weeds and the wheat not only to the church itself, but to each member: "In everyone, the weeds of sin will still be mixed with the good wheat of the Gospel until the end of time. Hence the Church gathers sinners already caught up in Christ's salvation but still on the way to holiness."[20]

When holiness refers to holiness *in* the church, it refers to the sanctification of individuals. The holiness *of* the church refers to the power of sanctification entrusted to the church through the power of the Holy Spirit working in it. This holiness exists despite the sinfulness of individual members of the church. Albert the Great refers to this meaning in his commentary on the Apostles' Creed:

> This article must therefore be traced back to the work of the Holy Spirit, that is, to "I believe in the Holy Spirit," not in himself alone, as the previous article states, but I believe in him also as far as his work is concerned, which is to make the Church holy. He communicates that holiness in the sacraments, the virtues and the gifts that he distributes in order to bring holiness about, and finally in the miracles and the graces of a charismatic type *(et donis gratis datis)* such as wisdom, knowledge, faith, the discernment of spirits, healings, prophecy and everything else that the Spirit gives in order to make the holiness of the Church manifest.[21]

16. *Catechism of the Catholic Church* (Collegeville, Minn.: Liturgical Press, 1994), #823.

17. *Catechism*, #824.

18. *Catechism*, #825.

19. *Catechism*, #827, citing *Lumen gentium* 8. See also *Unitatis redintegratio* 3.6; Heb. 2:17; 7:26; 2 Cor. 5:21.

20. *Catechism*, #827.

21. *De sacrificio missae* 2, c. 9, art. 9. Cited by Yves Congar, *I Believe in the Holy Spirit,* trans. David Smith (New York: Crossroad, 1983), 2:6.

The Second Vatican Council (1962-65) of the Roman Catholic Church reconciled the distinctions between earthly visible society and the spiritual community endowed with heavenly riches by asserting that these are not two realities, but "one complex reality which comes together from a human and a divine element," in an analogy to the mystery of the incarnate Word who is the union of a human and divine nature.[22] Ultimately the church is holy because it is the body of Christ (1 Cor. 12:27). Its holiness is inseparable from the holiness of Jesus Christ.

Catholic Church

Although already common in Eastern creeds, the word "catholic" only began to appear in Western creeds in the late fourth century.[23] The original meaning of "catholic" was "general" or "universal."[24] At the beginning of the second century Saint Ignatius was the first to use it as a predicate of the church to compare the local churches presided over by the bishops with the universal church directed by Christ: "Wherever the bishop shows himself, there shall the community be, just as wherever Christ Jesus is, there is the Catholic Church."[25] Ignatius was making the point that "the local community only had reality, life and power in proportion as it formed part of the universal Church with its spiritual head." This was also the meaning of the qualifier "catholic" in the *Martyrdom of Saint Polycarp*[26] (d. 156). Saint Cyril of Jerusalem (ca. 350) applied this meaning as well as others to the term:

> It is denominated Catholic because it *extends over all the world*, from one end of the earth to the other; and because it *teaches universally and completely one and all the doctrines* which ought to come to men's knowledge, concerning things both visible and invisible, heavenly and earthly; and because it *brings into subjection to godliness the whole race of mankind*, governors and governed, learned and unlearned; and because it *universally treats and heals the whole class of sins*, which are committed by soul or body, and *possesses in itself every form of virtue* which is named, both in deeds and words, and in *every kind of spiritual gifts*.[27]

22. *Lumen gentium* 8. *Vatican Council II: The Conciliar and Post Conciliar Documents*, ed. Austin Flannery, O.P., rev. ed. (Collegeville, Minn.: Liturgical Press, 1992).

23. Kelly, p. 385.

24. Kelly, p. 385.

25. *Smyrnaeans* 8.2 (Bihlmeyer, p. 108), cited by Kelly, p. 285.

26. *Inscriptio* 8.1; 19.2 (Bihlmeyer, pp. 120, 124, 130), cited by Kelly, p. 385.

27. *Catechetical Lecture* 18.23 (*Patrologia Graeca*, 22:1044), cited by Kelly, p. 385, emphasis

The dominant meaning of the term referred to the geographical extension of the church throughout the world.

A second meaning of "catholic" was the one orthodox church in contrast to heretical sects. The "catholic" faith represents the faith which comes to us from the apostles. This use probably first occurs in the Muratorian Canon, which listed the books of the Bible which were, or were not, "received in the Catholic Church."[28] This is also the meaning ascribed to it by Nicetas, who contrasted the catholic church with other "pseudo-churches."[29] More recently the use of "catholic" distinguishes the churches that accept the teachings of the seven ecumenical councils between Nicea I (325) and Nicea II (787) from such groups as the Nestorians and the Jacobites, which reject Ephesus, Chalcedon, and subsequent councils.[30] This second meaning of "catholic," although prominent at the time when Arianism, Donatism, and other heresies led to the emergence of rival churches, tended to be a secondary meaning of the term.

"Catholic" also designates "that type of Christianity that attaches particular importance to visible continuity in space and time and visible mediation through social and institutional structures, such as creeds, sacraments, and the historic episcopate."[31] This was the sense of the word "Catholic" at the Amsterdam Assembly of the World Council of Churches (1948), where the opposite was taken to be "Protestant."

Since the Reformation in the sixteenth century, "Catholic" is often associated with the particular church governed by the bishop of Rome, as successor of Peter, and by the bishops in communion with him. To distinguish this meaning from the various other meanings listed above, the term "Roman Catholic" refers to this group. Some confessional documents of the Protestant Reformation substitute "Christian" for "catholic" in translations of the Apostles' Creed. In England, those who considered themselves catholic distinguished themselves from those they termed "Roman Catholic."[32]

In contemporary theology "catholicity" has come to refer to fullness of communion. John Zizioulas holds that universality, not catholicity, is the counterpart to locality, for "catholicity" is in fact "an indispensable aspect of

---

added. See also Avery Dulles, "Representative Texts on the Church as Catholic" and "Meanings of the Word 'Catholic,'" in *The Catholicity of the Church* (Oxford: Clarendon, 1985), pp. 181-85.

28. Ibid.

29. *De symbolo* 10 (Burn, p. 48), cited by Kelly, p. 386.

30. *New Catholic Encyclopedia,* 10:789-801.

31. Dulles, *Catholicity of the Church,* p. 185.

32. Berard L. Marthaler, O.F.M. Conv., *The Creed* (Mystic, Conn.: Twenty-Third Publications, 1987), p. 316.

the local Church, the ultimate criterion of ecclesiality for any local body." Within a eucharistic ecclesiology the Eucharist transcends "not only divisions occurring within a local situation but also the very division which is inherent in the concept of geography: the division of the world into local places."[33] A local church must be in full communion with the rest of the local churches in the world in order to be truly a church. This requires the prayer and active care on the part of a particular church for all local churches, a certain common understanding of the gospel and the eschatological nature of the church, and certain structures to facilitate this communion. Such a communion does not collapse particular churches into a mega-church, but respects the diversity within communion in what might be called a "reconciled diversity" or a "diversified unity."[34]

Communion of Saints

In the Latin phrase *sanctorum communio*, *"sanctorum"* can either be interpreted as neuter plural or masculine plural. If it is neuter plural, the translation is "a sharing or partaking in holy things," the traditional term for the elements of the Eucharist. If it is masculine plural, the translation is "communion of saints," referring to the martyrs and confessors, living and dead, and all who make up the body of Christ. A translation forces a choice between the two possibilities, but the ambiguity of the Latin allows that the phrase can mean both. The two are not mutually exclusive, for in partaking of the one bread, we become one body (1 Cor. 10:16-17).

"The communion of saints" does not occur in the Creed of Constantinople or in the old Roman Creed, which was the precursor of the Apostles' Creed. Although the earliest use of the phrase may be the text commented on by Nicetas of Remesiana or possibly the so-called "faith of Saint Jerome," it certainly occurs in an imperial rescript of 388 banning Apollinarians from the communion of saints[35] and in a canon of a synod held at Nîmes in 394 or 396, in a context where it refers to the Eucharist.[36] Faustus of Riez (d. 490) and Caesarius of Arles (d. 541) attest to it as part of the creed known to them.

33. John Zizioulas, *Being as Communion: Studies in Personhood and the Church* (New York: St. Vladimir's Seminary Press, 1985), pp. 257-59.

34. Avery Dulles, "Catholicity," in *The New Dictionary of Theology* (Collegeville, Minn.: Michael Glazier, Liturgical Press, 1987), p. 174.

35. Kelly, p. 389.

36. Emilien Lamirande, *The Communion of Saints,* trans. A. Manson (New York: Hawthorn Books, 1963), p. 23.

Nicholas I (856-57) seems to have influenced the adoption of the phrase in Rome, although even in the twelfth century some Italian creeds do not include it. It is not included in Eastern creeds and was unknown to the African church in the time of Augustine (d. 430).

The origins of the phrase remain obscure. J. N. D. Kelly points to evidence that the clause was imported into the Western Church from the East: "While the expression *sanctorum communio* was rare and its meaning fluctuating in the West, the Greek equivalent, viz. *koinonia ton agion,* and related phrases were firmly established in the East and bore the clear-cut sense of 'participation in the holy things,' i.e. the eucharistic elements."[37] If, in fact, the phrase did originate in the East, as Harnack suggests, it certainly refers to the Eucharist. Another theory is that it was first admitted into the Creed by a Gaulish bishop and was passed on to Nicetas by Hilary. If it comes from South Gaul or another Latin-speaking region, the original meaning may have referred to "saints." In either case, it is certain that southern Gaul occupies an important place in its history.[38]

Its history reveals a rather wide variety of interpretations. Augustine applies the term to the Eucharist, as do the councils of Vienne (394) and of Nîmes (396). Faustus of Riez interprets *sanctorum communio* as a cult of the holy dead. A homily from the same period connects it with the cult of relics. In this interpretation we form a society with the saints in heaven.[39] This interpretation of the phrase as a communion of holy persons dominated the early Middle Ages (e.g., Alcuin, Rhabanus Marus, Walafrid Strabo).[40] Ivo of Chartres and Jocelin of Soissons connect the two meanings as a communion in the sacraments in which those saints who have departed from this life in the unity of faith also take part.[41] Abelard and John Fecamp continued to stress the neuter meaning, communion in holy things, while Peter Lombard and Bernard of Clairvaux interpreted it as an interchange of merit with the saints in heaven.[42] Alexander of Hales and Albert the Great combine the meanings of sharing in the sacraments and a sharing in communion with the members of the church. Thomas Aquinas interpreted it as a sharing in spiritual benefits: "Because all the faithful form one body, the benefits belonging to one are communicated to the others. There is thus a sharing of benefits *(bonorum communio)* in the Church, and this is what we mean by

37. Kelly, pp. 389-90; cf. pp. 174-75, 388-91.
38. Lamirande, p. 19.
39. See the Pseudo-Augustine sermon of the sixth century, sermon 242.
40. Lamirande, p. 26.
41. Ivo of Chartres, sermon 23, cited by Lamirande, p. 26.
42. Lamirande, p. 27.

sanctorum communio."[43] The interpretation became more polemical in the Counter-Reformation, with Bellarmine's understanding of it as a communion with the pope and Canisius stressing the sharing of good merits by the souls in purgatory.

The Apology of the Augsburg Confession (1531) comments that the phrase "the communion of saints" seems to have been added to the Creed "to explain what 'church' means, namely, the assembly of saints who share the association of the same Gospel or teaching and of the same Holy Spirit, who renews, consecrates, and governs their hearts."[44]

Calvin's *Institutes* (1559) interprets "the communion of saints" as signifying a community united in the fellowship of Christ sharing the mutually communicated blessing of God. This community among men, however, is not incompatible with a diversity of graces or a civil order by which each is permitted privately to possess his own means.[45]

The *Catechism of the Catholic Church* (1994) identifies the communion of saints as the church.[46] It identifies the two closely linked meanings: communion "in holy things *(sancta)*" and "among holy persons *(sancti)*," and recalls the association of the two meanings in the Eastern liturgy: "*Sancta sanctis!* ('God's holy gifts for God's holy people') is proclaimed by the celebrant in most Eastern liturgies during the elevation of the holy gifts before the distribution of communion. The faithful *(sancti)* are fed by Christ's holy body and blood *(sancta)* to grow in the communion of the Holy Spirit *(koinōnia)* and to communicate it to the world."[47] The communion of saints shares communion in spiritual goods, especially faith, the sacraments, charisms, and charity.[48] The communion of saints also refers to the communion of the church of heaven and earth.[49] This communion is ultimately a communion "in Christ who 'died for all,' so that what each one does or suffers in and for Christ bears fruit for all."[50]

One concludes from this history that whatever the original motive for inserting the phrase in the Creed and hence its original meaning, "communion of saints" can mean both communion in holy things and communion of

---

43. *Devotissima expositio super symbolum apostolorum* (vol. 3 of the 1643 Paris ed., p. 132). Quoted in Kelly, p. 394.

44. Apology of the Augsburg Confession, art. 7, in *The Book of Concord,* trans. Theodore G. Tappert (Philadelphia: Fortress, 1959), p. 169.

45. Calvin, *Institutes* 4.1.3.

46. *Catechism,* #946.

47. *Catechism,* #948.

48. *Catechism,* #949-53.

49. *Catechism,* #954-59.

50. *Catechism,* #961.

those people united in Christ inclusive of the dead. Moreover, these are not simply two different interpretations, but are interrelated insofar as through sacramental participation in Christ Christians are united with one another (1 Cor. 10:16-17). The unity of the two meanings is related to the unity of the three "bodies" of Christ: the historical Jesus of Nazareth, the sacramental presence of Christ in the Eucharist, and the ecclesial body of Christ. This last is the *totus Christus,* Christ as head united with the members of his mystical body. This communion which is the effect of incorporation into Christ is effected by the Holy Spirit and accomplished in baptism and the Eucharist. Furthermore, this union is a likeness of the union between the three divine persons — hence the aptness of the phrase "communion of saints" in the third article of a trinitarian creed.

A Contemporary Interpretation of "Holy, Catholic Church, Communion of Saints"

A contemporary interpretation of these terms considers their context in the third article of a creed recited in the liturgy and structured by belief in the triune God. The Creed is doxological, meaning it is praise of Father, Son, and Spirit and expressive of right relationships with God through adoration. As the Faith and Order Commission study of the Creed notes, "doxology is not merely the language of direct prayer and praise," but includes "all forms of thought, feeling, action and hope directed and offered by believers to the living God."[51] Doxology deflects attention from the self toward God and is oriented to the completion of the glory of God to be achieved eschatologically. Likewise, holiness, catholicity, and communion are achieved only eschatologically and God is praised in them.

The holiness, catholicity, and communion among the members of God represent significant challenges to our understanding of the church today. We are only too aware of the failings of many church leaders and the sinfulness of church members. We live in an ecumenically divided church where church divisions assume an aura of normalcy within a pluralistic culture. The original pain of mutual excommunications and condemnations is silenced, and the multiplicity of divided churches seems to be but another instance of infinite choices for the religious consumer. "Catholic" and

---

51. "The Filioque Clause in Ecumenical Perspective," in *Spirit of God, Spirit of Christ: Ecumenical Reflections on the Filioque Controversy,* ed. L. Vischer, World Council of Churches Faith and Order Paper 102 (London: SPCK, 1981), p. 10.

"postmodern" appear to be an oxymoron in a world where there is no longer a master narrative and truth claims are perceived to be in contradiction to individual freedoms. The "communion of saints" is challenged by spiritualities of individualized and privatized relationships between a believer and Christ without reference to how that relationship engages or is engaged by relationships with others. Consequently, profession of this part of the Creed constitutes a prophetic call to our dominant culture today to restore communion with God (holiness), communion among the churches (catholicity), and communion with each other around a common eucharistic table (communion of saints).

"Communion" is the common denominator which unifies and shows an interrelationship between "holy," "catholic," and "communion of saints." Holiness is above all an attribute of God. Any holiness attributed to persons accrues to them only by virtue of their communion with God. Holiness is only possible insofar as the Holy Spirit dwells within the members of the church and animates the church. Confession of the holiness of the church reminds us that it is more than a sociological institution subject to human limitations, but that it is the body of Christ and temple of the Spirit.

The church is "catholic" in the fullness of communion of the local churches with each other and the universal church and in the communion with the apostolic faith. However, it is also catholic when it encompasses the communion of saints. The universality represented by the concept "catholic" is neither a matter of geography nor of numbers of the baptized or saved. "Catholicity" is coterminous with "communion of saints" and "holy" in the eschatological completion of all in Christ.

The dynamics of doxology, holiness, catholicity, and communion come together in the second chapter of the Acts of the Apostles in the account of Pentecost. Pentecost is the great feast of the catholicity of the church represented by the mission to the Gentiles. The Spirit descends in tongues of flame on people gathered from every nation in a reversal of the Tower of Babel in Genesis (Gen. 11:1-9). The gift of the Spirit announces the inauguration of the eschatological time foretold by the prophet Joel (Joel 2:28-32). Peter preaches repentance and baptism for the forgiveness of sin. Those who were baptized devoted themselves to the apostles' teaching and fellowship, to the breaking of bread, apparently a common meal which included the Lord's Supper, and the prayers. The chapter ends with an account of life in common. The gift of the Spirit leads to praise of God and transformation of life.

Holiness, catholicity, and communion are the work of the Holy Spirit, the sanctifier and the bond of unity. Like doxology, they are characteristics of a

Christian manner of life. A test of right Christian living is whether it does or does not glorify God, whether it does or does not reflect the holiness of God, whether it does or does not serve communion among persons.[52] Right relationship with God leads to right relationship with other human beings. Doxology, orthodoxy, and orthopraxis are truly united in this third article of the Creed.

---

52. Catherine Mowry LaCugna, *God for Us: The Trinity and Christian Life* (San Francisco: Harper San Francisco, 1991), p. 343.

The Dream Church

Acts 4:32-37

THOMAS G. LONG

One of the problems with the book of Acts is that it insists upon giving us these snapshots of the life of the earliest church, and to tell you the truth, they are rather discouraging. They are discouraging not because they are bad news, but, quite to the contrary, because they are such rosy good news . . . so perfect, so idyllic, so dreamlike. The first of these vignettes is a description of the church immediately after the experience of Pentecost: "Awe came upon everyone, because many wonders and signs were being done by the apostles. All who believed were together and had all things in common; they would sell their possessions and goods and distribute the proceeds to all, as any had need. Day by day, as they spent much time together in the temple, they broke bread at home and ate their food with glad and generous hearts, praising God and having the goodwill of all the people. And day by day the Lord added to their number those who were being saved" (Acts 2:43-47).

Well, there you go. Awe, generosity, gladness, goodwill, not to mention three thousand baptisms at the nine o'clock service. All this good cheer and extravagant success make it difficult to get excited about the churches we know, the *real* churches, the ones where we worship, the ones where it's hard to get junior high advisers, where the praise band plays tug-of-war with the pipe organ, where people squabble over the color of the carpet, where theology is a fighting word, where the budget's an annual struggle, where people come every Sunday as long as the weather isn't too bad . . . or too good.

It's tempting to reassure ourselves by saying, "Look, this snapshot of the church as generous, awe-filled, joyful, and growing like a mushroom was, af-

233

ter all, taken right after *Pentecost*. That's different. You can't expect Pentecost every week, can you?" But what is doubly irritating about Acts is that it *does* seem to expect Pentecost every week. It insists that the church of Pentecost is not really all that different from the church down the block, that Pentecostal energy and fervor are the norm for the church, not the exception, that every Sunday is a kind of Pentecost, that every assembly of believers is full of Pentecostal fire and awe and gladness and generosity and praise and goodwill.

A case in point is this little account tucked into the fourth chapter of Acts. This is not Pentecost. This is two chapters after Pentecost, and the church has moved a long way in a short time. It has no stars in its eyes, because, as Acts makes clear, by now the church has already encountered urban poverty at its doorstep in the form of a lame beggar, uncertainty about theology, and trouble with the authorities. In fact, the leaders of the church have already done some jail time. No rose-colored glasses here. So, now that the Pentecostal fires have been dampened by a solid dose of reality, we have every reason to expect a realistic description of the church. But listen . . . "They were all filled with the Holy Spirit . . . spoke the word of God with boldness . . . were of one heart and soul . . . everything they owned was held in common . . . great grace was upon them all . . . there was not a needy person among them" (Acts 4:31-34).

Gee . . . another rosy portrait of a dream church. The only conclusion we seem forced to draw from these cheery descriptions in Acts is that, apparently, things have been downhill for the church ever since, unless . . . unless, there is something else, something deeper going on here. As is the case with every part of the Bible, whenever we read the book of Acts we have to know what we're reading and how to read it. One day in my preaching class at the seminary some students and I were looking at these passages in Acts, and you could sense a developing gloom forming over the students. Here they read of energized, Spirit-driven, grace-filled gatherings of believers, knowing full well they were heading out to serve graying congregations, many of them shrinking and fighting for their lives. Statisticians tell us that the average Christian congregation in America has fewer than seventy-five members and less than $1,000 in the bank. But we marched on through these passages in Acts rich with dreamlike churches, full of great power and praise and wonder and energy and joy, when suddenly one of the students said, "Gee, this reminds me of Eleanor Reynolds."

"Who's Eleanor Reynolds?" I asked.

"Aw, she's this old woman in my congregation back home who is our church's historian. She wrote the little booklet for our church's centennial. It's in the church library. You ought to read it. You can't believe the things she says; I mean, she tells about an ordinary family night supper, and she makes it sound like it's the messianic banquet."

That's it! Local church historians tell about family night suppers and make them sound like the messianic banquet. These portraits of the church in Acts are like local church history. Luke is the first Eleanor Reynolds. Local church historians may come across in the world of professional historians as amateurs and maybe as sappy and romantic, but the one virtue they have is that they love the church, and the one ability they have is the capacity to *see*, the capacity to see amid the ragged fortunes and foibles of real and struggling congregations the blessed community of Jesus Christ shining through. Theologically we could put it this way: they have the gift to see the church eschatologically, to sense in the everyday church the emerging presence of the kingdom of God.

You know how local church historians write. They say things like, "In August of 1932, the Rev. C. W. Hawthorne became the pastor of Macedonia Church. He and his wife Irene were adored by everyone in the community. Rev. Hawthorne preached his first sermon on Sunday evening, August 28, and the whole town was present. Every heart was touched by his stirring words, and the Spirit moved mightily in the service. Rev. Hawthorne served faithfully until his death in 1941, and his ministry continues to bear much fruit today." Really? Adored by *everyone*? The *whole town* was present? *Every heart* was touched? *Continues* to bear much fruit? Really? Why would someone say such things? Because they're true . . . because you know they are true if you have the ability to see the church eschatologically, the ability to see the church as a foretaste of things to come, the ability to see the kingdom happening in the life of the struggling church, the ability to look at a family night supper and know that it's an appetizer of the messianic banquet.

We know that Luke, the writer of Acts, is such a local church historian, and one of the ways we know it is because of how he describes the crowd at Pentecost. Who was at Pentecost? Luke tells us there were "Parthians, Medes, Elamites, and residents of Mesopotamia . . ." (Acts 2:9). Really? There were Medes at Pentecost? This was the first century, and there had not been any Medes around for hundreds of years. They were as extinct as mastodons. Elamites were at Pentecost? Really? They didn't wander over from the next county; they wandered over from the Old Testament. To say there were Medes and Elamites at Pentecost would be like saying, "You should have been at our church last Sunday. We had visitors from Florida, Michigan, Ohio, a whole van load of Assyrians, and a cute little Hittite couple who signed the Friendship Pad." Luke looks over the congregation at Pentecost and sees that the whole world — past, present, and future — was there. He looks at family night suppers and sees messianic banquets. He looks at ragged congregations struggling to be faithful and sees the blessed community of the risen Christ. He is a local church historian.

Sometimes people wonder, amid all the competition on Sunday and all the things one can find to criticize about the church, why they should even consider going, why they should take part in something so frail and faltering as a local congregation. I think it may well be one of the primary purposes of the life of the church to enable all of us to see through surfaces to the depths, to see the church and consequently the world, like a local church historian, to look at all the yearning places in human community and nevertheless to see the blessed community of God shining through. And when we see the church, and the world, this way, what do we see? We, too, look at family night suppers and see the messianic banquet, we look at every person we meet and see the image of God, we look at the ragged collection of folks who gather for worship and see the whole of humanity streaming to Mount Zion.

Garret Keizer, a minister in Vermont, tells of conducting a Saturday night Easter vigil service in his little church. Only two people, besides Keizer, have shown up for the service. Keizer lights the paschal candle and says the prayer. "The candle sputters in the half darkness," he writes, "like a voice too embarrassed or overwhelmed to proclaim the news: 'Christ is risen.'" He goes on: "But it catches fire, and there we are, three people and a flickering light — in an old church on a Saturday evening in the spring, with the noise of the cars and their winter rusted mufflers outside. The moment is filled with ambiguities of all such quiet observances among few people, in the midst of an oblivious population in a radically secular age. The act is so ambiguous because its terms are so extreme: the Lord is with us, or we are pathetic fools."[1]

The next morning, Easter, the church is packed with what Keizer calls "that deceptive Easter fullness." He knows that inevitably someone will say, "If only the church could be full like this all the time," and he knows he will reply, "Yes that would be so good. Maybe someday it will be." But to himself he whispers something else, something he has said to himself many times through the struggles of ministry, something that he sees and that sustains him, the words of Jesus: "Fear not, little flock, for it is your Father's good pleasure to give you the kingdom."[2]

But what is the point of seeing this way? What value is there in straining to glimpse the beloved community in the ragtag reality of the church? What is

---

1. Garret Keizer, *A Dresser of Sycamore Trees: The Finding of a Ministry* (New York: Penguin Books, 1991), p. 73.

2. Keizer, p. 78.

the point of taking the local church historian's point of view? Why try to squint and see the church and the world eschatologically? Isn't this just romantic piety, gazing through rose-colored stained glasses?

No, to the contrary, what we are seeing is not a romantic, make-believe church, but the deep truth about the real church, and ultimately the deepest truth about the whole creation: that the Holy Spirit is present and at work — at work in the halting and frail church and the broken places in the world — renewing, energizing, giving life, and forming us in the pattern of Christ. That is why Luke tells us about a man whose life was transformed, transformed in the church. In one way it is a very mundane story, and we are told very little about this man. His name was Joseph, he came from Cyprus, he was a Levite, and he owned some land. That isn't much information. But at another level, when we know a person's name, origin, family, and possessions, we know a great deal.

Several years ago when an uncle of mine died, my brother and I inherited twenty acres of farmland in Mississippi. As far as we can tell, the land is not worth a great deal; it's just a few acres of muddy pasture stuck in the middle of an old farm. There isn't even a road to provide access to our property. But as soon as we inherited it, our mother sat us down and said, "Whatever you do, never sell that land. That land has been in our family for years. That land is our land. Our sweat is in that soil, our blood is in that land. And if you do ever sell it," she added ominously, "do me the courtesy of waiting until I am dead and gone. I don't ever want to hear that you sold our land." In other words, just with a few facts, you know a great deal about us; we're the Longs, a family with roots in Oktibbeha County, Mississippi, and we own some land we're never going to sell because our blood's in the soil. Any questions?

So Luke tells us that this man named Joseph, who was from Cyprus, and who was a Levite, owned some land, land that his mama probably did not have to tell him never to sell because in that part of the world land is just about everything. But Luke tells us that something happened to Joseph in the church such that he opened his grasp on his possessions and sold the land, giving the proceeds to the apostles. Whatever happened to Joseph was not just about land or money; it was about *Joseph,* so much so that the apostles gave him a new name: Barnabas. Luke helpfully translates this for us, noting that "Barnabas" means "son of encouragement." Many commentators are quick to point out that this is wrong, that the Aramaic word "Barnabas" actually means "son of Nebo," not "son of encouragement." One commentator chortles, "Luke obviously does not know Aramaic." Maybe . . . what I am sure of is that Luke knows his church. Luke knows that when we are gathered, ragtag as we are, into a community where the resurrection is proclaimed, where

Christ is present, and where the winds of the Spirit blow, then sons and daughters of encouragement will be formed.

A friend of mine, Heidi Neumark, is the pastor of a Lutheran church in the South Bronx, in perhaps the poorest of all poor neighborhoods in America. Her first Sunday as pastor Heidi understood what kind of church she was serving when she found under the altar a box of rat poison next to the communion wafers. The leaders and officers of her congregation include former addicts and undocumented aliens and unemployed and the recently homeless. It is the kind of congregation Paul was talking about when he wrote, "Consider your own call, brothers and sisters: not many of you were wise by human standards, not many were powerful, not many of noble birth. But God chose what is foolish in the world to shame the wise."

During Holy Week several years ago this congregation decided to reenact in a passion play the whole sweep of Holy Week, from Palm Sunday to Easter. They began by dramatizing Jesus' entry into the city, borrowing a live donkey and, led by an actor playing the part of Jesus, parading in a long procession around the block of shabby storefronts and run-down apartments shouting "Hosannah!" When they got around the block and back to the door of the church, the Palm Sunday procession encountered in front of the church a street protest under way about police brutality. It was fitting, really, as Jesus and the protestors, the congregation and the street crowds, the cries of "Hosanna" and the cries of social outrage mingled together in a swirl of movement and noise. In fact, someone passing by on the street, seeing the confusion and fearing trouble, even called the police, whose arrival brought a bit of added color and drama.

Somehow the processional managed to make it inside the church where, as the play unfolded, Jesus was tried, condemned, and executed. But then, women came from the tomb early in the morning of the first day of the week, with an amazing word of an empty tomb and the astounding news, "He is risen!" The actors playing the disciples remained true to their assigned parts, expressing disbelief and confidence that this news from the women was but an "idle tale."

But then the script called for three members of the congregation to stand up and bear witness to the truth of the resurrection. "*I know* that he is alive . . . ," each one was to begin. The first was Angie. "I know that he is alive," she said, "because he is alive in me." She then told how she was abused by her father, how she fell into despair and alcoholism, became HIV positive. But then she responded to the welcome of the church, then she started attending worship, then a Bible study, and bit by bit she rose from the grave of her life. Now she is a seminary student, studying to be a pastor. "I am now alive because Jesus Christ lives in me and through me," Angie said, her face aglow. "I am a temple of the Holy Spirit."

The two other witnesses stood in turn, each reciting their part of the script: "I know that he is alive. . . ." Then that portion of the play was done, and it was time to move on. But others in the sanctuary began to rise spontaneously. "I know that he is alive," they would say, "because he is alive in me." Homeless people, addicts now clean, the least and the lost stood one by one. Nothing could stop them. "I know that he is alive," they shouted.[3]

Sons and daughters of consolation, all of them. It was like a dream, like a dream of a land where every tear is dried and death and pain are no more. Like a dream of the blessed community of God where people are free to let go of all that weighs them down, a blessed community where awe and blessing and joy and generosity and the praise of God are our daily bread.

May we all dream such dreams.

3. Heidi Neumark's church is beautifully described in her book *Breathing Space* (Boston: Beacon Press, 2003).

CHAPTER 13

The Forgiveness of Sins

Remissionem peccatorum

STEVEN D. PAULSON

The Problem with Forgiveness

The forgiveness of sins is rather easily confessed at the comfortable distance of the ancient Apostles' Creed. The problems arise when we attempt to practice forgiving particular sins and particular sinners here and now. Who, then, *can* forgive sins? Who even *wants* to?

When absolution is declared by a gospel servant authorized to forgive on earth as God forgives in heaven, the servant is using the keys (Matt. 16:19 and John 20:22-23) to unlock our prison's door and open heaven. Not surprisingly, even people in the church resist what seems to be the indiscriminate outpouring of God's "glorious grace that he freely bestows on us in the Beloved in whom we have redemption through his blood, the forgiveness of our trespasses according to the riches of his grace that he lavished on us" (Eph. 1:6-7). Who can approve publicizing such grace to the ungodly, who do not deserve or want it?

When Christians confess together their belief in the forgiveness of sin, it is like pinching themselves to make sure that what they heard is not a dream. Absolution seems somehow illicit, frightening, and joyful all at once. Can this be? May God just forgive? Can a word of promise accomplish what is promised? Is it right? Is it binding? Lasting? Legal? Is it even possible for the God who knows all things and counts the hairs on our heads to forget something — especially something as obvious as our sins?

Forgiveness of sins is frightening. Mercy disrupts order. It perverts our sense of justice. Doesn't forgiveness require the law, and the law its pound of flesh? If forgiveness is joined to proportional punishment (an eye for an eye, or at least a ritual sacrifice), how can the scales of justice ever be balanced? With forgiveness God appears to act freely — as if there were no divine law. "Freely" really means "unfairly" to those diligently practicing righteousness according to God's standard.

Scripture acknowledges the problem. The story of Jonah is the story of repentance worked by God's absolute demand and irresistible mercy. It not only takes up the troubling issues of mercy outside Israel and mercy for enemies (Nineveh), but of mercy outside the law. The God whose wrath kills and whose mercy brings new life asked Jonah, "Is it right for you to be angry?" Jonah thought so. So God "appointed a worm" to be his prophet. Jonah, if you care about the bush, God is saying, should I not care about Nineveh's people and even its animals? Forgiveness poses a special threat to the righteous.

Wisdom writings and the prophets agreed. The problem with God's *promise* of grace is the same as with God's demand: it is unilateral and so reminds us that God is God and we are not. God reminded Job: "Will you even put me in the wrong? Will you condemn me that you may be justified?" So Job repented in a way that makes us uncomfortable: "I had heard of you by the hearing of the ear, but now my eye sees you; therefore I despise myself, and repent in dust and ashes." God's relationship with Job does not change, whether God unfairly takes away his children or unfairly gives Job's new daughters an inheritance with their brothers (Job 40–42).

The forgiveness of sins is completely out of human control. We are utterly dependent on God's decision to forgive or not to forgive. Even the law gives us no place to stand from which we can demand forgiveness. There is no way around this, and so Israel was driven increasingly to its double eschatological conclusion: God's judgment on sin and God's salvation of sinners. On the one hand, "the LORD saw that the wickedness of humankind was great in the earth, and that every inclination of the thoughts of their hearts was only evil continually. And the LORD was sorry that he had made humankind on the earth" (Gen. 6). Furthermore,

> I hate, I despise your festivals,
>   and I take no delight in your solemn assemblies. . . .
> Let justice roll down like waters.
>
> (Amos 5:21, 24)

And again, "there is no one who does good, no, not one" (Ps. 14:3). Paul put the period on the end of that sentence: "Both Jews and Greeks are under the power of sin," and "all have sinned and fall short of the glory of God" (Rom. 3:23). All! On the other hand, there is the other eschatological conclusion that is even more breathtaking than God's judgment on sin: "Your faithfulness comes from me" (Hos. 14:2-8). "The days are surely coming, says the LORD, when I will make a new covenant with the house of Israel and the house of Judah. . . . I will put my law within them, and I will write it on their hearts. . . . For I will forgive their iniquity, and remember their sin no more" (Jer. 31:31-34). Can God forget? Yes, God promises to forget, but a costly memory remains:

> All we like sheep have gone astray;
>   we have all turned to our own way,
> and the LORD has laid on him
>   the iniquity of us all. . . .
> The righteous one, my servant, shall make many righteous,
>   and he shall bear their iniquities.
>
> (Isa. 53:6, 11)

All! Both absolutes in our relationship with God come crashing into the present when a preacher declares that we are forgiven on account of Christ: *No, not one is righteous,* and *Christ alone, the righteous one, shall make many righteous.*

To those who want to be right before God on other grounds, this kind of declaration sounds either like a farce or blasphemy against all that is sacred. God's forgiveness judges human achievement to be a vain hope for finding peace with God. It cuts the central nerve in the quest to motivate the masses to be moral. It rejects "spirituality" as an elevated life beyond creation and the body. If God forgives, all human hopes for an alternative righteousness are exposed as illusory — and unnecessary.

The God Who Forgives Sin

There are no partial steps toward forgiveness and away from sin. God deals in wholes. Just as sin involves the whole person, so repentance and forgiveness must be whole. To those who know there is no other hope, God's unthwartable power and boundless determination to forgive *is* the gospel itself: God forgives sinners! In Christ we know not only who God is, but what this God does. The Father did not spare his only-begotten Son, and he gave sinners his Holy Spirit, withholding nothing. "Take not thy Holy Spirit from me," we pray. "Done," says God.

The only way to overcome the fear of forgiveness is actually to be forgiven by the very one we offended. We have heard the preacher turn the key: "I absolve you." So we confess: "I believe the forgiveness of sins." We find ourselves always at this point of vacillating between the realities — in ourselves wholly idolatrous, in Christ wholly forgiven. In ourselves we belong to the old order, brought about by the sin of Adam and Eve; in Christ we belong to the new order, brought about by the forgiveness of sins.

Confessing faith in the forgiveness of sins rests on two biblical assumptions: "All have sinned" (Rom. 3:23) and Jesus is "the Lamb of God who takes away the sin of the world" (John 1:29). Throughout history the church has been inclined to diminish or adjust these assumptions, thereby compromising our confession that we believe "the forgiveness of sins." But God keeps coming to promise forgiveness. This God works in death and resurrection, law and gospel, judgment and forgiveness. First to our dismay, then to our eternal joy, the God who thus pours himself out for the unworthy is righteous.

The First Biblical Assumption: All Have Sinned

Who would not want what the church has to give? Why is forgiveness so difficult to receive when it is free? The law, whether given through Moses or available through experience, makes clear that love demands frequent ("daily") and serial ("not seven times, but seventy times seven") forgiveness. Forgiveness is necessary for life, but there is a perpetual problem with getting it done. A person cannot stay married, or raise children, or have parents, or teach, or buy and sell, or do any of the callings of life without having to forgive and be forgiven. In the crucible of life we must pray the old Jewish prayer that Jesus gave anew: "Forgive us our trespasses, as we forgive those who trespass against us." We could take this as a simple demand; we could then demand it when wronged, and it would coerce us to forgive when we have wronged others. Revenge would be forgotten. We could finally learn to live in peace if we used this simple rule for life: "As we have forgiven, forgive us."

But mercy is not so comfortable or practical. Applying this life-giving teaching is both difficult and dangerous. Acts of forgiveness are inconsistent. Even when they do happen, the world first praises them, then limits them because forgiveness is dangerous as public policy. At the end of a political term a president or governor may pardon criminals in a "Christmas" spirit; but making a habit of it would disrupt justice. Forgiveness cannot be made into a law or be perpetuated under a law. Sometimes the injustice of forgiving is just too great. When a leader such as Anwar Sadat actually forgives, he is assassinated by people with a righteous cause. More often, forgiveness as God's demand leaves us in real Catch-22s. A spouse who tries to forgive infidelity must both forget and not forget at the same time. Does one forgive a new Jewish settlement on the West Bank, or a suicide bomber at Passover? Do Armenians forgive Turks for genocide? Could God have meant that?

Forgiveness in the presence of evil creates legitimate conundrums. One solution includes proper punishment within the act of forgiveness. Forgiveness + punishment = mercy. But how much punishment is enough? Should forgiveness be given only if there is clear admission of guilt, accompanied by sorrow and shame? But therapeutic culture has determined that a chief problem, often perpetrated by Christians, is the creation of a guilt or shame complex. How do we raise children to have a conscience and yet not be overwhelmed by guilt? Forgiving on demand works, at best, fitfully.

David needed his Nathan, not to receive punishment, but to get out of the mire of partial self-accusations and partial self-defense into a real confession that understood God's kind of forgiveness as his only way out. From an actual sin, such as adultery, Nathan's accusation — "You are the man" — made David into a confessor that all sin is "original," and so he himself was inescapably under sin's rule:

> Indeed, I was born guilty,
>> a sinner when my mother conceived me.
>
>> (Ps. 51:5)

No reparation, no act of free will, no law could help him. The God who demands all must then give all; the God who kills must raise:

> Create in me a clean heart, O God,
>> and put a new and right spirit within me.
>
>> (51:10)

But, we may object, if we were born into sin, how can we be blamed? Thus we ultimately lay problems of forgiveness at God's own doorstep, since forgiveness seems to be God's bright idea in the first place. How does God manage to forgive real, active sinners like David? What kind of charade is it for God to "hide his face from my sins"? Doesn't God have a mighty dilemma too great even for divinity, an eternal struggle between two attributes that cannot be canceled or balanced — justice and mercy? The speculations about how God does this balancing act have produced not only our theories of atonement but also our ritual acts of repentance. Can God demand payment for sin and, at the same time, make the payment to himself?

Graded Repentance

A synthesis seems called for when we consider forgiveness apart from Christ, apart from the gospel, and according to the law. It appears that we need a via media between too much mercy and too little. But how can we get justice and mercy to kiss? When forgiveness becomes a matter of trying to do the right thing according to the law (especially in its "Christian" forms of turning the other cheek and forgiving seventy times seven), the demands of forgiveness are reduced to manageable proportions. We also find ourselves in a position of perpetual uncertainty about when to forgive, when not to, how much is enough, and who can do it. Over everything hangs the specter of our relationship with God determined by the little prayer, "Forgive me as I have forgiven others." How do we dare pray that when we know so little about what we have done and left undone? So we propose to take small steps toward successful forgiving, doing in parts what we can't seem to hold together as a whole. When the church entered the effort to adjudicate between God's wrath and mercy as the way to exercise the office of the keys, it made trouble for itself by diminishing its two proclaimed absolutes: all have sinned, and Christ is the Lamb of God who takes away the sin of the world.

Schism in the church often began with the "holy" trying to rid themselves of the "unholy" because forgiveness was found to be somewhere between difficult and impossible. The church then split between those who rigorously pressed for justice and those who pursued mercy. The "catholic" solution has been to find a middle road by using the law in moderation. Historically the church has called this middle approach "equity," as did the Council of Trent.[1] It should not surprise us that the phrase "forgiveness of sins" first appeared in public creeds with Cyprian. His churches found themselves in a crisis of forgiveness after the persecutions in North Africa. The church then attempted to step in as the "user" of the law, judging and adjudicating so that the conundrums of forgiveness could be moderated in a nervous kiss between mercy and justice.

Now it is true that confessing belief in the forgiveness of sins will, by the same token, renounce the series of rigorist heresies that keep springing up in churches (Donatism, Montanism, and Novatianism) and will also renounce their opposite (antinomianism). But overcoming heresy and schism remains

---

1. "For it is clear that priests could not have exercised this judgment if the case were unknown, nor could they have preserved equity *(aequitatem)* in imposing penance if the faithful had declared their sins only in general." *Decrees of the Ecumenical Councils*, ed. Tanner, vol. 2 (Washington, D.C.: Georgetown University Press, 1990), session 14, chap. 5, p. 706.

a struggle in the churches. The rigorists (from the time of James and the "superapostles" in Galatia right through the *Didache*, the letters of Clement, and the early form of *exomologesis* [rite of public confession]) always propose that we take God's law literally: we will be forgiven as much as we forgive. They are too optimistic about their achievement, as if Paul's "all have sinned" applied only before baptism, not after.

How could they get from parts to the whole? The fateful move to escape the conundrum of forgiveness was made in the North African churches of the third century and subsequently spread abroad. If nothing under the sun could escape both the *necessity* and *impossibility* of real, historical forgiveness, then forgiveness must be projected out of actual life into the role of an idea, specifically a goal toward which we ought to move. Forgiveness became a partial accomplishment of human striving cooperating with God's initial grace while moving toward the *goal* of whole repentance and forgiveness. Attempting to escape a schism over the issue of forgiveness, the church not only got schism, it also entered into another, deeper problem that finally erupted in the Reformation.

By at least the third century there is a movement from the preaching on forgiveness of sins (on account of what Christ has done) and its eschatological consequences to the attempt to control legalism and antinomianism. The catholic response to legalists was surely correct in one sense: preachers such as Chrysostom declared that God's mercy is infinite; one chance at repentance was not enough. But theologians argued that forgiveness may not be applied indiscriminately. Some repentance that symbolically reversed the act of treachery against the church should be required. Forgiveness became a sacrament offered under conditions controlled by church law. The secret mechanism of the moderate way was to apply the law to the sacraments as the way to forgive sin. The legal metaphor spread from Christ's atonement to the practice of compensating for sin by a symbolic, sacrificial exchange. In the words of Tertullian, "God offers release from penalty *(poena)* at the compensating exchange of penitence *(paenitentiam)*."[2]

With this reasoning, a casuistry concerning forgiveness appeared for both victim and perpetrator. The religious secret of sacrifice lay in offering a part for the whole *(pars pro toto)* with the clear implication that "I give that you will give" *(do et des)*. Pastoral involvement with repentance became a judicial decision about "satisfactions." The preacher/absolver was made into a judge (or "user") of God's law, and a process began that would separate baptism and repentance into two or more sacraments. Penance became the "laborious

2. Tertullian, *On Penance* 6.

baptism" described by Nazianzus,[3] and baptism's "once and for all" was confined to an act of the past whose forgiveness, once given, was used up.

Augustine began distinguishing "original" and "actual" sin by applying the first to baptism and the second to penance: baptism became the forgiveness of all original sin, but then a theory had to explain how Christians unexpectedly, but undeniably, did sin after baptism. Sin's "tinder" must remain, but not its essence. Still, *tinder* was enough to create great problems, which raised a whole new set of practical questions. How can churches repeat forgiveness without sponsoring antinomianism? How often and under what conditions? Penance was extended to all during Lent, and to all the sick and dying. Soon forgiveness as penance would have its own liturgy and its own three-step process of *contrition, confession,* and *satisfaction,* whose referee was the priest. The separation of baptism and confession was more rigorous in the West; but Eastern creeds usually kept the confession of forgiveness and baptism together, as in the Nicene Creed: "I believe in baptism for the forgiveness of sins." Nevertheless, the tendency to consider baptism as a "first plank" and repentance as a "second" (Tertullian in the West, Jerome in the East) spread widely.

The initial reaction to sin "after baptism" was rigorous, and for a time theologians argued for a onetime repentance. But sinners are extremely determined and inventive. By the sixth century the Irish monks not only saved Western civilization, but also offered a new possibility for the church in its casuistry on penance. It parceled out the law into what appear to be manageable portions (in penitentials) for those who are at least trying to become better. Private, specific confession to a holy one, repeated as often as necessary throughout life, became a solution to the problem of sin after baptism.

The Roman Catholic Church's genius was to set very moderate legal demands on people for their own good. One was that they had to confess their sins before a priest at least once a year (Fourth Lateran Council), which was part of a proper preparation for receiving the Lord's Supper as forgiveness. Sins were separated into manageable categories such as "venial" and "mortal." Then theologians rallied to the cause and developed theories to address anxiety about falling into mortal — or unforgivable — sin. Aquinas adapted the theory of character and virtue from Aristotle to conclude that, though it is always theoretically possible to lose grace, it is very difficult. Eventually a whole body of (canon) law grew up around these sacraments. Has a person properly repented? If so, then absolution can properly be uttered, much like placing an

---

3. Nazianzus, *Oration* 39, quoted by the Decrees of the Council of Trent, in *Decrees of the Ecumenical Councils*, session 14, chap. 3, p. 704.

accurate label on a product. Beyond that, in order to help the penitent *feel* forgiven, penance could be added in moderation.[4]

The via media between too much and too little mercy is a treacherous road indeed. It has always created more questions than it answered and has demonstrated two repeated tendencies: first, to diminish the law's demand to forgive as we have been forgiven, and second, to increase uncertainty about how much repentance is enough. The extension of the judgment by a priest and the need to reduce the anxiety of the penitent flowered into more elaborate theories outside the everyday need to forgive others. Indulgences, petition of the saints, purgatory, the sacrifice of the mass, the office of the papacy all became intertwined in the fruitless effort to answer the question: How much repentance is enough? When is forgiveness finally real, on earth as it is in heaven?

What does the church do with sinners? It cannot be too rigorous, or too free. This dilemma launches the project of putting the church's good Christology into a synthesis with a very bad anthropology: on the one hand, preaching forgiveness apart from the law in Christ alone, and on the other, preaching the law as the form of forgiveness. That produces a confusion between God's demand and God's promise, which makes forgiveness into a process of approaching a goal by small steps that God's grace accepts as "enough."

The Promise Does What It Says

In the end the attempted synthesis forgot two things: sin always involves the whole person, and Jesus Christ alone is the Lamb on whom all sins are laid. Luther disrupted the historic church's process of repenting and being forgiven by actually doing it. By repenting according to church practice, he found uncertainty and self-righteous pride in himself at the same time. Penance afforded a righteousness according to the (manageable) new law of the church, and so it blocked Christ's promise of absolute forgiveness in the here

---

4. One of the important movements of our time has been the Roman Catholic Church's attempt to reorganize the sacrament of penance under the rubric of "reconciliation." The new rite of reconciliation considered some of the dangers and problems of distinguishing mortal and venial sins, though the distinction remained necessary. It made steps to place reconciliation back in the community and in light of God's word, though law and gospel remain combined in a synthesis of equity. It is for this reason that sin "after baptism" remains the identifiable sticking point between Lutherans and Catholics concerning the doctrine of justification, but this is no small matter.

and now. Luther's was not a revolt against indulgences or even a mere challenge to the penitential system; he was grasped by the apostolic preaching in terms of both the demands of the law (forgive as you have been forgiven) and God's promise apart from the law in Jesus Christ (you have been forgiven). When the priest absolved someone, he was not acting as judge on a prior movement of the heart as measured by the law; he was interrupting life as usual — with its partial forgiveness and numerous failures — by a direct promise of God. This promise accomplishes what it says: it puts the old sinner to death and raises a new saint. The preached word forgives. Since this is hidden to our eyes, available only to faith, both the sinner and the saint remain whole. Both absolutes are true at the same time: all have sinned and fall short of the glory of God; apart from the law, Christ has wrapped himself in all our sins, and there they died when he was nailed to the cross. God has forgiven and forgotten them. The word of God through the earthly preacher's mouth and the earthly things of water, wine, bread do this. When the preacher said, "I absolve you on account of Christ and by his authority," a collision occurred. The announced word is whole, absolute, and without remainder, and its effect is eschatological — a new creation, though hidden in faith itself.

Forgiveness must finally break away from the law into accomplished fact. It cannot remain a series of theological theories meant to reassure sinners and keep them trying to become better at the same time. Who gets forgiven? Actual sinners wholly opposed to God, even in their righteousness. Who can forgive? Whoever has received these words through faith, though God's unthwartable will to go public with forgiveness creates a special office for it — the office of the preacher, or local "forgiveness person."[5] What if the old Adam doesn't die, being such a good swimmer (Barth)? Does it invalidate the promise? No, it necessitates it again as the only end to self-righteousness and despair simultaneously.

For this reason Reformers used a public form of absolution in worship services so that God's words that kill and make alive go out widely. They often debated the ongoing place of private confession. Luther knew how this could be abused, but he also knew what great benefits could come from a specific use of the gospel: "I would not give up confession for all the riches in the world . . . save for the sacrament I know of no greater treasure and comfort than confession." But Luther also demanded that the normal tables be turned: "We must not look to our work but to the treasure, which we hear from the priest's mouth, which makes us go gladly and *force the priests and not vice*

---

5. Edgar Carlson, "The Doctrine of the Ministry in the Confessions," *Lutheran Quarterly*, n.s., 7 (spring 1993): 79-91.

versa."[6] Stop being forced by priests to confess; instead, force the priest to confess the promise!

Baptism was the first way this promise entered a person's life. So all repentance and forgiveness, or the whole of Christian life, was marked as a return to baptism's promise, a promise that was never used up and never became only an event of the "past." Confession, whether in a public or private form, returned to its proper place in baptism.

Some who adopted aspects of the Reformation came back to repentance and forgiveness only under the form of the law; thus the old struggle between legalism and antinomianism returned in the likes of Menno Simons. This re-created a problem with baptism, which was no longer the solution to original sin because original sin was essentially denied. Baptism was the external label for the internal, prior movement of the heart, thus giving birth to an anti-papal form of the same church problem that preceded the Reformation. The promise of forgiveness had become empty, the Christian a judge, the church a communion of like-minded people directed toward increased holiness measured by the law. Then the need to reassure the anxious created not a second plank of penance but a need for rebaptism. Thus Christ was buried again beneath the steps to holiness.

The Second Absolute: Jesus, the Lamb of God,
Takes Away the Sin of the World

Jesus Christ came forgiving: "The time is fulfilled, and the kingdom of God has come near; repent, and believe in the good news" (Mark 1:14). This split the times into old and new. When Jesus was on trial, the high priest asked him, "'Are you the Messiah, the Son of the Blessed One?' Jesus said, 'I am; and "you will see the Son of Man seated at the right hand of the Power," and "coming with the clouds of heaven"'" (14:61-62).

The trouble with Jesus Christ, one might say, started when John the forerunner and preacher pointed his long, bony finger at Christ and said: "Behold, the lamb of God, who takes away the sin of the world." It is not just that humans have found this a bewildering proposition — that one person could bear the world's sin — but that Jesus actually proceeded to act like this was

6. From Luther's Palm Sunday sermon, 1529, in *Sermons of Martin Luther,* ed. and trans. John Nicholas Lenker (Grand Rapids: Baker, 1983), 1:17-18, and *The 1529 Holy Week and Easter Sermons of Dr. Martin Luther,* trans. Irving L. Sandberg, edited and introduced by Timothy J. Wengert (St. Louis: Concordia, 1999), p. 34, emphasis added.

really true. To the paralytic Jesus says, "Son, your sins are forgiven," and murmuring arose: "It is blasphemy! Who can forgive sins but God alone?" (2:4-6). To those suspended between heaven and earth, new and old, clinging to the law's clear demand as the way to righteousness ("Forgive, if you have anything against anyone; so that your Father in heaven may also forgive you your trespasses," 11:25), Jesus was a puzzle, then a threat.

Jesus' last supper with the Twelve was "in the night in which he was betrayed"; nevertheless, to those betrayers he gave his new testament as a promise, and Matthew adds the obvious: "for the forgiveness of sins" (Matt. 26:28). What was the result of all this forgiving by Christ, his eating with sinners, his eschatological signs of healing and exorcism? It got him killed! Christ's naked and unqualified forgiveness of sin acted outside divine law, as one who had authority.

In the cross, where the old and new are finally distinguished, the only question left is, where can I find a gracious God? Can this particular sin, a complete and final act of human "freedom," be forgiven? The question is not neutral, but interested, involved, full of care. We are dying under God's wrath, after all. That is why we have found the crux of all Scripture in the Christian confession of belief in the "forgiveness of sins": God, who *forgives sin*. The Father does this through his Son, Jesus Christ, in whom "God was reconciling the world to himself, not counting their trespasses against them, and entrusting the message of reconciliation to us" (2 Cor. 5:19). In Christ there is a new creation.

Alarms should go off, then, when we confess this dangerous belief in the actual forgiveness of sins accomplished in our midst. Belief in the forgiveness of sin signals among us a new kingdom of the Spirit in which the living who have not forgiven as they have been forgiven nevertheless have been made white as snow. That is, Christ's own betrayers are forgiven by a God who, though knowing all, has accomplished what we could not: God absolutely forgot! God made a forgiveness kingdom in which he does not see or know our sin because it has been covered by Christ alone, not by our ability first to forgive.

Now, forgiveness by God burns like coals to a trampled conscience that holds its guilt before its eyes and sees no way to be washed white as snow. True forgiveness also only fuels the inner fires of the righteous, whose passion for justice does not really want forgiveness but restitution and reward. That is why the law teams up with sin and death to oppose Christ alone as our forgiveness. We prefer balance, order, and righteousness according to God's natural or eternal law, even if God must die on its behalf. But God, who forgives sin, is none other than this very man Jesus Christ, who came forgiving. In Christ the Father did not merely provide an example of how to forgive enemies. The cross was not a deal between God's attributes of mercy and justice for God to get his pound of flesh from beggars who had no means of paying. Christ, who knew no sin, became sin for us (2 Cor. 5:21). Christ redeemed us from the curse of the law by becoming an actual curse for us (Gal. 3:13). Such was the cost, not to ourselves, but to God. That cost will never be forgotten by God, though humans frequently forget. But God doesn't remember our sin anymore, so that sinners can be made alive in the new kingdom.

This was "right." The triune God was, is, and will be right. When God forgave in Christ, it was no longer a demand, a covenant, or a prophecy. It was something that had come to be. Forgiveness was not a speculative idea, it was a historical fact; indeed, forgiveness came in as a person. By that means, rather than as a general goal, forgiveness has become inescapable for those the Father has placed in the hand of his Son.

When we hear John's proclamation, "Behold, the lamb of God, who takes away the sin of the world," we are forced to conclude that Christ was not only found among sinners but wanted to be there, by free will — the only will that is really free. If God's will has chosen this, then the law has no choice but to attack him as the only one who freely wills to be a sinner. All others are merely doing what they are bound to do. Thus Jesus' death is not a case of mistaken identity, an accident, or an unnecessary grief the disciples could have averted had they opened themselves to God or transacted some other transcendental business. The cross is necessary for the Lamb of God to take away the sin of the world. The curse of God has come to duel with the blessing. But it is the blessing that is God's final, irresistible desire, and so Christ's death becomes the death of death, the law to the law, sin to sin — in an eschatological collision in Christ's own person.

Christ did this out of love in the form of mercy for actual, specific sinners. Because he is God by nature, his blessing cannot be conquered, even by his own wrath or law. That blessing is a burning love, even when no distinction can be made between me and my sins — as David, Peter, and Paul all found. The Father did not spare his Son; the Son did not count equality with God a thing to be grasped; the Holy Spirit was not ashamed to proclaim even through the local preacher and give this to us as the inviolable promise that creates new life out of nothing.

Back to Earth

Christ, as distinguished from the law, must be made known. He alone is the Lamb of God who takes away the sin of the world. John is not that one; he only bears witness to Christ, on whom lies the sin of us all absolutely, wholly, once and for all. Thus we can return to our daily lives with two absolutes: sin and Christ. Sinners in ourselves, righteous in Christ, we come back to the situation in which David found himself. We are subject to sin in ourselves, but God sends a preacher. Otherwise, how would we hear? Nathan declared: "Now the LORD has put away your sin; you shall not die" (2 Sam. 12:13). Commonly the preacher is the local "forgiveness person," who absolves real sinners by a simple promise: "I forgive you all your sins." And in this exercise of the office of the keys, though we ourselves are remarkably bad at the law's requirement to forgive, our own prison is opened. Forgiveness is a real end and a new beginning. Applied to us, that means death and resurrection, or the end to the futility of taking little steps toward the big forgiveness. Sinners in ourselves, saints in Christ, we are allowed by this freedom to live in the old world with its partial forgivenesses and petty mercies. This freedom allows us to live in the world that either forgets its sin too easily or can't seem to let it go. So we trust God absolutely when we pray, "Forgive us our sins as we forgive those who sin against us." We take God at his word. Forgiveness then finds its way through us as servants to everyone, while in Christ we remain subject to none — having sin, death, and the power of evil behind us. For where there is forgiveness of sins, there is not only "salvation" but life, real life as spouses, parents, children, teachers, students, farmers, politicians — and all the relationships in life where *daily* forgiveness is desperately needed.

Reviving Forgiveness

Matthew 18:21-25

CYNTHIA L. RIGBY

"Should you not have had mercy on your fellow slave, as I had mercy on you?" (v. 33)

It was the first anniversary of 9/11, and I was participating in a panel discussion at a United Methodist church in Austin, Texas. We had just finished presentations on the theological implications of what had happened and "where we need to go from here." The floor was opened for Q and A. A hand shot up from the back row. The man sat on the edge of his seat, leaning forward, his face twisted in anguish. I had the distinct sense that he had come, that night, hoping for an opportunity to speak his mind. "Those people who destroyed the towers . . . ," he began, forcing his voice to stay measured, "the Bible says I have to forgive them. But I'm telling you, I *just can't* do it! What does this mean for me, since Jesus said we had to forgive others in order to be forgiven?"

This man clearly thought that forgiveness is, at times, impossible. He seemed uncertain that it was even desirable, post-9/11. In the short time I talked with him, he told me he understood forgiveness to mean that we have to forget, to let go of all feelings of anger, to put aside injustices that have been done. I've got to hand it to him — he was honest enough to admit that, in his view, we human beings are simply not wired to forgive, by this definition. We are programmed to remember. To get angry when people hurt us. And we want justice to prevail, particularly when injustice is directed against *us.*

What complicates matters significantly is that we do not always stand on the receiving end of wrongdoing. When we are wronged, we want justice. When we are in the wrong, we want mercy. When we need forgiveness, we hope others are better forgivers than we are. We concentrate on believing that God forgives. Though we are unable to forget evildoing, God *is* able, we assure ourselves. "To err is human, to forgive is divine," the saying goes. Scripture teaches us that God removes our transgressions from us as far as the east is from the west (Ps. 103:12). God cleanses us from all unrighteousness, seeing us as holy and blameless in Jesus Christ (1 John 1:9; Eph. 1:4). God's capacity to forgive surpasses anything we can conceive of. Ten thousand talents' worth, the parable says. Figuring a talent to be worth approximately fifteen years of wages, this is the equivalent of *150,000 years* of paychecks. If a person made $65,000 a year, that would mean the canceled debt would be $9,750,000,000! As far as I know, this is a bit more than the average servant would borrow from the average king on an average day in New Testament times. The figure is simply inconceivable, by any standards. It is there to remind us that God's graciousness runs deeper than anything we could ever imagine.

In light of this it might be tempting to throw up our hands in awe, vowing to leave all matters related to forgiveness in the generous hands of God. But then we are confronted by that pesky creed. "I believe in the Holy Spirit, the holy catholic church, the communion of saints, *the forgiveness of sins. . . .*" "Wait a minute!" we may think. "The 'forgiveness of sins' seems to be in the wrong place. Shouldn't it be in one of the first two articles? Doesn't it better describe the work of the 'almighty Father' or 'Jesus Christ'"? (After all, it's clear that *they are* the ones who handle forgiveness.) Instead, "forgiveness of sins" comes near the end, in the section about the Holy Spirit's work in the context of the Christian community. Forgiveness seems to be a trademark of the communion of saints, an aspect of what it is to be holy. Leaving forgiveness to God, then, does not appear to be an option.

The idea that the divine work of forgiveness includes our forgiving of one another is a persistent theme in the New Testament. Paul urges members of the church at Ephesus to forgive each other, even as God in Christ has forgiven them (Eph. 4:32). Jesus treats God's forgiveness of us and our forgiveness of one another as inextricably connected. In the Lord's Prayer and in the parable in Matthew 18, it even looks as though God's forgiveness of us is in some way *contingent upon* our forgiveness of others. "Forgive us our debts, *as we* forgive our debtors," Jesus teaches us to pray (Matt. 6:12; Luke 11:4). When the servant does not show mercy to his fellow servant, the king seems to take back forgiveness that has already been given.

God *taking back* forgiveness? Could anything strike greater fear in our hearts? The idea that God would withdraw forgiveness from those who do not forgive others seems incompatible with everything we know of God's grace. Don't we hear from our pastors, every Sunday, that we are saved by grace, and not because of anything we have done (Eph. 2:8)? Don't we rely on the promise that nothing can separate us from the love of God in Christ (Rom. 8:38-39)? Or should we modify this to read, "Nothing can separate us from the love of God . . . except when we don't forgive others"? Surely, it couldn't be the case that we are unconditionally forgiven of all sins except the sin of not forgiving.

On the other hand, however, one could argue that the parable lays out a pretty straightforward formula for maintaining the favor of God. It is a formula that seems seriously slanted to our advantage. We forgive someone a hundred days' worth of wages, God forgives us 150,000 years' worth. What a deal! At times I read this parable and wonder what this king can possibly teach me about the unconditional love of God. At other times I read it and think to myself: Why all the complaining? How much easier can it get? All the servant has to do is forgive some piddling debt and he's home free.

And then I come back to earth and remember what human beings are really like. Forgiveness does not come easily for us, even when the debt owed is relatively small. Even in the context of the communion of saints, it doesn't come easy. Sometimes forgiveness seems *harder* in the life of the church. Why *is* that? Maybe it's because our expectations of each other are so high. We don't expect our Christian friends to offend us, so we hold it twice as much against them when they do. Or maybe it's because Christians are always pressuring each other to forgive. As well intentioned as we are, we too often try to force each other to push aside feelings of anger. We're more comfortable when wrongdoing is named with a discreet *whisper* than with a SHOUT. And we communicate that it is best to forget the ways we have been violated.

Perhaps we are not always wrong in making such demands. Certainly we should resist the litigious culture in which we live. We should let minor infractions drop without a great deal of fanfare. The problem is, though, that not all injustices weigh in at a measly 100 denarii. How do we relate to the person in our lives who causes us pain on a day-to-day basis? What does forgiveness look like, in that case?

A woman in her early forties recently told me she is a survivor of incest. A revered family member had raped her, repeatedly, from the time she was a little girl until she was thirteen. As soon as she was old enough and strong enough to fight him off, she did. He, still living, has never admitted his fault. This story, as horrific as it is, is a very common one. But just as tragic, and common, is the theological overlay that often accompanies it. This woman had grown up in a Christian family and had attended church her entire life. She wept as she confessed to me that she had spent thirty years trying to forgive this man, and had yet to conquer her sin of being unforgiving. She knew the incest was not her fault, but she blamed herself for how long the pain had stretched on. "All my life people at church have told me I need to forgive him," she said. "And they're right. If I could just forgive him, everything would be fine." As far as I could tell, members of the Christian community had never allowed her to name the wrongdoing, presumably for fear that to do so would look unforgiving and therefore unchristian.

I wonder if that man from the back row, the one who asked about forgiveness, felt some of the same pressures this woman did. Were people in the church telling him he had to "get over" his pain? Did he finally decide he was unable to forgive because he thought the church was asking him to be a passive, silent "doormat"?

Contrary to what we may have been taught, forgiveness does not require us to overlook sin, injustice, and pain. Certainly forgiveness is about mercy. It does not demand compensation for wrongdoing. But this does not mean the wrongdoing goes unnoticed. To be forgiving is, in fact, to be *hypersensitive* to the pain and injustices that surround us. Just look at the parable. The servant is miserably aware of his own debt, pleading for mercy. The king recognizes this pain and is moved by it. He takes an interest in the servant and in the servant's well-being. Later, a group of servants complains to the king about how the forgiven servant did not himself forgive. Notice that the king does not throw up his hands and say, "Sorry, but I don't know what you are talking about. The moment I canceled his debt, I forgot the details of the entire matter." On the contrary, the king is infuriated. A man he tried to free has gone out and insisted that another be in bondage. The king responds emotionally because, as someone who forgives, his senses are heightened to the lack of forgiveness that surrounds us and the pain this lack causes. The king berates the servant, throwing him in jail, because he recognizes that forgiveness has failed to occur. Despite his best efforts, forgiveness is not something he can accomplish alone. Rather, it is fully realized only in the context of the community, when mercy is shown and reconciliation and transformation are taking place.

The parable is actually, then, not a story about a king who gave the gift of forgiveness and then took it back. Rather, it is a story of a servant who does not participate in the forgiveness that is extended, and so hurts himself and the community. The servant does not stop to revel in the mercy of the king, getting caught up in its implications. He is not revived by the experience. Perhaps he thinks of his canceled debt matter-of-factly, as a fortuitous transaction, as something the king does for him that simply gets him ahead of the game. He seems oblivious to the fact that the king is not merely handing him a gift, but inviting him to participate in a whole new way of being. In a world built on transactions, exchanges, rights, and "getting ahead," the servant is probably stunned to be identified as "wicked." After all, what did he really do wrong? The hundred denarii is owed to him; he is perfectly within his rights to throw the debtor in jail.

This logic, though impeccable, reveals that forgiveness has not actually taken root. Sure, the king cancels the servant's debt. But what the king is offering the servant, with this cancellation, is more than the break of a lifetime. The king is not giving the servant a life-changing gift, but the gift of an entirely new life.

Sometimes television sitcoms play with the idea of what it would be like to receive a new life. The standard plot of such episodes is that a lead character saves the life of another character. Next thing you know, the one who has been saved is obsessed with trying to even the score with the one who saved him. Running errands, bringing gifts, being sweet and subservient — eventually driving up a wall the one who saved him. Inevitably the saved person tries to stage a way the indebted one can save her life, in order to get the grateful one off her back. Usually the plan backfires and the lead character is forced to rescue the other a *second* time. Now the saved one has to do something to pay back for *two* lives! What makes this plot funny is the audience's underlying awareness that there is really no way to even the score. No amount of shoe shining can earn back a life. But the point I want to make here is this: the shoe shining is still very important. It shows that the one who is saved has "gotten it," entering into the new life that was proffered.

When I think of what it looks like to enter into a life marked by forgiveness, I often think of Scrooge. Ebenezer Scrooge, from Charles Dickens's *Christmas Carol*. Think of Scrooge, waking up on Christmas morning, amazed that he has been given another chance. He is not dead, after all. He has not missed Christmas. Now, before raising his head off his pillow, he could have calculated that the extension of his life was fortuitous, giving him more time to build his profit margin. He could have chosen to engage the day in the stingy way he engaged every other. If he had responded this way, it wouldn't have made a bit of difference whether or not Marley and the other ghosts had been real, or whether they had actually handed him a new life on a silver platter. He still would be dead. Instead, of course, Scrooge rises from bed a changed man. He buys a Christmas goose and a sackful of presents, giving away all that he can, as quickly as he can. He does these things not because he is obligated to, but because he can't help himself. He can't believe how lucky he is.

If only the servant had been a bit more like Scrooge. What if he had run out of his meeting with the king with a full heart, reaching out to those around him? Then we would know he had gotten it. Then we would see the fruits of forgiveness. It's not a matter of the servant, or Scrooge, or us *doing something* to ensure that forgiveness "takes." But it is a matter of living into and out of that which it is impossible to pay back.

So — where does this leave our back-row questioner and the woman who wanted so badly to forgive her abuser? They, with all of us, are called to engage with the community as those revived by forgiveness. But this does not mean they are called to be doormats, to overlook injustices, or to forget wrongdoing. On the contrary, deep engagement with life will lead them to be even more determined to challenge the brokenness that marks our existence. It will include moments of rage and disappointment when others betray the magnanimous grace that has been extended to all. As Desmond Tutu explains, forgiveness is emotionally exhausting work. He writes: "In forgiving, people are not being asked to forget. On the contrary, it is important to remember, so that we should not let such atrocities happen again. Forgiveness does not mean condoning what has been done. It means taking what happened seriously . . . drawing out the sting in the memory that threatens our entire existence." Like the king in the parable, like Jesus in the Gospels, to live as those who are forgiven means naming wickedness for exactly what it is. To name, to remember, to be angry, and to grieve — all are corollaries of hoping for new life. To close ourselves off from experiencing these, as though they are antithetical to forgiveness, is to forget that forgiveness compels engagement with the real, nitty-gritty details of life. Forgiveness wrestles with the difficult stuff in the hope that others, too, may come to participate.

We believe in the communion of saints. We believe in the forgiveness of sins. We live in community with those who have tasted God's boundless graciousness. We've been given a new chance at life. We've been given new life. May each of us have the strength and the courage to be revived by this gift. May we wake in the morning reveling in our good fortune. May we learn to live in gratitude, forgiving one another even as we have been forgiven. Amen.

CHAPTER 14

The Resurrection of the Body

Carnis resurrectionem

RICHARD B. HAYS

Resurrection Turns the World Upside Down

By raising the man Jesus — who had been given the death penalty by the duly constituted civil authorities — God turned the world upside down. The resurrection upsets the world because it gives us a glimpse of a truth more fundamental than common sense — a glimpse of a world no longer ruled by the power of death.

When the first Christian missionaries began their work of proclamation in the ancient Mediterranean world, the story they told struck their hearers as strange and disturbing. In Acts 17 we read an account of the resistance Paul and Silas met when they began preaching in Thessalonica. They went to the synagogue and began expounding Israel's scripture to demonstrate that "it was necessary for the Messiah to suffer and to rise from the dead" (17:3a). Initially they attracted a few followers, but it didn't take long for the backlash to materialize. Soon an angry mob was at the door of Jason, their host. Not finding Paul and Silas, the mob dragged Jason and some other believers before the city authorities, shouting, "These people who have been turning the world upside down have come here also. . . . *They are all acting contrary to the decrees of the emperor, saying that there is another king named Jesus*" (17:6-7).

What was so alarming about the message of Paul and Silas? Clearly the posse of agitators was not alarmed by a message about how individuals might secure otherworldly immortality. Rather, the message the apostles preached posed a threat to public order. They were "turning the world upside down" because they were proclaiming that Jesus, who had been put to death by the authority of Caesar, is Lord; therefore, Jesus is Lord and Caesar isn't. The claim was provocative because the imperial propaganda machine was pressing the Roman emperor's claim to hold universal sovereignty. For example: a first-century inscription acclaims "Divine Augustus Caesar, son of a god, imperator of land and sea, the benefactor and savior of the whole world."[1] Against this background, it can be no coincidence that the apostolic speeches in Acts repeatedly interpret the resurrection of Jesus as the definitive sign that Jesus has now been enthroned above every other authority. Peter's Pentecost sermon in Acts 2 climaxes by declaring that the resurrection of Jesus proves that God has put Jesus on the throne of David and reduced all other human rulers to subservience at his feet. Jesus has reclaimed the title "Lord," which Caesar had falsely usurped, and he is the "Christ" — the anointed King for whom God's people had hoped, the one who will bring the reign of God's justice on earth (2:22-36).

It is not hard to see why this sort of claim sounded like "turning the world upside down." Indeed, it sounded like treason against the empire. The thing that is harder to understand is why, according to Luke's account, the *Jewish* crowd in Thessalonica became so agitated about a perceived affront to the authority of Caesar. After all, as Jews, did they not share Israel's ancient hope for God to raise up a Davidic ruler once again and to place the other nations under his feet? Apparently not. They had made their peace with the Pax Romana. They were comfortable with the lives they knew. Talk of resurrection threatened to destabilize their accommodations.

But it is by no means Jews only who wanted the present order of things to continue without interruption. Two chapters later in Acts, Luke tells the story of a riot among the pagan silversmiths in Ephesus. They dragged two of Paul's companions into the great public amphitheater, and for two hours they protested against the Christian preachers by chanting over and over, "Great is Artemis of the Ephesians" (19:23-41). Why were the silversmiths staging this public demonstration? Because they realized that Paul's message about Jesus' resurrection threatened to depose all other gods — and therefore ruin their business of selling silver idols of Artemis. The resurrection of Jesus is not good news for business-as-usual.

These two stories — the mob action in Thessalonica and the silversmiths' riot in Ephesus — show in different ways how the message of Jesus' resurrec-

---

1. David C. Braund, *Augustus to Nero: A Sourcebook on Roman History, 31 BC–AD 68* (London: Croom Helm, 1985), #66. Cited in Joel B. Green, *The Theology of the Gospel of Luke* (Cambridge: Cambridge University Press, 1995), p. 120.

tion challenges the way the world conducts its affairs. Indeed, the message of the resurrection upsets the world so much that the world will go to outrageous lengths to suppress or supplant that message.

Perhaps that explains in part why our proclamation of the resurrection in the church is so halting. We are up against serious resistance — resistance from outside forces and resistance from within ourselves. In order to take the measure of that resistance, we must first take a step back to clarify what the classical Christian teaching about the resurrection actually is.

Clarifying Christian Teaching: The Resurrection of Jesus and the Resurrection of the Body

The early Christians proclaimed that God had broken the power of death by raising Jesus bodily from the grave; therefore, the New Testament writers and the early Christian creeds looked forward to *the resurrection of the body* as the consummation of God's redemptive action in the world. They believed that when the risen Lord returned in glory, the dead would be raised to new life. Thus the resurrection stood at the heart of early Christian preaching and faith.

Every time Christians repeat the Apostles' Creed, they declare, "I believe in . . . the resurrection of the body." Yet in our time few Christian doctrines are more neglected and misunderstood than this one. Many devout Christians expect their souls to "go to heaven" when they die, without realizing how little the Bible says about any such idea, and without understanding what the church has historically taught about the resurrection of the body. The resurrection of the dead is not at all the same thing as the immortality of the soul, although many Christians confuse them.[2] Resurrection has a physically embodied character. It is neither an escape from the material world nor a merely subjective experience in the hearts of the disciples; rather, it is a physical event in the future of the time and space that we inhabit.

To understand the conceptual world in which the early Christians preached the resurrection, we must consider the story of the seven martyred brothers in 2 Maccabees 7. When the tyrant Antiochus Epiphanes threatened to cut out their tongues and cut off their hands, one of the brothers stretched forth his hands and said, "I got these from Heaven, and for the sake of his laws I disdain them, and from him I hope to get them back again" (2 Macc. 7:11). The resurrection will restore the body: that is what many first-century Jews

---

2. For a classic delineation of this distinction, see Oscar Cullmann, *Immortality of the Soul or Resurrection of the Dead? The Witness of the New Testament* (London: Epworth, 1958).

believed, and it is what Jesus' earliest followers understood when they testi-fied that he had been raised from the dead.[3]

All this may seem reasonably clear. Yet a confusion between resurrection and disembodied immortality arose very early in the history of the church, as Christian preachers moved out from the Jewish communities where the gospel was first proclaimed and began addressing the Gentile world. The distinctively Jewish idea of bodily resurrection seemed puzzling and even offensive to many people in Greco-Roman culture — as Paul's correspondence with the church at Corinth attests. (See also Acts 17:30-32, which depicts a crowd of Athenians, including Epicurean and Stoic philosophers [17:18], scoffing at Paul's message of resurrection and final judgment.) Ancient Stoicism, which had a monistic understanding of the cosmos, did not encourage expectations of individual postmortem existence; Stoics generally believed that the elements of which human beings are composed would disintegrate and become reabsorbed into "the continuing, ordered process of the universe."[4] On the other hand, much first-century Greek thought, under the influence of Platonism, tended toward dualism: the concrete physical world was seen as an imperfect and corrupted shadow of a nonmaterial reality, and the body was seen as a prison for the soul. A standard pun equated the physical body *(sōma)* with a tomb *(sēma)* in which the true human self was trapped. In order to attain truth and freedom, on this view, it was necessary for a wise person to transcend the realm of the senses and to become, as the Greek writer Plutarch put it, "pure, fleshless, and unde-filed."[5] Celsus, a Middle Platonist critic of Christianity, scorned the hope of resurrection of the body as "the hope of worms." He asked derisively, "[W]hat sort of human soul would have any further desire for a body that has rotted? . . . For the soul [God] might be able to provide an everlasting life; but, as Heraclitus says, 'corpses ought to be thrown away as worse than dung.'"[6] In this cultural setting, it was not long before some people began to reinterpret Christianity as a message about how to escape from the body.[7]

---

3. For a full discussion of the evidence, see George W. Nickelsburg, *Resurrection, Immortal-ity, and Eternal Life in Intertestamental Judaism* (Cambridge: Harvard University Press, 1972); N. T. Wright, *The Resurrection of the Son of God* (Minneapolis: Fortress, 2003).

4. Brian E. Daley, "A Hope for Worms: Early Christian Hope," in *Resurrection: Theological and Scientific Assessments*, ed. T. Peters, R. J. Russell, and M. Welker (Grand Rapids: Eerdmans, 2002), p. 138.

5. Plutarch, *Romulus* 28.6.

6. Quoted by Origen in *Against Celsus* 5.14, trans. Henry Chadwick (Cambridge: Cambridge University Press, 1965), p. 274. For this reference I am indebted to Daley (p. 138).

7. Daley provides a helpful survey of the complex and various ways in which patristic writ-ers — and their Gnostic rivals — understood the meaning of resurrection.

Justin Martyr, the second-century Christian apologist, protested stoutly against this tendency. He wrote that there are "some who are called Christians . . . who say there is no resurrection of the dead, and that their souls, when they die, are taken to heaven." He calls such people "godless, impious heretics" and warns his readers not to be deceived by them: "Do not imagine that they are Christians." In contrast, he insists, "I and others, who are right-minded Christians on all points, are assured that there will be a resurrection of the dead."[8]

Justin is simply echoing the apostolic message of the New Testament. Paul, in writing to the church he had founded at Corinth, also had to contend with people who were saying "there is no resurrection of the dead (anastasis nekrōn)" (1 Cor. 15:12): no raising of corpses. They thought the crude apocalyptic idea of resurrection could be replaced by an exalted spiritual wisdom — or, as we might call it today, "spirituality." But Paul insists that without the resurrection of the body, the whole gospel is in vain and those who have believed the gospel are "of all people most to be pitied" (15:19). The bodily resurrection of Jesus is the firstfruits, a sign of the cosmic consummation when the risen Christ will triumph over all other powers, including death, and hand over the kingdom to God the Father (15:20-28). Paul insists, therefore, that the resurrection for which we hope remains a future event: "For as all die in Adam, so all *will* be made alive in Christ. But each in his own order: Christ the first fruits, *then at his coming* those who belong to Christ" (15:22-23).

When Paul writes in Romans 8 of the present as a time of longing for redemption, he says that "we ourselves, who have the first fruits of the Spirit, groan inwardly while we wait for adoption, the redemption of our bodies" (8:23). Note carefully: he does not say "redemption *from* our bodies," but "redemption *of* our bodies." The difference is enormous and crucial for Christian theology. God the creator will not abandon what he has created. The doctrine of the resurrection of the body affirms that God will finally redeem creation from its bondage to death and decay. But Paul is very clear that we do not yet see that for which we hope. We groan along with the unredeemed creation (8:18-25). This, too, is part of the truth that Christians must tell as we confront the reality of death.

To be sure, a handful of NT passages (Luke 23:43; John 14:2; Phil. 1:21-24) suggest that those who believe will be "with Christ" immediately upon death. This expectation — which is quite a minor note in the NT in contrast to the dominant expectation of resurrection at the last day — should not be understood as an alternative to the hope of resurrection of the body. Rather, these

---

8. Justin, *Dialogue with Trypho* 80.

texts envision an intermediate state of being in the presence of God while still awaiting the resurrection. A vivid image of this intermediary condition appears in Revelation 6:9-11, where the souls of the martyrs are portrayed as "under the altar" in the heavenly throne room, still awaiting final vindication. They are told to "rest a little longer" until the appointed time for the final revelation of God's justice. Passages such as this provide the background for the classic Christian teaching that those who die in Christ enter the communion of the saints and exist in the presence of God. This image of "life after death," however, does not replace the expectation of a final resurrection; indeed, the intermediate state is conceived as anticipatory, looking forward to the resurrection of the body, which remains the focal point of hope.

Resurrection as the focal point of Christian hope may be illustrated by recalling Paul's response to the Thessalonian believers, who were confronting the death of loved ones. "But we do not want you to be uninformed, brothers and sisters, about those who have died, so that you may not grieve as others do who have no hope. For since we believe that Jesus died and rose again, even so, through Jesus, God will bring with him those who have died" (1 Thess. 4:13-14). Paul goes on to explain that the dead in Christ will rise first and be gathered into a great reunion with those who are left alive, and so they will be together forever, with Christ and with one another. At the conclusion of the passage Paul writes simply, "Therefore comfort one another with these words" (4:18). Notice that Paul *does not* say to the grieving Thessalonians, "Your loved ones are already in heaven with Jesus." Instead he holds out the promise of the resurrection of the body, based on the sure ground of Christ's resurrection. That is the ground of the apostolic message of comfort.

One more thing must be said, however, about the NT's teaching on resurrection. The resurrection of the dead must be distinguished from mere resuscitation of the mortal body. Paul insists that "flesh and blood cannot inherit the kingdom of God" (1 Cor. 15:50); consequently, resurrection must involve both continuity with our present embodied existence and *transformation* of our bodies into a glorified state beyond our imagining: "For the trumpet will sound, and the dead will be raised *imperishable*, and *we will be changed*" (15:52). It is *our* bodies that will be raised and redeemed, but they will be transformed by the power of God to be "conformed to the body of [Christ's] glory" (Phil. 3:21). How can there be both continuity and transformation? Paul grapples with this issue at length in 1 Corinthians 15:35-58. He gestures toward the mystery of resurrection by pointing to the analogy of the seed buried in the earth: it grows into a living plant that could never have been imagined just by looking at the seed. That is only an analogy, of course, not an explanation. Somehow in the freedom and power of God, God will conform our resurrected bodies to Christ's glory in such a way that we will be (unimaginably) like him and yet at the same time fully ourselves, at last made whole.

The Message of Resurrection Today

There is much confusion today in the church's speech and practice about resurrection. American Protestant churches have come to surround death with a sentimental nineteenth-century hymnody and piety that in effect deny its reality and the "not yet" dimension of redemption. When we confront death, we tend to focus on the fate of the individual soul (conceived as going to heaven immediately), not on the resurrection of the body, and certainly not on God's restoration of the whole creation. Regrettably, this kind of individualistic, dualistic piety is closer to ancient Gnosticism than to historic orthodox Christianity. Many funeral services offer an incoherent hodgepodge combining biblical teaching on resurrection with dualistic ideas about the flight of the soul to heavenly bliss, and sometimes also with New Age, quasi-Eastern notions that the deceased has not really died but has simply been merged into nature, so that she is now present in the sunset and the gentle rain and so forth. (It is as though the ancient traditions of Platonist dualism and Stoic monism, having been held in check for centuries by biblical and trinitarian teaching, have finally burst the doctrinal dam and flooded into our funeral practices.) It is a matter of urgent importance for the church to resist such corruptions of the gospel.

In addition to these sentimental "spiritual" heresies, the biblical understanding of resurrection faces another powerful source of resistance in our time on a very different front: rationalist materialism. In modernity secular rationalism became the default governing paradigm for public discourse, especially among the intellectual elite in the West. From the point of view of rationalist materialism, a human being is nothing other than a complex biochemical organism; therefore, death is simply the end of that organism. Any talk of life after death is meaningless, unless it is simply a poetic way of describing how we live on in the memory of those whose lives we have touched. For many people who do not attend churches, and for some who do, scientific materialism frames their worldview.

I recently heard a lecture given by a distinguished medical researcher who is seeking to understand the genetic causes of heart disease. At one point in his talk he offered the following description of his working assumption about human beings: "We are disposable packages designed for the successful transmission of gametes." In other words, our only purpose in the world is to re-produce ourselves and pass along our genetic material to future generations. I wanted to ask him why, if that is so, he cared so deeply, as he obviously did, about prolonging the lives of his patients long past their reproductive years. There was a deep philosophical tension between the scientific materialism that governed his research and the inarticulate human compassion that moti-vated it. This sort of unresolved tension is rampant in our culture. Rationalist materialism governs public accounts of what is "real"; therefore, in this frame of reference "resurrection," like all religious language, can only be a meta-phorical description of some sort of affective state in our own consciousness.

Matters are made still worse by the fact that a significant body of *NT scholarship* has fallen under the spell of rationalist materialism. The recent history of theology is replete with attempts to reinterpret the meaning of the NT's resurrection stories — or even to rewrite them — in ways that will not conflict with a modern scientific worldview. The most abidingly influential approach to this problem in the twentieth century was offered by Rudolf Bultmann, who offered the lapidary explanation that "Jesus rose in the kerygma." This, or some variation of it, remains a widely held solution to the problem. According to Bultmann, the NT's stories about a bodily resurrec-tion and empty tomb are not in any sense factual descriptions of something that happened to Jesus of Nazareth, who had been put to death; rather, they are to be understood as expressions of the "Easter faith" of the first disciples. They are inadequate, primitive attempts to express in mythic imagery the conviction that Jesus' death was in fact an expression of the grace of God.

Bultmann's demythologized account of Easter faith continues to prevail in many circles of NT scholarship, including the work of Gerd Lüdemann[9] — who eventually took the step of renouncing any claim of Christian faith — and of the scholars who have marketed themselves as "the Jesus Seminar." Some interpreters who follow this line, such as John Shelby Spong and Marcus Borg, regard "Easter faith" as spiritually authentic and true, while others, such as Lüdemann, regard it as "only a pious wish" that ultimately has produced deceptive and destructive consequences.[10] Lüdemann asserts that the body of Jesus either rotted in the tomb or "was devoured by vultures and jackals." How then did the story of the resurrection of Jesus arise in the first place? Lüdemann, Spong, and Robert Funk — the founder of the Jesus Semi-

9. G. Lüdemann, *The Resurrection of Jesus: History, Experience, Theology* (Minneapolis: For-tress, 1994).

10. For Lüdemann's public statement renouncing Christian faith, see his book *The Great Deception: And What Jesus Really Said and Did* (London: SCM Press, 1998), esp. "A Letter to Je-sus" (pp. 1-9). The phrase "only a pious wish" appears on p. 3.

nar — have produced speculative accounts of the psychological states and experiences ("mass ecstasy," "grief work," etc.) that might have given rise to "Easter faith" among Jesus' followers.[11]

The fundamental problem with studies of this kind is their methodological circularity. They begin by thinking inside the box of modernist epistemology, which rules out a priori the possibility of the resurrection of the body of a man crucified, dead, and buried. They then scrutinize the Gospels and produce speculative revisionist accounts of the history behind them. These speculations are then offered for sale as scientific historical findings that should supplant the canonical narratives. But what if the premise is wrong? What if the testimony of the witnesses is true, and the tomb really was empty? How would that force us to think differently about history? As Jürgen Moltmann has suggested, the key problem is not to reconsider the resurrection in light of history, but to reconsider history in light of the resurrection.

What would be the implications of reevaluating the world in light of the resurrection? The final part of this essay will offer some theological reflections in response to that question.

First, *the resurrection undermines the myth of human autonomy.* As long as we ignore or deny the resurrection, we can maintain the illusion that we are self-sufficient and in control of our own lives. Autonomy is held in extremely high value in our culture. We may make mistakes, of course, and we don't *yet* know everything or control everything, but surely given enough time and scientific progress, we believe that human ingenuity can solve the problems we face. But the resurrection exposes the lie of autonomy. The resurrection brings us face-to-face with our creator, the God "who gives life to the dead and calls into existence the things that do not exist" (Rom. 4:17b). Further, through the death and resurrection of Jesus, this God has reached out to save us, through an act beyond all human capacity, beyond all human understanding. Therefore, the resurrection makes it unmistakably clear that we are not our own; we are not capable of saving ourselves. In light of the resurrection, our self-salvation projects, such as the Human Genome Project, start to look disturbingly like the Tower of Babel.

Second, *the resurrection dismantles the dichotomies we employ to erect walls to keep "religion" safely sealed off in its own compartment.* We build walls between body and soul, between secular and religious, between political and spiritual. The resurrection tears them down. Against all dualisms, ancient and modern, the resurrection declares that bodies matter, that God's power is

---

11. For an extended imaginative reconstruction, see John Shelby Spong, *Resurrection: Myth or Reality?* (San Francisco: Harper San Francisco, 1994), pp. 242-60.

present, and will ultimately prevail, in the material world. God intends to redeem the created order, not beam us up out of it. In Romans 8 Paul hears the whole creation groaning in travail, but in light of the resurrection he affirms that we can look forward to the day when "the creation itself will be set free from its bondage to decay and will obtain the glorious freedom of the children of God" (Rom. 8:21). One might suppose the world would want to hear this, but it is not always so. The dichotomies are comforting; they allow us to keep God at arm's length, on the margins of our experience. In particular, the walls allow those with power to abuse the creation and to dismiss the voices of protesting prophets as the voices of an otherworldly idealism that fails to reckon "realistically" with the world as it is — that is, the world as it is inside the walls we have built to keep God out. The resurrection rolls away the stone and tears down the walls.

Third, *the resurrection portends God's judgment of the world.* When we stand before the risen Lord, we find ourselves summoned to judgment.[12] After Paul escaped the mob in Thessalonica that accused him of turning the world upside down, he went on to Athens, where he delivered a public speech at the Areopagus. It was an artful piece of oratory and things were going well, until he got around to the climax, where he condemned idolatry and spoke of the connection between resurrection and judgment: "While God has overlooked the times of human ignorance, now he commands all people everywhere to repent, because he has fixed a day on which he will have the world judged in righteousness by a man whom he has appointed, and of this he has given assurance to all by raising him from the dead" (Acts 17:30-31). The reaction of the Athenians was predictably divided. "When they heard of the resurrection of the dead, some scoffed; but others said [cautiously], 'We will hear you again about this'" (17:32). Either way, this was hardly a welcome message for a city like Athens that liked to think of itself as prosperous, enlightened, devoted to education and the arts, the high point of human culture. For such a city the idea of divine judgment could only come as a disturbing prospect.

The same was true of the Sadducees in Jerusalem, who rejected belief in the resurrection of the dead (see, e.g., Mark 12:18-27). They were closely linked with the temple establishment, and they collaborated with the Roman authorities. In this privileged position they had everything to lose in a future judgment by God. Their rejection of the resurrection was probably linked, therefore, with a desire to preserve the political and economic status quo.

The Bible repeatedly links judgment with resurrection. The linkage is a

---

12. For a nuanced discussion of this theme, see Rowan Williams, *Resurrection: Interpreting the Easter Gospel* (Harrisburg, Pa.: Morehouse, 1994), pp. 7-28.

necessary one. Why? In the history we know, justice does *not* prevail. The righteous suffer, the wicked prosper, and the poor have justice denied them. If God is going to make all things right and establish justice, it will necessarily be in the life of the world to come, a world in which God will swallow up death forever, and wipe away the tears from all faces, and take away the disgrace of his people (Isa. 25:7-8). That is the world for which we pray every time we say, "Thy kingdom come, thy will be done on earth as it is in heaven." It is not a prayer that should be lightly prayed — especially by the comfortable and privileged. But the resurrection of Jesus is a sign that God's day of reckoning is coming, whether we welcome it or not.

Fourth, *the resurrection transforms our seeing*. The resurrection challenges what we take to be the clear evidence of our senses. It calls into question our seeing, our perception of what is "real." The epistemological shift is nicely illustrated by Paul's incredulous rhetorical question in his speech before Agrippa: "Why is it thought incredible by any of you that God raises the dead?" (Acts 26:8). Paul, already trained as a Pharisee to expect the resurrection, now finds himself living in a world in which the truth of Jesus' resurrection shapes his commonsense view of daily reality. The idea that someone might find resurrection incredible seems as odd to him as it might seem to us today to encounter someone who still believed the earth to be flat. The resurrection has produced a "conversion of the imagination" that causes us to understand everything else differently.[13] But those who still live in the flat-earth frame of reference may find it distinctly threatening to be told that their perceptions are distorted. Recognizing the difficulty of coming to this new way of seeing, the theologian Sarah Coakley makes the intriguing proposal that the resurrection of Jesus might bring about "a transformation of the believer's actual epistemic *apparatus*."[14] Learning to see properly in this new world requires a retraining of our senses: the resurrection purges the death-bound illusions that previously held us captive and sets us free to perceive the real world of God's life-giving resurrection power. But, like the dwellers in the dim darkness of Plato's cave, those who have not seen the world illumined by the resurrection often prefer the darkness. They reject the disciplines required to see in a different way.

13. See Richard B. Hays, "The Conversion of the Imagination: Scripture and Eschatology in 1 Corinthians," *New Testament Studies* 45 (1999): 391-412. For further reflection on the hermeneutical implications of such a conversion, see Hays, "Reading Scripture in Light of the Resurrection," in *The Art of Reading Scripture,* ed. Ellen F. Davis and Richard B. Hays (Grand Rapids: Eerdmans, 2003).

14. Sarah Coakley, *Powers and Submissions: Spirituality, Philosophy, and Gender* (Oxford: Blackwell, 2002), p. 131.

Fifth, *the resurrection inaugurates a new community that embodies a counterpolitics.* The resurrection of Jesus calls into being an alternative community that represents God's coming kingdom. The earliest resurrection traditions in the Old Testament (such as Ezekiel's vision of the valley of dry bones [Ezek. 37:1-14]) express the ardent hope that God will restore the fortunes of exilic Israel. The prophetic word that God tells Ezekiel to speak to the bones is this: "I am going to open your graves, and bring you up from your graves, O my people; and I will bring you back to the land of Israel. And you shall know that I am the LORD" (37:12b-13a). Thus, from the first, resurrection and national restoration were closely linked. It is no accident that the hope of resurrection — only dimly suggested in most of the OT — comes into sharpest focus in the late literature associated with political resistance to an oppressing power, i.e., in books such as Daniel and 2 Maccabees. The same is probably to be said of a recently published fragment of the Dead Sea Scrolls (4Q521) which prophesies that the Lord will "make the dead live, he will proclaim good news to the meek, give lavishly to the needy, lead the exiled and enrich the hungry." Resurrection is both a symbol and a literal hope for the faithful remnant community that continues to hope God will set things right in the end.

Resurrection upsets the world because it creates and sustains this kind of countercommunity, a community that has its own distinctive politics. As Paul puts it in Philippians 3, Christ's people belong to an alternative *politeuma* — the word means a colony or political jurisdiction — whose life together is destined finally to be conformed to the image of the risen Lord (Phil. 3:20-21). That is a threatening state of affairs for a world that would like to have everyone conformed to the commonsense values and norms of the empire. In contrast to those norms, the eschatological community of the resurrection is marked by practices such as these: forgiveness, reconciliation between different ethnic groups, peacemaking, sharing possessions, fidelity in marriage, holiness in body, and keeping Sabbath as a sign of the world to come.

Finally, *the resurrection of the body gives us hope.* The same message of resurrection that upsets the world is, in the end, also the only true answer to the world's longing, the only true source of comfort in the face of death. Apart from the hope of resurrection, our lives in this world are either random and meaningless or ordered toward death and decay. The gospel, however, declares that God will not abandon us: we will be raised to new life in imperishable bodies. That message of hope enables us to live faithfully and courageously in the present age. It is no accident that Paul's lengthy discussion of resurrection in 1 Corinthians 15 concludes with a hopeful word of encouragement: "Therefore, my beloved, be steadfast, immovable, always excelling in the work of the Lord, because you know that in the Lord your labor is not in vain" (15:58). The one who raised Jesus from the dead is faithful; therefore, we his creatures look to him to give life also to our mortal bodies.

The Resurrection of the Body

1 Corinthians 15:35-36

FLEMING RUTLEDGE

One of the oddities of this present era in the church is our attitude toward the body in time of death. The numerous small cemeteries that sprinkle our Berkshire Hills testify to the traditional importance of Christian burial. As we all know, there has been a sweeping change in funeral and burial customs in the church. It is explicitly stated in the Episcopal prayer-book service that the body will be present in the church (in a closed coffin), but this is widely disregarded today as memorial services replace funerals. Cremation was very rare in the Christian community until the 1960s, but it is commonplace now. After cremation, ashes are scattered on beaches or buried in gardens. It's as though an unspoken agreement has taken shape among us; we aren't going to do it the old way anymore. To be sure, there is much to be said for cremation. It is much cheaper, and it takes up much less space. Still, the shift has been remarkable, and even more remarkable is that it has taken place with a near-total lack of discussion. Thousands of years of Christian symbolism seem to be vanishing without a thought.

The oddity is that two things are happening at once. In a time when we seem to be giving no attention to the body in the ceremonies of the church, at the very same time we are seeing more attention given to bodies than ever before. The newspapers are full of stories about the use of DNA to identify remains. The painstaking search for bodies at Ground Zero went on for almost a year. The media went to extraordinary lengths to describe — with remarkable respectfulness in many cases — the recovering, examining, documenting, storing, labeling, and so forth. The whole nation shared the anguish of the families who desperately longed to receive back some identifiable, tangible token of their loved ones. This concern for the bodily remains of those who have died has been equally conspicuous during the recent war. The bodies of fallen soldiers are retrieved by helicopter at great expense and brought home with solemn ceremony. A central feature of the military funeral is the draping of the coffin with the flag and the hallowed ceremony of folding it and presenting it. As all of this takes place in various locations all over America, civilian memorial services continue to be held where there is no coffin to be seen. We seem to have a divided mind on the subject of the body at the time of death.

Here are two stories from Ground Zero. One year after 9/11 I watched an anniversary program on TV. I'm sure many of you saw this too, the interview with two surviving firefighters, a father and son who spent weeks at the site hunting for Tim, their lost son and brother. After several agonizing weeks, the body was found. The younger man related, "They told my father to come down to the pile. When he came, they saluted him. I hadn't seen that before. My father knelt and said, 'We got you, buddy.'" Then, the young man said, concluding his story, "Tim was heavy when we carried him out; he was all there."[1] I think that we, hearing this testimony, can feel the weight of that body ourselves, and the gravity of its meaning.

The second story is from the newspaper. John C. Hartz was in the south tower on the phone with his wife, describing the scene in the north tower, when the second plane struck his floor. His widow, some months later, told a reporter that she had never previously understood why people were so intent on recovering bodies. "Now I understand," she said. "It's a basic human need. We are tactile."[2]

So perhaps, in this time of confusion and contradiction concerning bodies, it would be a good thing, this Eastertide, to remember what we say in the Apostles' Creed: "I believe in the resurrection of the *body*." What does that mean?

First of all, let's make absolutely sure that everyone understands that our Lord's promise of eternal life does not in any way depend upon bodies being intact. This was obvious from the beginning, since many of the early Christians were burned to death, leaving nothing but ashes behind. Obviously the power of God to raise the dead was not restricted to those whose bodies remained whole. There can be no objection to cremation on those grounds.

---

1. This is from my notes. I did not record the channel or the program.

2. Eric Clapton and James Glanz, "Limits of DNA Research Pressed to Identify the Dead of 9/11," *New York Times*, April 22, 2002.

Christian burial was always *symbolic;* it pointed beyond itself to something ineffable.

Behind the traditional prominence given to the body of the Christian in death was a teaching that characterized the Hebrew faith from the time of the patriarchs when, we are told, Joseph's body was carried all the way back to Israel from Egypt. Theologians and biblical scholars have repeated this Hebrew teaching so often and so regularly that it seems unnecessary to keep on saying it, but since there are so many pressures on the church to give it up, we need to raise the issue again. In the Hebrew Bible the body and the self are a psychosomatic unity. The Judeo-Christian tradition teaches that without a body, there is no person. John Updike, the novelist, is not always a reliable guide to Christian doctrine, but he has always had a clear understanding of this particular point. In his novel *A Month of Sundays,* the lascivious clergyman who is the main character muses, "Our faith insists . . . that we and our bodies are one . . . our body looks up at us from a cloudy pool; but it is us, our reflection. . . . nothing less galvanic than the Resurrection of the dead will deliver our spirits to eternity."[3]

The idea of a soul or spirit that intrinsically belongs to eternity, independent of the body, was never part of the original Christian gospel. The idea came into Christianity from Hellenistic philosophy, and it pervaded the church so totally that to this day people are shocked to hear that the immortality of the soul is not a biblical idea. More to the point on this Eastertide morning, the idea that the soul lives on when the body dies is so dear to many Christians that it is genuinely distressing to hear it challenged, as though our Easter faith were being undermined. Indeed, some of you may be feeling distressed at this very moment. I will never forget when I was a know-it-all young clergyperson teaching this subject in a class, and people were so upset by it that I had to spend weeks, if not months, trying to undo the damage. I've been more careful since then. The point being made is that we love people precisely *in their bodies,* not as spiritualized abstractions, and the promises made to us by God in Christ have to do with our *bodily* existence. God, it appears, *cares* about those human remains even though he does not *need* them.

The place to look in the New Testament for all of this is the first letter of Paul to the Corinthians. That particular congregation was a case study in this whole issue. Paul was quite upset when he wrote to them; he could see that they were in danger of going off the theological rails. He had learned that the resurrection of the body did not interest the Corinthians. They believed in something called the "medicine of immortality," and they were convinced

---

3. I have taken the liberty of switching the order of the sentences for rhetorical effect.

that they had received a blockbuster dose of it, enough to last them into eternity. You may very well ask if that idea isn't very similar to what Christians believe about baptism, and what difference does it make anyway? Isn't that close enough? Why make such an issue of it?

Paul obviously thought it was an extremely serious error. He wrote to the congregation that if they didn't believe in the resurrection of the body, then they didn't believe in the resurrection of Christ either. Here's how he put it:

> If there is no resurrection of the dead, then Christ has not been raised; if Christ has not been raised, then our preaching is in vain and your faith is in vain. We are even found to be misrepresenting God, because we testified of God that he raised Christ, whom he did not raise if it is true that the dead are not raised. For if the dead are not raised, then Christ has not been raised. If Christ has not been raised, your faith is futile and you are still in your sins. Then those also who have fallen asleep in Christ have perished. If for this life only we have hoped in Christ, we are of all [people] most to be pitied. (1 Cor. 15:13-19)

When Paul says "for this life only," he doesn't just mean "this life that we live before we die." He means something very much more penetrating than that. He means this *unredeemed* life, this life in sin and death, this life full of grief and pain, a life lived without the transforming power of God. He means life as "the old Adam," lived with all its gaping fault lines, its bitter disappointments and failures. The Corinthians believed they had already left that behind. They were a lot like the "New Age" spiritual enthusiasts of today. They thought they had already drunk the medicine of immortality. No, you haven't, Paul says. If human beings had immortal souls, there would be no need for a resurrection, and therefore no need for Christ. On the contrary, the Christian hope lies concretely and specifically in the resurrection of Christ and in the future resurrection that he will give.

Only Christ can give this gift; it is not an intrinsic possession of the human being. Paul says quite emphatically, "Flesh and blood cannot inherit the kingdom of God, nor does the perishable inherit the imperishable" (v. 50). The eternal life of the resurrection must be received as a completely new creation fresh from the hand of the Creator, independent of anything we are able to contribute to it. And moreover, scandalous as it may seem, this humanly inconceivable gift will be a *bodily resurrection* from the dead. It is therefore in some ineffable way recognizably continuous with our human identity in this life, yet entirely discontinuous with it because it is the gift of the *divine* life.

At this point the apostle anticipates all the arguments and questions he will get — precisely because his announcement is inconceivable in ordinary human terms. He writes, "But some one will ask, 'How are the dead raised? With what kind of body do they come?'" Paul's response is not very polite. He says, basically, Those are stupid questions. "You foolish person!" You've gone off on the wrong track, he tells them. You're being too literal-minded. Where's your imagination?

A story was told me recently that might be apocryphal but might well be true. The two people in question, both clergy, are very well known in the American church. One of them is a prolific writer of skeptical books calling the orthodox faith into question. The other is a famous preacher of the gospel. The skeptic, seeking to provoke the preacher, says, "My daughter has two Ph.D.s. How can I expect her to believe anything so unacceptable to the modern mind as the resurrection of the body?" The preacher says, thoughtfully, "I don't know your daughter. How limited is her imagination?"

In a way, we can say Paul was concerned with the Corinthians' lack of imagination. "How are the dead raised? With what body do they come?" Will I still be wearing contact lenses? Will I weigh what I weigh now, or what I weighed at sixteen? Will I get a new set of teeth? Will I be married to my first wife or my second? These are the kinds of questions that made Paul impatient. "You foolish person!" You are missing the whole point.

One person who did not miss the point was Emily Dickinson of Amherst. It is hard to believe that there was a time when people thought of her as a dotty recluse writing pretty little poems about birds and flowers. Everybody now knows that she had one of the most powerful intellects in American literary history. If we want to talk about imagination, she lived at the outer reaches of it. As we now know, she was engaged in a lifelong struggle with the great questions of Christian faith. She wrote a number of poems about the resurrection. Most of them have an ironic edge, as though she wanted to believe but could not. There is one poem, though, that simply leaps across the terrain of doubt on a gust of joy. It begins with the very quotation from Paul that we have been considering. "With what body do they come?" Note Dickinson's response. This text from 1 Corinthians has lodged in her mind. Had she heard it in church that morning? More likely, had she read it that day? How does it work upon her imagination? Does she ask the "foolish" questions about what sort of body it will be? Does she get on her high horse and ask how a person with an intellect like hers could possibly believe such a thing?

Here is her poem:

"And with what body do they come?" —
Then they *do* come — Rejoice!

What Door — What Hour — Run — run — My Soul!
Illuminate the House!

"Body!" Then real — a Face and Eyes —
To know that it is them! —
Paul knew the Man that knew the News —
He passed through Bethlehem.[4]

The verses from 1 Corinthians caught Dickinson's imagination and simply swept away all her skepticism. The apostle knew, because he knew the Man. The poet responded to Paul's words as we are all meant to, with rapture. *"Body!"* Paul said. "Then *real*"! We will "know that it is them," our very beloved ones themselves, not abstractions, not shadows, not spirits, not ideas, not vapors — but solid, tactile, *real.* Tim is *all there.* Tim *will be* all there. We have this promise from the Word of God.

Then they *do* come! Run, run, my soul!

---

4. Emily Dickinson, *Collected Poems*, #1492.

CHAPTER 15

The Life Everlasting

Et vitam aeternam

GABRIEL FACKRE

The renowned nineteenth-century church historian Philip Schaff observed that the Apostles' Creed "follows the historical order of the revelation of the triune God, the Father, the Son, and the Holy Ghost . . . from creation to the life everlasting . . . in a grand liturgical epic for the edification of the church."[1] In a parallel figure the Creed has been thought of as a drama in three acts — God creating, reconciling, and redeeming — with *life everlasting* as the close of the final scene in act 3. It's the last of "the last things." As the very "end," it has to do with the closure of the tale *(finis)* and its purpose *(telos)*.

The full meaning of that purpose can only be understood by following the plot of the "grand liturgical epic," this ancient church's version of "the unfolding drama of the Bible."[2] Both share a common narrative. While the Bible takes us through seven chapters of God's story: creation, fall, covenant, Christ, church, salvation, consummation,[3] the Creed captures this biblical movement in three great acts. Why three? *Apostolicum* wants to make clear confessionally that God *is* what God *does.* Creating, reconciling, and redeeming are the missions of the Father, the Son, and the Holy Spirit, who as one

---

1. Philip Schaff, *History of the Christian Church*, vol. 1 (New York: Scribner, Armstrong and Co., 1872), p. 262.

2. Bernhard W. Anderson's much-reprinted *The Unfolding Drama of the Bible*, 3rd ed. (Philadelphia: Fortress, 1988).

3. Gabriel Fackre, *The Christian Story*, vol. 1, 3rd ed. (Grand Rapids: Eerdmans, 1996), passim.

GABRIEL FACKRE

God involves all persons in each act. The "economic Trinity" is the "ontological Trinity" at work.

Because *life everlasting* is the end point of the economy of the triune God, and thus reflective of the ontology of God, we discern who this God is from what transpires in the unfolding drama. So, a quick tracking of the tale, using both magisterial Scripture and ministerial tradition (the Creed) as our guides. As Jesus Christ is the heart of Christian Scripture, and thus his creedal paragraph is the central and longest in this "rule of faith," the narrative is read through a christological lens.[4]

The world is brought to be by Another. The triune God creates heaven and earth, willing into existence a partner to the divine purposes. The Genesis accounts speak of a steward of creation, the creature with the human face gifted with, and called to, image God (Gen. 1:26), beckoned to a life together with the Maker, humanity, and all creation. But Adam refuses partnership, choosing not to love God but to "play God" (3:5), reaping the consequences of estrangement from Creator, neighbor, and nature; the intended life together is lost, the wages of sin, death (Rom. 6:23). Yet the Creator does not give up on creation, making a rainbow covenant with the world (Gen. 9:8-16), with glimpses of the purposes of God granted by a "common grace" in order to keep the drama moving toward its goal. And more: yet another covenant with a special people chosen to see and live out the vision of *shalom,* the peace of God that on our plane is a life together of wolf and lamb, nation and nation, Creator and creature.

Amidst its trials and tribulations the *shalom* that God is comes to dwell among us in Jesus the Jew. He is "our peace" (Eph. 2:14). The divinely intended life together is enacted in his life and ministry; his death takes away our sin; his resurrection and ascension declare and make possible by grace through faith our participation in the life together, a good news announced by and accessed through the church, pointing toward the "last things" that consummate the divine purposes.

The God at work in this drama in three acts is the Father, Son, and Holy Spirit, no different in the divine being from the divine doing, the trinitarian economy disclosing the triune ontology of a coinherent life together. The end of the tale, "everlasting life," is consonant with who God is, a life together of all the parties to the divine drama. To that culmination we turn.

For all the illumination we have on the very last thing, Scripture cautions reserve. What is to be discerned is seen "in a mirror dimly" . . . "through a glass darkly" (1 Cor. 13:12, NRSV, KJV). So Luther's wise counsel: "As little

4. Fackre, *The Christian Story,* pp. 14-26.

children in their womb know about their birth, so little do we know about life everlasting."[5] Barth echoes this modesty, assuring us, however, that it will be no less than Jesus Christ himself that constitutes what will be.[6] With such counsels in mind, we follow the biblical glimpses of life everlasting, not seen through clear-glass views of the world to come, but in the colored light and vivid figures of stained glass windows.

The everlasting life to come so viewed is a "big picture." It has to do with a new heaven and a new earth (Rev. 21:1), a kingdom to come within it (Matt. 6:10), and new persons to inhabit this transformed cosmos and everlasting reign (John 3:16). All three dimensions are marked by the purposes of the God who does just what God is. Any life that lasts forever is a mirror of God's own life together sought by the Creator for creation itself, and embodied in the incarnate Word. We follow these crucial clues of the shape of things to come.

Personal Destiny

The third paragraph of the Creed gives pride of place to the goal of God for persons, reflecting their status as made in the divine image. It speaks of our appearance before the judgment seat of Christ, and for Christian believers the forgiveness of their sins, the resurrection of their bodies, their communion as saints in this world and the world to come.

In like manner, the Reformation catechisms point to the everlasting future of persons: Luther's *Small Catechism:* "The Holy Ghost . . . will raise me up and all the dead, and will grant everlasting life to me and to all who believe in Christ."[7] The Heidelberg Catechism: "I shall possess, after this life, perfect blessedness, which no eye has seen nor ear heard, nor the heart of man conceived, and thereby praise God forever."[8] Comparably so, the Roman Catholic tradition speaks of the "beatific vision . . . the immediate knowledge of God which constitutes the primary felicity of Heaven. The souls of the blessed see God, directly, and face to face."[9]

---

5. Martin Luther, WA TR 3:276, 26-27, quotes by Hans Schwarz, "Eschatology," in *Christian Dogmatics*, ed. Carl Braaten and Robert Jenson, vol. 2 (Philadelphia: Fortress, 1984), p. 586.

6. Karl Barth, *Credo* (New York: Charles Scribner's Sons, 1962), pp. 166-67.

7. "Small Catechism," in *Martin Luther's Basic Theological Writings*, ed. Timothy F. Lull (Minneapolis: Fortress, 1989), p. 485.

8. *The Heidelberg Catechism*, trans. Allen O. Miller and M. Eugene Osterhaven (New York: United Church Press, 1962), p. 60.

9. "Beatific Vision," in *A Catholic Dictionary*, ed. Donald Attwater (New York: Macmillan,

While we begin with the destiny of persons granted everlasting life, it's important to keep in mind that we cannot separate the final future of the blessed from the corporate and cosmic setting in which the full drama of the Creed places it, faithful as it is to the biblical story behind it.

And just what is "life"? The Greek terms *zoe* and *psyche* are used throughout the New Testament, the former tending to be associated with our physical life as such, and the latter our life with God, though the former can sometimes include the latter.[10] Our focus is the person's life with God in its ultimate sense, the last scene in the final act of the creedal drama. A thread of New Testament allusions to personal life everlasting speak of "seeing" and "knowing" God "face to face" (1 Cor. 13:12; Rev. 22:4). But what poor words we have in expressing this encounter. How different and deeper is it than our conventional seeings and knowings. Hints of it do exist in our Christian life, yes, for eternal life/everlasting life begins in time, even as it comes to flower in eternity. As we see and know Jesus, God is among us as the Son . . . in his promised real presence in Word and sacrament . . . in ad hoc encounters of eternal life. But all this is seeing and knowing "in a mirror, dimly." What surprises we have in store!

Probing another biblical metaphor, theologians have spoken about the unspeakable in terms of "light" — seeing it, radiated by it (Rev. 21:23-25; 22:5), "the beatific vision" of the Catholic tradition. Yet even Protestant Charles Hodge speaks this way of the "radiancy of glory . . . the incomprehensible blessedness of heaven shall arise from the vision of God. This vision is beatific."[11] The Orthodox tradition has its own depiction, life eternal as participating in the very being of God as *theosis*, deification. All this stirs the heart while it boggles the mind.

A refrain in the theologians of the church, and giving it body (literally), is the assurance that we have to do with Jesus Christ himself in his "glorified humanity." What better finale than to meet our Lord, not now in the end of the end as judge of the quick and the dead, but as "friend" (John 15:14-15), even as we bow our knee to the "King of kings and Lord of lords"? Life everlasting is life together with Jesus Christ! — life together in the body, dimly seen and anticipated in eucharistic communion with the risen Lord, yet now in everlasting life in the "spiritual body" of the believer with eyes of heavenly

---

1961), p. 48. See also *Catechism of the Catholic Church* (Liguori, Mo.: Liguori Publications, 1994), paras. 1023, 2550.

10. "Zao, zoe . . . ," in *Theological Dictionary of the Bible*, ed. Geoffrey W. Bromiley, abridged in 1 vol. (Grand Rapids: Eerdmans, 1985), pp. 290-96.

11. Charles Hodge, *Systematic Theology*, vol. 1 (New York: Scribner, Armstrong and Co., 1874), p. 860.

sight entranced by the one known on earth by eyes of faith as the body and blood given in bread and wine. Again, we are thinking the unthinkable about what is to be, our seeing infinitude from finite perspective, not through transparencies but translucencies.

Life together in the triune Being is love in its purity. What else can communion with Christ everlasting be than eternal love? Indeed, a life together with the ultimate life together is one in which "love never ends" (1 Cor. 13:8).

The love of Christ for us in this world is a busy one. In the Gospels, ever and again, he reaches out to those with manifold needs. So too at the end he will finally "wipe away every tear" from our eyes, and "mourning and crying and pain will be no more," for life everlasting has come when "death will be no more" (Rev. 21:4). He does this as the "Alpha and Omega" who promises that "to the thirsty I will give water as a gift from the spring of the water of life" (21:6). And our response is one of unending praise and thanksgiving to God (7:15), and a loving outreach to others (a christologically read Isa. 11:6-9; 40:31). Can the never ending love not include loving God with the mind, as well as heart and soul (Matt. 22:37), perhaps sitting under one's "vine" and "fig tree" (Isa. 36:16) with a good theological book? Or in our association with others, as Barth once remarked: his anticipation of a vigorous give-and-take with Schleiermacher, getting things cleared up?

Such rich images suggest a lively world to come. Serenity and contentment, surely, but no bovine serenity or armchair contentment. Isaac Dorner, an earlier theologian who thought much about "the future state," puts it this way:

> The highest activity of the will is to be in perfected worship (Rev. 7:12, 22:3), consisting in adoration, thanks, and praise, and also in joyous obedience, making itself in godlike love an organ of God's continuing work. This leads to the relation of blessedness to *rest* and *enjoyment* on the one hand, on the other, to *action*. . . . It follows then from this, that in the rest, which is conceived as the goal, as an eternal Sabbath (Heb. 4:11, Rev. 7:16, 17, 21:4) there will be no inactivity; and also no unrest in the activity.[12]

In a similar vein, a contemporary theologian, Miroslav Volf, questions the erasure of time from eternity: "*Ultimate fulfillment is not only compatible with temporality but also unthinkable without it,* partly because any intelligi-

---

12. *Dorner on the Future State: The Doctrine of the Last Things,* translated with an introduction and notes by Newman Smyth (New York: Charles Scribner's Sons, 1883), p. 141.

ble notions of both reconciliation and contentment in fact *presuppose* change. Whatever the virtues of taking up time into eternity, its inadequacies are major: with the erasure of temporality in the 'life' of the world to come, it takes away the possibility of communal peace and personal joy."[13] Even Edmund Fortman, a Roman Catholic theologian who strives to stay close to magisterial teaching, says, "But a more recent theology is moving in the direction of a more 'dynamic heaven' that admits growth and progress in perfection throughout eternity. Is such a theological view compatible with the teaching of Sacred Scripture and of the Church? It seems to many of us that it is."[14]

Theologians, however, may get carried away with what all this movement might mean. The otherwise cautious Fortman peers through the biblical stained-glass windows of the world to come. Finding some transparencies, more than Scripture's translucencies, he sees that the redeemed

will have telepathic powers by which they will be able to communicate thoughts and desires and feelings to one another. . . . They will have clairvoyant powers by which they will be able to perceive objects and scenes and forms that are distant in space and time . . . precognitive powers by which they can have advance knowledge of future occurrences . . . psycho-kinetic powers by which they can affect and move and most likely transform matter even at a distance. . . . They will be agile, able to move easily from place to place, perhaps from planet to planet and from one part of the cosmos to another — with the speed of thought.[15]

Of course, such heavenly speculation has a long history, as in Origen, who declared that "the redeemed will apprehend the nature of the stars and the reasons for their respective positions."[16] And some have been quite sure there will be "degrees of the bliss of heaven."[17] Well, a few inferences from the biblical data might be apt, as with Dorner's hope that the blessed will have to do with "Paul, John and the Prophets, and have the noblest enjoyment in an infi-

---

13. Miroslav Volf, "Enter into Joy! Sin, Death and the Life of the World to Come," in *The End of the World and the Ends of God: Science and Theology on Eschatology*, ed. John Polkinghorne and Michael Welker (Harrisburg, Pa.: Trinity Press International, 2000), p. 270.

14. E. J. Fortman, S.J., *Everlasting Life after Death* (New York: Alba House, 1976), pp. 313-14.

15. Fortman, pp. 312, 313.

16. See J. N. D. Kelly, *Early Christian Doctrines* (New York: Harper and Brothers, 1958), pp. 485ff., for this and for other teachings of the early church fathers on "life everlasting."

17. Louis Berkhof, *Systematic Theology*, 4th ed. (Grand Rapids: Eerdmans, 1938, 1982), p. 737.

nitely manifold communion and love."[18] However, overall, better a devout agnosticism about the shape, size, and contours of things to come, settling for the metaphorical modesties of Scripture.

Social Destiny

"Seeing the Light" as the personal goal of the redeemed is inseparable from seeing *in* the Light others who share that end. Sociality is also destiny. We've already anticipated that in the comments above.

The early church fathers, with their strong sense of a social Trinity, regularly included the human-life-together aspect of the final state. Gregory of Nazianzus, taking up the light imagery, spoke of heaven as a "perpetual festival, illuminated by the brightness of the Godhead of which here we can only catch fleeting glimpses, and it will be our joy to gaze on the Trinity of divine Persons."[19] Ambrose, Jerome, and others stressed the fellowship we will have with "the saints," reflecting the "communion of saints" that appears in the Apostles' Creed itself.

Scripture and tradition range through the continuum of ultimate social destinies, from the most intimate to the most corporate. There is no strict counterpart in heaven to earth's one-flesh union, for the very Christ who declared it sacred (Matt. 19:5-6) also reminds us that "in the resurrection they neither marry nor are given in marriage" (22:30). Yet the blessing that concludes the solemnization of marriage in one tradition appeals for "the Lord [to] mercifully with his favour look upon you, and fill you with all spiritual benediction and grace; that ye may so live together in this life, that in the world to come ye may have life everlasting."[20] And if God "setteth the solitary in families" (Ps. 68:6 KJV), granted as an "order of preservation" for this world, why would the redemption of that life together not be part of the eternal purposes too?

Then there is the family of faith. Again we have the qualifier regarding too simple a continuity between earth and heaven, with the word from John that "I saw no temple in the city, for its temple is the Lord God the Almighty and the Lamb" (Rev. 21:22). But what of the "church triumphant" gathered for the

18. *Dorner on the Future State*, p. 140.

19. Kelly, p. 486.

20. *The Book of Common Prayer: According to the Use of the Protestant Episcopal Church in the United States of America* (Philadelphia: Church Pension Fund, 1940), p. 304. This version of the words, especially treasured by the writer and spouse, as having been spoken over them at their 1945 "solemnization of matrimony."

"marriage feast of the Lamb" (Rev. 19:7, 9; Matt. 22:2), the promise of Christ to share the Supper, face-to-face, the "fruit of the vine . . . when I drink it new with you in my Father's kingdom" (Matt. 26:29)? An eternal life together could not exclude the communion of saints around the Table, a body of Christ in heaven, whatever temple-less form the brothers and sisters in this family of faith might take.

And the circle widens. Many biblical metaphors of the end have to do with a polis-to-be. We look forward to an "everlasting" kingdom come, and in it the ultimate city of God (2 Pet. 1:11; Luke 11:2; 13:29; 18:25; 22:16; 2 Tim. 4:18; Rev. 21:10-26). Again the qualifier about the eschatological commonwealth, for we have to do with a realm like nothing we've seen on earth of ordinary flesh and blood (1 Cor. 15:50), a *new* Jerusalem, "coming down out of heaven from God" (Rev. 21:10), not of human manufacture. The light imagery contrasts with the shadowy structures we inhabit: "It has the glory of God and a radiance like a very rare jewel. . . . And the city has no need of sun or moon to shine on it, for the glory of God is its light, and its lamp is the Lamb" (Rev. 21:11, 23). And the coming together of often warring states is so new to us, for "the nations will walk by its light, and the kings of the earth will bring their glory into it" (21:24). In every systemic setting, justice will "roll down like waters, / and righteousness like an ever-flowing stream" (Amos 5:24). Every social flaw shall be mended, the mighty brought down and the lowly exalted (Luke 1:52). *Shalom*, as the peace of a new world, will come to be. All social suffering will come to an end, the tears from tyranny, war, hunger, and poverty wiped away, for "they will not hurt or destroy on all my holy mountain for the earth will be filled with the knowledge of God as the waters cover the sea" (Isa. 11:9).

The last scene of the final act of God's drama speaks to the age-old issue of theodicy, the problem of evil. The question is: How can we hold together the three Christian nonnegotiables, God as all-good and all-powerful, and evil as real? The Holocaust? Millions starved, killed in wars, oppressed by the malice of the fallen powers that be? The eschatological answer, surrounded though it be with mystery for those still in not-yet times: nothing "will be able to separate us from the love of God in Jesus Christ our Lord" (Rom. 8:39). Paul's future tense tells us that the absolute power of God is in the future: the all-good God will prevail in the end, mending every flaw in creation's sin-wracked and painful history.

Pie in the sky bye and bye? Compensation in heaven for earth's travail that prompts us to accept without protest the world's wrongs? Nothing could be further from the truth. The world we anticipate makes us restless for what will be. It calls into question the things that are and drives us in turn to critique, challenge, and overturn all those circumstances short of God's intended and promised purposes. Social eschatology is inseparable from social ethics. Hence the importance of a full vision of what is to be, the corporate as well as the personal end, with moral mandates consonant therewith.[21]

Nature's Destiny

The life that lasts forever includes the redemption of a fallen nature. We have to do in the end with a "new heaven and a new earth" (Rev. 21:1), as well as a new Jerusalem and new saints. The latter live in a new city and kingdom settled on a new earth under a new heaven. In such a redeemed creation the struggle for survival will be all over, for "the wolf will live with the lamb and the leopard will lie down with the kid" (Isa. 11:6). The animosity between human nature and cosmic nature is finished, for the "nursing child shall play over the hole of the asp, and the weaned child shall put its hand on the adder's den" (11:8).

While the Western tradition had a place for the natural dimension of everlasting life,[22] certainly so in its teaching of the resurrection of the body, it was the Eastern Church that gave it special accent: "The whole of nature is destined for glory. . . . The divine Spirit which in all its fulness is poured out from Christ on those who believe in him, whose spirits are thereby kindled anew, does not fill only their bodies with new life, making them transparent for what is heavenly, but transforms nature and the cosmos, too."[23] For all its limitations (the missing Lutheran stress on annihilation of the old or the Calvinist transformative theme, matters to which Moltmann points),[24] the Orthodox reminder cannot be forgotten. In contemporary terms, in "the Shalom that shall be, there is no fellowship with Christ that is not fellowship with the earth."[25] Biblically stated, how can there be solace for a "groaning" creation (Rom. 8:22), one that "waits with eager longing" (8:19) for freedom from "its bondage to decay" (8:21), if there is no cosmic life that lasts forever rather than a destiny of death?

---

21. Set forth early in his writing by Jürgen Moltmann in his *Theology of Hope*, trans. James W. Leitch (London: SCM Press, 1967), pp. 329-38 and passim, and all his works since.

22. See especially Anthony A. Hoekema, "The New Earth," in *The Bible and the Future* (Grand Rapids: Eerdmans, 1979), pp. 274-87.

23. D. Staniloe, *Orthodox Dogmatik* I (Gütersloh, 1985), pp. 294, 369, quoted in Jürgen Moltmann, *The Coming of God: Christian Eschatology*, trans. Margaret Kohl (Minneapolis: Fortress, 1996), p. 273.

24. Moltmann, *The Coming of God*, pp. 267-72.

25. Moltmann, *The Coming of God*, p. 279.

James Luther Adams taught a generation of his students that what we hold to be true eschatologically will be what we work for ethically. In this case it means that a passionate ecological ethic rises out of the conviction that God will bring a nature renewed.

*   *   *

Miroslav Volf summarizes the comprehensive Christian belief in life everlasting we have been describing in this way: "the final reconciliation of 'all things,' grounded in the work of Christ the reconciler and accomplished by the Spirit of communion, is the process by which the whole creation along with human beings will be freed from transience and sin to reach the state of eternal peace and joy in the communion with the triune God."[26]

Ancillary Issues

All biblical images of life everlasting imply, indeed portray, its opposite. While appropriate to the exploration of the creedal phrase "final judgment," how can we not make passing reference to the alternative future implied in our present topic?

What would everlasting death be but the things contrary to everlasting life? First and foremost, a life apart, rather than life together, everlasting estrangement from the relationships God intended for the world: no blessed participation in the life together of the triune Being; no joyful celebration of the same; no rapturous bonding in the unities God intended for us — familial, ecclesial, political; no reconciliation with or of the natural cosmos. Everlasting death of this sort is more horrible than popular portrayals of fiery pain; our worst anthropomorphic imaginings are so far short of the hell of life apart.

The fearsomeness of everlasting death, however conceived, has prompted some to argue for more hospitable endings. The most generous is that of universalism in which all will be brought to eternal life, given God's universal desire for all to be saved (1 Tim. 2:4) and every hellish region disallowed. The case for such is made variously: because God is too good to consign any to perdition; because humans are too good to be so consigned; the fires of hell are real and lasting but not everlasting, for their role is rehabilitation where the dross is burned away in preparation for the purity of heaven; with or

26. Volf, p. 278.

without such cleansing, the trajectory of God's story cannot but end with the fulfillment of God's promise that God shall be all and in all, none excepted. Karl Barth's thesis that all have died with Christ, and all have been exalted in him, sounds like that, moving ineluctably to the doctrine of universalism, too, but not so. Barth's commitment to the divine sovereignty rightly will not allow us to tell God what finally must be done. But we do have "a command . . . to hope and to pray cautiously . . . that . . . His compassion should not fail, and that in accordance with His mercy which is 'new every morning' He 'will not cast off for ever' (La. 3:22f., 31)."[27]

Yet others, believing the fearsome portrayals of hell do not comport with divine love, and seem an inordinate recompense for the outcome the damned do deserve, propose annihilation as their prospect, everlasting death as simply the end of our life in time, the "perish" of John 3:16 understood as extinction.

Neither universalism nor annihilationism has come close to becoming the mind of the church ecumenical, the latter finding deficient their biblical warrants, being wary of diminishing the weightiness of sin, and honoring the persistent classical juxtapositions.

More recently, questions raised by religious pluralism have impacted Christian thinking about our subject. How can the multitudes who have never heard of Christ, or the true telling of the story, be consigned to everlasting death? Holding otherwise are a variety of proposals that range from "pluralist" camps, with little or no biblical warrant, which hold that all religions or people of good will are in touch with the same eternally saving Reality, to particularist perspectives that see Christ himself as the absolute Savior who offers everlasting life anonymously to those in other religions who respond in good conscience to the truth granted them.[28] Taking another tack, Mark Heim elaborates on earlier themes of Joseph DiNoia and Gavin D'Costa, with some precedents in Dante's *Divine Comedy,* holding that people of deep devotion in Buddhism, Hinduism, Islam, and other world religions will achieve their desired religious fullfillments through graces related to the dimensions of the triune God in a world ordered for such diversity . . . though not the fullness of everlasting life accessible through Christian faith.[29] Are there warrants in Scripture for such a view? The case has yet to be made. Are these

---

27. Karl Barth, *Church Dogmatics* IV/3/1, trans. G. W. Bromiley (Edinburgh: T. & T. Clark, 1961), p. 478.

28. For a spectrum of pluralist and particularist views, see Gabriel Fackre, "Christ and Religious Pluralism: The Current Debate," *Pro Ecclesia* 7, no. 4 (fall 1998): 389-97.

29. S. Mark Heim, *The Depths of the Riches: A Trinitarian Theology of Religious Ends* (Grand Rapids: Eerdmans, 2001).

fulfillments the "suburbs of heaven" or "the suburbs of hell" — subsets of everlasting life or everlasting death? Heim's answer is ambiguous, inviting a lively dialogue about his proposal.

Also impacted by pluralism, yet with roots in patristic thought as reflected in the "descent of Christ to the dead" phrase in our creed, another theory asserts that God does not deny to any the good news of everlasting life by justifying faith. Christ, the Hound of Heaven, pursues those who have not heard the gospel either to the gates of death (a Roman Catholic theory of "final decision")[30] or beyond them (a Protestant theory of divine perseverance),[31] each offering a yes or no choice to the Christ so met.

Related to the foregoing is the question of the special destiny of the Jewish people, brought to the fore after the Holocaust, and the exposure of the "teaching of contempt" so long an undercurrent in traditional Christianity. With a growing consensus about an "antisupersessionist" view of the purposes of Israel in the plans of God, especially in the fresh exegesis of Romans 9–11, the question comes of the fate of Jews who do not know or confess Christ.[32] Some believe that Jews of Abrahamic faith, not only those who are Old Testament believers (declared saved retroactively by Christ's work by some strands of the Reformation, or of meeting Christ after death to hear of their savior, as in much patristic thought), but Jews *after* Christ, are graced with everlasting life, learning of the source of their salvation by the Christ they will meet in the eschaton. This view is the counterpart of the Jewish judgment that Christians faithful to Noah's covenant will be redeemed, learning that their everlasting life is a gift of the God of Abraham, Isaac, and Jacob and not Jesus Christ.

These latter ancillary proposals are yet theories with no official status, efforts to think through, often on biblical grounds, unanswered questions that bear on the last phrase of the Creed. However, as doctrine develops, who knows whether someday one or another of these views may prove to the church at large its grounding in Scripture and coherence with historic teaching.

---

30. Fortman, pp. 79-82.

31. For an outworking of this point of view by the writer, see Gabriel Fackre, Ronald H. Nash, and John Sanders, *What abouth Those Who Have Never Heard?* ed. John Sanders (Downers Grove, Ill.: InterVarsity, 1995), pp. 56-61, 71-95, 150-55.

32. See *The Theology of the Churches and the Jewish People: Statements by the World Council of Churches and Its Member Churches* (Geneva: WCC Publications, 1988), and the formulations of antisupersessionism in one church (the United Church of Christ), *New Conversations: God's Unbroken Covenant with the Jewish People*, vol. 12, no. 3 (summer 1990).

Conclusion

What better way to conclude the Creed's narrative than with the music that will mark the end, and the meeting with the one who awaits us there?

> What joy to know, when life is past,
> The Lord we love is first and last, the end and the beginning! . . .
> Oh let the harps break forth in sound!
> Our joy be all with music crowned
> Our voices gaily blending!
> For Christ goes with us all the way —
> Today, tomorrow, ev'ry day!
> His love is never ending!
> Sing out! Ring out!
> Jubilation! Exultation!
> Tell the story! Great is he, the King of glory![33]

33. Philipp Nicolai, 1556-1608, "O Morning Star, How Fair and Bright!" in *Lutheran Book of Worship* (Minneapolis: Augsburg; Philadelphia: Board of Publications, Lutheran Church in America, 1989), no. 76.

The Life Everlasting

1 Corinthians 15:50-58

CRAIG C. HILL

"And they lived happily ever after." That is the fairy-tale ending we read to our children before switching off the light at bedtime. We reassure them that dragons and witches and bullies do not finally triumph, that virtue is rewarded and that love endures. We reinforce their belief in a moral universe in which happiness is the offspring of goodness and not its chance acquaintance or certain competitor.

But life soon confronts our children with other narratives, stories in which every wrong is not righted nor every injustice overturned. They discover danger, witness prejudice, and experience failure. They learn that things do not always work out as they hope and that they cannot always get what they want. Eventually they encounter death, and with it loss that is not reversed by a wizard's spell or a heroine's kiss.

Life thus schools us in doubt. We cannot believe everything we hear. It is right to doubt that we can "lose twenty pounds while eating whatever we want," or "look ten years younger overnight," or "get rich working only a day a week from home." It is right for us to question such extravagant claims, lest we be swindled, lest we be injured, lest we be disappointed. Prudence demands that we become wary of strangers and suspicious of even our own motives. On one level this is no more than an awareness of sin, in others and in ourselves. More deeply it is a recognition of the mystery of evil, whose embassy is to thwart and cheapen and diminish human life.

"If it sounds too good to be true, it probably is." For many people today, that advice applies preeminently to religion, whose hopes are dismissed outright as wishful thinking. The "real world" consists only of what is accessible to scientific verification. Therefore, meaning itself is an illusion. The universe has no creator, no purpose, and ultimately no future. According to today's most popular cosmology, in the end there will be only a burned-out and dissipated universe: not noise and fury, but silence and futility, signifying nothing. In this scenario there can be no "happily ever after." According to microbiologist Jacques Monod, "[T]he choice of scientific practice, an unconscious choice in the beginning, has launched the evolution of culture on a one-way path: onto a track which nineteenth-century scientism saw leading infallibly upward to an empyrean noon hour for mankind, whereas what we see opening before us today is an abyss of darkness."[1] Persuasive as it may be to some, the "wishful-thinking argument" is a nonstarter. One might just as well contend that atheism is a projection of the human will. After all, a world without God is a world without absolute obligations, which is just the sort of world in which many would prefer to live. One can always impugn the motives of one's intellectual opponents, but such rhetoric proves nothing except, perhaps, its own arrogance. Reasonable, intelligent people of good will have long been divided on these, as on so many other, questions.

Retrospectively, I might regard as wishful thinking a material universe whose physical characteristics, such as electromagnetism and gravity, are so finely balanced as to make possible the emergence of life and, even more extraordinary, sentience. Who could have predicted a cosmos whose rock would birth Pythagoras's theorem, Beethoven's *Fifth Symphony,* Chartres cathedral, and Shakespeare's *Hamlet?* Nevertheless, such a universe exists. Not every desirable object is an illusion.

Our desire for purpose, order, and meaning is fundamental to our existence. Many of the earliest cultural artifacts are religious in nature, and belief in life after death is nearly universal. This does not prove the validity of religion, but it certainly weighs in its favor. As C. S. Lewis put it, "If I find in myself a desire which no experience in this world can satisfy, the most probable explanation is that I was made for another world."[2] Or, to use Huston Smith's analogy, wings do not prove the existence of air, but they surely count as evidence. We know instinctively that we are something more than the sum of our parts and part of something more than ourselves. Consider the final chorus of Joni Mitchell's "Woodstock":

---

1. Cited in Huston Smith, *Why Religion Matters: The Fate of the Human Spirit in an Age of Disbelief* (New York: Harper Collins, 2001), p. 41.

2. C. S. Lewis, *Mere Christianity* (New York: Macmillan, 1960), p. 119.

We are stardust, million-year old carbon
We are golden, caught in the devil's bargain
And we've got to get ourselves back to the garden.

On the one hand, we are quite literally stardust, assemblies of primordial carbon. On the other hand, we are something more, something "golden." Yet we are not now fully ourselves; we are "caught in the devil's bargain." To get "back to the garden" is to go to the place of wholeness and innocence for which we long.

Christianity is grounded in the hope that we shall indeed arrive at such a place — not the garden but that for which the garden is the prefiguring image, the kingdom of God. The core affirmation of Christian faith is that God — not evil, futility, and death — is the final reality in the cosmos. This belief encompasses not only the hope of eternal life but also the expectation that creation itself will be redeemed (Rom. 8:18-25). Why believe in the happy ending? For the first Christians the answer was obvious: because of Jesus' resurrection.

Several years ago my wife, Robin, became increasingly ill over a period of weeks. She was tested for numerous ailments, nearly all of which would have proved fatal. After two months she could scarcely get out of bed, and I began to take seriously the possibility that she would die. My faith was hard pressed. Did I truly believe with Paul that "in all these things we are more than conquerors through him who loved us," that "neither death . . . nor anything else in all creation, will be able to separate us from the love of God in Christ Jesus our Lord" (Rom. 8:37-39)? It was not easy.

As I meditated on Scripture, I came to value particularly 1 Corinthians 9:1, in which Paul declares, "Am I not free? Am I not an apostle? Have I not seen Jesus our Lord?" This is one of only a handful of places where Paul refers back to his experience of seeing the resurrected Jesus at his conversion. Moreover, Paul's letters provide the only undisputed primary-source testimony composed by an eyewitness of the resurrection. His writings would be invaluable for this reason if for no other.

It is worth noting that the pre-Christian Paul had no cause to wish for Jesus' resurrection. As a Pharisee he would have expected the resurrection of the righteous on the last day, not the resurrection of a particular individual — a criminal, at that — in the recent past. What's more, Paul rejected Christian claims about Jesus in the most forceful way possible: he persecuted those who held them. The appearance of Christ turned Paul's life upside down and set him on a path of almost unparalleled hardship. (See the catalogue of his sufferings in 2 Corinthians 11:23-33.) In other words, Paul had every self-interested reason in the world not to believe, but believe he did. The same could be said of other early Christian leaders, such as James, who appears not to have been a follower of Jesus, his brother, prior to the resurrection. Like Paul, James was martyred in the early 60s for his Christian witness.

In the course of my wife's illness, I learned to borrow from the faith of Paul and other early Christians who paid with their lives for their unyielding conviction that God in Christ had triumphed over death, in whose victory they believed they would one day share. Fortunately Robin eventually recovered, but I have never forgotten what it was like to pass so near to death.

Concerning death the Bible is remarkably unsentimental. Paul and other New Testament authors do not tell us that deceased believers will become angels or stars, nor do they say that we shall be melded with some divine force. There is no greeting-card sentiment about God needing more company in heaven. Instead, death is seen as that great enemy which, apart from God's ultimate and undeserved act of re-creation, would unmake us all. In short, death is real.

According to Paul, "The wages of sin is death, but the free gift of God is eternal life in Christ Jesus our Lord" (Rom. 6:23). The hope is for the resurrection of the body, not the immortality of the soul. Eternal life is not a given; it is a gift bestowed only by God. The one who created conscious beings is able to re-create such beings by resurrection. Hence 1 Corinthians 15:50: "Flesh and blood cannot inherit the kingdom of God, nor does the perishable inherit the imperishable." Christians are not required to believe in an immortal soul that exists independent of the body. Instead, Paul writes, we will be changed (v. 51), given bodies like that of the resurrected Jesus himself. On this point the New Testament is clear and yet sensibly reserved. Compare 1 John 3:2: "Beloved, we are God's children now; what we will be has not yet been revealed. What we do know is this: when he is revealed, we will be like him, for we will see him as he is."

John Polkinghorne, Cambridge physicist and Christian author, contemplates these matters in his book *The God of Hope and the End of the World*. He emphasizes that resurrection involves a measure of both continuity and discontinuity. We will be the same persons, but also changed beings. Writes Polkinghorne,

> Whatever the human soul may be, it is surely what expresses and carries the continuity of living personhood. . . . It is certainly not merely material. The atoms that make up our bodies are continuously being replaced in the course of wear and tear, eating and drinking. We have very few atoms in our bodies today that were there even two years ago. What does appear to be the carrier of continuity is the immensely complex

"information-bearing pattern" in which that matter is organized. This pattern is not static; it is modified as we acquire new experiences, insights and memories, in accordance with the dynamic of our living history. It is this information-bearing pattern that is the soul.[3]

According to Polkinghorne, this pattern remains in the mind of God and can be reproduced, much as software can be moved from one computer to another. To extend this (admittedly inadequate) analogy, the software itself may be enhanced by the capabilities of the new computer. Also, it may continue to be upgraded.

That a future life might include our "upgrading" is much discussed by theologians. If we are to live in the presence of God, we must be holy as God is holy. That implies a bit more than a move up from version 1 to version 1.1. Christian thinkers have speculated for centuries about whether moral perfection will be instantaneous or gradual, the second option being one basis for belief in some form of purgatory.[4] A similar debate surrounds depictions of life in heaven. Most theologians today reject the notion that heavenly existence will be static, represented at its silliest by the sitting-on-clouds-playing-harps stereotype. They see heaven not only as a place of endless praise, joy, and fellowship, but also as a realm of ceaseless fascination and development. I am in no position to evaluate these claims, nor, beyond a certain point, do I find such speculations helpful. More concrete and much more useful is Paul's advice about the present-day implications of our future hope: "But thanks be to God, who gives us the victory through our Lord Jesus Christ. Therefore, my beloved, be steadfast, immovable, always excelling in the work of the Lord, because you know that in the Lord your labor is not in vain" (1 Cor. 15:57-58).

The gospel places demands upon us that conflict at many points with our worldly self-interest. To love our enemies is not necessarily going to make us happy. To serve the poor is unlikely to advance us socially or economically. It is no accident that the radical ethic of Jesus is situated within an equally radical proclamation of the coming kingdom of God. That is the only context within which it makes sense. To attempt to follow Jesus' teaching while denying its core affirmation is an exercise in futility. "Eschatological demands require eschatological commitments and eschatological resources."[5]

3. John Polkinghorne, *The God of Hope and the End of the World* (New Haven: Yale University Press, 2002), pp. 105-6.

4. A fascinating defense of purgatory is found in Jerry Walls's excellent *Heaven: The Logic of Eternal Joy* (Oxford: Oxford University Press, 2002), pp. 34-62.

5. Craig C. Hill, *In God's Time: The Bible and the Future* (Grand Rapids: Eerdmans, 2002), p. 198.

Paul urged the Corinthians to be steadfast and immovable, "always excelling in the work of the Lord." But being "steadfast and immovable" implies meeting opposition, and "the work of the Lord" is endlessly sacrificial. Is it worth it? Yes, "because you know that in the Lord your labor is not in vain." Good deeds may be undone, faithful choices may be frustrated, and loving acts may be rejected; nevertheless, they are not wasted. The Christian philosopher Jerry Walls put it this way: "To recover heaven as a positive moral source is to recover our very humanity. . . . It allows us to hope that the worst things that happen can yet come to a good end rather than to dread the prospect that the best things will come to a bad end. And if it is indeed the Holy Spirit who inspires this hope, it is a hope that will not be disappointed."[6]

"Where, O death, is your victory? / Where, O death, is your sting?" Is death the end, the final page in the story of our lives? Or can we believe in a happy ending? "Thanks be to God, who gives us the victory through our Lord Jesus Christ" (1 Cor. 15:55, 57). Amen!

6. Walls, p. 200.